UPnP Design by Example

A Software Developer's Guide to Universal Plug and Play

Michael Jeronimo
Jack Weast

INTEL
PRESS

ISBN 0-9717861-1-9

This book is printed on acid-free paper. ♾

Publisher: Richard Bowles

Editor: David J. Clark

Managing Editor: David B. Spencer

Content Manager: Stuart Goldstein

Text Design: Marianne Phelps

Composition: Octal Publishing, Incorporated

Graphic Art: Donna Lawless (illustrations), Ted Cyrek (cover)

Printed in the United States of America

10 9 8 7 6 5 4 3 2 1

First printing, April 2003

To Jenni. Thanks for believing in me. I appreciate your patience, support, encouragement, and sacrifice during the many months it took to write this book.

To Matty, Sean, and Portia. Thanks for keeping me smiling. You're the best bunch of heffalumps a dad could have. ☺

To Jan and John (Nana and Papa). Thanks for taking care of the kids during those Sunday afternoon writing sessions and for providing a home away from home.

—Michael

To Papa. The original Weast engineer who started it all; it is your life story that has taught me the value of hard work and dedication against even the greatest of odds.

To Aaron, whose natural ability to do everything better than your older brother continues to provide inspiration and drive for my own success.

—Jack

Contents

Foreword xv

Preface xix

Acknowledgments xxvii

Part I Introduction to the UPnP Architecture 1

Chapter 1 It Just Works 3

Why the UPnP Standard? 4
The Foundation for Home Networking 4
What Is the UPnP Standard? 5
User Scenarios 6
  Watching a Movie 7
  Home Maintenance 7
  Key Themes 8
The UPnP Forum 8
  A Brief History of UPnP 9
The Committees of the UPnP Forum 10
  Steering Committee 10
  Technical Committee 10
  Marketing Committee 10
  Working Committees 10
Security and the UPnP Architecture 13
  The UPnP Security Working Committee 13
  The SSDP Service Bug 14
The UPnP Implementer's Corporation 15
Summary 16

Chapter 2 UPnP Concepts 17

Terminology 17
UPnP Phases 21
  Addressing 23
  Description 23
  Discovery 23
  Control 24
  Eventing 24
  Presentation 24
The UPnP Object Model 24
  The Device 25
  The Service 25
  Events and Subscriptions 28
  The Built-in Web Server 31
The UPnP Stack 31
  Point-to-Point Communication 32
  Multicast Communication 32
  Addressing Protocols 32
Summary 33

Chapter 3 The Technical Foundation 35

Uniform Resource Identifiers 35
  Uniform Resource Locators 36
  Uniform Resource Names 36
  The UPnP Architecture and URIs 36
IP Multicast 37
  The Host Group 37
  Network Infrastructure Support for IP Multicast 38
  The Reach of UPnP Network Traffic 38
  UPnP and IP Multicast 39
Hypertext Transfer Protocol 1.0 40
  HTTP Request/Response Model 40
  Structure of HTTP Transactions 40
  Initial Request Line 41
  HTTP Status Codes—Initial Response Line 41
  Header Lines 42
  The Message Body 43
  Sample HTTP Exchange 43
HTTP 1.1 44
  Host: Header 45
  Accepting Absolute URLs 45
  Chunked Transfer-Encoding 45
  Persistent Connections and the "Connection:close" Header 47
  The "100 Continue" Response 47

Caching 48
Client and Server Requirements 49
HTTP over UDP—HTTPMU and HTTPU 50
The MX Request Header 50
The S (Sequence) General Header 51
The AL (Alternate Location) General Header 51
The "*" Request URI 52
Extensible Markup Language 52
XML Documents 53
The Document Prolog 53
XML Elements 56
XML Attributes 57
CDATA Sections 57
XML and UPnP 57
The Document Object Model 58
The Tree Structure 58
DOM Levels 58
DOM Objects 59
DOM and UPnP 60
Summary 61

Part II UPnP Protocols 63

Chapter 4 Addressing 65

Addressing Challenges 66
Dynamic Host Configuration Protocol 66
Acquiring a Lease 67
Renewing a Lease 68
Releasing a Lease 69
Auto-IP 69
Address Selection 69
Resolving Address Conflicts 70
Ad-Hoc Networks 70
Limitations 71
Steps in UPnP Device Addressing 71
1. Try to Obtain an Address via DHCP 71
2. Failing DHCP, Proceed with Auto-IP 72
Summary 74

Chapter 5 Discovery 75

The Discovery Problem 76
Service Discovery Solution 76
Design Decisions 76
Simple Service Discovery Protocol 78
Service Identification 78
Communication Model 79

Discovery Requests and Presence Announcements 80
Network Transport 81
SSDP Discovery Request 81
SSDP Discovery Response 84
Presence Announcements 87
Device Available: ssdp:alive 89
Device Unavailable: ssdp:bye-bye 91
Expiration Information and Cache Control 91
Summary 92

Chapter 6 Description 93
UPnP's Description Phase 94
Description Document Standards 95
UPnP Device Description Document 97
Basic Device Information 98
UPnP Service Description Documents 103
Retrieving Device and Service Descriptions 108
Validity of the Information in Description Documents 110
Summary 110

Chapter 7 Control 111
Remote Procedure Calls 112
The Simple Object Access Protocol 113
SOAP Namespaces 114
The SOAP Message Envelope 115
The SOAP Header Element 115
The SOAP Body Element 115
SOAP Encoding Rules 116
Conventions for SOAP over HTTP 117
The SOAP HTTP Request 117
The SOAP HTTP Response 119
SOAP Exceptions 120
The Control URL 121
Action Request 122
Action Response 124
Action Error Response 126
QueryStateVariable 127
Summary 128

Chapter 8 Eventing 129
Events in a Distributed System 129
Publisher/Subscriber Model 130
General Event Notification Architecture 131
The Communication Transport 131
HTTP Methods and Headers 132

Using GENA with UPnP Devices 132
Service Description and Evented State Variables 134
The UPnP Template Language for Eventing 135
Moderation of Events 136
Event Keys 137
Subscription Processes/Mechanics/Examples 137
Subscriber List 137
Subscribing to Events 138
Renewing a Subscription 141
Canceling a Subscription 143
Cancellation Response 145
Event Messages 145
Event Keys 146
The NOTIFY Message 147
The NOTIFY Message Response 149
Summary 150

Chapter 9 Presentation 151

The UPnP Presentation Page 151
Getting a Device's Presentation Page 152
Presentation Page Requirements 152
HTML/HTTP-based Presentation 153
Implementation Choices 154
Localization 155
Language Tags 156
Accept-Language and Content-Language Headers 157
Character Encodings 157
Summary 159

Part III Developing a UPnP Device 161

Chapter 10 Introducing the UPnP Super Toaster 163

Who Needs a New Toaster? 164
Physical Product Description 164
Software Requirements Specification 165
Introduction 165
Information Description 165
Functional Description 167
Summary 171

Chapter 11 Choosing a UPnP SDK 173

What to Look For 173
The Implementations 174
Allegro Software 174
Atinav Incorporated 174
Lantronix 175

Metro Link 175
Microsoft 175
Siemens 176
Intel 176
The Choice for This Example: The Intel SDK 176
Installation 177
Source Tree 181
Using the Intel SDK in Your Applications 182
Where to Go for Help 182
Intel® Tools for UPnP Technologies 184
Summary 186

Chapter 12 Adding Device Discovery 187

Problem Description 187
UPnP Device Description 188
Device Implementer Responsibilities 188
UPnP Namespace Requirements 189
Mapping our Requirements 189
Device Namespace 190
URLBase 193
The Super Toaster Device 193
Super Toaster Services 195
The Complete Device Description Document 199
Device Registration 201
Cleaning Up 209
What about the IP Address? 212
Programmatic Description Document Creation 217
Intel Tools for UPnP Technologies 217
Summary 225

Chapter 13 Defining Device Services 227

Introduction 227
Service Characteristics 229
Service Description Documents 230
UPnP Data Types 230
Super Toaster SCPDs 232
Lifetime Statistics Service 232
Toaster Control Service 240
Supporting Service Action Invocation 244
Multiple Out Parameters 259
The Complete Service Action Handlers 261
Intel Tools for UPnP Technology 274
Summary 282

Chapter 14 Handling Subscriptions and Events 283

Problem Description 283
UPnP Service Subscriptions 284
  Event Subscription URL 285
  Subscription Semantics 286
  Subscription Events 288
UPnP Super Toaster 290
  Toaster Status SCPD 291
Implementation 292
  Upnp_Subscription_Request 295
  The API 297
  The Code 300
Super Toaster Improvements 306
  Lifetime Statistics 306
  Toaster Control Service 310
Alternate APIs 311
Intel Tools for UPnP Technology 313
Summary 317

Chapter 15 Creating Device Presentation Pages 319

Problem Description 319
UPnP Presentation Pages 319
  Presentation URL 320
  Localization 321
Creating a Presentation Page 322
  Viewing the Presentation Page 322
Dynamic Presentation Page Creation 324
  Using the DOM 324
  Copy and Paste 334
Advanced Topics 340
  Invoking Actions 340
  Server Scripts 341
Summary 341

Chapter 16 Putting It All Together 343

The Four Steps of Device Development 343
  Device Description 343
  Device Services 344
  Subscriptions and Eventing 345
  Presentation 346
Advanced Topics 346
  Embedded Devices 346
  Other Stuff 348
Using the MAC Address for the Device UDN 350
  Updating the Device Description Document 351

Testing with Device Validator 355
Device Spy Trick 356
Summary 356

Part IV Advanced Topics 357

Chapter 17 UPnP Audio/Video 359

Problem Statement 359
UPnP A/V Architecture Overview 360
A_ARG_TYPE 362
LastChange 362
UPnP A/V Media Server 363
ContentDirectory Service 363
ConnectionManager Service 368
AVTransport Service 370
UPnP A/V Media Renderer 375
ConnectionManager Service 375
RenderingControl Service 376
AVTransport Service 380
UPnP A/V Control Point 381
End User Scenario: Audio Playback 382
Summary 383

Chapter 18 Adding UPnP A/V Support to the Super Toaster 385

Super Duper Toaster 385
Ground Rules 386
Writing the Code 393
Connection Manager Service 397
AVTransport Service 402
Intel Tools for UPnP Technology 411
Summary 411

Chapter 19 Developing Control Point Applications 413

Problem Description 413
UPnP Control Point Applications 414
Discovery 416
Invoking Actions 420
Subscriptions and Eventing 423
Advanced Topics 431
Summary 432

Part V Future Topics 433

Chapter 20 Simple Control Protocol 435

Why SCP? 435
SCP Device Architecture 436
  Communication Subsystem 436
  Application Subsystem 436
SCP Discovery 437
SCP Logical Device Model 438
SCP and UPnP Differences 441
  Property Routes and Subscriptions 442
Event Source Property 443
Security 443
SCP and UPnP Interoperability 444
SCP SDK 445
Summary 447

Part VI The Appendixes 449

Appendix A UPnP API Quick Reference 451

Appendix B References 457

Glossary 463

Index 475

Foreword

Imagine being able to use your home PC as a control center from which you can direct audio or video content (music, movies, and so on) from the Internet or your hard drive to play on your stereo or TV. Further imagine sitting on your couch with friends and family viewing your latest vacation pictures on your TV—a slide show streamed directly from your PC. Digital content, broadband access, and wired and wireless home networks are ushering in a new digital media age that will make such things possible.

This networked lifestyle increasingly demands more self-configuring networks that allow devices to easily join and leave networks and to learn about other connected devices. Home networks, without the benefit of full-time IT departments, require new technologies that can automate device and service discovery and control without a network administrator.

In October 1999, 20 or so companies from many industries, including computers, consumer electronics, home automation, networking, appliances, and others, formally launched the UPnP Forum. This cross-industry initiative has now gathered more than 500 member companies working together to develop interoperability specifications and standards for easy home networking. Intel is a founding member of the UPnP Forum and has successfully led several working committees, including Audio/Video, Internet Gateway, Security, Remote I/O, and QoS, in the Forum.

UPnP technology has the potential to change the way we live and work forever. In recent years we've come to rely on a plethora of convenience devices that didn't exist a decade ago; UPnP technology takes advantage of TCP/IP and web technologies to build easy connectivity into these now-common electronic appliances.

However, the UPnP standard is more than just a simple extension of the plug-and-play peripheral model. The UPnP architecture leverages Internet protocols, including IP, TCP, UDP, HTTP, SOAP, and XML, to support automatic discovery for a variety of device categories from a wide range of vendors. This means that a device can dynamically join a network, obtain an IP address, convey its capabilities, and learn about the presence and capabilities of other devices. Devices can also leave a network smoothly and automatically without leaving any unwanted state behind.

What makes the UPnP architecture universal is that it uses common device control protocols instead of vendor-specific device drivers. The UPnP standard does not specify or constrain the design of an API for applications running on control points; OS vendors can create APIs that suit individual customer needs. The UPnP architecture enables vendor control over device UI and interaction using the browser as well as conventional application programmatic control. As a result, UPnP technology enables peer-to-peer network device connectivity that is independent of operating systems, programming languages, or physical network connections.

I am honored to have been asked to write the foreword for this book. As a charter member of the UPnP Forum steering committee and UIC Board of Directors, and spearheading UPnP efforts at Intel, I've long felt that there was a great need for a well-written book illustrating UPnP technologies. This book satisfies that need: First, it provides a solid background and contextual framework within which to understand the design philosophy and protocol components in the UPnP architecture. Then, Michael and Jack draw on their extensive and pragmatic experiences in projects related to UPnP technology at Intel to provide developers with the right level of detail and guided tours about how to build robust UPnP software for their devices. Whether you are new to UPnP technology, or consider yourself an expert, you will learn things from this book.

Intel is working across several industries to create a common digital home vision and the standards to support it. This collaboration will allow devices in the home to seamlessly work together through widely accepted open standards such as IEEE 802 networks, IP networking protocols, and UPnP device protocols. I believe that this book, our work in the UPnP Forum, Intel's Digital Home vision, the Intel SDK, and other related Intel R&D efforts will accelerate the industry's delivery of UPnP products that will make the UPnP vision a reality in every home.

Charlie Tai
Principal Engineer, Corporate Technology Group
Intel Corporation
January 2003

Preface

I was at my father-in-law's house recently, helping him to set up his new Internet gateway. He was concerned about security and having his computers directly accessible from the Internet over his DSL connection and had purchased an Internet gateway with integrated firewall. We set up the gateway and plugged in the computers. Hoping for the best, we started networking applications on the PC, such as the browser. No luck. We reviewed information about ports, DHCP, and packet filtering. Ten minutes stretched to an hour. An hour stretched to two. It became a challenge—surely I could get this thing to work. After all, I was a software developer who had worked in the networking field for years. We continued configuring and eventually got most applications to work—browser, e-mail, and so on. Then we tried to print to the network printer. Nothing. Something that we had done along the way had caused the printer to stop working. At that point, we stopped for the evening, discouraged and short of our goal.

I did learn a simple, obvious fact from this experience: It is far too difficult for home users to add networking equipment like this to their home networks. It is too complex and requires the user to know too much about the underlying technology. We cannot continue to introduce complex networking devices into the home. In fact, we must reverse the trend and reduce the complexity for the end user. Technology should fade into the background, supporting activities in the home in a transparent way.

The concept of Universal Plug and Play as implemented in the UPnP standard is part of the answer. The UPnP architecture is a technology for transparent network device connectivity. It allows devices to "just work" when plugged into the network, eliminating the administrative hassle typically associated with networking devices.

This book is a practical guide to developing software for UPnP devices. It will provide you, the UPnP developer, with the background you'll need to understand the UPnP technology by introducing you to the protocols that comprise the UPnP architecture. The book will also guide you in the process of using Intel's open source SDK to implement UPnP devices. The style is pragmatic—"developer to developer." We incorporate packet traces, code samples, and screen shots as needed to teach you how to add UPnP support to your devices.

Intended Audience

This book is intended for software developers—both those curious about UPnP technology and those who are planning to develop software for a UPnP device. Perhaps you are a developer new to the UPnP architecture. You may have questions such as: How does UPnP technology work? How do I add UPnP support to my device? What SDKs must I use? What pitfalls should I be aware of? This book answers your questions and provides the technical information you need.

We assume that you are comfortable with network programming concepts: TCP/IP, sockets, and so on, and as a result, we don't cover these topics in this book; many excellent resources are already available.[1] We also assume that you are familiar with HTTP, IP Multicast, XML, and the Document Object Model (DOM), but we do include review material on these subjects. The code samples in the second half of the book are in C, but the protocol material is programming-language independent and is applicable to any UPnP implementation. Most of all, we assume that you have a strong desire to understand how UPnP works and want to jump right in and get started.

We look forward to the many UPnP devices that will be developed and the simpler home networking experience for the end user that will result. We hope that this book becomes an invaluable reference for you as you bring your devices from concept to market.

---

1 See Appendix B for a list of references.

Organization

The book is divided into six parts as follows:

Part I: Introduction to the UPnP Architecture

Chapter 1: It Just Works provides practical information about the UPnP architecture, such as where it came from, why it was created, and what it does. This chapter doesn't require any detailed technical background; rather, it provides an orientation to the world of UPnP technology.

Chapter 2: UPnP Concepts covers basic UPnP concepts, such as control points, devices, and services, and introduces other common UPnP jargon. It also discusses the UPnP object model, shows the relationships between the objects, and gives an overview of the UPnP protocol stack.

Chapter 3: The Technical Foundation covers prerequisite technical material. UPnP is built upon many existing protocols and standards including HTTP, XML, the Document Object Model, and IP Multicast. Chapter 3 provides basic information about these topics to allow the reader to understand the rest of the book.

Part II: UPnP Protocols

Chapter 4: Addressing discusses the foundation of UPnP networking—how a UPnP device automatically acquires an IP address. The chapter first discusses the operation of the Dynamic Host Configuration Protocol (DHCP) used by devices to acquire an address in a managed network environment. It then covers the Auto-IP protocol, a method used by devices in the absence of a DHCP server that specifies how the UPnP device chooses an IP address from a set of reserved addresses.

Chapter 5: Discovery presents an overview of the discovery process. It discusses the general problem of discovery of network-based resources; takes a look at the service discovery protocol adopted for use by the UPnP architecture, the Simple Service Discovery Protocol (SSDP); and then elaborates on discovery in UPnP technology—how UPnP devices use SSDP to advertise their services and to discover other UPnP devices and services.

Chapter 6: Description covers the format of the XML documents used to describe UPnP devices and the services they provide, and how client programs learn about the devices and invoke actions on the services by retrieving and parsing these documents. Chapter 6 also describes different ways UPnP device implementers can organize the interfaces their devices provide, including embedding devices within other devices.

Chapter 7: Control describes the network-based remote procedure call mechanism used by clients to invoke the services provided by UPnP devices, the Simple Object Access Protocol (SOAP). The chapter details the control messages and responses of the protocol as well as the data representation it uses to encode function parameters.

Chapter 8: Eventing describes how clients are notified of state changes in the services provided by UPnP devices—both the XML format used to describe the messages themselves and the General Event Notification Architecture (GENA) protocol used to carry the messages.

Chapter 9: Presentation shows how a UPnP device may use standard web protocols to provide a web page for browser-based control of its operation, allowing users to interactively control the device and view its status.

Part III: Developing a UPnP Device

Chapter 10: Introducing the UPnP Super Toaster defines a sample UPnP device that we will take from concept to fully functional implementation in subsequent chapters.

Chapter 11: Choosing a UPnP SDK surveys the different UPnP SDKs available, including Intel's open source UPnP SDK. It compares each SDK's features and capabilities, helping the reader to understand which SDK is applicable to his or her situation. The chapter also provides installation instructions for the Intel's open source SDK.

Chapter 12: Adding Device Discovery walks through the creation of a device description document for the sample device and introduces the APIs needed to programmatically support device discovery.

Chapter 13: Defining Device Services covers the definition of our device service description documents and shows how to implement support for UPnP actions.

Chapter 14: Handling Subscriptions and Events completes the services defined in the previous chapter by adding support for subscriptions. We show how subscriptions relate to state variables and events.

Chapter 15: Creating Device Presentation Pages adds the last bit of functionality to our device: its presentation page.

Chapter 16: Putting it All Together summarizes the process we've taken to arrive at a fully functional UPnP Super Toaster, focusing on what we've learned, pitfalls we've encountered along the way, and what we can do to improve our device.

Part IV: Advanced Topics

Chapter 17: UPnP Audio/Video explains the UPnP A/V 1.0 standard produced by the UPnP A/V working committee. It gives an overview of the A/V architecture and describes each of the A/V services and their interactions.

Chapter 18: Adding UPnP A/V Support to the SuperToaster shows how to incorporate A/V support into an existing UPnP device. In particular, we'll demonstrate how to add the ability to play audio files to the UPnP device we developed in Part 3.

Chapter 19: Developing Control Point Applications demonstrates how to write a simple control point applications suitable for the discovery of devices, invocation of actions, and subscription to services.

Part V: Future Topics

Chapter 20: Simple Control Protocol explains the Simple Control Protocol (SCP), a lightweight protocol, compatible with the UPnP standard, that will allow devices with otherwise minimal resources to interact in a UPnP technology-based network. The chapter suggests how, in the future, many device designs may incorporate inexpensive SCP silicon.

Part VI: The Appendixes

Appendix A: UPnP API Quick Reference is a quick reference guide to the Intel UPnP SDK. It provides a compact synopsis of the functions and data structures provided by the SDK and used by UPnP device implementers. It can serve as a reference guide when reading the implementation sections of the book or when using the book to guide UPnP device implementation.

Appendix B: References lists recommended resources, including sources of more information about UPnP technology as well as pointers to UPnP technology-related tools to aid in the process of developing UPnP devices.

The *Glossary* is an extensive listing of terms associated with UPnP technology.

How to Use This Book

This book was written to support a wide variety of technical backgrounds, from the UPnP professional to those new to UPnP technology.

- For readers who have little or no experience with UPnP technology, we recommend reading the book from cover to cover. This will present the most complete view of the UPnP architecture, leaving nothing out.
- For readers with some familiarity with UPnP technology and home network technologies, we recommend skipping the first three chapters and going directly to the details of the UPnP device architecture starting with Chapter 4.
- For advanced readers (or for those on tight deadlines who must implement devices *now*), we recommend heading right to Part III, where we show, step by step, how to implement a real UPnP device using the Intel open source SDK.
- Finally, for readers who already have experience developing UPnP devices with the Intel SDK but want to know more about UPnP A/V and how to add A/V support to their device, we recommend heading directly to Part IV of the book, where we cover UPnP A/V and other advanced topics.

Part V presents topics related to the future of the UPnP standard. Although not necessary for understanding the details of UPnP device implementation today, this section will help you to understand upcoming technologies and the implications they may have for your devices.

Accompanying CD-ROM

The CD-ROM has source code, tools, and information that will assist you in developing your UPnP device, including

- Source code and binaries for Intel's open source UPnP SDK
- Sample programs, including all of the samples from the book
- UPnP tools, such as a utility to view and interact with any UPnP device, a tool to monitor UPnP protocols, and a tool to generate skeleton code from a device description
- UPnP specifications and related documents

Typographic Conventions

Throughout this book we use the following typographic conventions:

Bold is used for emphasis.

Italic is used to introduce new terms or concepts.

`Fixed width font` is used for program listings and URLs.

Comments and Questions

We hope that we have produced a book that you will find useful. Please let us know how we can improve it in future printings. You can reach us directly by e-mail at `michael.jeronimo@intel.com` and `jack.weast@intel.com`. For more information, examples, and updates to the book, please visit the book's web site at `http://www.intel.com/intelpress/upnp/`.

Acknowledgments

We would like to thank all of the people who have helped us on this project, both the many UPnP experts within Intel Corporation and others throughout the industry. Our job was just to explain what many other people have already created.

From Intel, we would like to thank Dan Baumberger and the UPnP SDK team, for producing the open source UPnP SDK for Linux that we and many others have used; Vijay Rao, for supporting the idea for a UPnP book and sponsoring the project; Charlie Tai, for his UPnP expertise and writing the foreword, John Ritchie and Mark Walker, for their work on UPnP A/V and their input on the A/V chapters; Ylian Saint-Hilaire, Bryan Roe, and Nelson Kidd, for the excellent UPnP tools that are included on the CD-ROM; and Ken Knowlson and Jim Edwards for allowing us to dedicate some work time to this effort.

For bringing the Super Toaster to life on the page, we would especially like to thank Jeremy Emerson, whose striking artistic talents, vision without direction, and supportive friendship took a boring sample device into something much greater than we could have ever created on our own.

Special thanks go to James Marshall for letting us use his excellent tutorial on HTTP as the foundation for the sections on Hypertext Transfer Protocol 1.0 and HTTP 1.1 in Chapter 3.

We would also like to sincerely thank our reviewers, Rajendra Bopardikar, Dan Baumberger, Matt Delco, Bob Dunstan, Ken Geer, Andrew Grover, Tom Halpenny, Jamie Jason, Bryan Roe, Daniel Slightam, Jim Stanley, Michael Walz, and Paul Zurcher, for providing feedback on early drafts of the book. Your input was an integral and valued part of the successful completion of the book.

We would especially like to thank Intel Press for giving us the opportunity to write this book and help us through the writing process. Special thanks go to Stuart Goldstein, our content manager, for helping us to improve the technical content of the book; David Clark for doing an excellent job at editing our manuscript and reminding us to use the term "UPnP" correctly; and David B. Spencer, the managing editor, for teaching us about the publishing process and helping us to improve the quality of the text.

Finally, we offer our heartfelt thanks and gratitude to our families, whose patience, support, and encouragement provided that extra bit of motivation and drive to see this project through. We could not have completed this book without you.

Part I

Introduction to the UPnP Architecture

Chapter 1

It Just Works

It's kind of fun to do the impossible.

—Walt Disney

People expect that when they bring a television or DVD player home, they can just plug it in, hook up a few cables, and the device will "just work." These devices perform their functions well and are easy for consumers to install. PC peripherals, on the other hand, have not been as easy to install. Users must be concerned with gory details such as device drivers to get devices to work properly. Recently, Universal Serial Bus (USB) and Plug-and-Play have improved the situation for PC peripherals so that devices can now be automatically detected and device drivers automatically installed. But networked devices, such as an Internet gateway or a networked printer, still require complicated manual setup and configuration.

The UPnP[1] standard brings the PC peripheral Plug-and-Play concept to the home network, with the same ease of use and automatic configuration that users have come to expect with Plug-and-Play devices. Just

[1] UPnP is a certification mark of the UPnP Implementers Corporation.

as devices can be plugged into the PC and automatically detected and configured, consumers of home networking equipment can now easily add UPnP devices to their home networks and have them just work.

Why the UPnP Standard?

When USB devices are plugged into a PC they are automatically detected by the operating system, which loads the appropriate software and makes the device available for applications to use. This automatic detection and configuration of devices makes it easy for the end user to add and use new devices.

Similar to a PC and its peripherals, there are various home networking devices, such as an Internet gateway or a networked printer, that the user may wish to connect to the local network. However, these devices usually require an administrator to configure them before they can be used. The difficulty of configuring home networking equipment has been a problem for consumers and a barrier to the adoption of home networking. With UPnP, users can add devices to the home network without installing drivers or configuring the devices before using them.

The Foundation for Home Networking

UPnP technology, along with other emerging technologies such as wireless networking and high-speed Internet connections, is transforming the home. Many devices, such as digital televisions and home audio equipment, are becoming UPnP technology-enabled. In time, other existing networks in the home, such as the power line, home entertainment, and telephone networks, will have bridging software that automatically makes devices on those networks appear as UPnP devices. The result will be a single, logical network of UPnP devices—a kind of "digital home platform" for entertainment, home automation, and other kinds of applications, as shown in Figure 1.1.

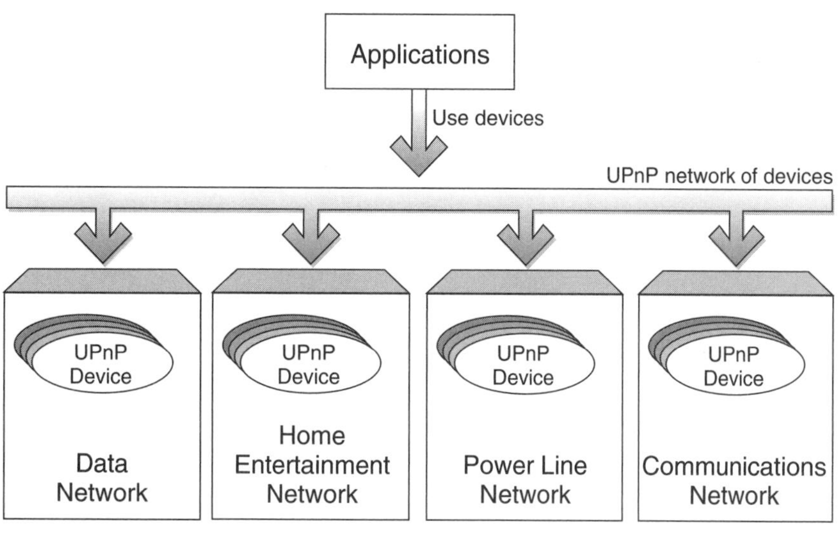

Figure 1.1 UPnP Technology Is the Foundation for Home Networking

What Is the UPnP Standard?

The UPnP architecture is designed to connect networked devices, such as PCs, entertainment equipment, and intelligent appliances. It defines a base set of standards for all devices to adhere to and conventions for describing devices and the services they provide.

The UPnP architecture leverages existing standards such as TCP/IP, HTTP, and XML instead of inventing new underlying mechanisms. The architecture consists of a set of standardized protocols that each UPnP technology-enabled device implements to provide for discovery, control, and data transfer between UPnP devices. UPnP technology can be supported on any common operating system or hardware platform, and it works with almost any type of physical networking media—wired or wireless—providing maximum user and developer choice.

The UPnP architecture provides:

- *Device Connectivity.* The UPnP architecture defines the protocols for devices to interact with other devices. UPnP devices can join and leave the network transparently, advertise their services, discover other devices and services, send events, and control other devices.

- *Ad-Hoc Networking.* UPnP devices can come together to form a network dynamically, without the need for dedicated networking infrastructure services, such as a server to manage address assignment. These *ad-hoc* networks are created on-the-fly and enable device connectivity without manual configuration.
- *Zero-Configuration Networks.* The UPnP architecture supports zero-configuration networking where the user is not required to configure devices before they are used on the network. The non-technical user will find it simple to add and use devices.
- *Standards-Based Architecture.* The UPnP architecture is based on open standards, including a foundation of existing and proposed standard Internet Engineering Task Force (IETF) and World Wide Web Consortium (W3C) protocols such as IP, TCP, UDP, HTTP, XML, and SOAP. Leveraging existing Internet-based technologies simplifies the design of UPnP devices.
- *Platform Independence.* The UPnP architecture is primarily a set of protocols and is not an API definition. The UPnP architecture keeps the implementation of the protocols private and does not require vendors to develop their implementations on any specific operating system, language, or hardware. With this approach, UPnP devices can be developed on any platform—a desirable trait in a network full of devices from many vendors, including consumer electronics companies.
- *Media and Device Independence.* UPnP technology can run on any medium for which there is an IP stack, including phone lines, power lines, Ethernet, RF, and IEEE 1394.
- *Programmatic and Manual Device Control.* The UPnP architecture enables applications to programmatically control home networking devices. In addition, users can manually control devices using the device's browser-based administrative interface.

User Scenarios

Many futuristic automation scenarios can be developed using UPnP devices. Here are a couple of examples that illustrate the power and flexibility of UPnP technology in the home of the future.

Watching a Movie

Arriving home after a long day at work, George decides to watch a movie. He happens to be in the kitchen getting a glass of juice from the fridge, so he calls up a list of recent movies on the screen near to him on the kitchen counter. George checks out some previews and then selects the movie to watch. The movie selection program turns on the home theater system and automatically starts the movie. The controlling program also dims the lights and adjusts the volume of the speakers. Settling in, George watches the movie for a while. Twenty minutes later, an alert pops up on the home theater screen indicating activity in the front yard. George puts the porch camera on the screen and sees the local pizza delivery man walking up the path to his door, delivering the pizza ordered earlier. George meets the delivery man at the door, takes the pizza, pays him, including a generous tip, and returns to the home theater room. Some time after the delivery man leaves, the kitchen lights and porch lights turn themselves off to conserve energy, having not detected any motion.

Home Maintenance

Every New Year's Day, Shannon does home maintenance. With her wireless PDA in hand, she walks through her house, examining the status of various systems and devices. The PDA displays the list of systems to be inspected in the house and tells Shannon what to look for, displaying instructions and pictures as needed.

Shannon starts in the garage with the water heater. She uses her PDA to view the operational parameters of the water heater. Using that information, she optimizes the heater's energy use, updating the heater's settings to monitor activity over a period of time and anticipate peak loads and off periods.

Shannon moves on to the kitchen where she uses the PDA to review the state of the dishwasher and the refrigerator. The dishwasher hasn't been working very well lately, so she uses the PDA to invoke the dishwasher's self-test. The test doesn't turn up any problems, so she calls up the dishwasher manual. The manual has a troubleshooting section that Shannon reads to find out what might be the problem. Shannon doesn't find any answers, so she uses the PDA to send an e-mail message to the manufacturer explaining the problem.

Shannon continues through the house, inspecting, calibrating, and making notes of things that she needs to buy for the house. She eventually completes this year's maintenance inspection and goes to the store to pick up the items she needs.

Key Themes

With a little playful daydreaming, you can probably envision many more scenarios like these that simplify life in the home, limited only by your imagination. Some key themes appear in many of the scenarios, such as automation, where devices automatically respond to events generated from other devices, and convenience, where the user is able to easily accomplish tasks. While the scenarios seem futuristic, one thing is certain—having a standard, open platform for home networking will inspire creativity. The UPnP standard is the underlying technology to help make scenarios like these real.

Let's take a step back from the future now and take a look at the UPnP Forum, the organization responsible for the UPnP standards.

The UPnP Forum

Microsoft Corporation introduced the UPnP initiative at the Consumer Electronics Show in January of 1999. The initiative was originally supported by companies such as Microsoft, Intel, Hewlett-Packard, Compaq, Dell, and many others, and was considered the next phase of the Plug-and-Play initiative introduced by Intel, Compaq, and Microsoft in 1992.

To guide the creation of the standards, a cross-industry group, the UPnP Forum, was created. Today, the Forum consists of more than 550 companies, including industry leaders in consumer electronics, computing, home automation, home security, appliances, printing, photography, computer networking, and mobile products.

The primary activities of the UPnP Forum include:

- Defining device standards based on the UPnP architecture
- Providing for the certification of devices
- Facilitating joint member promotion of UPnP

Device descriptions are XML documents, based on a device description document schema, that describe a particular kind of device. By defining and publishing UPnP device descriptions, members of the UPnP Forum create standard building blocks for home networking. The standards defined by the UPnP Forum are platform-neutral. Membership and participation in the design of device schema templates are open to any member companies. Companies interested in standardizing particular device classes are encouraged to join the UPnP Forum and participate in working committees to design schema templates for their devices.

Vendors can implement devices that conform to these standards, but they must then demonstrate that their devices pass the tests in order to receive a logo for their device. The UPnP Forum provides the means for vendors to certify their devices.

The UPnP Forum also seeks to promote the UPnP standard in the industry and with the general public. It provides a framework for companies to get together and define building block standards: both technical standards, like the UPnP architecture, and legal standards, such as a broadly signed and carefully scoped joint development agreement. These technical and marketing objectives are pursued to advance the entire home networking industry.

A Brief History of UPnP

The core UPnP architecture was originally developed by Microsoft and contributed to the UPnP Forum in the form of the UPnP Device Architecture specification. The specification was approved by UPnP Forum Technical Committee on June 13, 2000. Version 1 of the specification enumerates the UPnP core protocols and establishes the foundation that working committees use to develop their specific devices.

Table 1.1 gives a timeline of activity in the UPnP Forum.

Table 1.1 UPnP Timeline

Date	Event
1/99	UPnP standard publicly announced
10/99	UPnP Forum officially formed
6/00	UPnP version 1 architecture finalized
6/00	Microsoft Windows† ME with UPnP version 1 support ships
7/00	Intel's open source UPnP SDK released
5/01	UPnP version 1 toolkits announced
10/01	Microsoft Windows XP with UPnP version 1 support ships
11/01	First UPnP device standard published
12/01	First UPnP-enabled devices ship
1/02	Microsoft Windows CE with UPnP version 1 support ships

The Committees of the UPnP Forum

The UPnP Forum consists of four organizational elements. Three are permanent committees: the Steering Committee, the Technical Committee, and the Marketing Committee. The fourth is a set of Working Committees formed as needed by participants to define standard device types.

Steering Committee

The UPnP Steering Committee is the high-level directing body of the UPnP Forum. It has about 20 members from various companies, including Microsoft. The composition of the Steering Committee can change over time as new members are added. The Steering Committee provides business leadership and makes decisions for the UPnP Forum. As the organization's management team, the Steering Committee oversees the working committees for defining device descriptions (DCPs). The Steering Committee launched a separate company, the UPnP Implementer's Corporation (UIC), responsible for the certification of devices.

Technical Committee

The UPnP Technical Committee is a group of technical representatives from various companies who process technical issues from working committees. The Technical Committee reviews these issues and produces architectural requirements. They are responsible for the "big picture" technically for the UPnP standard.

Marketing Committee

The UPnP Marketing Committee undertakes joint member promotion of the UPnP standard, including representing the UPnP Forum at industry trade shows.

Working Committees

The nitty-gritty technical work gets done in the Working Committees of the UPnP Forum. These groups define the device descriptions that describe the interfaces that the device provides to the network. The working committees define the syntax and semantics of a particular device type so that implementations of that device type will be interchangeable.

To start a new working committee in the UPnP Forum, members must first make a proposal to the UPnP Steering Committee. The proposal consists of a set of user scenarios to demonstrate the usefulness of the new device type, a schedule of the proposed work, and a commitment from three independent groups to implement the device type. Having multiple independent implementations demonstrates interoperability of the new device type standard. The group is formed with a particular charter, expressed as a set of objectives to be accomplished. Once the group satisfies their charter, its work is complete and the group is disbanded. If the group decides to continue work on a subsequent version of the device type, the group must be re-chartered and meet the same requirements as any other new group to be chartered. This process is summarized in Figure 1.2.

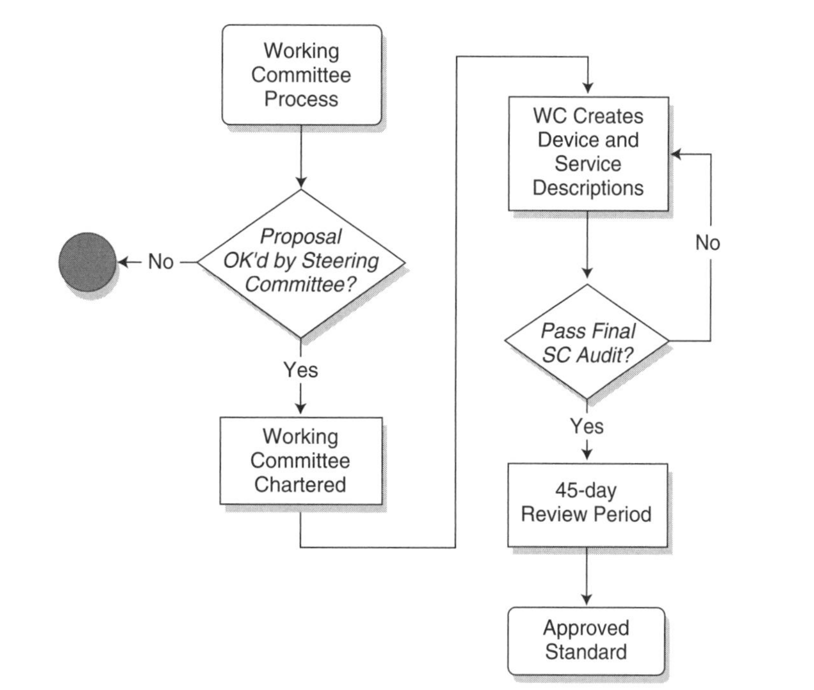

Figure 1.2 Standardization Process Flowchart for UPnP Device Descriptions

All working committees follow the same basic timeline. The working committee members first collaborate to design the device description. This process usually involves weekly conference calls and periodic face-to-face meetings as the group's members work through the issues with the design for the device type. Once the device description is completely designed, test suite development can begin. Sample implementations are typically developed, tracking the development of the standard. Once the test suites are finalized, the implementations can be validated. Working committees often gather for interoperability events to test their independent implementations against one another. After the implementations pass the test suites, the standard moves to the Steering Committee for a final audit. Upon passing this audit, the standard goes into a 45-day review period. At the close of this period, it becomes an approved standard of the UPnP Forum. Figure 1.2 illustrates the standardization process followed by working committees of the UPnP Forum.

The Internet Gateway: The First Certified Device Type

The Internet Gateway Device was the first device standard produced by one of the UPnP Forum working committees. The Internet Gateway Device (IGD) 1.0 working committee included representatives from companies such as Intel, Alcatel, Microsoft, Sony, and Linksys. The IGD supports sharing of Internet connections, advanced connection-management features, management of host-configuration services, and support for transparent Internet access by non-UPnP-certified devices.

Before IGD 1.0, most gateways allowed a single Internet connection to be shared by multiple computers in the home. Unfortunately, this technology prevented many compelling applications, including multiplayer games, file sharing, and real-time communications (such as Internet phone), from working correctly without extra tools and advanced knowledge of gateway and networking configurations.

Currently, the UPnP Forum has many working committees, including Internet Gateways, Audio/Video, Home Automation, Printers and Imaging, Remote I/O, and Security. The committees are formed to meet specific objectives and then are disbanded when their work is done. They are often re-chartered to meet new objectives, but must meet the same criteria as a new working committee, including commitment from three independent groups to implement the device type. For a list of committees at any give time, visit the UPnP Forum web site at `http://www.upnp.org`.

Security and the UPnP Architecture

UPnP technology helps to make networking automatic—people will bring home networking devices, turn them on, and have them just work, with no technical expertise required. One potential impediment to this vision, however, is the need for security. There is a trade-off between security and ease of use. Implementing security tends to require administration—setting up passwords, defining access control lists, and so on—which gets the user involved again and makes the process of using networked devices less automatic.

In version 1 of the UPnP architecture, there is no built-in security: All UPnP devices on the network can be controlled by any control points. Recently though, a new working committee of the UPnP Forum has been established that is developing a standard security infrastructure compatible with current and future versions of the UPnP architecture.

The UPnP Security Working Committee

The UPnP architecture enables simple networking in the home and small office. "Home and small office" can include many different settings, from single-family homes, apartments, college dorms, and hotel rooms to a local coffee shop providing wireless Internet access for its customers. UPnP devices will enter and leave these dynamic network environments and, as always, unscrupulous people will look for opportunities to take advantage of a lack of security.

The UPnP Security working committee is a new group in the UPnP Forum that has been chartered to provide a security solution for the UPnP architecture that will be common to all device types. The Security working committee includes members from Intel, Microsoft, Siemens, IBM, Sony, and others. In early 2001, the group specified the requirements for a UPnP security solution and defined the user scenarios it intends to support.

Securing the UPnP architecture may eventually expand the use of UPnP technology to new fields, such as providing high-value services. The security solution developed by the working committee will give users choice and control over their network, but will introduce an inevitable trade-off: security with configuration versus no security with no configuration. The group will undoubtedly try to strike a balance and minimize the configuration required in its security solution.

Requirements of the Security Solution

The UPnP security solution will use standard encryption and digital signature algorithms to protect all of the UPnP protocols. It will include a powerful trust model with non-public key infrastructure authorization certificates, avoiding the heavy infrastructure requirements associated with public key infrastructure (PKI) solutions. It will also be sensitive to the processing capabilities likely to be found on networking devices and will require only moderate processing power to implement.

The UPnP Security working committee will introduce security concepts to the basic UPnP architecture. These additions will likely include principals, permissions, authorization certificates, and access control lists. In addition, the Security working committee will also specify how to secure the basic UPnP protocols, including discovery, control, eventing, and presentation. For example, digital signatures and encryption will be used to maintain confidentiality and to enforce any access control policy.

The SSDP Service Bug

Even with a system that has been designed to be secure, security vulnerabilities can arise from weaknesses in the implementation. These vulnerabilities can result in denial-of-service attacks, preventing systems from being able to offer their services, or provide on opening for an intruder to gain unauthorized access. Microsoft Windows ME and Windows XP contain an implementation of the UPnP protocols and a corresponding API that allows developers to create UPnP control points and devices. Microsoft's Internet Gateway implementation, for example, uses this API to provide the services required of a UPnP Internet Gateway device. Unfortunately, there were two bugs discovered with the implementation of the UPnP protocols shipped with these operating systems[2] (which since have been fixed with subsequent service packs). Both bugs involve how UPnP technology-capable computers handle the discovery of new UPnP devices on the network.

---

[2] The bugs are also present on Windows 98 and Windows 98SE systems that have the Internet Connection Sharing client installed.

The first bug is an unchecked buffer in the implementation of the Simple Service Discovery Protocol (SSDP). When the SSDP service receives a message from a device that has joined the network, the code processing the messages does not check the input for length. An unchecked buffer, one of the most common and most serious of implementation flaws, allows an attacker to provide more data on an input channel (an SSDP socket in this case) than is expected, overwriting the program stack and allowing the attacker to run any arbitrary code in the context of the application. In this case, the attacker could cause code to be run in the context of the SSDP service, which has system privileges on Windows XP.

The bug's official title was: "Unchecked Buffer in Universal Plug and Play Can Lead to System Compromise" and was documented in Microsoft Security Bulletin MS01-059, which was originally posted on December 20, 2001, at the following URL:

```
http://www.microsoft.com/technet/treeview/
default.asp?url=/|technet/security/bulletin/MS01-059.asp.
```

The second bug introduced by the implementation of the SSDP service provides an opportunity for attackers to use the service to perform two kinds of denial-of-service attacks—a distributed denial-of-service attack where many hosts simultaneously request a device description document from a single host, and a simple denial-of-service attack where many devices may simultaneously request a device description from a single host. The details of these attacks are contained in the Security Bulletin.

The UPnP Implementer's Corporation

The UPnP Implementer's Corporation (UIC) is an independent non-profit corporation created by the UPnP Steering Committee that administers the UPnP device certification process.

The UIC owns and licenses the UPnP certification mark. Companies with devices that pass conformance tests may license the UPnP logo for use with their device. The UIC licenses conformance tests to UIC members, reviews test results, and issues certificates of conformity to devices that pass the tests. The UIC tests cover the device-dependent features specified in the UPnP device standard and the device-independent features specified in the UPnP version 1.0 architecture.

Summary

- The UPnP standard helps to reduce complexity and simplify home networking for the end user.
- UPnP technology-based products "just work" when they are connected to the network.
- The UPnP architecture is the unifying device abstraction layer for the home of the future, with proxies and bridges spanning to other networks in the home, such as the power line, telephone line, and home entertainment networks.
- With the UPnP architecture, the same kind of open, standard design target we have enjoyed with PC peripherals is coming to the home networking platform.
- UPnP standards will allow devices from different vendors to interoperate.
- UPnP Forum working committees define standard XML-based device and service types that devices may implement.
- Work has begun in the Security working committee of the UPnP Forum to define a security solution for the current and any future versions of the UPnP architecture.

Chapter 2

UPnP Concepts

The mother art is architecture. Without an architecture of our own we have no soul of our own civilization.

—Frank Lloyd Wright

There are a few basic concepts introduced by the UPnP architecture. This chapter introduces these concepts and the underlying UPnP object model, describing each of the different UPnP entities and their corresponding roles and responsibilities. Once you understand this basic object model, you will see some of the common activities that occur on a network of UPnP devices, activities that form the building blocks for futuristic scenarios like those in the previous chapter. The chapter then delves a bit further into UPnP technology, reviewing the UPnP protocol stack and giving a quick overview of each protocol that is part of the UPnP device architecture.

Terminology

Devices, services, and control points are the basic abstractions of the UPnP device architecture. A *UPnP device* can be any entity on the network that implements the protocols required by the UPnP architecture. Because UPnP standardizes the protocols through which a device communicates rather than the APIs that a programmer uses, any entity that behaves as a UPnP device by speaking the required protocols *is* a UPnP device. Thus, a device either can be a dedicated physical device, such as an Internet gateway, or a logical device, such as a PC, that has implemented the functionality required of an Internet gateway.

A UPnP device contains zero or more services. A *service* is a unit of functionality implemented by a device. Each service has a set of methods, or *actions*, each with a set of optional input and output parameters and an optional return value, much like a function in the C programming language. The specifics of a service, as defined by a UPnP Forum working committee, define each action in detail, listing its required input and output parameters and whether the action returns a value.

An Analogy to Component-based Systems

If you are familiar with a component-based system such as Microsoft COM, a UPnP device is like a class object, while the UPnP service is like an interface that the object supports. A UPnP action is similar to a method in a COM interface—it has input and output parameters and may have a return value.

The services that a device must implement are determined by the device's type. The working committees of the UPnP Forum standardize the set of services that particular device types must support.[1] For example, an audio rendering device, such as a CD player, might have a service that provides the ability to play, stop, and pause audio content.

A *control point* is an entity on the network that works with the functionality provided by a device. In the terminology of client/server computing, the control point is the client and the device is the server. Control points can invoke actions on services, providing any required input parameters and receiving any output parameters and possibly a return value. Control points can also request that devices notify them when the device state changes. Figure 2.1 shows a control point invoking an action on a UPnP device. The device has implemented a single UPnP device type that contains two services.

---

[1] Nonstandard device types may have any set of services and methods as defined by their implementer. It is possible to create proprietary devices and services using UPnP technology, but, by definition, nonstandard services will not be interoperable with devices from other vendors.

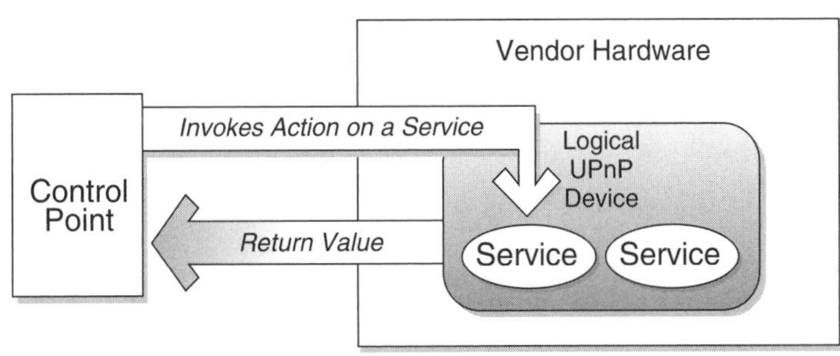

Figure 2.1 Control Point Invoking an Action

Any entity that invokes the services of a UPnP device is a control point. In fact, UPnP technology-enabled devices may have control point functionality built in, so that they can invoke the services or monitor state changes in other devices. With this capability, devices can form a peer-to-peer network where devices take advantage of each other's services.

Figure 2.2 shows a UPnP technology-enabled device that contains a control point that can invoke the services of other UPnP devices.

A device such as an electronic picture frame could implement this pattern by having control point functionality built in, so that when a user presses buttons on the side of the picture frame to navigate through the pictures to be displayed, the control point application on the picture frame retrieves digital images from another UPnP device on the network.

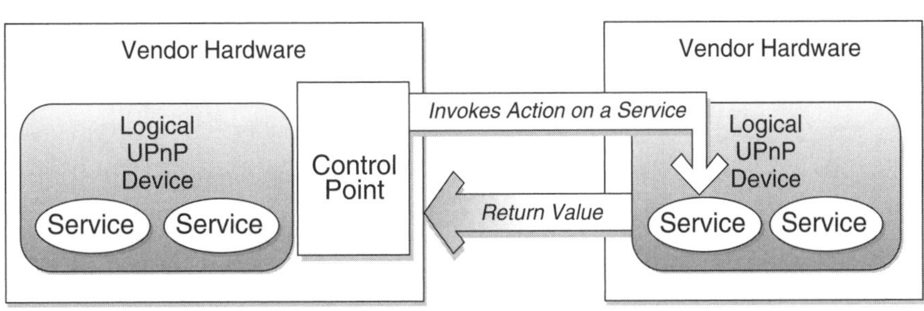

Figure 2.2 Peer-to-Peer: A Control Point in a UPnP Device

Root and Embedded Devices

A UPnP device may also contain other devices. This logical composition of devices gives the UPnP developer flexibility when determining how to implement the device. It also allows the embedded device to be discovered and used independently from the main containing device.

For example, imagine a UPnP television with an embedded UPnP VCR. In this case, the VCR device might have tape transport, tuner, and clock services. The UPnP television device could have a channel control service and a picture adjustment service while containing an embedded VCR device. In UPnP terminology, the top-level device is called the *root device* and the contained device is called an *embedded device,* as shown in Figure 2.3.

A UPnP-enabled device can also implement more than one root device. The UPnP developer has great flexibility in designing the logical structure of devices and services.

State Associated with a Service

Services group the actions provided by UPnP devices. They can also maintain associated states. Like an instance of a C++ class with its member variables, each service may have a *state table*, which is a grouping of its *state variables*. Each state variable has a name, a type, and a value.

UPnP control points can request to receive indications of state variable changes from the service. When a service detects a change to one

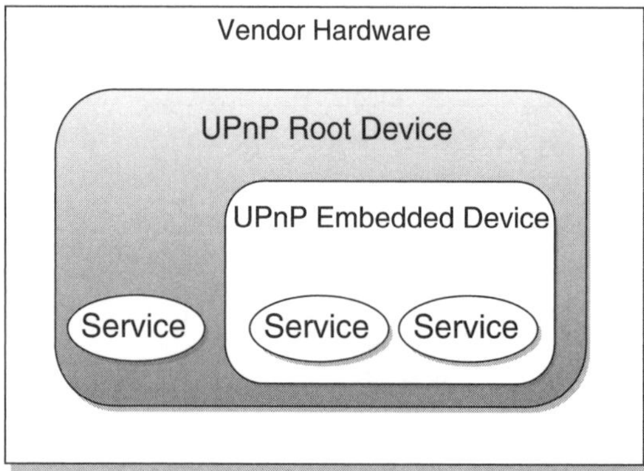

Figure 2.3 Root Device Containing an Embedded Device

of its state variables, the service notifies any registered control points of the change. For example, a service that renders audio tracks might keep a state variable that has the URL of the current track being played. When the track changes, the service sends a state change notification with the new URL to all control points that have registered to receive events from the service.

Figure 2.4 shows how a control point communicates with a service to subscribe to and receive notifications for state variable changes.

UPnP Phases

As you have seen so far, in a network of UPnP devices, control points can discover devices, invoke actions on a device's services, and subscribe to events. Devices, on the other hand, respond to invoked actions and send events when state variables change. To make this basic functionality possible, all UPnP devices follow the same basic pattern, or *phases*, of operation:

- *Addressing.* The device joins the network, acquiring a unique address that others can use to communicate with it.
- *Description.* The device summarizes its services and capabilities in a standard format.

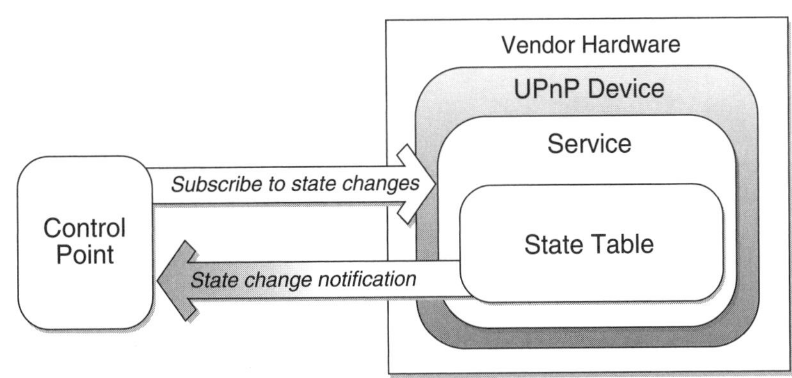

Figure 2.4 State Changes and Notifications

- *Discovery.* The device is found by control points and the device's description information is retrieved.
- *Control.* The device handles requests from control points to invoke actions.
- *Eventing.* The device's services notify registered control points when internal state changes occur.
- *Presentation.* The device optionally provides an HTML-based administrative interface to allow for direct manipulation and monitoring.

Together, these steps define how all UPnP devices behave on a network. Figure 2.5 shows the UPnP phases and their dependencies. A device first acquires an address, then is able to provide a description of its capabilities to control points that have discovered it. Once a control point has discovered a device and retrieved the description of its services, it is able to either control the device, request that it receive notification of events (changes to state variables), or an administrator may manually monitor or configure the device.

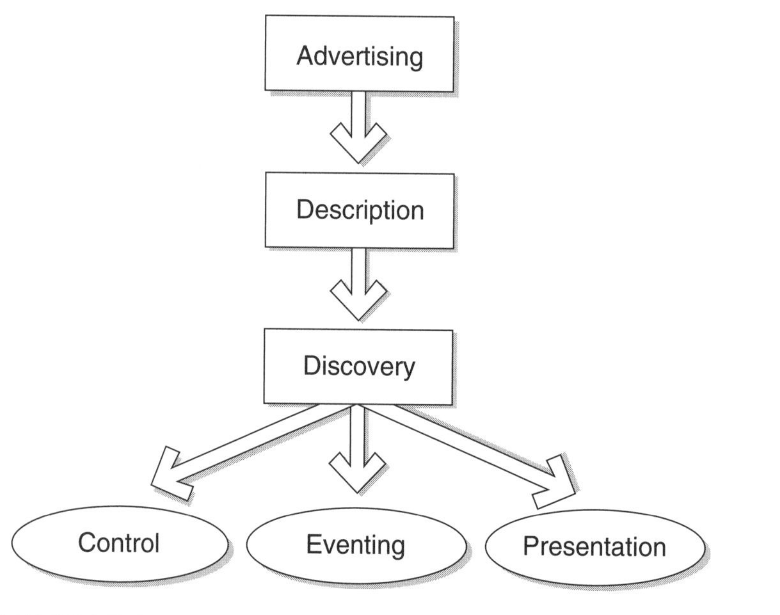

Figure 2.5 UPnP Phases

Each UPnP phase has related network protocols that each device must support. The protocols are described in detail in subsequent chapters, but are briefly introduced here to give you and idea of the scope of a UPnP device.

Addressing

The foundation for UPnP networking is *addressing*, the process by which a device automatically acquires an IP address. As the first step of UPnP, addressing allows devices to join the network and to communicate with other UPnP devices.The addressing protocols built in to UPnP devices allow them to join an IP network dynamically and to acquire an address without user configuration.

Addressing takes into account whether a device is operating in an unmanaged or managed network. An unmanaged, or *ad-hoc*, network is a network where there are no preexisting infrastructure devices (or they are currently inoperable) and the network nodes themselves make up the network. A managed, or infrastructure, network allows devices to acquire an IP address from a DHCP server on the network.

Description

Description allows devices to list the functionality they provide. Descriptions of devices and their services are contained in XML-based *description documents*. The *device description document* contains device information such as manufacturer, make, model, and serial number; a list of services provided by the device; and a list of embedded devices. *A service description* document contains detailed information about the service, the actions it provides, and their parameters and return value.

Discovery

The discovery process enables control points to find devices and services and retrieve information about them. Also, once a device has acquired an IP address, the device may advertise itself and its services on the network. Devices include a URL for their device description document in their advertisements and discovery responses. The URL provides control points with the information they need to retrieve the device and service descriptions, enabling the control points to learn all about the device and the services it offers.

Once a control point has discovered a device and has retrieved the device and service description documents, it may control the device, subscribe to events sourced by the device's services, or retrieve the device's presentation page.

Control

Control is the phase of UPnP where control points invoke the actions provided by a device's services. A device's service receives a control message and acts upon it. The device may change state as a result of the operation, leading to the next UPnP phase, eventing.

Eventing

Eventing allows control points to monitor state changes in devices. The UPnP architecture uses a publisher/subscriber model where control points may subscribe to a service provided by a device. The device's service notifies all registered control points upon changes in state variables. Responding to state changes in this way enables a UPnP network of devices to be a dynamic, responsive, event-driven system.

Presentation

Presentation is the process by which a device presents a browser-based user interface for manual user control and to allow viewing of device status. Each device contains a web server and may provide a web page for browser-based clients. This web page serves as the manual interface for the device as opposed to the device's programmatic control interface. This browser-based interface can be used to control the device, to change operational parameters, to view device and service information, or for any other device-specific functionality implemented by the manufacturer.

The UPnP Object Model

A UPnP developer must be intimately familiar with the basic UPnP objects and their attributes, interfaces, properties, and relationships. Understanding the UPnP object model will give you a conceptual frame of reference for understanding UPnP device implementations.

The Device

By itself, a device does nothing more than provide self-describing information such as the manufacturer, model name, and serial number. A device's set of zero or more services provides its real functionality.

A root device may contain a number of embedded devices. For example, a digital television device might have an embedded audio player device.

Each device can have a set of icons to depict the device in control point user interfaces. The icons are available in different sizes to satisfy different UI requirements.

The device also maintains the URL of its device description document. During the discovery process, the device returns the URL for its description document[2] to allow control points to learn the details of the device.

Figure 2.6 summarizes the relationship between the device, its services and icons, and any embedded devices.

The Service

A UPnP service is conceptually similar to a Java interface, C++ virtual base class, or COM interface in that it provides a set of function signatures that are grouped into a logical whole. In the UPnP architecture, the methods are called actions. In general, each action has a name and may have input and output arguments. Each argument has a name, value, and a direction. The direction may be either input or output (but not both), depending on whether the argument is passed into the action or is returned from the action to the caller. Each action may also have a return value that provides the result of the action.

Services without Actions

Services don't require any actions; they can have only state variables, just as a C++ class can have member variables without having any methods. In this case, the service would only support control points subscribing to state changes and control points querying for the current value of state variables.

---

[2] The *device control protocol*, or *DCP*, is an earlier name for a device description document. DCP emphasizes the fact that the description document provides the interface, or *protocol*, for the device.

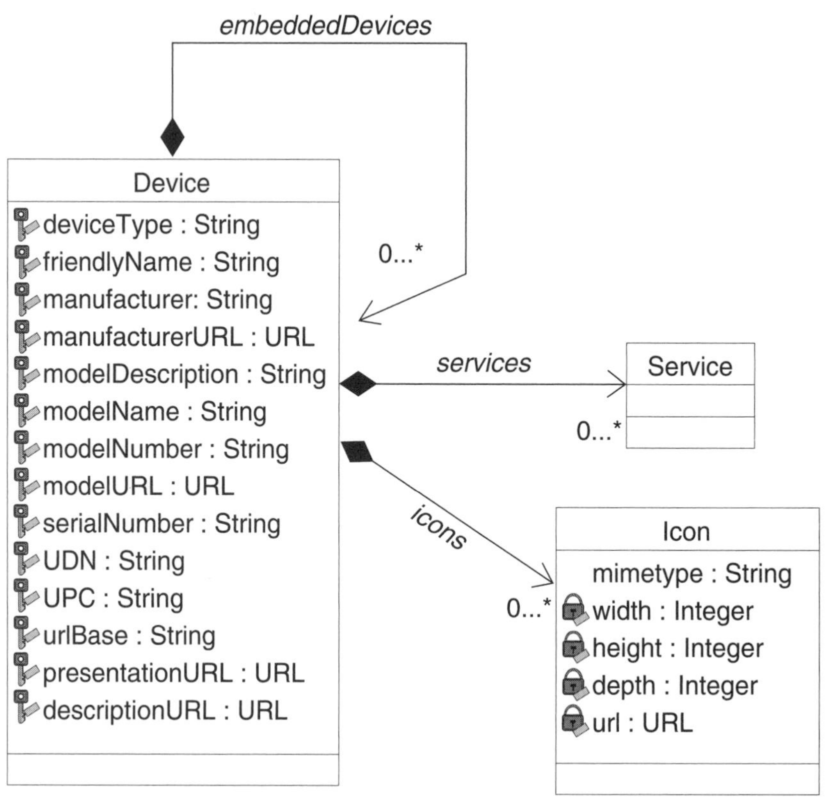

Figure 2.6 Class Diagram: The UPnP Device

The Service's URLs

Each UPnP service has a *service type* Uniform Resource Identifier (URI)[3] that uniquely identifies the service. Standard service types are defined by a UPnP Forum working committee and begin with `urn:schemas-upnp-org:service` followed by a service type suffix, colon, and an integer service version.

For example, the following service type URI is for the UPnP A/V Connection Manager Service, version 1:

```
urn:schemas-upnp-org:service:ConnectionManager:1
```

[3] A Uniform Resource Identifier can be either a name or a URL. Think of it as a unique identifier. Chapter 3 has more information about URIs.

Every service also has a *serviceId* URI that uniquely identifies the service among all of a device's services. No two services may have the same serviceId. For standard services defined by a UPnP Forum working committee, the serviceId must begin with `urn:upnp-org:serviceId:` followed by a serviceId suffix. For example, the serviceId for the Connection Manager Service could be specified as follows:

```
urn:upnp-org:serviceId:cmgr
```

Every service maintains three URLs that provide the information necessary for control points to communicate with services, as follows:

- The `ControlURL` is where control points post requests to control this service. The UPnP vendor specifies one for each device.
- The `EventSubURL` is where control points post requests to subscribe to events. The event subscription URL must be unique within the device; no two services may have the same URL for eventing. If the service has no evented variables, it should not have eventing; if the service does not have eventing, this element must be present but should be empty.
- The `DescriptionURL` tells control points the location from which they can retrieve the service description document. The service description is an XML document that summarizes the information about a service, including each of its actions. This document is returned upon an HTTP GET request.

Each service has zero or more state variables. Each state variable has a name, a type, and a current value. The UPnP Device Architecture specification recommends that a state variable also have a default value, but does not require it. A state variable also has a set of allowed values used to describe the range of permissible values for the variable.

Any of the state variables can trigger events on state changes as determined by the implementer of the service. If the variable does trigger an event when its state changes, it is said to be evented.

Every input argument to an action is associated with one of the service's state variables. This is called the argument's *related state variable*. Figure 2.7 adds the state variable class to the previous diagram of the service and its actions. Only one of an action's arguments may be designated as the action's *return value*. The return value provides the result of the action to the caller.

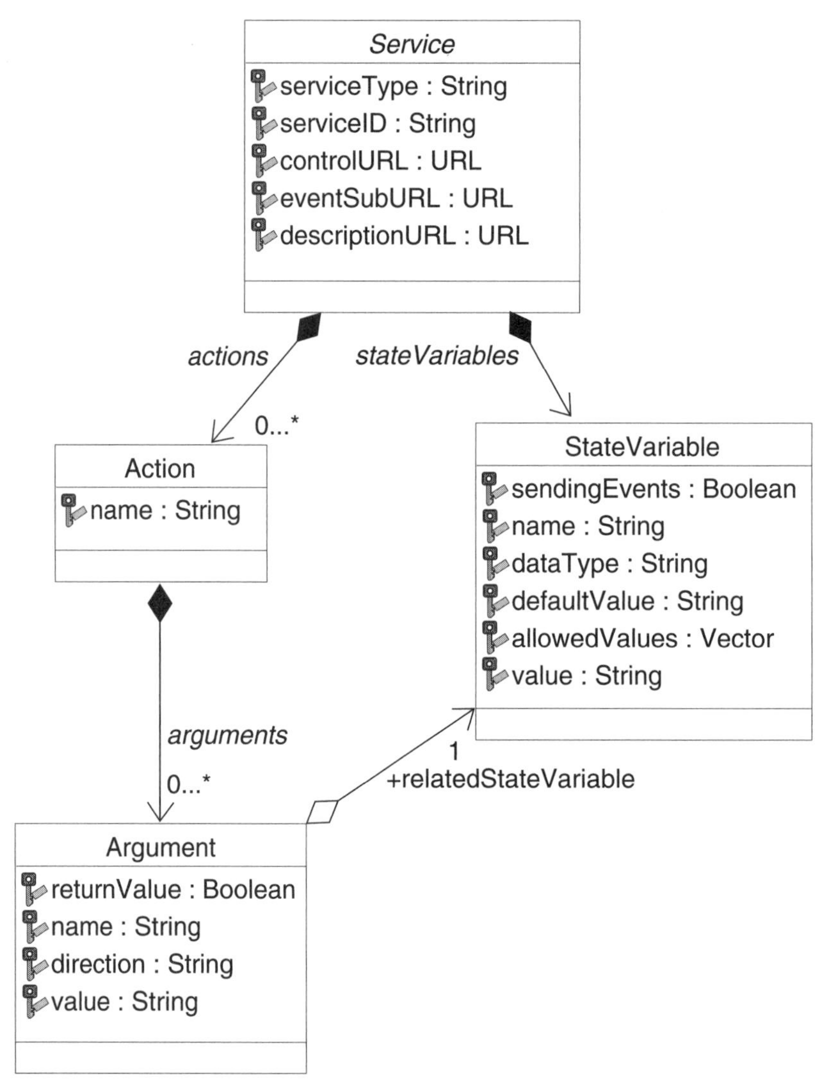

Figure 2.7 Class Diagram: Service, Actions, and State Variables

Events and Subscriptions

UPnP architecture employs an event notification system using a publisher/subscriber model, where control points assume the role of subscribers and services the role of publishers. Services publish event notifications to control points that have subscribed to receive them. The event notification message from the service has the current value of all of the service's state variables. The UPnP architecture provides no mechanism to subscribe on a variable-by-variable basis.

A subscription is a request from a control point to a service to receive a notification when any of the service's state variables change state. A control point subscribes by sending a subscription request that includes:

- The service of interest
- A URL to which the events can be sent
- A subscription time for the event notification

Accepting the Subscription

If the service accepts the subscription, the service responds with a unique subscription identifier and a duration for the subscription. The unique identifier allows the control point to refer to the subscription in subsequent requests to the service, such as renewing or canceling the subscription. The duration specifies the length of time that the subscription is valid and will be maintained by the service.

Initial Event Message

As soon as possible after the subscription is accepted, the service also sends the first, or initial, event message to the subscriber. This event message contains the names and current values for all evented variables and allows the subscriber to initialize its model of the state of the service.

Modeling a Device

A control point typically maintains an image of the state of devices with which it is working. When the control point receives an event message notifying it of a state change with a device, it updates its internal representation of the device, keeping it in sync with the devices it is monitoring. The control point can use this information in subsequent actions to guide its operation.

State Variables Don't Have to Be Evented

Not all state variables must be evented. A service may designate one or more state variables as *non-evented* and not send event messages to subscribers when these variables change values.

State Change Events

If one or more of a service's state variables are evented, the service publishes updates to the subscribers when the variables change. An event is a message from a service to subscribed control points that is used to keep the control points informed of changes in state associated with the service. Control points subscribe to events and the service notifies them when the event has occurred.

All subscribers are sent all event messages. Subscribers receive event messages for all evented variables, and event messages are sent regardless of the reason that the state variable changed, for instance, in response to an action request or due to an internal state change.

Subscription Expiration

If a subscription expires, the subscription identifier becomes invalid, and the service stops sending event messages to the control point. If the control point tries to send any message other than a subscription request message—a subscription renewal request, for example—the service rejects the message because the subscription identifier is invalid.

Subscription Renewal

All subscriptions must be renewed periodically for the control points to continue to receive notifications (unless they are initially requested for "infinite" duration). To keep the subscription active, a control point must send a renewal message before the subscription expires. The renewal message is sent to the same URL as the original subscription message, but the renewal message does not include a delivery URL for event messages. Instead, the renewal message includes the subscription identifier received in the initial message accepting the subscription.

Subscription Cancellation

When a control point no longer wants to receive events from a service, the control point should cancel its subscription. Generally, canceling a subscription reduces service, control point, and network load. If removed abruptly from the network, the control point might be unable to send a cancellation message. As a fallback, the subscription eventually expires on its own unless renewed.

The Built-in Web Server

Every UPnP device has a built-in web server that is used as the underlying communication mechanism for much of the device's functionality. The web server receives the messages related to description, control, presentation, and event subscription. It provides access to the device's description document, the service description documents, the device presentation page, device control, and event registration.

UPnP devices build on web technologies to move from a manual web browsing system to a dynamic, distributed system of programmable components on the local network.

The UPnP Architecture and Web Services

The UPnP architecture has a lot in common with Internet-based web services. Devices are like containers for web services, making functionality available in the home that can be composed to create new kinds of distributed applications. In fact, both UPnP and Internet-based web services use the SOAP protocol to invoke methods/actions. However, as you will see in Chapter 5, UPnP uses a local discovery mechanism while web services use an Internet-scale discovery system called UDDI. In the future, as discussed in Chapter 19, UPnP 2.0 will adopt the Web Services Description Language, replacing its current syntax for device and service description. This will bring UPnP another step closer to Internet-based web services.

The UPnP Stack

The TCP/IP protocol suite and HTTP provide the basic network connectivity for the UPnP device architecture. Communication between control points and devices is built upon HTTP as the foundation, over both connection-oriented and connectionless transport protocols. The connection-oriented Transmission Control Protocol (TCP) is used as the transport when a control point is communicating directly with a device or when a service is communicating to a control point. The User Datagram Protocol (UDP) is used when a control point or device needs to communicate to many recipients simultaneously.

Point-to-Point Communication

Each UPnP device provides a set of HTTP URLs for control points to retrieve the device description document, control the device, subscribe to events, and get the devices presentation page. Figure 2.8 shows the basic UPnP protocol stack.

Multicast Communication

A few aspects of the UPnP architecture require the sender to communicate with many recipients simultaneously. For example, UPnP discovery mechanism allows devices to send presence announcements to all of the other devices on the network, letting them know that the device is now available. For this purpose, the UPnP architecture uses a form of HTTP that is sent over multicast UDP, called HTTPMU. In some cases, response messages are sent directly back to the source using HTTP over unicast UDP, called HTTPU. These protocols are illustrated in the Figure 2.9.

Addressing Protocols

The UPnP architecture devices must support both the Dynamic Host Configuration Protocol (DHCP) and the dynamic configuration of private link-local addresses ("Auto-IP"). A device first attempts to contact a DHCP service to acquire an address. If it fails to locate a DHCP server, the device uses Auto-IP, which enables devices to select addresses without a DHCP server being present to assign the address.

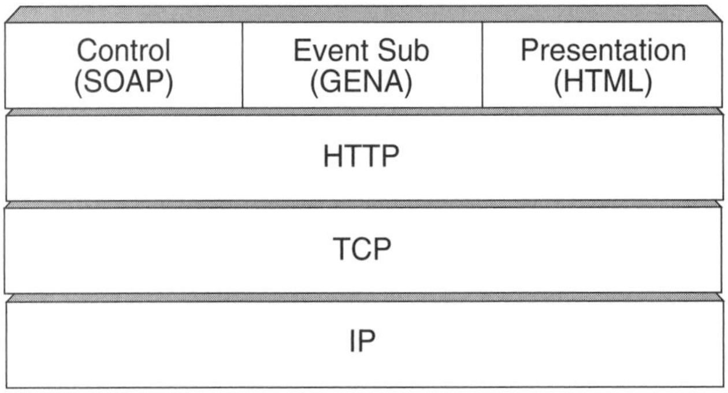

Figure 2.8 The UPnP Architecture Protocol Stack

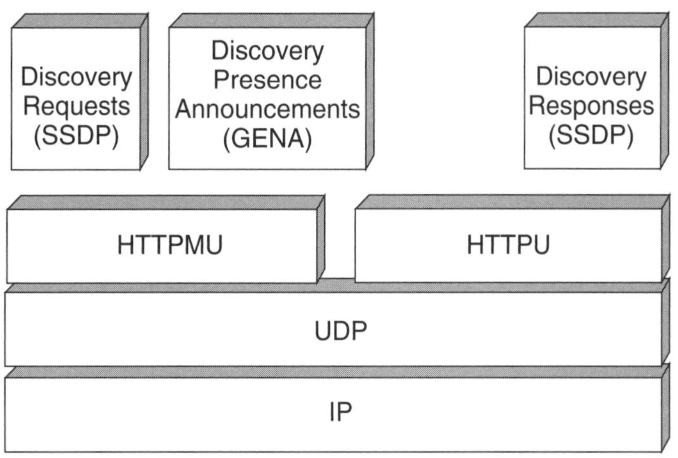

Figure 2.9 HTTPMU and HTTPU Protocol Stack

Summary

- The UPnP architecture is a powerful and flexible software architecture that makes use of existing standard protocols, combining them to provide a zero-administration networking capability for the home or small office network.
- Standard device and service types enable devices from various manufacturers to interoperate.
- All UPnP devices follow the same pattern in their operation and support protocols for addressing, discovery, description, control, eventing, and presentation.
- The UPnP object model that includes devices, services, actions, events, and subscriptions is simple.
- The basic set of operations for this object model allows control points to retrieve information about devices, to invoke device services, and to manage event subscriptions.
- UPnP devices can join an existing managed network or can form ad-hoc networks without the support of networking infrastructure services.

Chapter 3

The Technical Foundation

A wise man builds his house upon the rock.

—Matthew 7:24

The UPnP device architecture builds upon existing protocols rather than inventing new mechanisms to do the same thing. For example, the protocol used by UPnP devices to implement device discovery uses HTTP over UDP over IP multicast to send search messages to all hosts listening on the local network. This chapter covers the technological foundation upon which the UPnP architecture is built, including URIs, IP Multicast, HTTP, HTTPU, HTTPMU, XML, and DOM. This is not an exhaustive treatment of each subject, but provides the UPnP developer with enough background on the UPnP architecture's technical foundation to prepare for subsequent chapters.

If you are already familiar with this material, you may proceed directly to Chapter 4, the first chapter of Part 2 of this book, to begin the overview of UPnP protocols.

Uniform Resource Identifiers

The World Wide Web has information, in the form of *resources*, and links among the resources. The resources are either physical resources, such as a file stored on a server, or abstract resources, such as a CGI script that reads fields from a database and formats the data into an HTML page to return to the client. A *Uniform Resource Identifier* (URI) is a compact string of characters used to identify a resource on the Web.[1] The URI provides a conceptual mapping from an identifier to a resource on the Web. For example, the contents of a web page can change over time, while the URI for the page stays the same. URIs are further classified as Uniform Resource Locators and Uniform Resource Names.

Uniform Resource Locators

A *Uniform Resource Locator* (URL) is a URI that identifies a resource by specifying its location rather than identifying the resource by name or some other attribute. Many URL schemes are named after protocols. For example, URLs using the HTTP scheme begin with `http://` and specify to use the HTTP protocol to retrieve the resource. URLs beginning with `ftp://` specify to use the FTP protocol to retrieve the resource.

Uniform Resource Names

A *Uniform Resource Name* (URN) is a label for a resource that is required to remain globally unique and persistent even when the resource ceases to exist or becomes unavailable. Therefore, URNs cannot be reused; once a URN is used to name a resource, it is never used again to name another resource.

The URN does not describe the location of the resource, but provides only its name. The name is drawn from one of a set of defined namespaces, each of which has its own structure and procedures for assigning names. The `urn` prefix, for example, is used in a standardized URN namespace for naming resources.

The UPnP Architecture and URIs

URIs—both URLs and USNs—have many uses within UPnP devices. UPnP devices, for example, use URNs to uniquely identify both the type of device, like a UPnP printer, and the particular instance of device, such as a printer from a particular manufacturer. UPnP services use URNs in the same way—to identify both the type and name of the

[1] The precise syntax for URI is defined in RFC 2396.

service. URLs are used by devices to define locations that control points can use to send requests to devices, such as when invoking an action provided by one of a device's services.

IP Multicast

IP multicast provides an efficient means to implement a group communication model as is required by some phases of UPnP (discovery, for example, uses multicast to find devices on a network and to inform control points of a device's presence). Using IP multicast, a host can simultaneously send data to many other hosts on the network without having to send a copy of the data to each host individually.

Conceptually, multicasting consists of the following components:

- A group of hosts to receive data
- A mechanism for hosts to join and leave the group
- Multicast-capable routers for managing and relaying group membership information and efficiently forwarding multicast traffic
- Protocols and APIs for applications to create, send, and manage data

The Host Group

The group of hosts that receive multicast data from the sender is called the *host group*. The host group is a logical entity whose membership can change over time. Each host in the group shares a common multicast address and receives any data sent to the multicast address.

The sender does not need to be a member of the group to send data to it, nor does the sender need to know the specific members of the group. From the sender's point of view, multicast is just like unicast; the sender simply sends data to a specific address and port, and the underlying network handles the communication with the members of the group. The only difference is the address used. For unicast, the address belongs to a particular host; for multicast, the address is a special multicast address shared by potentially many hosts.

Multicast Addressing

Internet Protocol, version 4 (IPv4) multicast addresses are Class D Internet addresses. Class D Internet addresses start with 1110 in the high-order bits and cover the range of addresses from 224.0.0.0 to 239.255.255.255.

Many addresses in this range are reserved for specific purposes. For example, 224.0.0.1 is the *all hosts group*, which is used to address all of the multicast hosts that are directly connected to the same network as the sender, and 224.0.0.2 is used to communicate with all routers on a subnet. UPnP control points and devices use the multicast address 239.255.255.250, and port 1900. Using this address and port, any source can send data to all UPnP devices and control points on a local network.

Network Infrastructure Support for IP Multicast

IP multicast requires the support of multicast-capable IP routers. These routers implement the protocols required to manage groups and to determine the best paths for forwarding data among other multicast routers. The routers share information with each other about group membership, communicate with endpoints to accept requests for joining and leaving groups, and forward multicast data to other multicast routers on the network.

The Reach of UPnP Network Traffic

While most details of IP multicast need not concern developers of UPnP devices, one detail should be understood: how far multicast traffic is allowed to propagate on the local network. There are two ways multicast routers limit the range of multicast packets: the IP datagram's TTL field and administratively scoped IP multicast.

Time to Live Field

The Time to Live (TTL) field of the IPv4 header controls the number of times, or "hops," that an IP datagram is allowed to traverse a router. Each time a router forwards a datagram, the datagram's TTL field is decremented by 1. If a datagram's TTL field is greater than 1, the multicast router forwards the packet, but if the TTL field is 0, the multicast router drops the packet without sending an error notification to the sender.

Changing the TTL value used at the source of multicast communication extends or contracts the reach of the packets. Making the TTL value too small may unnecessarily restrict the reach of the multicast traffic, while making the TTL value too large may make the multicast traffic available to unintended hosts. By default, the UPnP Device Architecture specification requires that the TTL field defaults to 4, but allows this value to be locally configurable. This means that multicast communication sent by a UPnP control point or device reaches other UPnP devices and control points within four router hops.

Administratively Scoped IP Multicast

There is another way to limit the reach of multicast data. There is a special range of IP Multicast addresses, 239.0.0.0 to 239.255.255.255, that is called the *administratively scoped IPv4 multicast address space*. Within this range, addresses are partitioned to have predefined semantics about the scope or how broadly the data will propagate. Administrative scoping provides a simple way to contain IP multicast communication within the administrative boundaries of an organization. Network administrators may configure a scope region whenever limiting the distribution of multicast data is required. For example, the routers at the edge of an organization can be configured as administrative boundaries and will not forward multicast datagrams to routers outside this boundary, regardless of the datagram's TTL value.

The IP multicast address used by UPnP devices, 239.255.255.250, is an administratively scoped multicast address. This address falls within the *IPv4 Local Scope* and is the smallest of the administrative scopes.

UPnP and IP Multicast

As you'll see in subsequent chapters, the UPnP architecture uses IP multicast as a transport to send messages to many recipients simultaneously. For example,

- Control points use a IP multicast-based discovery mechanism to find out which devices are present on the local network.
- Devices announce their presence on the network using messages carried over IP multicast.
- Services send state change event messages over IP multicast to control points that have registered to receive the events.

The UPnP architecture makes extensive use of IP multicast. Many of the messages of the UPnP device architecture are carried in an extended version of the HTTP protocol designed specifically for IP multicast. However, before you take a look at the modified HTTP, here is a review of HTTP basics.

Hypertext Transfer Protocol 1.0

With the tremendous success of the World Wide Web, the Hypertext Transfer Protocol (HTTP) has become a ubiquitous transport protocol.[2] HTTP started out as a simple text-based request-response protocol designed to carry various web-based resources, such as HTML pages and image files. HTTP's limited set of commands allowed a web browser to perform simple interactions with web servers—retrieving web pages, posting data to a server, and so on. Because of its simplicity, and the fact that most network administrators permit HTTP to pass through their routers, the use of HTTP grew. Pragmatic engineers began to use HTTP for other applications, running their protocols over HTTP to penetrate the firewall. HTTP has since evolved to become a generic, stateless, extensible, object-oriented protocol that can be used for many tasks, from name servers to distributed object management systems.

HTTP Request/Response Model

HTTP uses a simple request/response model of communication: an HTTP client opens a connection with an HTTP server and sends a *request message* to the server. The server returns a *response message*, usually containing the resource that was requested by the client. After delivering the response, the HTTP 1.0 server closes the connection.[3] No connection state is maintained by the server between requests, making HTTP a *stateless protocol*. State can be maintained at the client in the form of *cookies*, which are presented to the server with each request.

Structure of HTTP Transactions

The format of HTTP request and response messages is similar. Both message types consist of:

- An *initial line* that specifies the *method*, or action, to be taken
- Zero or more *header lines* that specify variables and their values

---

[2] See `http://www.jmarshall.com/easy/http/`. Also, for a complete specification of HTTP 1.0, see RFC 1945, and for HTTP 1.1, see RFC 2616. Both of these specifications are on the accompanying CD-ROM.

[3] As you will see in the next section, HTTP 1.1 servers can keep the connection open after sending a response. Their connections are "persistent" and result in increased performance.

- A blank line (that is, a CRLF combination by itself)
- An optional *message body* (for example: a file, or query data, or query output)

The initial line and message headers should end in CRLF, although any web browser or web server should gracefully handle lines ending in just LF (CR and LF here mean ASCII values 13 and 10, even though some platforms may use different characters.)

Initial Request Line

The initial line is different for the request and for the response. A request line has three parts separated by spaces: a method name, the local path of the requested resource, and the version of HTTP being used. For example, a typical request line looks like:

```
GET /path/to/file/index.html HTTP/1.0
```

`GET` is the most common HTTP method. It requests the server to return the indicated resource specified in the second field, the Request-URI. The final field of the initial request line is always the HTTP version used in the form `HTTP/`*`major.minor`* in uppercase characters. In this case, the version is `HTTP/1.0`.

HTTP Status Codes—Initial Response Line

The initial response line, called the *status line*, also has three parts separated by spaces: the HTTP version, a *response status code* that gives the result of the request, and an English *reason phrase* describing the status code. Typical status lines are:

```
HTTP/1.0 200 OK
```

or

```
HTTP/1.0 404 Not Found
```

The HTTP version is in the same format as the request line, HTTP/x.x.

The status code is meant to be computer-readable; the reason phrase is meant to be human-readable, and may vary. The status code is a three-digit integer, and the first digit identifies the general category of response:

- 1xx indicates an informational message only.
- 2xx indicates success of some kind.

- 3xx redirects the client to another URL.
- 4xx indicates an error on the client's part.
- 5xx indicates an error on the server's part.

The most common status codes are listed in Table 3.1.

Header Lines

Header lines provide information about the request or response, or about the object sent in the message body. The header lines appear in the message one per line and are of the form "*Header-Name: value*," ending with CRLF. It is the same format used for e-mail and news postings and is defined in RFC 822, section 3. The details include the following:

- Header lines should end in CRLF, but you should handle LF correctly.
- The header name is not case-sensitive (although the value may be).
- Any number of spaces or tabs may be between the ":" and the value.
- Header lines beginning with space or tab are actually part of the previous header line, folded into multiple lines for easy reading.

Table 3.1 HTTP Status Codes

Status Code	Description
200 OK	The request was successful.
404 Not Found	The requested resource was not found.
301 Moved Permanently	The requested resource has been permanently moved and is not currently available.
302 Moved Temporarily	The requested resource has been temporarily moved and is not currently available.
303 See Other (HTTP 1.1 only)	The resources has moved to another URL (given by the `Location` response header) and should be automatically retrieved by the client. This is often used by a CGI script to redirect the browser to an existing file.
500 Server Error	An unexpected server error. The most common cause is a server-side script that has bad syntax, fails, or otherwise can't run correctly.

For example, the following two headers are equivalent:

```
Header1: some-long-value-1a, some-long-value-1b


HEADER1: some-long-value-1a,
         some-long value-1b
```

HTTP 1.0 defines 16 headers, although none are required. HTTP 1.1 defines 46 headers, and one of these, the `Host:` header, is required for all requests.

The Message Body

An HTTP message may have a body of data sent after the header lines. In a response, this is where the requested resource is returned to the client (the most common use of the message body), or perhaps it contains explanatory text if there is an error. In a request, this is where user-entered data or uploaded files are sent to the server.

If an HTTP message includes a body, there are usually header lines in the message that describe the body. In particular,

- The `Content-Type` header gives the MIME-type of the data in the body, such as text/html or image/gif.
- The `Content-Length` header gives the number of bytes in the body.

Sample HTTP Exchange

To retrieve the file at the URL

```
http://www.intoast.com/path/file.html
```

the client first opens a socket to the host `www.intoast.com`, on port 80. (It uses the default port because no port number is specified in the URL.) Then the client sends the following through the socket:

```
GET /path/file.html HTTP/1.0
From: someuser@intoast.com
User-Agent: HTTPTool/1.0
(blank line)
```

The initial request line asks the server for the file `/path/file.html`. The two headers `From:` and `User-Agent:` tell the server which user and program are requesting the file. The server responds with something like the following, sent back through the same socket:

```
HTTP/1.0 200 OK
Date: Fri, 20 Nov 2002 23:59:59 GMT
Content-Type: text/html
Content-Length: 1354

<html>
<body>
<h1>Sample Header Text</h1>
(more file contents)
.
.
.
</body>
</html>
```

The initial response line tells the client that the request for the file was successfully processed. The headers in the response include the `Date` header to specify the date and time the server received the request, and the `Content-Type` and `Content-Length` headers to specify the MIME type and the length of the returned file, respectively. After sending the response, the server closes the socket.

HTTP 1.1

Like many other protocols, HTTP has evolved over the years. HTTP 1.1 was introduced to address new needs and overcome shortcomings of HTTP 1.0. Generally speaking, it is a superset of HTTP 1.0 that has specific improvements for faster server responses, including:

- Allowing multiple transactions to take place over a single *persistent connection*
- Cache support, which also reduces required bandwidth
- Support for dynamically-generated pages using *chunked encoding*, a technique that allows a response to be sent before its total length is known

In addition, HTTP 1.1 makes efficient use of IP addresses, allowing multiple domains to be served from a single IP address.

Host: Header

Starting with HTTP 1.1, an HTTP server at one IP address can be *multi-homed*, that is, the home of server web domains. For example, `www.host1.com` and `www.host2.com` can be hosted by the same server.

Hosting several domains on the same server is like several people sharing one phone: a caller knows who they are calling, but whoever answers the phone does not. Thus, every HTTP request must use the `Host` header to specify the host name (and possibly port) for which the request is intended. For example, a complete HTTP 1.1 request looks like this:

```
GET /path/file.html HTTP/1.1
Host: www.host1.com
(blank line)
```

After the initial request line, `Host` is the only required header in an HTTP 1.1 request. HTTP 1.1 severs are not allowed to accept HTTP 1.1 requests without it. If a server receives such a request, it must return a `400 Bad Request` response.

Accepting Absolute URLs

The `Host` header is actually an interim solution to the problem of host identification. In future versions of HTTP, requests will specify the host name in the initial request line by using an absolute URL instead of a pathname, as follows:

```
GET http://www.intoast.com/path/file.html HTTP/1.2
```

The HTTP 1.1 requirement to include a `Host` header in requests applies only to clients using HTTP 1.1 and not clients of any future version of HTTP. If the request uses an HTTP version later than 1.1, the server can accept an absolute URL instead of a `Host` header. If the request uses HTTP 1.0, the server may accept the request without any host identification.

Chunked Transfer-Encoding

If an HTTP server wants to start sending response data before it knows the total length of the response (like with long, dynamically generated output), it can use the simple *chunked transfer-encoding*. Chunked encoding breaks the complete response into smaller chunks and sends them in series. Such responses are identified by including the `Transfer-Encoding` header with the value set to `chunked`. Servers are not required to generate chunked messages, but all HTTP 1.1 clients and servers must be able to process them.

A chunked message body contains a series of *chunks*, followed by a line with "0" (zero), followed by optional footers (just like headers), and a blank line. Each chunk consists of two parts:

- A line with the size of the chunk data, in hexadecimal notation, possibly followed by a semicolon and extra parameters (the "size-line parameters"), ending with CRLF
- The data itself, followed by CRLF

For example, a chunked response might look like the following:

```
HTTP/1.1 200 OK
Date: Fri, Dec 2002 23:59:59 GMT
Content-Type: text/plain
Transfer-Encoding: chunked

1a: ignore-stuff-here
abcdefghijklmnopqrstuvwxyz
10
1234567890abcdef
0
some-footer: some value
another-footer: another value
(blank line)
```

Note the blank line after the last footer. The length of the text data is 42 bytes (1a + 10, in hex), and the data itself is

```
abcdefghijklmnopqrstuvwxyz1234567890abcdef
```

The footers should be treated like headers, as if they were at the top of the response.

The chunks can contain any binary data and may be much larger than the examples here. The size-line parameters are rarely used. Footers are also rare, but might be appropriate for things like checksums or digital signatures.

For comparison, here is the equivalent to the above response without using chunked encoding:

```
Date: Fri, Dec 2002 23:59:59 GMT
Content-Type: text/plain
Content-Length: 42
```

```
some-footer: some value
another-footer: another value

abcdefghijklmnopqrstuvwxyz1234567890abcdef
(blank line)
```

Persistent Connections and the "Connection:close" Header

In HTTP 1.0 and before, TCP connections are closed after each request and response, requiring a new connection for each resource retrieved. Opening and closing TCP connections takes a substantial amount of CPU time, bandwidth, and memory. In practice, most web pages consist of several files on the same server, so much can be saved by allowing several requests and responses to be sent through a single *persistent connection*.

Persistent connections are the default in HTTP 1.1, so nothing special is required to use them. A client just opens a connection and sends several requests in series (called *pipelining*), and reads the responses in the same order as the requests were sent. The server sends responses back in the same order as the requests—this is all it takes for a server to support persistent connections. Clients must be very careful to read the correct length of each response and to separate them correctly.

Because requests can be pipelined, HTTP 1.1 introduces a new mechanism, the `Connection: close` header, for clients to explicitly tell servers when there will be no more requests on the connection. If a client uses the `Connection: close` header in the request, then the connection will be closed after the corresponding response. Similarly, the server can include the `Connection: close` header to inform the client that the server will close the connection following the response, and the client should not send any more requests through that connection. (Servers can also close idle connections after some appropriate timeout period.) Because a server might close the connection before all responses are sent, clients must keep track of requests and resend them as needed. However, when resending, a client should not pipeline the requests until it knows that the connection is persistent.

The "100 Continue" Response

During the course of an HTTP 1.1 client sending a request to a server, the server might respond with an interim `100 Continue` response. This means the server has received the first part of the request and can be used to aid communication over slow links. In any case, HTTP 1.1 clients must handle the 100 response correctly (perhaps by just ignoring it).

The `100 Continue` response is structured like any HTTP response, that is, it consists of a status line, optional headers, and a blank line. Unlike other responses, it is always followed by another complete, final response.

So, further extending the last example, the full data that comes back from the server might consist of two responses in series, such as

```
HTTP/1.1 100 Continue

HTTP/1.1 200 OK
Date: Fri, 31 Dec 2002 23:59:59 GMT
Content-Type: text/plain
Content-Length: 42
some-footer: some-value
another-footer: another-value

abcdefghijklmnopqrstuvwxyz1234567890abcdef
```

To handle this, a simple HTTP 1.1 client might read one response from the socket; if the status code is 100, discard the first response and read the next one instead.

When an HTTP server receives the first line of an HTTP 1.1 (or later) request, it must respond with either `100 Continue` or an error. If it sends the `100 Continue` response, it must also send another, final response, once the request has been processed. The `100 Continue` response requires no headers, but must be followed by the usual blank line, such as:

```
HTTP/1.1 100 Continue
(blank line)
(another HTTP response goes here)
```

Caching

To support caching, HTTP 1.1 servers must time-stamp every response with a `Date` header containing the current time (all time values in HTTP use Greenwich Mean Time), in the form

```
Date: Sun, 1 Nov 2002; 14:34:22 GMT
```

All responses except those with 100-level status must include the `Date` header. Including a `Date` header in the response allows clients to cache responses along with the date and time that they received from the server.

Clients may use the `If-Modified-Since` or `If-Unmodified-Since` headers to specify time-based conditions for servers to return resources. For example, a client may use the `If-Modified-Since` header to ask the server for a newer version of the resource if it has been modified since the last time it retrieved it. Using these headers, clients can determine that they have a current version of the specified resource and do not have to waste network bandwidth by unnecessarily retrieving a resource that is the same as the one they already have.

Client and Server Requirements

HTTP 1.1 requires a few additional features from both clients and servers. To comply with HTTP 1.1, clients must

- include the `Host` header with each request
- accept responses with chunked data
- either support persistent connections, or include the `Connection: close` header with each request
- handle the `100 Continue` response

To comply with HTTP 1.1, servers must:

- require the `Host` header from HTTP 1.1 clients
- accept absolute URLs in a request
- accept requests with chunked data
- either support persistent connections or include the `Connection: close` header with each response
- use the `100 Continue` response appropriately
- include the `Date` header in each response
- support at least the `GET` and `HEAD` methods
- support HTTP 1.0 requests

The UPnP device architecture makes extensive use of HTTP (version 1.1), and IP multicast is often the underlying transport. Now take a look at an extended version of HTTP that was designed to be carried over IP multicast.

HTTP over UDP—HTTPMU and HTTPU

HTTP is a generic request/response protocol that is carried over TCP. However, TCP is a stream-oriented protocol between two communicating peers. There are many other kinds of communication that cannot be efficiently modeled using TCP, such as sending a single message to a group of recipients. A host would have to send the same message to all recipients individually. What is needed is a way to keep the benefits of HTTP while using either unicast or multicast UDP as the transport.

HTTP over unicast UDP, HTTPU, affords the benefits of HTTP along with the simplicity of UDP. With HTTPU, a host can send an HTTP-formatted message to another host without the expense of setting up a TCP connection.

HTTP over multicast UDP, HTTPMU, allows the sending of HTTP messages, but to many recipients simultaneously. HTTPMU enables a group communication model using HTTP-style request/response messages.

Although there are clear benefits to being able to send HTTP over UDP, doing so introduces a few problems that must be resolved:

- If a host sends to many recipients, they may all respond at the same time, perhaps overwhelming the sending host's ability to process the responses.
- If a host sends multiple requests to many recipients, it must match the responses, received asynchronously, with the original request.
- HTTP's `Location` header is used to identify a URI in a response message, such as when redirecting the client to a new URI. HTTP only supports a single `Location` header in response messages. New models of communication enabled by HTTP over UDP may require multiple locations to be specified in a response.

HTTPU and HTTPMU introduce three new HTTP headers to address these issues: the `MX` request header, the `S` general header, and the `AL` general header.

The MX Request Header

The `MX` request header is used to help spread out, over time, responses to HTTPMU requests so that they do not come at a rate greater than the requestor can handle. The `MX` header specifies the maximum number of seconds that a multicast UDP HTTP resource can wait before it sends a response initiated by a multicast request.

If a resource has a single response to a request, it generates a random number between `0` and `MX` that represents the number of seconds the resource waits before sending the response. If a resource has multiple responses to the request, it should send these resources spread over the interval `[0..MX]`.

The client will receive responses from the various resources spread out over the time interval specified in the `MX` header, lowering the chances of the client becoming overwhelmed by the responses.

The S (Sequence) General Header

Because UDP is connectionless, there is no way for an HTTPU/HTTPMU client to associate a response from a server with a request the client has previously sent. The `S` header provides this ability. The `S` header contains an absolute URI that is unique across the entire URI namespace. When an `S` header is sent by a client on a HTTPU/HTTPMU request, the server simply returns the same value in the response.

If a client receives multiple responses with the same `S` header, then the client may assume that all the responses refer to the same request. However, because the responses are carried by UDP, there are no ordering guarantees for the responses. Multiple responses with the same `S` header can come in any order. Clients are not required to send the `S` header; it is purely for the convenience of the client to match responses with requests.

The AL (Alternate Location) General Header

HTTP's `Location` response header allows a single URI to be returned in a response. For example, for HTTP `201 (Created)` responses, the `Location` header specifies the new resource that was created by the request. The `Location` header's value consists of a single absolute URL, as follows:

```
Location: http://www.intoast.com/index.htm
```

Using HTTPMU and HTTPU, there are many instances in which a resource needs to provide location information using multiple URIs. The standard `Location` header is not sufficient in this case. The `AL` header is a new header for HTTPMU/HTTPU that has the same semantics as the location header but can contain multiple URIs.

The contents of an `AL` header are ordered. If both a `Location` header and an `AL` header are included in the same message, then the URI in the `Location` header is to be treated as if it were the first entry in the `AL` header.

The "*" Request URI

Besides specifying new headers, another modification is required to standard HTTP in order to send HTTP over IP multicast. In the HTTP protocol, the client sends a request to the server that consists of a request method, a request URI field, and the HTTP protocol version. For example,

```
GET http://www.intoast.com/index.htm HTTP/1.1
```

The `Request-URI` field of an HTTP request specifies the resource to be retrieved. In the previous example, the client the request was for a web page on the host `www.intoast.com`.

However, when used with a multicast HTTP request, the request URI has a slightly different meaning. Instead of specifying a resource to be retrieved, the `Request-URI` specifies for whom the request is intended. HTTPU and HTTPMU use "*", which means "to everyone who is listening to this IP address and port." For example,

```
M-SEARCH "*" HTTP/1.1
```

In the future, other values for the `Request-URI` may be defined that allow the sender to specify different subsets of the listening hosts. UPnP devices using HTTPU and HTTPMU only use the "*" value for the request URI.

Later chapters show how various protocols used by UPnP devices use HTTPU and HTTPMU, which tie together the simplicity of HTTP messages with the ability of IP multicast to efficiently reach many hosts simultaneously. HTTP and IP multicast provide the transport for the messages. The next topic in the list of technologies that provide the foundation for the UPnP architecture, XML, provides the means to format messages.

Extensible Markup Language

The Extensible Markup Language (XML) is fast becoming the de facto Internet standard for the representation of information. XML is a meta-language that allows customized markup languages to be developed that specify the structure of data and how various elements relate. XML also provides for easy data exchange, as XML documents contain self-describing information about the rules used to compose them. XML is detailed in the XML 1.0 specification provided by the World Wide Web Consortium[4] (W3C), the body that defines standards for the Web.

---

[4] See `http://www.w3c.org` for more details.

XML Documents

XML documents consist of *markup* and *character data*. Markup refers to those parts of the XML document that give it its structure, such as the start and end tags that delimit the elements of an XML document, the comments that are included to describe the document, or the processing instructions that give the XML processor instructions on how to process the document. Character data is all of the data in an XML document that is not markup; it is the content of the document.

Syntactically, XML documents must be *well-formed* and *valid*. A well-formed XML document follows the syntax established for XML documents by the W3C. For example, according to the XML specification, an XML document consists of three parts: a prolog, a root element, and a miscellaneous part. In addition, to be valid, an XML document must conform to an associated *document type definition* (DTD) or XML schema that provides the detailed syntax for a particular type of document.

The Document Prolog

XML documents begin with a document *prolog* that may contain an XML declaration, processing instructions, comments, white space, and document type declarations. The document prolog is optional. However, the W3C recommends that XML documents include at least an XML declaration.

The XML Declaration

The XML declaration is the first line of the document and identifies it as an XML document, as follows:

```
<?xml version="1.0" encoding="UTF-8" standalone="no"?>
```

The XML declaration has the following three attributes:

- *Version.* This attribute is required for all XML declarations. It specifies the XML version used to compose the document. Currently, only "1.0" is possible.
- *Encoding.* The encoding attribute specifies the language encoding for the document. The default is UTF-8. Other encodings include Unicode, UCS-2, and UCS-4. This attribute is optional.
- *Standalone.* This optional attribute is set to "no" if the document does not refer to any external entities. Otherwise, the value is "yes."

Processing Instructions

The <? and ?> pairs of characters used in the XML declaration identify processing instructions for the XML processor. These instructions, except for `<?xml?>` and `<?XML?>` which are reserved, are specific to the XML processor. For example, the processing instruction `<?xml-stylesheet?>` is understood by both Microsoft Internet Explorer version 5 and Netscape Navigator version 6, and is used to connect an XML document with an external stylesheet.

Comments

The prolog often contains comments that describe the XML document. XML comments use the same convention as HTML comments: They start with `<!--` and end with `-->`. Comments may appear anywhere in a document except before the XML declaration and not within markup. For example, the following comment is embedded within a tag and is not allowed:

```
<TAG attribute="value" <!--comments can't go here -->>
```

Instead, comments should appear outside of any other markup:

```
<!-- comments work better here -->
<TAG attribute=" value" >
```

White Space

XML documents may contain the typical white space characters such as spaces, carriage returns, line feeds, and tabs. By default, the XML processor ignores the white space in the document's markup, but preserves it outside of the markup (in the document's content). Ignoring white space in the document markup allows the document writer to format the document to make it easier to read. For example, nesting conventions can be followed to help human readers more easily understand the relationships expressed by the document.

Document Type Declarations and XML Schema

Both Document Type Definitions (DTDs) and XML schema are methods for specifying the syntax of XML documents. A particular DTD or XML schema defines a new type of document. For example, a "memo" DTD could define the structure of a business memo within an organization.

Although both methods allow a document designer to specify the elements, attributes, and other characteristics of a valid document type, each method has its own syntax. DTDs came first and use a syntax that is not based on XML. The much more powerful XML schema syntax was defined later by the W3C, and XML schema are themselves valid XML documents.

The UPnP device architecture uses the XML schema method for specifying the different document types used by UPnP devices and control points. Working committees within the UPnP Forum define standard device and service templates for each standard UPnP device type. Implementers use these standard device and service templates and may augment them with additional functionality specific to their implementation.

XML Namespaces

Because XML permits the creation of new markup languages, each with their own set of tags and attributes, name conflicts inevitably arise. For example, consider an XML document that uses two XML schema—one for specifying information about books and one for specifying information about magazine articles. Both XML schema define the `<author>` tag, but each defines a different set of attributes for this tag. The document designer is not able to use both of these schema at the same time because of the name conflict.

XML namespaces provide a mechanism for using otherwise incompatible schema. An XML document simply lists the namespaces it is using, with the `xmlns` attribute, and provides an identifier for each namespace. The tag name now includes a prepended namespace identifier, differentiating it from other tags with the same name in other namespaces. For example,

```
<?xml version="1.0"?>
<items xmlns:book="http://www.intoast.com/book-schema"
 xmlns:mag="http://www.intoast.com/mag-schema">
  <book:book>
    <book:title>How to fix things</book:title>
    <book:author>Jonathan Goode</book:author>
  </book:book>
  <mag:magazine>
    <mag:title>40 days to a better you</mag:title>
    <mag:author>Dr. Bill</mag:author>
  </mag:magazine>
</items>
```

If a namespace attribute is provided without a namespace identifier prefix, the namespace is the default namespace. Tags and attributes in the default namespace can be used without any prefix.

Besides specifying the prefix to use for a given XML schema, using a namespace attribute causes the XML processor to include the referenced schema file. Using XML namespaces has the effect of pulling in new syntax and confining that syntax to a particular prefix in the referencing document. For example, in Chapter 6, "Description," a UPnP device description starts as follows:

```
<?xml version="1.0"?>
<root xmlns="urn:schemas-upnp-org:device-1-0">
```

and a UPnP service description starts like this:

```
<?xml version="1.0"?>
<scpd xmlns="urn:schemas-upnp-org:service-1-0">
```

In the first case, the device description XML document is including the device description schema, specified by the URN, urn:schemas-upnp-org:device-1-0. In the second case, the service description XML document is including the service description schema, urn:schemas-upnp-org:service-1-0.

XML Elements

Elements are the most common form of XML markup. Like elements in HTML, XML elements have a start tag and an end tag, each of which are delimited by angle brackets. For example, a book element might look like this:

```
<book>
   sub-elements here
</book>
```

Some elements may be empty. In this case, the characters "/>"are used to close the empty tag, effectively merging the start and end tags. For example, an empty book element looks like: <book/> .

XML tag names are case-sensitive; that is, the tags <ELEMENT>, <Element>, and <element> are all distinct.

The Root Element

The root element is the single element of an XML document that holds all of the other elements of the document. The root element comes directly after the document's prolog. For example, a simple XML document that describes a magazine article might look like this:

```
<?xml version="1.0"?>
<article>
  <title>How to write XML Documents</title>
```

```
  <author>Justin Smith</author>
  <ref>http://www.intoast.com/WritingXML.html</ref>
</article>
```

In this example, the document starts with the prolog, consisting of just the XML declaration, followed by the root element, `<article>`, which contains the article's sub-elements.

XML Attributes

XML attributes are name/value pairs that occur inside start tags and empty tags after the tag name. Values are assigned to attributes using the equals sign and must be quoted. For example, the following start tag

```
<article available="true">
```

specifies that the `article` element has an attribute, `available`, that has the value `true`. Although both single (' ') and double (" ") quotes are allowed, it is common practice to use double quotes. If single quotes are used, double quotes may appear in the string. If double quotes are used, single quotes may appear in the string.

CDATA Sections

CDATA sections are a way to include text that contains characters that would otherwise cause the XML processor to interpret the text as markup. The text inside the CDATA section is not interpreted by the XML processor; it simply passes over the text looking for the closing tag. For example, the following element contains a CDATA section containing the characters "<" and ">."

```
<SourceCodeExample>
<![CDATA
#include <stdio.h>
int main(){ return 0; }
]]>
</SourceCodeExample>
```

XML and UPnP

XML is used by the UPnP device architecture to describe UPnP devices and the services they provide, to carry UPnP action requests and responses, and to specify the format of events sent by services to control points. Subsequent chapters describe each of these uses in detail.

The Document Object Model

The Document Object Model (DOM) is an API for HTML and XML documents that defines the object model for these documents. The W3C has specified the DOM API in a language-independent way, and it has been implemented in many different programming languages, including C, C++, Java, and JavaScript. With the Document Object Model, programmers can access, change, delete, or add just about anything found in an HTML or XML documents.

The Tree Structure

In DOM, a document is treated as a tree of nodes. Everything in a document becomes a node—elements, attributes, text, CDATA sections, and so on. For example, consider the following XML document:

```
<?xml version="1.0" encoding="UTF-8"?>
<Book>
  <Title>Hello, it's me</Title>
  <Author>Otto B. Graphy</Author>
</Book>
```

This document has a node corresponding to the processing instruction on the first line and a root node corresponding to the `<Book>` element. The `<Book>` element has two sub-nodes, the `<Title>` and `<Author>` nodes. These nodes are *child nodes* of the `<Book>` node. Both the `<Title>` and `<Author>` nodes have a sub-node that contains the text of each element.

The DOM API is a programmer's view of a document with its own object model and related terminology. Where an XML or HTML document has elements, attributes, and so on, a DOM programmer views the same document in terms of nodes of a tree and the set of attributes and functionality of each node.

DOM Levels

The Document Object Model is divided into many different levels, each of which implements a particular set of objects.

- *DOM Level 1.* This specification, at `http://www.w3.org/TR/REC-DOM-Level-1/`, includes methods that manipulate a document's structure and content. It includes functionality to work with HTML and XML documents.

- *DOM Level 2.* This specification, at `http://www.w3.org/TR/DOM-Level-2/`, includes the object model for style sheets and adds functionality for manipulating style information in documents. Other features of DOM Level 2 include a built-in event model and support for XML namespaces.
- *DOM Level 3.* Future levels of the DOM specification will provide features such as document loading and saving, document validation against a schema, and an object model for DTDs and schemas.

DOM Objects

In DOM's object-oriented model, all of the various node types derive from a single base class, Node. The Node base class has the attributes listed in Table 3.2, which are inherited by all of the derived node types.

Each node also inherits methods to allow changing the relationships between a node and its children. These methods include `insertBefore`, `replaceChild`, `removeChild`, and `appendChild`. The derived node types defined by DOM Level 1 are listed in Table 3.3.

Table 3.2 The Attributes of a DOM Node

Object	Description
nodeName	The node's name
nodeValue	The node's value
parentNode	The parent of the node
childNodes	The set of children of this node. The children are provided in a NodeList object that allows iteration over each of the objects and indexing to particular objects
firstChild	The first child of this node
lastChild	The last child of this node
previousSibling	The previous sibling of the node
nextSibling	The next sibling of the node
attributes	The attributes of the current node. The attributes are provided in a NamedNodeMap object that allows indexing by name of the attribute and iteration over all of the attributes
ownerDocument	The top-level document object that includes this node.

Table 3.3 DOM Level 1 Node Types

Object	Description
Document	The document object. This is the root node of the XML file.
DocumentFragment	A fragment of an XML document
DocumentType	The <!DOCTYPE> element
EntityReference	A reference to an entity
Element	An element
Attr	An attribute
ProcessingInstruction	A processing instruction
Comment	A comment
Text	The text of an element or an attribute
CDATASection	The contents of a CDATA section
Entity	A parsed or unparsed entity in the XML document
Notation	A notation

DOM and UPnP

Because the UPnP device architecture makes extensive use of XML, implementations of UPnP devices have many opportunities to use the DOM API. For example, a device implementer can use the DOM API to compose a device description document to send to a control point. The control point can then use the DOM API to parse the incoming device description document. Potential uses of DOM correspond with the use of XML documents by the UPnP device architecture—description documents, events, SOAP requests and responses, and so on.

Summary

This chapter has provided a quick overview of the foundational technologies of the UPnP device architecture. Familiarity with these subjects simplifies learning UPnP by providing the conceptual foundation upon which to build your understanding of UPnP. You won't need to be an expert in XML, for example, to successfully develop UPnP devices, but knowing enough about XML to read device and service descriptions and their related schema will definitely help. For you convenience, Appendix B has a list of references for you to find more information about the technologies mentioned in this chapter.

Part II

UPnP Protocols

Chapter 4

Addressing

"Hallo, Rabbit," said Pooh, "is that you?"

"Let's pretend it isn't," said Rabbit, "and see what happens."

—A. A. Milne, *Winnie-the-Pooh*

Postcards are a simple means of communication. You write your message on a card, address it, put on a stamp, and then drop it in the mailbox. However, if the address you wrote on a postcard was not unique, you might end up sending the card to someone you did not intend. In any communication delivery system, communicating endpoints need to be able to clearly identify to whom they wish to send data. To do so, each endpoint must have a unique address. How UPnP devices acquire, manage, and release addresses is called *addressing*. Addressing is the first step in UPnP networking; without an address, a device cannot proceed with subsequent UPnP phases, such as discovery where it offers its services to control points on the network.

UPnP devices are built upon the foundation of the TCP/IP protocol suite, which provides the network layer connectivity devices needed to communicate. Each endpoint on an IP network has an address that uniquely identifies it among all of the endpoints on the network. There are two addressing protocols used by UPnP devices, the Dynamic Host Configuration Protocol (DHCP) and the Dynamic Configuration of IPv4

Link-Local Addresses ("Auto-IP"). This chapter briefly covers how each of these protocols operates, under which circumstances each is needed, and how each is used by UPnP devices.

Addressing Challenges

The IP protocol is a ubiquitous network protocol and is a good choice for network layer connectivity for UPnP devices. By itself, IP requires configuration that other protocols such as IPX and AppleTalk do not, including configuring each endpoint's IP address. However, in keeping with the zero configuration goal, you don't want the user to have to manually configure each UPnP device with its IP address, but would prefer an automatic addressing mechanism instead. There are two addressing protocols available to resolve this conflict between the need to configure the IP stack and the desire to avoid end-user configuration of device parameters: DHCP and Auto-IP. Each has its strengths and weaknesses, and together they provide complementary solutions to UPnP device addressing.

Dynamic Host Configuration Protocol

Dynamic Host Configuration Protocol (DHCP) provides a framework for passing configuration information to hosts on a TCP/IP network, including the host's IP address, subnet mask, default gateway, and domain name server. It is a client/server protocol that uses UDP as its transport. DHCP clients send messages to DHCP servers on port 67 and receive responses from servers on port 68. A DHCP server manages a pool of IP addresses, automatically assigning addresses to network hosts, and reuses addresses that have been released. Using a DHCP server to assign addresses to IP endpoints centralizes the management of IP addresses, ensuring that each endpoint receives a unique address and avoids problems that arise with manual configuration.

There are three mechanisms DHCP can use to assign IP addresses to clients.

- *Automatic allocation.* The DHCP server assigns a permanent IP address to a client.
- *Manual allocation.* The network administrator determines the address assignment for each host, and the DHCP server simply conveys the address to the clients when they request an address from the DHCP server.

- *Dynamic allocation.* In this most common mode of operation, the DHCP server assigns an IP address to the client for a limited period of time. The client is said to have a *lease* on the address. Once the lease expires or is released by the client, the server may assign this address to another client.

Each UPnP device is required to have a built-in DHCP client. When a UPnP device is first connected to a network, it searches for a DHCP server to acquire an IP address. In theory, a DHCP server servicing a network of UPnP devices could use any of the three mechanisms. However, dynamic allocation provides the best match as it requires no administrative configuration per client.

Acquiring a Lease

The DHCP protocol begins with a DHCP client broadcasting a DHCPDISCOVER message on its local network segment. This message has various tags that can be set to indicate what options the DHCP client is requesting. In the DHCPDISCOVER message, the client may optionally suggest the IP address it wants to use and the desired lease duration. Allowing the client to suggest an address enables the client to acquire the same IP address it had last time it successfully booted. The server responds with a DHCPOFFER message that includes the IP address it is offering to the client along with other parameters such as the subnet mask.

Once the client receives the DHCPOFFER in response to its DHCPDISCOVER, it proceeds to accept the address by sending a DHCPREQUEST message that includes a *server identifier* value. The server identifier tells the server that the client has accepted its offer and implicitly tells other servers it has declined their offers.

The selected server receives the DHCPREQUEST and acknowledges with a DHCPACK message containing the configuration parameters. (If the server has already allocated the IP address, it sends a DHCPNAK instead, which causes the client to reinitiate the DHCP protocol.) The client should then perform a check to make sure the IP address is correct and is not already in use by another host on the network. If the client detects that the address is already in use, it sends a DHCPDECLINE message and starts the process from the beginning.

Figure 4.1 shows the sequence of messages in a typical DHCP session.

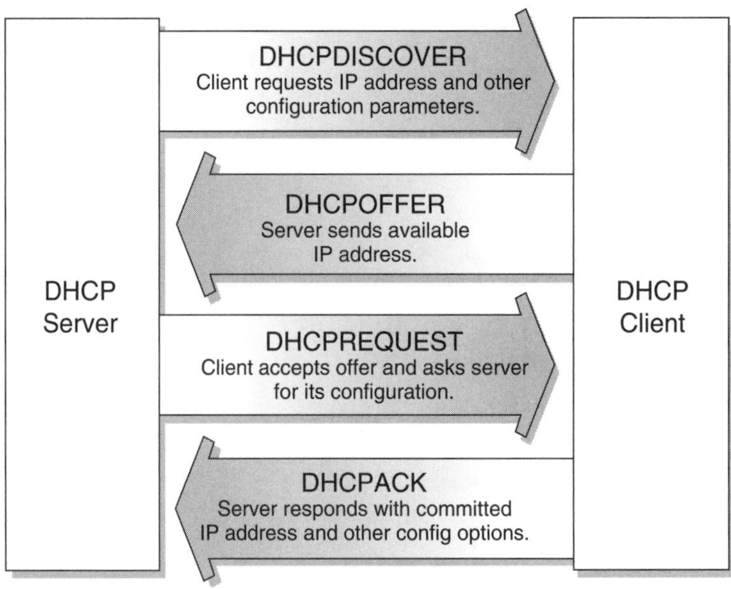

Figure 4.1 The DHCP Protocol

Renewing a Lease

Eventually, a client's lease approaches expiration.[1] If the client wants to extend its lease, it sends a DHCPREQUEST to the server. In this message, the client sets its current IP address but does not include a server identifier in the message. The server responds with a DHCPACK message that includes the new duration for the lease. At this point the client has successfully reacquired its address with a new duration.

Rebooting

When a client is rebooting and has a previous lease from a DHCP server, the client tries to renew the lease. If the lease hasn't expired, the DHCP server renews it. If the lease hasn't expired, but for some reason the client can't contact the DHCP server, the client first tries to "ping" its default gateway by sending an ICMP echo request. If the client receives a response, the client assumes that it is still located on the same

[1] Some clients attempt to renew as soon as they reach 50 percent of the lease's expiration.

network where it had previously obtained the lease and continues to use the lease, as normal. If the client does not receive a response from the gateway, the client assumes it is no longer on the same network and that the new network is unmanaged, so it then uses Auto-IP to select an address.

Releasing a Lease

If the client no longer needs its IP address, the client sends a DHCPRELEASE message to the server, giving up the address and allowing the server to assign it to another host.

Auto-IP

Using DHCP to assign addresses to a dynamically changing set of devices requires a DHCP server to be continuously available. To run continuously, the server must be on a machine that is always on, such as an Internet gateway or a PC home server. It may not always be possible to have a DHCP server running, especially in homes or small offices without administrative support. In keeping with the zero-administration philosophy, the designers of the UPnP architecture needed another addressing mechanism to ensure that UPnP devices could acquire addresses even on networks without a DHCP server. Auto-IP was the solution.

Auto-IP is a method by which an endpoint on an IP network may automatically choose an IP address and subnet mask in the absence of a DHCP server. Auto-IP does not replace DHCP, but augments it, making clients more robust by allowing them to acquire addresses in the absence of DHCP services. UPnP devices use the Auto-IP mechanism only if a DHCP server is not present, or if the DHCP process fails. In addition, the UPnP device architecture specifies how a UPnP device that has configured its address using Auto-IP must periodically check for the presence of a DHCP server so that it can smoothly transition to using a DHCP-assigned address.

Address Selection

Once a UPnP device has determined it must use Auto-IP to get an IP address, it starts by selecting a candidate address. While the actual address selection algorithm is implementation-dependent, the address must fall within a range of addresses, 169.254/16, that are non-routable

IP addresses.[2] Addresses in this range will not cross gateways, so they will never make it outside of an organization and onto the Internet. After selecting an address, the client also configures itself with a default class B subnet mask of 255.255.0.0.

Resolving Address Conflicts

Once the UPnP device has selected an address, it must verify that the address is not already being used by another device on the network. To do this, the UPnP device uses the Address Resolution Protocol in an unusual way.

ARP maps any network-level address, such as an IP address, to its corresponding data link address, such as an Ethernet address, so that a networking stack can encapsulate an IP datagram in an Ethernet frame and send it to its intended destination. A network host, upon receiving an ARP request, checks to see whether it is configured with the IP address in the request. If so, the host responds with its data link address to the originator. The originator then uses the data link address to compose a header for the packet it is about to send to the host. Figure 4.2 summarizes this exchange.

In attempting to find out whether an address is currently in use, a UPnP device configuring itself using Auto-IP sends out an ARP request for the address it has chosen. If none of the hosts on the network are currently using the IP address, there will be no response to the ARP message, and the device assumes that it is free to use the address.

Ad-Hoc Networks

Using Auto-IP for address assignment, it is possible for hosts to come together and form an *ad-hoc network*[3] without having the assistance of preexisting network infrastructure, including DHCP and DNS servers. This feature enables many interesting scenarios with UPnP devices. For example, consider two users with wireless PDAs meeting in an airport who want to share files. If the users are not in proximity to a DHCP server, each PDA assigns itself an address from the 169.254 network. At that point, each device has network connectivity and is able to discover the services, such as file sharing, offered by the other device.

---

[2] The Internet Assigned Numbers Authority (IANA) has reserved this range for private IP addressing, so no one can use it on the Internet. This range is known as the LINKLOCAL net. Also, the first and last 256 addresses are reserved for future use and must not be selected.

[3] This system of devices comes together to form a short-lived network without the support of any preexisting network infrastructure.

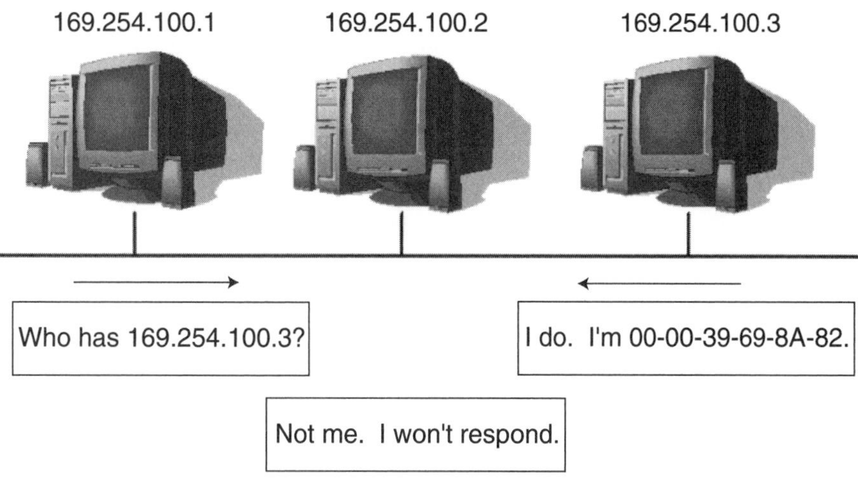

Figure 4.2 ARP: Finding the Owner of an Address

Limitations

Address selection using Auto-IP does have some limitations. While DHCP-assigned addresses can be routed throughout the organization, addresses allocated by Auto-IP cannot. Addresses allocated by Auto-IP are special, link-local addresses that are restricted to the local network segment. As a result, devices with Auto-IP addresses cannot be seen by control points beyond the local network segment.

Steps in UPnP Device Addressing

All UPnP devices must follow the same steps in acquiring an IP address. The steps, as specified by the UPnP device architecture, are presented in the flowchart in Figure 4.3.

1. Try to Obtain an Address via DHCP

First, a UPnP device must try to get an address from a DHCP server. If the device successfully acquires an address, it is ready to continue with subsequent UPnP phases. It must thereafter only be concerned with renewing its lease when the time comes.

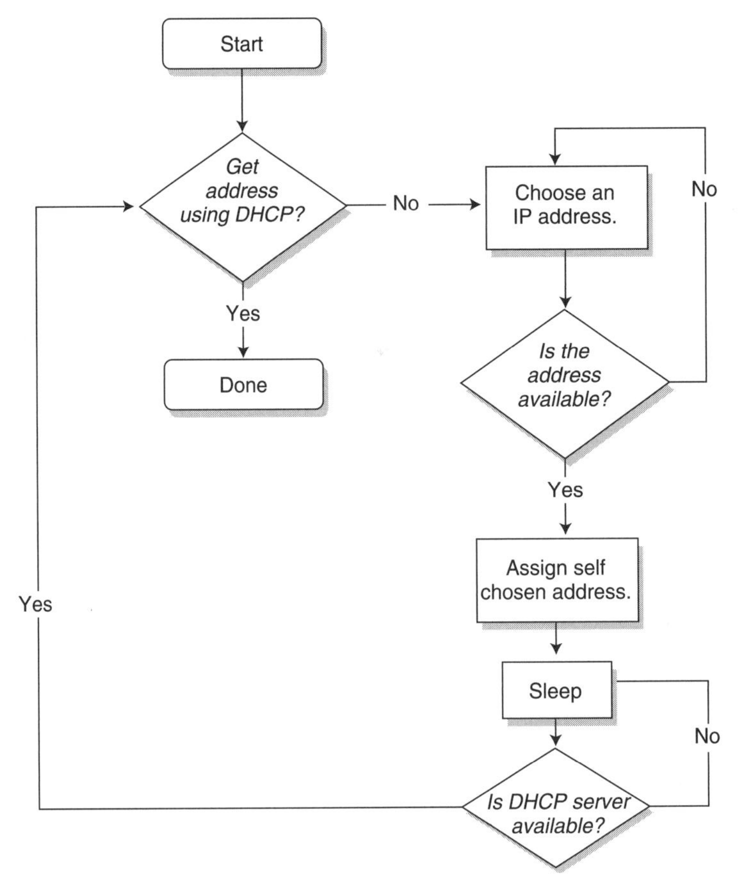

Figure 4.3 UPnP Device Addressing Flowchart

2. Failing DHCP, Proceed with Auto-IP

If the UPnP device fails to acquire an address from a DHCP server, it begins the process of selecting and testing an IP address.

2a. Choose an IP address

To help keep clients from becoming stuck in a loop with other clients while trying to allocate an address, clients implementing Auto-IP are expected to randomize their IP address selection algorithm. Otherwise, clients could potentially get stuck in phase with other clients selecting and testing the same sequence of addresses.

2b. Test Whether the Address Is Available

When using Auto-IP to select an address, the client tests to determine whether the address is already in use. If so, the client chooses another address and tries again. The client keeps choosing addresses either until it finds one or has tried more times than its configured retry count. The number of retries is implementation-specific and should be based on the algorithm used for choosing an IP address. This retry count is present to make sure that clients auto-configuring on busy auto-configured network segments do not loop infinitely looking for an IP address.

2c. Periodically Check for a DHCP Server

Clients may come into proximity of a DHCP server or a DHCP server may have previously been unavailable when the clients were booting and acquired addresses. Whatever the reason for the availability of the DHCP server, if it becomes available, devices must switch to a DHCP-assigned address. UPnP devices configured using Auto-IP must therefore periodically test for the availability of a DHCP server. When rechecking, if the device determines that no DHCP server is available, it waits for a period of time and then tries again. The suggested default for this interval is 5 minutes for Ethernet-based implementations.

2d. Upon Finding a DHCP Server, Switch to a DHCP-assigned Address

Receiving a response from a DHCP server, the UPnP device must respond and obtain a lease from the server. If the client successfully obtains the lease, it must drop any existing automatically configured IP addresses unless the device supports multiple addresses on the interface being configured.

How the device drops existing connections is defined by the implementation, but it should allow existing connections to be completed before closing them. In addition, the device should not allow new connections on the old, automatically configured address. Once all connections on the old address are closed, it can remove the address from the interface and will be entirely transitioned to the new address.

Summary

- Addressing is the first step for UPnP devices; each device must acquire an IP address before it can discover other devices or offer its services on the network.
- UPnP devices support two methods for acquiring addresses, DHCP and Auto-IP. Using both DHCP and Auto-IP allows the UPnP architecture to scale from simple, on-the-fly ad-hoc networks to small business environments.
- All UPnP devices follow the same steps to acquire an IP address. These steps allow devices to transition between networks with DHCP and those without DHCP.
- Ad-hoc networks allow wireless devices to communicate even without preexisting network infrastructure.
- Auto-IP addresses are not routable, limiting communication to the local network segment.

Chapter 5

Discovery

"Oh! Piglet," said Pooh excitedly, "we're going on an Expotition, all of us, with things to eat. To discover something."

"To discover what?" said Piglet anxiously."

"Oh! just something."

"Nothing fierce?"

"Christopher Robin didn't say anything about fierce. He just said it had an 'x'."

—A.A. Milne, *Winnie the Pooh*

Once a UPnP device acquires an address, it is ready to provide its services to control points on the network. Discovery, the next phase in UPnP device operation, allows control points to search for devices and services on the network and find ones that meet its search criteria. This chapter first looks at service discovery in general and then examines the Simple Service Discovery Protocol, the discovery protocol used by UPnP devices.

The Discovery Problem

In the future, many devices will be available in the home and small office, including hardware devices such as home audio players and televisions, and software-only services that implement functionality without actually controlling underlying hardware. Networks will become flexible, dynamic, distributed systems of users, devices, and services. However, this distributed service scenario introduces a couple of problems: How do clients find the network-based services they need? Also, when searching for devices and services, the clients may find many that will satisfy their requirements. How do they select which is best or most appropriate? In addition, users should not have to load device drivers or configure IP addresses in order to add new devices to the network and make them available to other programs.

Service Discovery Solution

A mechanism for discovering network-based services must allow clients to query the network to find out whether required services are currently present and available, and must provide clients with the information they need to select a particular service from the set of those available.

To do this, devices and services can advertise their functionality on the network and provide information to clients about themselves to facilitate the client's selection. Devices and services *advertise* and *inform*, letting clients know about their presence and the functionality they provide. Clients, on the other hand, *discover* and *select*, finding the services they need and then choosing the one that meets their requirements, as shown in Figure 5.1.

Design Decisions

There are many details to be concerned with when designing a service discovery solution, such as:

- How do resources join the network?

  How does a resource become capable of participating in the discovery process? For example, given an IP-addressable network device, how does it acquire its address?

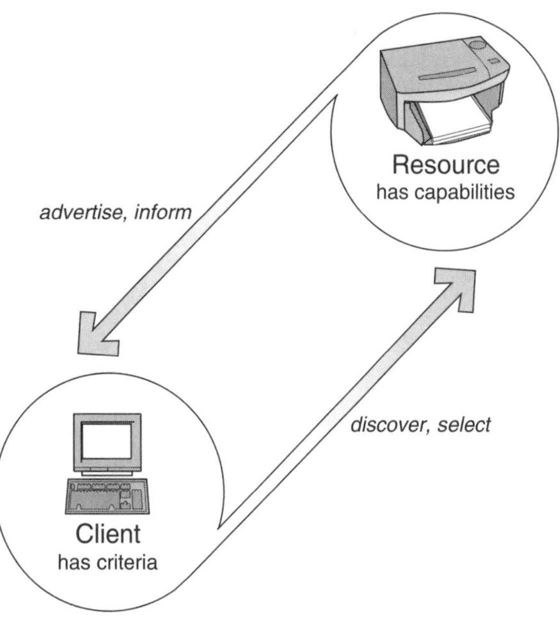

Figure 5.1 Responsibilities of Devices and Control Points in Discovery

- How does the discovery system identify resources?

  In other words, what does a client request when searching for a particular resource? Are these identifiers unique? What prevents different resources from using the same identifier?

- How do clients specify the details of what they are looking for?

  Can clients search by type only, or can they include other attributes in their search criteria? Allowing a full-features search capability increases the complexity of the discovery solution but makes the job easier for clients. Providing a simple search capability tends to shift the burden to clients to interpret information they have received in order to make a selection. At a minimum, clients must be able to find resources and gather information about them so that they can select which they will use. Some clients, such as general-purpose network administration tools operating in a diagnostic or troubleshooting capacity, may need to browse for all services on the network. The search mechanism may also provide this capability.

- What communication model is used?

  Is there a central facility that keeps track of all the available services on the network and responds to discovery requests, or is there a decentralized system where every resource responds to these requests?

- Clients discover resources on the network. How long is the information they receive about the resource valid?

  What if a device fails after advertising its services? How does the client find out? How long does it take the system to notice that the device is no longer functioning? The information returned to clients about the available resources and their locations should be up-to-date and should contain information to tell the client how long it is valid.

Simple Service Discovery Protocol

The Simple Service Discovery Protocol (SSDP) was designed to be a simple discovery solution for HTTP-based resources on the local area network that doesn't require any configuration, management, or administration. SSDP doesn't attempt to address the problem of Internet-wide HTTP-based resource discovery. That problem is left to other protocols, such as Universal Description Discovery and Integration (UDDI). For more information see `http://www.uddi.org`.

Service Identification

SSDP introduces two concepts related to service identification, the *service type* and the *Unique Service Name (USN)*. A service type is a URI that identifies the type, or function, of a particular resource—a printer service, for example. SSDP does not define service types, but provides the mechanisms for discovering them. Service types for UPnP devices and services are defined by UPnP working committees for each standard device type.

A Unique Service Name is a URI that is used to uniquely identify an instance of a particular service, allowing SSDP clients to differentiate between two services with the same service type. A USN typically contains a universally unique identifier (UUID)—a 128-bit number used to uniquely identify an object. UUIDs are created by utility programs based on the network address of the host generating the UUID, a time-stamp, and a randomly generated component.

The pairing of a service type URI and a Unique Service Name URI uniquely identifies SSDP services. For example, one SSDP service might have

```
service type: "printer"

USN: "uuid:399766A8-B2F5-436d-8B45-0B5BE1F3CA40"
```

while another device on the network has the same service type with its own unique service name, such as:

```
service type: "printer"

USN: "uuid:B007B924-1DD0-40b9-B825-20811077BEF1"
```

Communication Model

SSDP uses a decentralized approach to service discovery whereby no central store maintains information about resources, their location, and their availability. Instead, each client directly queries the network and each resource responds directly to these requests, as shown in Figure 5.2.

Hey! I'm Over Here!

The decentralized approach to service discovery is a bit like trying to find your friend in a crowd. You might yell out your friend's name loud enough so that everyone can hear. If your friend hears you, he yells back to you. In other words, you are broadcasting a search request to everyone on a group communication channel, and the search target, if present, is responding back directly to the originator. If your friend leaves the crowd, he might yell over to you let you know. Likewise, if a new friend appeared, she might tell you that she is now present.

The decentralized discovery is robust in that it does not require any central knowledge or configuration by a network administrator. The information is always up-to-date since resources respond directly to queries and issue updates to clients about their status. However, this system requires every resource to listen for and process the discovery requests. As the number of resources on the network grows, this approach becomes less attractive—state information is duplicated across clients, more network bandwidth is consumed with discovery traffic, and computational power is wasted as every resource has some processing dedicated to listening for and processing discovery messages.

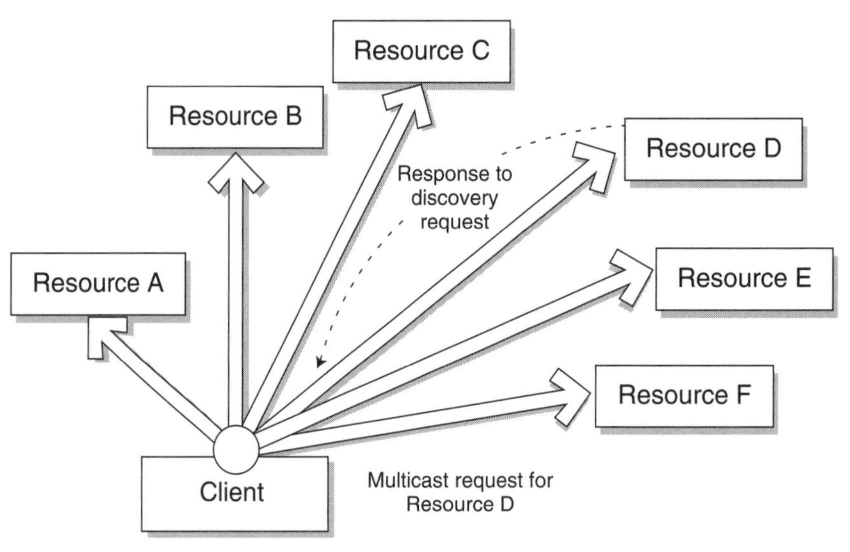

Figure 5.2 Decentralized Discovery—Broadcast for a Resource

Discovery Requests and Presence Announcements

There are two types of SSDP requests. The first, *discovery requests*, allow SSDP clients to look for SSDP resources. The second, *presence announcements*, allow SSDP resources to announce their presence on the network. SSDP's balance of discovery requests and presence announcements is designed to make the protocol efficient, reducing network traffic.

When a resource comes on-line, it announces its presence. This lets all clients know that the resource is available. From then on, the resource does not need to send out any other presence announcements, except when it is going off-line. Any clients that come on-line after the resource has announced its presence send out discovery requests. If the resource supports the requested service, it responds to the client. The client does not need to repeat the discovery request because any resources that come on-line after it has issued the request will announce their presence. The result is that neither client nor server need send out steady streams of messages.

Balancing Act

If either the discovery requests or the presence announcements are omitted, the protocol becomes much less efficient. For example, without presence announcements, UPnP control points would have to periodically send out discovery requests to find UPnP devices and services of interest. They couldn't be sure new devices hadn't come on-line since their last discovery request. Likewise, omitting the discovery requests and relying on the presence announcements would cause UPnP devices to continually broadcast their presence—new control points could have come on-line and would not be aware of the devices yet.

Network Transport

Since SSDP is concerned with the discovery of Web-based resources, it is reasonable to consider HTTP as the transport. However, HTTP runs over TCP, a connection-oriented, reliable, peer-to-peer protocol. Since SSDP requires its discovery requests and presence announcements to be sent to every peer on the local network, using direct HTTP connections to every host on the network is not feasible. Instead, SDDP uses HTTP over multicast UDP to send messages to every SSDP peer on the network.

SSDP clients multicast HTTPMU discovery requests to the address 239.255.255.250:1900, which is SSDP's reserved multicast address and port that has local administrative scope, limiting the delivery of the multicast packet to an administrative domain. No provision is made for the reliability of the discovery messages sent over UDP, a datagram protocol that does not provide reliability guarantees.

SSDP services listen to the SSDP multicast channel to hear the discovery requests. If an SSDP resource receives a multicast HTTPMU discovery request that matches the service it offers, it responds by sending a response directly to the SSDP client that issued the search using the HTTPU.

SSDP Discovery Request

The SSDP discovery request introduces an HTTP request method, `M-SEARCH`, and a header to identify the search target, `ST`. The client sets `ST` to the URI of the desired service type. Multiple `ST` headers are not allowed. More complex searches such as specifying logical operations or name/value pairs are not supported. SSDP only supports basic searches to keep it an easy-to-implement and easy-to-use discovery protocol. Table 5.1 lists the headers used in a UPnP SSDP request.

UPnP control points and devices use SSDP's URI search capability, but use particular conventions for the ST header in discovery messages. By setting different values of the ST header of the discovery request message, UPnP control points can search for all devices, root devices, specific device types, or specific service types. Table 5.2 lists the different values for the ST header in a UPnP discovery request.

Take a closer look at a real SSDP discovery request issued by a UPnP control point looking for an Internet gateway device:

```
M-SEARCH * HTTP/1.1
Host: 239.255.255.250:1900
Man: ssdp:discover
MX: 3
ST: urn:schemas-upnp-org:device:InternetGatewayDevice:1
```

The request line has the M-SEARCH method indicating a search request with the Request-URI set to "*" to indicate that the search is intended for all listening hosts.

Table 5.1 SSDP Request Headers

Header	Required	Type	Description
Host	Required	Domain name or IP address and optional port	If the port is not specified, port 80 is assumed. For UPnP discovery requests, the value is "239.255.255.255:1900."
Man	Required	Must be "ssdp:discover"	The SSDP client sets the Man header to "ssdp:discover" to indicate that this is a an SSDP discovery message that must be understood by the recipient.*
MX	Required	integer	Maximum number of seconds in which to respond. To reduce the load on the client receiving many responses to the request, the responder sends the reply at a random point during this time interval.
ST	Required	Single URI	Search target for the discovery message. This is what the client is looking for.

* The Man header is part of the HTTP extension framework. The recipient must understand and process the mandatory extension or return a "510 (Not Extended)" status code. See the "HTTP Extension Framework" Internet Draft for more information.

Table 5.2 UPnP Search Types

Type of Search	Syntax	Description
All devices	`ssdp:all`	Searches for all UPnP devices.
Root devices	`upnp:rootdevice`	Searches for all UPnP root devices. Only root devices will respond; embedded devices will not.
Specific device	`uuid:`*device-uuid*	Searches for a particular device by the device's unique ID. The unique ID is supplied by the device vendor.
Devices of a specific type	`urn:schemas-upnp-org:device:`*deviceType-version*	This kind of search will locate all devices of a given type. The device type is as defined by a working committee of the UPnP Forum.
Services of a specific type	`urn:schemas-upnp-org:service:`*serviceType-version*	Like the device type search, this search will find all services of a given type.

The `Host` header, required in HTTP 1.1 requests, specifies the name of the recipient. This information is redundant for UPnP SSDP requests, as the `Host` header is not specifying anything the recipient doesn't already know—SSDP uses the multicast address of 239.255.255.250 and port 1900.

The `Man` header must be included and set to `ssdp:discover` for all SSDP discovery requests to show that the recipient must understand this header.

The `MX` header specifies that the services have 3 seconds to respond. As discussed in Chapter 3, each service chooses a random time within this interval to respond. This helps to balance the load for the control point when it processes responses. This value is specified by the UPnP device vendor.

Every `ssdp:discover` request must contain an `ST` header that is a single URI that specifies the service being searched for. In this case, the search is for Internet gateway devices, so the `ST` header is set to `urn:schemas-upnp-org:device:InternetGatewayDevice:1`.

SSDP Discovery Response

Once a device or service detects that it is being searched for, it responds with a unicast message directly to the sender. In addition to providing both a service type and a unique service name for the discovered service, discovery results provide expiration and location information. Table 5.3 lists the headers used in UPnP SSDP discovery response messages.

Table 5.3 SSDP Response Headers

Header	Required	Type	Description
Cache-Control	Required	various	There are various cache control settings described in RFC 2068, "Hypertext Transfer Protocol — HTTP/1.1." UPnP discovery responses use max-age = *seconds* to specify how long until the advertisement expires. The max-age directive is required and must be set to > 1800 seconds (30 minutes).
Date	Recommended	RFC1123 date	When the response was generated.
Ext	Required	no value	Confirms that the `Man` header in the request (`ssdp:discover`) was understood.
Location	Required	Single URL	Value is a URL to the device description document of the root device.
Server	Required	String	A concatenation of the OS name, OS version, UPnP/1.0, product name, and product version that is specified by the UPnP vendor.
ST	Required	Single URI	Search target for the discovery message. The response contains the same ST value as the corresponding request message.
USN	Required	Single URI	This is the unique service name for the discovered device or service. The ST and USN values together uniquely identify an instance of a service.

For UPnP devices, the USN field may take many different forms depending upon the type of request in the original ST header, as shown in Table 5.4.

Getting back to our example, the following response might result from the discovery request:

```
HTTP/1.1 200 OK
Location: http://192.168.0.1:2869/upnphost/udhisapi.dll?
 content=uuid:6859ddde-89cd-46df-bab8-1394523aec23
Ext:
USN: uuid:6859ddde-89cd-46df-bab8-  1394523aec23:
  :urn:schemas-upnp-org:device:InternetGatewayDevice:1
Server: Microsoft-Windows-NT/5.1 UPnP/1.0
  UPnP-Device-Host/1.0
Cache-Control: max-age=1800
ST: urn:schemas-upnp-org:device:InternetGatewayDevice:1
Content-Length:0
```

Table 5.4 Format of USN Response Header

Format	Description
`uuid:`*device-UUID*`:upnp-rootdevice`	This form is used when the request specified `upnp-rootdevice`. There can be many responses to this kind of search, each matched device including its own unique device ID.
`uuid:`*device-UUID*	This form is used when a specific device is being search for by its device ID. There should be at most one response to a message of this kind.
`uuid:`*device-UUID*::`urn:schemas-upnp-org:device:`*deviceType:ver*	This form is used in response to a search for a particular kind of device, say, an Internet gateway. All gateway devices will respond with the USN header set in this format.
`uuid:`*device-UUID*::`urn:schemas-upnp-org:device:`*serviceType:ver*	This form is used in response to a search for a particular kind of service, such as an AVTransport service of a media rendering device. Many different device types could include the same kind of service. All instances will respond in this form.

Discovery responses like this one start with the typical HTTP success response and are followed by a few additional headers to convey information about the discovered resource.

The `Location` header contains the location where the client can actually use the discovered device. In this case, the Internet gateway is implemented on a Microsoft Windows NT[†] host.

The `Ext` header is returned, without a value, to indicate that the recipient has understood the mandatory header in the request.

Because the original search request was looking for all Internet gateway devices, the USN uses the form that includes the matched device's unique ID, concatenated with "::", concatenated with the original search target, `urn:schemas-upnp-org:device:InternetGatewayDevice:1`.

The `USN` header contains the identifier for the matched resource.

The `Server` header provides information the operating system of the device and the product name and version.

The `Cache-Control` header tells the requestor how to cache the returned information. In this case, the discovery response is valid for 5000 seconds.

The `ST` header contains the same `ST` value as the original request. This is what the requestor was searching for.

This response has no associated content, so the `Content-Length` header is set to 0.

There are a few rules SSDP discovery responses must respect:

- Only SSDP services with a service type that matches the value in the `ST` header may respond to an `ssdp:discover` request on the SSDP multicast channel.
- A successful response to an `ssdp:discover` request must include the `ST` and `USN` headers.
- Responses to `ssdp:discover` requests sent over the SSDP multicast channel must be sent to the same IP address and port that made the `ssdp:discover` request.
- A response to an `ssdp:discover` request should include the service's location expressed through a `Location` and/or `AL` header. Location information identifies how one should contact a particular service. One or more location URIs may be included in a discovery response or a presence announcement.
- According to the SSDP draft standard, responses to `ssdp:discover` requests should contain a `Cache-Control:max-age` or `Expires` header. When both are present, they are processed in the order

specified by HTTP/1.1, that is, the `Cache-Control` header takes precedence over the `Expires` header. If neither the `Cache-Control` nor the `Expires` header is provided on the response to a `ssdp:discover` request, the information contained in that response must not be cached by SSDP clients.

- Expiration information identifies how long an SSDP client should keep information about the service in its cache. Once the entry has expired, it must be removed from the SSDP client's cache.

Presence Announcements

Discovery requests are one side of the coin—how clients actively search for services. SSDP presence announcements are the other side—how SSDP services communicate information about their availability to clients. Presence announcements, or *advertisements*, allow SSDP services to:

- Let interested SSDP clients know when they join or leave the network
- Notify interested SSDP clients when their location changes
- Update expiration information regarding them in client cache entries

SSDP presence announcement use the GENA's `NOTIFY` method over the same HTTPU/HTTPMU transport used by discovery requests. There are two kinds of advertisements: device available and device unavailable.

When a device joins the network, it advertises all of its devices, both the root device and any embedded devices, and all of the services that it provides in any of these devices. This lets control points know about all of the functionality provided by the device and all of the various ways it can be found.

The advertisements take the form of a `NOTIFY` message that include the following elements:

- An `NT` header that has a potential search target—how the control point can search for this device or service.
- A `USN` header that has a composite identifier for the advertisement. This is a concatenation of the device ID and the value in the `NT` header.

- A `Location` header that contains a URL for more information about the device. If the `NT` header specifies a service, the Location header contains a URL for the service's containing device.
- A `Cache-Control` header to specify the duration of the advertisement—how long the advertisement is valid.

A UPnP device may send out many presence announcements to completely advertise all of its devices, both root and embedded, and all of its services. For example, there are three discovery messages for root devices, corresponding to the three ways it can be discovered. Table 5.5 summarizes all of the `NT` and `USN` header values for different kinds of advertisements.

There are three advertisements for the root device: two advertisements for each embedded device and one advertisement for each service. If a root device has *d* embedded devices and *k* services, this results in $3 + 2d + k$ advertisements for a device to completely advertise all of its devices and services. The advertisements are sent out individually and have roughly the same expiration times. Because of the unreliable nature of the underlying UDP transport, devices should send out each advertisement more than once.

Table 5.5 NT and USN Header Values Device and Service Advertisements

	NT	USN
Root device advertisements:		
1	root device UUID	root device UUID
2	device type: device version	root device UUID`::device type:device version`
3	`upnp:rootdevice`	root device UUID`::upnp:rootdevice`
Embedded device advertisements:		
1	embedded device UUID	embedded device UUID
2	device type: device version	embedded device UUID::device type:device version
Service advertisements:		
1	device type: device version	enclosing device UUID::service type:service version

Device Available: ssdp:alive

When joining the network, SSDP services advertise their presence by sending a NOTIFY method over the SSDP multicast channel. The request line of this message simply has

```
NOTIFY * HTTP/1.1
```

to indicate that this is a GENA notification message. Table 5.6 lists the associated headers for this message.

Table 5.6 ssdp:alive Headers

Header	Required	Type	Description
Host	Required	Multicast address and host	Must be 239.255.255.250:1900
Cache-Control	Required	Must have `max-age` directive	Specifies the number of seconds that the advertisement is valid. Should be > 1800 seconds.
Location	Required	Single URL	This URL points to the location of the UPnP device description document of the root device.
NT	Required	Notification type	May take one of the forms listed in Table 5.2: `upnp:rootdevice` `uuid:`*`device-UUID`* `urn:schemas-upnp-org:device:`*`deviceType:ver`* `urn:schemas-upnp-org:service:`*`serviceType:ver`*
NTS	Required	Single URI	Must be `ssdp:alive`
Server	Required	String	Concatentation of OS name, OS version, `UPnP/1.0`, product name, and product version.

Continues

Table 5.6 ssdp:alive Headers *(Continued)*

Header	Required	Type	Description
USN	Required	Single URI	As listed in Table 5.2, the USN value takes one of the following forms, depending on what is being advertised: `uuid:`*`device-UUID`*`::upnp:rootdevice` `uuid:`*`device-UUID`* `uuid:`*`device-UUID`*`::urn:schemas-upnp-org:device:`*`deviceType:ver`* `uuid:`*`device-UUID`*`::urn:schemas-upnp-org:service:`*`serviceType:ver`* Consider the NT header that which may be discovered, and the USN header as the way that it may be discovered.

Now look at a real UPnP device advertisement. The following advertisement is from an Internet gateway device:

```
NOTIFY * HTTP/1.1
Host: 239.255.255.250:1900
Cache-Control: max-age=1800
Location: http://192.168.0.1:2869/upnphost/udhisapi.dll?
  content=uuid:6859ddde-89cd-46df-bab8-1394523aec23
Server: Microsoft-Windows-NT/5.1 UPnP/1.0
  UPnP-Device-    Host/1.0
NTS: ssdp:alive
ST:urn:schemas-upnp-org:device:InternetGatewayDevice:1
USN:uuid:6859ddde-89cd-46df-bab8-1394523aec23::
  upnp:rootdevice
```

The interesting headers in this response include the highlighted `NTS`, `ST`, and `USN` headers. The `NTS` header simply identifies this GENA notification as an SSDP presence announcement. The `ST` header lists the discoverable device or service. In this case, it has the root device, the Internet Gateway. The `USN` header has one of the ways this device can be discovered: by searching for root devices. Other advertisements will have the same headers but different values, depending upon the details of the matched device or service.

Device Unavailable: ssdp:bye-bye

When a device is removed from the network, it must notify control points that it is going away by sending an `ssdp:bye-bye` message corresponding to each of the `ssdp:alive` advertisements it has previously sent out. This notifies the control points that the device and its services are no longer available. If a device happens to experience a failure and is unable to deliver its bye-bye messages, the advertisements previously sent out will eventually expire and be removed from any control point caches. Table 5.7 provides a full description of these headers.

For example, the following bye-bye message cancels the advertisement of the Internet gateway root device. It lets control points know that the device is no longer available. This message would be sent along with other messages to cancel any other embedded devices and services.

```
NOTIFY * HTTP/1.1
HOST: 239.255.255.250:1900
NTS: ssdp:bye-bye
ST:urn:schemas-upnp-org:device:InternetGatewayDevice:1
USN:uuid:6859ddde-89cd-46df-bab8-1394523aec23::upnp:
  rootdevice
```

Expiration Information and Cache Control

Expiration information, such as that provided in the `Cache-Control` header, tells the client how long it should keep information about the service in its cache. Once the entry has expired, it must be removed from the client's cache. An `ssdp:alive` message is used by services to prevent a cache entry from expiring, allowing it to be continuously available. An `ssdp:bye-bye` message causes clients to update their caches, removing the service.

Table 5.7 ssdp:bye-bye Headers

Header	Required	Type	Description
Host	Required	Multicast address and host	Must be 239.255.255.250:1900
NT	Required	Notification type	Same as `NT` header value in corresponding `ssdp:alive` advertisement
NTS	Required	Single URI	Must be `ssdp:bye-bye`
USN	Required	Single URI	Same as `USN` header value in corresponding `ssdp:alive` advertisement

When the SSDP client receives an `ssdp:alive` request whose USN matches the USN of an entry already in the cache, all information regarding that USN is replaced with the information on the `ssdp:alive` request.

Summary

- Service discovery is the mechanism by which devices and network-based services make themselves available to clients, and clients can discover devices and services.
- SSDP is the discovery protocol used by UPnP devices.
- SSDP was designed to be discover HTTP-based resources based on Uniform Resource Identifiers.
- SSDP uses a decentralized model of communication that requires no user administration.
- SSDP's balanced scheme of discovery requests and presence announcements minimize network traffic.
- UPnP adds conventions for using SSDP, including predefined service types and the composition of URIs to search for devices and services.

Chapter 6

Description

Calvin: "My life needs a rewind/erase button."

Hobbes: "And a volume control."

—Bill Watterson, *The Authoritative Calvin and Hobbes*

After a UPnP control point discovers a device, it has only the information contained in the discovery message—the device's type, its universally-unique identifier, and a URL to its description document. To find out more about the device, including the services and actions it supports, the control point retrieves description documents from the device. This chapter explains the description process and details about UPnP description documents, with information about

- How devices are described, including vendor-specific information, embedded devices, and URLs for control, eventing, and presentation
- How services are described, including actions, arguments, state variables, and properties of the variables
- How control points retrieve device and service descriptions from devices

UPnP's Description Phase

The description phase is the link between UPnP's discovery and control phases. In the discovery phase, devices advertise their presence to control points on the network, while control points search for devices. Once a control point receives these advertisements and finds a device of interest, it gets the description documents directly from the device to learn more about the device and its services. Once a control point has processed the description documents and understands the device's capabilities, it is ready to control the device, as shown in Figure 6.1.

Description documents allow control points to dynamically adapt to devices. For example, a control point can detect the presence of a preferred vendor-specific service on a device and use that instead of a standard service.

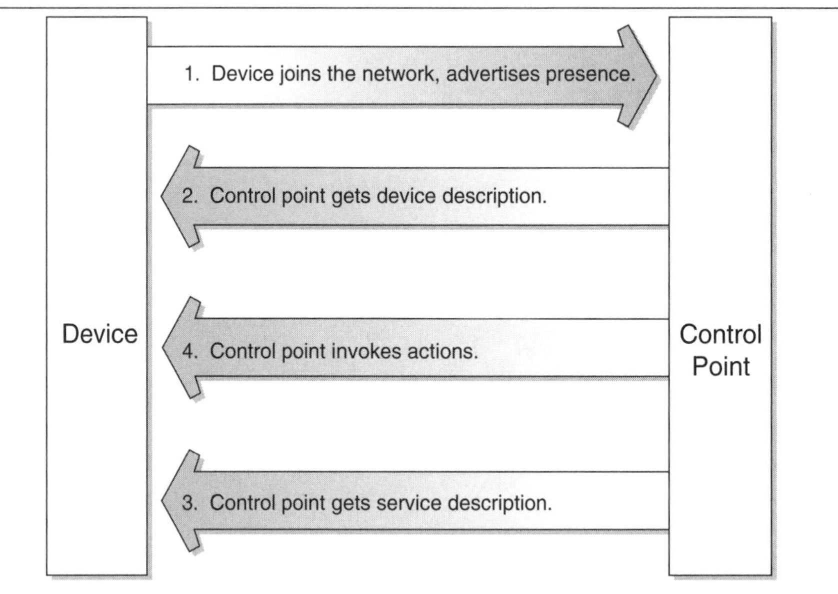

Figure 6.1 Retreiving Device and Service Descriptions

Discovery, Description, and Control

These abstract phases of discovery, description, and control are fundamental to the service-providing process; you must first find a provider, then learn more about the provider to ensure it meets your needs, and then actually receive service from the provider.

For example, have you ever had a problem with your car and needed service? Chances are you looked for an auto mechanic in the local telephone directory. Finding one, perhaps you placed a call to find out more about the company and whether they worked on your type of car. After that, you may have made an appointment to bring the car in and have the work done. If so, you followed the discovery, description, and control phases.

Description Document Standards

Device and service descriptions are simply XML documents that conform to the UPnP Template Language, the XML syntax defined by the UPnP Forum for creating device and service descriptions. This basic template language is used by the various working committees of the UPnP Forum to define standard devices and the services they must contain.

UPnP Forum working committees start with the UPnP Template Language and create description document templates for a particular device type and its services. When implementing UPnP devices, device vendors fill in the placeholders in the description document templates, providing vendor-specific information. Conceptually, the UPnP device template defines the type of device, while the device description document instantiates the template with vendor-provided information.

The device and service templates include information about a standard device and its services, actions, parameters, variables, and so on. For example, the Internet Gateway working committee has standardized the device and service templates for an Internet gateway device. Vendors implementing standards-compliant devices start with these templates defined by working committees and fill in vendor-specific information, perhaps differentiating their devices by included additional services, extending existing services, or embedding additional devices.

The resulting description document returned from a particular UPnP device therefore conforms to a UPnP Forum-defined syntax, implements device and service types defined by a UPnP Forum working committee, and includes information specific to the vendor and hardware, as pictured in the stack in Figure 6.2.

There are a few rules governing UPnP description documents:

- All elements and attributes are case-sensitive.
- All other values, except URLs, are case-insensitive.
- The order of elements is not significant. The elements can be in any order without changing the meaning of the description document.
- Required elements must occur exactly once with no duplicates.
- Recommended or optional elements may occur at most once.
- As specified by the Flexible XML Processing Profile (FXPP), control points must ignore any unknown elements and their sub-elements or content, and any unknown attributes and their values, when processing device and service descriptions.
- The ampersand character (&) is not allowed in XML. If required, it must be converted into `&` or `%26` (URL escape code).

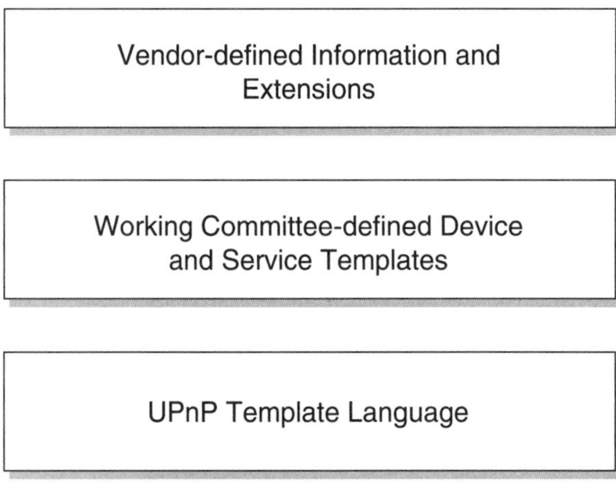

Figure 6.2 Contributions to Description Documents

- Binary data may not be directly included in an XML document. It must first be converted into text using formats such as base64 or binhex. Binary data can be referenced indirectly by using a URL to the data in the document.
- Devices standardized by UPnP Forum working committees must have an integer version number. Later versions must be a superset of earlier versions.

UPnP Device Description Document

A device description document mirrors the logical structure of a device, as discussed in Chapter 2. A device description document has three top-level elements, the <specVersion>, <URLBase>, and <device>, as shown in the following listing (values in *italics* are placeholders for actual values):

Note As we present code and XML through the book, there will be instances where the page width is not wide enough to hold the entire line. Long lines will be cut up into multiple lines, and we'll try to use indentation to make it clear where the line of text is continued.

```
<?xml version="1.0"?>
<root xmlns="urn:schemas-upnp-org:device-1-0">

  <specVersion>
    <major>1</major>
    <minor>0</minor>
  </specVersion>
  <URLBase>base URL for all relative URLs</URLBase>
  <device>
    basic device information elements
    service list
    embedded device list
  </device>

</root>
```

As with any XML document, the device document begins with the xml processing directive.

The <root> element of the device description, the top-level representation of the device, has an xmlns tag that includes the standard device description schema, identified by the URI, urn:schemas-upnp-org:device-1-0. This tag references the UPnP Template Language for devices, the schema that defines the syntax for device descriptions.

The <specVersion> element contains two required sub-elements, <major> and <minor> that must be set to 1 and 0, respectively, for UPnP 1.0. The optional <URLBase> element is a single URL that defines the base URL for the device. All relative URLs in the document are appended with this base URL. If the <URLBase> is empty or is not provided, the base URL for the document is the URL from which the device description was retrieved.

Basic Device Information

The device element has many sub-elements that provide details about the device—both manufacturing-related information and information about the functionality provided by the device. This section of the device description document has the following form:

```
<device>
  <deviceType>urn:schemas-upnp-org:device:deviceType:v
    </deviceType>
  <friendlyName>short name for the device</friendlyName>
  <manufacturer>manufacturer name</manufacturer>
  <manufacturerURL>URL to the manufacturer's Web site
    </manufacturerURL>
  <modelDescription>description of the device
    </modelDescription>
  <modelName>model name</modelName>
  <modelNumber>model number</modelNumber>
  <modelURL>URL to model site</modelURL>
  <serialNumber>manufacturer's serial # for the device
    </serialNumber>
  <UDN>uuid:UUID</UDN>
  <UPC>Universal Product Code</UPC>
  <iconList>information about icons</iconList>

  <serviceList>description of services provided by
    the device</serviceList>

  <deviceList>description of embedded services contained
    in this device</deviceList>

  <presentationURL>the URL for the device presentation
    page </presentationURL>

</device>
```

The <device> element contains the sub-elements described in Table 6.1. The strings and URLs in the device description may be, and in some cases should be, localized. In this way, the device can respond with the correct language when a control point specifies a preferred language using the `Accept-Language` header.

Table 6.1 Device Sub-elements

Element	Required	Type	Description
deviceType	Required	Single URI	The kind of UPnP device this is. Standard device types defined by one of the UPnP Forum's working committees must begin with `urn:schemas-upnp-org:device:` and are followed by the device type suffix, '`:`', and an integer device version.
friendlyName	Required	String	A short text description of the device. This string should be localized and is specified by UPnP vendor.
manufacturer	Required	String	The name of the manufacturer. This string may be localized and is provided by the UPnP device vendor.
manufacturerURL	Optional	Single URL	The URL for the manufacturer's web site. This URL may be relative to base URL and is specified by UPnP vendor.
modelDescription	Recommended	String	A long text description of the device for an end user. This string should be localized and is specified by UPnP device vendor.
modelName	Required	String	The name of this model of the device. This string may be localized and is specified by UPnP vendor.
modelNumber	Recommended	String	The model number of the device. The string may be localized and is specified by UPnP vendor.
modelURL	Optional	Single URL	The URL of the Web site for this model of the device. The URL may be localized and may be relative to the base URL. Specified by UPnP vendor.

Continues

Table 6.1 Device Sub-elements *(Continued)*

Element	Required	Type	Description
serialNumber	Recommended	String	The serial number of the device. May be localized and is specified by UPnP vendor.
UDN	Required	Single URI	The Unique Device Name for the device. This is a unique identifier for the device that doesn't change, even across device reboots. The UDN must begin with `uuid:` followed by a UUID suffix. The value is specified by the UPnP device vendor.
UPC	Optional	Single UPC	Universal Product Code. A UPC is a 12-digit, all-numeric code that identifies the consumer package. It is specified by UPnP vendor.
presentationURL	Recommended	Single URL	URL for the device presentation page. The URL may be relative to base URL and is specified by UPnP vendor.

A device can have icons associated with it that are used by control point user interfaces to represent the device. A device vendor can supply many icons for a device, with different qualities for different kinds of UIs. After a control point reads a device description document, it can retrieve one of the icons for the device to render in its user interface. To represent this information, the device description has an `<iconList>` element that consists of a sequence of `<icon>` elements as shown in the following listing:

```
<device>
...
  <iconList>
    <icon>
      <mimetype>image/format</mimetype>
      <width>horizontal pixels</width>
      <height>vertical pixels</height>
      <depth>color depth</depth>
      <url>URL to icon</url>
    </icon>
     other icons here
</iconList>
...
</device>
```

The `<icon>` element has the sub-elements listed in Table 6.2.

Table 6.2 Icon Sub-Elements

Element	Required	Type	Description
mimetype	Required	RFC 2387 MIME type	Single MIME image type
width	Required	Integer	Horizontal width of the icon in pixels
height	Required	Integer	Vertical height of the icon in pixels
depth	Required	Integer	Number of color bits per pixel
url	Required	Single URL	Pointer to the icon image. May be relative to the base URL.

The UPnP device architecture recommends one icon in each of the following sizes (width × height × depth): 16 × 16 × 1, 16 × 16 × 8, 32 × 32 × 1, 32 × 32 × 8, 48 × 48 × 1, and 48 × 48 × 8.

The Service List

After the icon list, the device description document contains a list of all of the services the device provides. This is not complete information about the service (that is, what the service description is for), but it does provide the service's type, identifier, URL for retrieving the service description, and a URL for eventing services, as shown in the following listing:

```
<device>
  ...

  <serviceList>
    <service>
      <serviceType>urn:schemas-upnp-org:service:
        serviceType:v</serviceType>
      <serviceId>urn:upnp-org:serviceId:serviceID
        </serviceId>
      <SCPDURL>URL for the service description</SCPDURL>
      <controlURL>URL for controling the service
        </controlURL>
      <eventSubURL>URL for event messages</eventSubURL>
    <service>
    Other standard services here
    Other vendor-defined services here
  </serviceList>

  ...

</device>
```

The required <serviceList> element contains one or more <service> elements with the sub-elements listed in Table 6.3.

Table 6.3 Service Sub-elements

Element	Required	Type	Description
serviceType	Required	Single URI	UPnP service type. For standard service types defined by one of the UPnP Forum working committees, the service type is in the following format: `urn:schemas-upnp-org:service:`*`serviceType:v`*, where *`serviceType`* is the type as defined by the working committee and *v* is an integer service version. Nonstandard service types conform to the following format: `urn:`*`domain-name`*`:service:`*`serviceType:v`*, where *`domain-name`* is an ICANN domain name owned by the device vendor, *`serviceType`* is defined by the vendor, and *v* is an integer service version.
serviceId	Required	Single URI	The serviceId is a identifier for this service that is unique within the device description—no two services may have the same ID. The serviceId for standard services are defined by working committees and have the following format: `urn:upnp-org:serviceId:`*`serviceId`*. Nonstandard services look like: `urn:`*`domain-name`*`:serviceId:`*`serviceId`*, where *`domain-name`* is the ICANN domain name owned by the vendor.
SCPDURL	Required	Single URL	URL for service description (formerly known as Service Control Protocol Definition URL). May be relative to base URL. Specified by UPnP vendor.
controlURL	Required	Single URL	The URL for control messages for the service. This URL may be relative to base URL. Specified in the <URLBase> element. The controlURL is specified by UPnP device vendor.

Continues

Table 6.3 Service Sub-elements *(Continued)*

Element	Required	Type	Description
eventSubURL	Required	Single URL	The URL for event-related messages, such as subscription, renewal, and cancellation. This URL may be relative to base URL. No two services in the device may have the same eventing URL. If the service has no evented state variables, this element must be present, but should be empty. This value is specified by the UPnP device vendor.

The Embedded Device List

A device can contain embedded devices. To describe the embedded devices, the device description document has a `<deviceList>` element that has a `<device>` sub-element for each embedded device. The format of the `<device>` element is the same format as the root device. The `<deviceList>` element is required if and only if the root device has embedded devices.

UPnP Service Description Documents

The service description contains detailed information about a service. Like a device description template, the service description template is created by a working committee of the UPnP Forum. The device vendor fills in the placeholders in the template to create a service description. A service description starts much like a device description:

```
<?xml version="1.0"?>
<scpd xmlns="urn:schemas-upnp-org:service-1-0">
  <specVersion>
    <major>1</major>
    <minor>0</minor>
  </specVersion>
  ….
</scpd>
```

The `<scpd>` element identifies this as a service description (service control protocol document). The `<scpd>` element must have an `xmlns` attribute of `urn:schemas-upnp-org:service-1-0`. This attribute references the UPnP Template Language for services.

Like the device template, the <specVersion> element must have the required <major> and <minor> sub-elements that give the major and minor versions of the UPnP Device Architecture specification to which the device is conforming.

The Action List

After the standard version information, the service description has an <actionList> element that lists of all of the actions (zero or more) that the service supports. In addition to standard actions, UPnP vendors may add their own actions and services. The following listing shows the layout of the <action> elements:

```
<scpd>
  ...
  <actionList>
    <action>
      <name>actionName</name>
      <argumentList>list of arguments</argumentList>
    </action>
    Other standard actions here

     Other vendor-defined actions here

  </actionList>

<scpd>
```

Table 6.4 describes the two <action> sub-elements.

Each action may have zero or more arguments in its <argumentList> element. Each argument in the argument list has a "direction" and may be either an input or output parameter. One of the output arguments

Table 6.4 Action Sub-elements

Element	Required	Type	Description
name	Required	String	Name of action. May not contain any hyphen or '#' characters. For standard actions defined by a UPnP Forum working committee, must not begin with X_ or A_. For nonstandard actions specified by a UPnP vendor and added to a standard service, must begin with X_.
argumentList	May be required		Each action may have zero or more arguments. If an action has arguments, the argumentList element must be present.

may be marked as the action's return value. Each argument must correspond to a state variable (its related state variable). The following listing shows how these elements are described for each argument:

```
<scpd>

  ...
  <actionList>
    <action>
      <name>actionName</name>
      <argumentList>
        <argument>
          <name>formalParameterName</name>
          <direction>in xor out</direction>
          <retval />
           <relatedStateVariable>stateVariableName

                </relatedStateVariable>
        </argument>
       Other arguments
      </argumentList>
    </action>
    Other standard actions here

     Other vendor-defined actions here

  </actionList>

<scpd>
```

Table 6.5 provides the details for the <argument> sub-elements.

The Service State Table

The next major section of service description is the service state table—a list of the service's state variables. State variables are used to model the state of the service at run time. The <serviceStateTable> element of the service description is required and must have one or more state variables. Each state variable is described using the <stateVariable> element. This element has a required sendEvents attribute that may be set to either "yes" or "no" to specify whether the state variable is evented. Each <stateVariable> element has sub-elements to specify the state variable's name, type, and default value, as described in Table 6.6.

There are two ways that the values for a state variable may be specified—by listing the allowed values or by specifying the range of allowed values.

Table 6.5 Argument Sub-elements

Element	Required	Type	Description
name	Required	String	Name of formal parameter. Should be name of a state variable that models an effect the action causes. Must not contain a hyphen character (-, 2D Hex in UTF-8). Should be < 32 characters.
direction	Required		Whether argument is an input or output parameter. Must be in or out, but not both. Any in arguments must be listed before any out arguments.
retval	Optional		Identifies at most one out argument as the return value. If included, must be the first out argument. (Element only; no value.)
relatedStateVariable	Required		Must be the name of a state variable.

Table 6.6 StateVariable Sub-elements

Element	Required	Type	Description
name	Required	String	Name of state variable. Must not contain a hyphen character (-, 2D Hex in UTF-8). For standard variables defined by a UPnP Forum working committee, must not begin with X_ or A_. For nonstandard variables specified by a UPnP vendor and added to a standard service, must begin with X_.
dataType	Required		Same as data types defined by XML Schema, Part 2: Datatypes. Defined by a UPnP Forum working committee for standard state variables; specified by UPnP vendor for extensions.
defaultValue	Recommended		Recommended. Expected, initial value. Defined by a UPnP Forum working committee or delegated to UPnP vendor. Must match data type. Must satisfy allowedValueList or allowedValueRange constraints.

The Allowed Value List for String Variables

If a state variable is of type String, the possible values that the variable may take can be specified using a list of allowed values. In this case, the <allowedValueList> element has one or more <allowedValue> subelements that specify a legal value for this variable. The following listing shows a state variable with its name, type, and default value, along with a list of allowed values:

```
<scpd>
  ...
  <serviceStateTable>

    <stateVariable sendEvents="yes">
      <name>variableName</name>
      <dataType>variable data type</dataType>
      <defaultValue>default value</defaultValue>

      <allowedValueList>
        <allowedValue>allowed value #1</allowedValue>
        <allowedValue>allowed value #2</allowedValue>
        <allowedValue>allowed value #3</allowedValue>
        Other standard allowed values
      </allowedValueList>

    </stateVariable>
    Other standard state variables
    Other vendor-defined state variables
  </serviceStateTable>
</scpd>
```

The Allowed Value Range for Numeric Variables

For numeric variables, the range of acceptable values can be specified using an <allowedValueRange> element. This element has three subelements: <minimum>, <maximum>, and <step>, as follows:

```
<scpd>

  ...
  <serviceStateTable>
    <stateVariable sendEvents="yes">
      <name>variableName</name>
      <dataType>variable data type</dataType>
      <defaultValue>default value</defaultValue>

      <allowedValueRange>
        <minimum>minimum value</minimum>
```

```
        <maximum>maximum value</maximum>
        <step>increment value</step>
      </allowedValueRange>
    </stateVariable>
    Other standard state variables
    Other vendor-defined state variables
  </serviceStateTable>
</scpd>
```

Retrieving Device and Service Descriptions

Control points retrieve device and service description documents by issuing HTTP GET requests to the appropriate URL. To retrieve a device description, the control point uses the URL contained in the discovery advertisement or response to a discovery query. (Remember, the discovery response has the type, uuid, and URL for the device description document.) The device returns the device or service description in the body of an HTTP response.

For example, consider that a control point has received the URL `http://192.168.1.1/device/toaster` in a discovery response. To get the device description document for this device, the control point issues an HTTP GET as follows:

```
GET device/toaster HTTP/1.1
Host 192.168.1.1:8080
Accept-Language: language preferred by control point
(blank line)
```

The `Host` header gives the name or IP address and optional port of the device description URL. This URL can be from the `Location` header in the discovery message or from the <SCPDURL> element of the device description. If the port value is not supplied, it is assumed to be port 80.

The `Accept-Language` header specifies the preferred language of the control point. If the device does not have a description available in this language, it may return the device description in a default language. The values for this header are from the set of RFC 1766 language tags.

This HTTP request to the device's URL causes the device to return its device description in the following HTTP response (values in *italics* are placeholders for actual values):

```
HTTP/1.1 200 OK
Content-Language: language used in description
Content-Length: length of body in bytes
```

```
Content-Type: text/xml
Date: when responded

<?xml version="1.0"?>
XML device description
```

Like other UPnP responses, the device must respond within 30 seconds, including expected transmission time. Once the control point has the device description, it can parse the document and have URLs to retrieve each of the service descriptions. A similar request is made to each of the SCPDURLs.

```
GET service/foobar HTTP/1.1
Host: 192.168.1.1:8080
Accept-Language: language preferred by control point
(blank line)
```

This HTTP request to the SCPDURL results in the following:

```
HTTP/1.1 200 OK
Content-Language: language used in description
Content-Length: length of body in bytes
Content-Type: text/xml
Date: when responded

<?xml version="1.0"?>
XML service description
```

The body of this response is a UPnP device or service description as explained in detail above. Table 6.7 lists the headers used in a description document response.

Table 6.7 Description Document Response Headers

Header	Required	Type	Description
Content-Language	Required if and only if an Accept-Language header was provided in the request.	RFC1766 language tag	Description documents can be returned in one of many languages.
Content-Length	Required	Integer	Length of body in bytes
Content-Type	Required	Must be `text/xml`	Description documents are XML documents
Date	Recommended	RFC1123 date	Date the response was generated.

Validity of the Information in Description Documents

Device and service descriptions are valid for as long as the device remains on the network with a discovery advertisement that has not expired. As long as the discovery advertisements from a device have not expired, a control point may assume that the device and its services are available. If the discovery advertisement expires or is canceled (receives a "bye-bye" message) and a new one is issued, the control point must reread the description documents for the most current information about the device.

Rules on using the information are:

- If a device cancels its advertisements and re-advertises, it may change information in its description documents.
- Control points must not assume that the descriptions remain unchanged.

Summary

- The description phase of UPnP comes after discovery and enables control points to find out details about devices and the services that they implement. Once control points have this information, they are ready to invoke actions on the device's services.
- Description enables subsequent phases of UPnP: control, eventing, and presentation.
- Device and service description documents are XML documents that follow a standard schema defined by the UPnP Forum.
- The contents (elements) of specific device and service descriptions are defined by various working committees of the UPnP Forum and correspond to the required information that a standard UPnP device must have.
- Description documents are retrieved using a simple HTTP GET to a device's URL or a service's SCPDURL.

Chapter 7

Control

There's nothing remarkable about it. All one has to do is hit the right keys at the right time and the instrument plays itself.

—Johann Sebastian Bach

After a UPnP device has acquired an IP address and advertised its presence on the network, control points can then discover the device and invoke any of the actions provided by the device's services. In UPnP terminology, this invocation process is called *control*.

The control protocol used between UPnP control points and devices is the Simple Object Access Protocol (SOAP). As a UPnP developer, you will not typically be required to compose SOAP messages directly (this will be handled by the particular SDK you are using), but understanding SOAP and its operation will be helpful to you when debugging and tracing control messages between control points and devices.

This chapter begins by discussing the important characteristics of remote procedure call (RPC) mechanisms such as SOAP. Then you will take a closer look at SOAP and how it brings remote procedure calls into the realm of web-based resources. The chapter presents the details of the protocol and will show you some sample messages. The last part of the chapter discusses how SOAP is used by UPnP devices and discusses some potential pitfalls to be aware of.

Remote Procedure Calls

In a computer program running as a single process on a single computer, individual program components can refer to each other directly because they are in the same memory address space. If a component needs to access a data structure, the component simply references it directly. Also, when calling other functions, parameters are simply pushed on the stack or passed in registers, and control is passed directly to the function. However, when programs are partitioned into many components on potentially many different machines, the components can no longer directly reference each other, but must use some intermediate inter-process message-passing system to achieve the same result. Like a function or procedure call in a nondistributed program, the client process issues a request to a server and the response is transmitted back to the client from the server. Each component becomes like a mini-server, exposing its programmatic interface and allowing clients to invoke functions from across the network.

Remote procedure call mechanisms that support this distributed computing model must, at a minimum, have the following:

- *A Message-Based Protocol.* Includes requests, responses, and error responses to allow a caller to remotely invoke a function, procedure, or method at the server.
- *Platform-Independent Data Representation.* Used to package function call parameters. The representation may include predefined types to allow the user to specify commonly used types, such as an integer or a character sequence, and may have extensibility mechanisms to allow user-defined types.

The model may also have optional features such as:

- *Security.* Using various means such as digital signatures, signed messages, encryption, and client authentication can achieve confidentiality, integrity, and authentication.

RPC implementations can range from a simple, low-budget request/response protocol with fixed data types and no security features to a full-blown system with user-definable types and secure messaging using digital signatures and a public key infrastructure. In either case, the basic functionality is the same: Make a simple call to a network-based remote entity as if it was a local component, as shown in Figure 7.1.

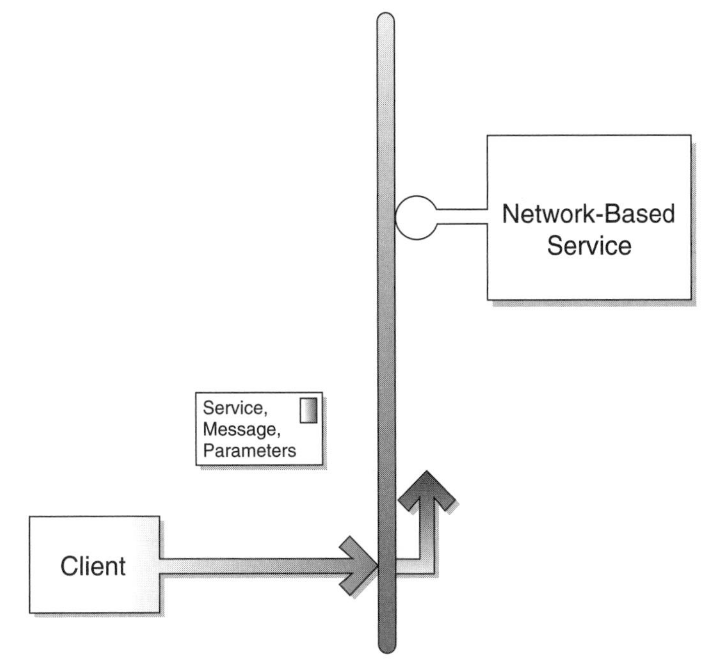

Figure 7.1 Client Issuing an RPC to a Network-based Service

Remote procedure call mechanisms have been around for a long time and the issues surrounding them are well understood. However, bringing these ideas to the web, including the home and small office, is a recent innovation.

The Simple Object Access Protocol

The Simple Object Access Protocol (SOAP) is a protocol that brings together XML and HTTP to provide a Web-based messaging and remote procedure call mechanism. XML is used to express the contents of the messages, while HTTP is used to send the messages to their destination. This section describes SOAP in general and not specifically how SOAP is used to allow control points to invoke the services provided by UPnP devices. Later sections explain the conventions introduced by the UPnP architecture for using SOAP as its control protocol.

SOAP is specified as a set of conventions that govern the format and processing rules of SOAP messages. SOAP consists of four parts:

- *The SOAP envelope.* An XML schema that defines a framework for describing what is in a message, how to process it, and whether it is optional or mandatory.
- *The SOAP encoding rules.* Another XML schema that defines a set of rules for expressing instances of application-defined data types.
- *The SOAP binding.* A convention for using different transport protocols. SOAP can potentially be used in combination with a variety of other transport protocols. (However, SOAP is most commonly carried by HTTP.)
- *The SOAP RPC representation.* A convention for representing remote procedure calls and responses.

The SOAP message is the basic unit of communication between peers. SOAP messages are written in XML, making SOAP platform-independent (any system capable of creating and parsing XML documents can send and receive SOAP messages). Because of the power of XML, SOAP messages can be fairly complex in structure and can transmit highly complex data types.

SOAP Namespaces

XML namespaces, like namespace constructs in programming languages like C++ and Java, ensure uniqueness among XML elements, avoiding collisions among elements from different sources with the same name. There are four namespaces used in SOAP, each of which is independent of the others, as shown in Table 7.1.

Table 7.1 SOAP Namespaces

Namespace	Description
http://www.w3.org/2001/06/soap-envelope	SOAP envelope namespace. The envelope is the outermost container for SOAP messages.
http://www.w3.org/2001/06/soap-encoding	SOAP encoding namespace. The encoding rules specify how to encode data types in SOAP messages.

Continues

Table 7.1 SOAP Namespaces *(Continued)*

Namespace	Description
http://www.w3.org/2001/XMLSchema-datatypes	XML schema for data types. The basic set of types for SOAP messages.
http://www.w3.org/2001/XMLSchema-instance	XML schema for instances defines several attributes for use in any XML documents.

The SOAP Message Envelope

The *SOAP message envelope* is the outermost container of SOAP messages. It is a well-formed XML document that comes right after the standard HTTP headers in the body of an HTTP message. The `<Envelope>` element contains two child elements: `<Header>` and `<Body>`. The SOAP `<Header>` element is optional, but the `<Body>` element is required. The `<Header>` and `<Body>` elements each contain SOAP blocks, which are valid XML data. A block within the SOAP header is called a header block and a block within a SOAP body is called a body block.

The SOAP Header Element

The *SOAP header* is an optional element for carrying auxiliary information for authentication, transactions, and payments. It is a collection of zero or more SOAP blocks. The SOAP `<Header>` element can contain an unlimited number of child elements that support the message in some way and enable developers to extend SOAP messages in very powerful ways.

The SOAP Body Element

The *SOAP body* is a collection of zero or more SOAP blocks. The SOAP `<Body>` element contains the core of the message—a remote method call and its associated arguments, a method response, or error information for failed calls.

By convention, a method response is contained in a child element that is named by appending the word "Response" to the name of the remote method.

Figure 7.2 illustrates the composition of a SOAP message.

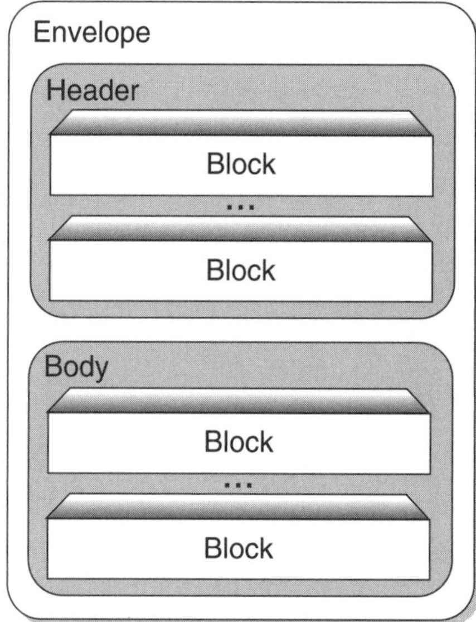

Figure 7.2 SOAP Encapsulation Model: Envelope, Header, Body, and Blocks

For example, the following SOAP message has a body that has a call to a `GetInformation` method of some fictitious Web service. This particular message does not use a header.

```
<?xml version="1.0" encoding="utf-8" ?>
<soap:Envelope xmlns:soap="http://schemas.xmlsoap.org/
soap/envelope/" xmlns:xsi="http://www.w3.org/2001/
XMLSchema-instance" xmlns:xsd="http://www.w3.org/2001/
XMLSchema">
  <soap:Body>
    <MethodName />
  </soap:Body>
</soap:Envelope>
```

SOAP Encoding Rules

The SOAP encoding rules allow you to actually pass useful data to a SOAP endpoint by defining how to encode data types in a SOAP message. The encoding rules provide a representation for a type system that can be used to encode data into XML. The encoding rules attempt to include many common features found in programming language type systems, databases, and semi-structured data, including simple scalar types and compound types.

You don't *have* to use the SOAP encoding rules for encoding your data, but they do provide a complete type system for you. This chapter does not go into detail on the types available in the SOAP encoding rules. Table 7.2 lists some of the simple scalar types available.

Table 7.2 SOAP Scalar Types

Type	Example
32-bit signed integer	–27
Boolean	0 or 1
ASCII string	this is a string
Signed floating point number	–27.327
date/time	2001-03-27T00:00:01-08:00
base64-encoded binary	eW91IGNhbid0IHJlYWQgdGhpcyE=

Conventions for SOAP over HTTP

SOAP is not dependent upon any particular underlying transport protocol and can be carried by a variety of transport protocols, including HTTP, SMTP, and FTP. However, for each particular transport protocol, conventions must be established to allow the transport to carry SOAP's XML payload. For example, binding SOAP to HTTP is relatively simple because SOAP's request/response message model matches HTTP's model, making it easy to encapsulate SOAP within HTTP. However, conventions such as how to set HTTP's content type, what additional HTTP headers should be used, and how errors are handled also need to be agreed upon.

The SOAP HTTP Request

A SOAP message is sent as an HTTP `POST` with the content type set to `text/xml` to indicate that the content of the message is an XML document. SOAP request messages include a new HTTP header, `SOAPAction`, whose value is a URI that indicates the intention of the SOAP request—to let the receiver know that this is a message for a particular service, for example. SOAP does not require this field to point to an actual web resource, however. The information is provided to allow intermediate processors, such as a web server receiving all SOAP messages, to route or filter incoming SOAP messages.

The SOAPAction header can be set to either an empty string, the name of the SOAP method, or it can have no value. The empty string ("") means that the intent of the SOAP message is provided by the HTTP Request-URI, and no value means that there is no indication provided for the intent of the message.

The following example shows a sample SOAP request. The example highlights the HTTP POST request, the Content-Type header set to text/xml, and the SOAPAction header set to indicate you're calling a fictitious book checkout service. (As you will see shortly, the UPnP device architecture defines a particular format for the value of the SOAPAction header, specifying the service and action to invoke.) The body of the message depends on the particular action being invoked.

```
POST /Checkout HTTP/1.1
Host: library.intoast.com
Content-Type: text/xml; charset="utf-8"
Content-Length: length of body in bytes
SOAPAction: http:// library.intoast.com/checkout

<s:Envelope
xmlns:s="http://www.w3.org/2001/06/soap-envelope/
    " s:encodingStyle="http://www.w3.org/2001/06/
    soap-encoding/">
  <s:Body>
  Body of message here...
  </s:Body>
</s:Envelope>
```

M-POST, HTTP Extensions, and the MAN Header

SOAP uses the HTTP Extension Framework to extend HTTP. To ensure that the introduced SOAPAction header is not confused with other HTTP extensions, SOAP conforms to the HTTP Extension Framework by specifying a unique URI in the MAN header and attaching the prefix M- to the POST method. Using the M-POST method requires the HTTP server to find and understand the URI in the MAN header and to understand the SOAPAction header.

The SOAP specification requires that requests must first be attempted *without* the MAN header or M- prefix. If the request fails with 405 Method Not Allowed, then a second request must be sent using the MAN header and M- prefix. If that request fails with 501 Not Implemented or 510 Not Extended, then the request fails.

The SOAP HTTP Response

The SOAP HTTP response, like the request, is an XML document contained in a standard HTTP message whose content type is `text/xml`. The XML document for the response is structured just like the request, using the `<Envelope>` and `<Body>` tags, but the Body itself contains the encoded method result instead of the method call. Methods that do not return a value (void methods) simply omit the `<return>` part of the Body.

SOAP over HTTP follows the semantics of the HTTP status codes. For example, `2xx` status code[1] indicates success—the client's request was successfully received, understood, and accepted. There are five values for the first digit of the HTTP return code, as summarized in Table 7.3.

The following example shows a successful SOAP response, including the 200 result code, the `Content-Type` header, and the SOAP envelope containing the response.

```
HTTP/1.1 200 OK
Content-Type: text/xml; charset="utf-8"
Content-Length: length of body in bytes

<s:Envelope xmlns:s='http://www.w3.org/2001/06/
    soap-envelope'>
  <s:Body>
  Body of response message here...
  </s:Body>
</s:Envelope>
```

Table 7.3 HTTP Return Code Categories

Number Range	Meaning	Description
2xx	Success	The action was successfully received, understood, and accepted.
3xx	Redirection	Further action must be taken in order to complete the request.
4xx	Client Error	The syntax of the request is invalid or cannot be fulfilled.
5xx	Server Error	The server failed to fulfill an apparently valid request.

[1] The first digit of the status code defines the kind of response. The last two digits are not significant in categorizing the response, but provide further information about the error.

SOAP Exceptions

If an error occurs while the server is processing the SOAP request, the server issues a `500 Internal Server Error` response and returns a SOAP message containing a SOAP fault in the response. The SOAP fault appears within the Body of a SOAP message and carries error and/or status information. There are four sub-elements of the `<Fault>` element, `<faultcode>`, `<faultstring>`, `<faultactor>`, and `<detail>`.

The `<faultcode>` sub-element provides a value that indicates the reason for the fault and is intended to provide information that an application can use to recover from the fault without user intervention. The `<faultcode>` values include those listed in Table 7.4.

The `<faultstring>` sub-element contains an explanation of the fault. Typically, the `<fault>` sub-element would be used by the application to recover from the fault, while the `<faultstring>` sub-element contains more detailed information for the user to assist in recovering from the error.

The `<faultactor>` sub-element is a URI that identifies the source of the fault.

The `<detail>` sub-element carries application-specific error information related to the SOAP Body.

The listing in Figure 7.3 shows all of the SOAP Fault sub-elements in a SOAP fault returned to a caller.

Table 7.4 Values of the `<faultcode>` Sub-element

Name	Description
VersionMismatch	Returned when the server detects an invalid namespace in the request.
MustUnderstand	Returned when the server does not understand an immediate child element of the SOAP header and the SOAP mustUnderstand attribute was set to "1" on the request.
Client	Returned when the message was not correctly formed or did not contain required information.
Server	Returned when the server cannot complete the request for some reason. The message itself is not the problem, but the server's processing of it.

```
<s:Envelope

xmlns:s='http://www.w3.org/2001/06/soap-envelope'
xmlns:f='http://www.w3.org/2001/06/soap-faults'>
  <s:Body>
    <s:Fault>
      <faultcode>MustUnderstand</faultcode>
      <faultstring>One or more mandatory headers not
        understood</faultstring>
      <faultactor>fault actor</faultactor>
      <detail>more detail </detail>
    </s:Fault>
  </s:Body>
```

Figure 7.3 A Sample SOAP Fault

The Control URL

In a UPnP device description document, each service element has a <controlURL>—an element that contains a URL where all control messages for that service are to be sent. Control points send SOAP-based control messages to this control URL and, in response, the service returns any results or errors from the action. The following listing highlights the location of the <controlURL> element in a device description document.

```
<xml version="1.0"?>
<root xmlns="urn:schemas-upnp-org:device-1.0">
  <specVersion>
    <major>1</major>
    <minor>0</minor>
  </specVersion>
<URLBase>base URL for all of the relative URLs</URLBase>
device>
  other device description elements
  <serviceList>
    <service>

      <controlURL>URL for control requests</controlURL>

    </service>
  </serviceList>
</root>
```

Action Request

To invoke an action using the POST method, a control point must send a request in the following format to the service's controlURL.

```
POST controlURL HTTP/1.1
Host: controlURL host:port
Content-Length: length of body in bytes
Content-Type: text/xml; charset="utf-8"
SOAPAction: "urn:schemas-upnp-org:service:
  serviceType:v#actionName"

<s:Envelope xmlns:s="http://schemas.xmlsoap.org/soap/
  envelope/"
s:encodingStyle="http://schemas.xmlsoap.org/soap/
  encoding/">
  <s:Body>
    <u:actionName xmlns:u="urn:schemas-upnp-org:service:
      serviceType:v">
      <argumentName>in arg value</argumentName>
      other in args and their values go here, if any
    </u:actionName>
  </s:Body>
</s:Envelope>
```

The request line for this message uses the POST method. The controlURL sub-element will be the path component of the URL for control for this service. Table 7.5 lists the headers used when invoking an action on a service.

The body of the HTTP message consists of a SOAP envelope. The required namespace attribute for this element,

```
http://schemas.xmlsoap.org/soap/envelope/
```

includes the schema for the SOAP envelope. The encodingStyle attribute must also be present and must be

```
http://schemas.xmlsoap.org/soap/encoding/
```

All SOAP requests follow this pattern.

The Body element contained in the SOAP envelope contains the body of the action request and is qualified with the SOAP envelope namespace. It contains the required <actionName> sub-element, which contains the name of the action in the service the caller wishes to invoke. This element must include the XML namespace of the service being called. The format for this attribute is urn:schemas-upnp-org:service:serviceType:v.

Table 7.5 Action Request Headers

Header	Required	Type	Description
Content-Length	Required	Integer	Length of the body of the message in bytes.
Content-Type	Required	Must be `text/xml`	Should also include the `charset` attribute to specify the character encoding used, such as UTF-8.
Host	Required	Domain name or IP address and optional port of the control URL for the service	Given in the `<controlURL>` sub-element of the service element in the device description. If the port is not supplied, port 80 is assumed.
Man	Required for M-POST only	Value is set to the XML schema for SOAP envelopes. Contains a namespace directive that is then used on the `SOAPAction` header.	No Man header is required with the `POST` method. Required with `M-POST`.
SOAPAction	Required	Single URI.	Must be the service type, "#", and name of action to be invoked, enclosed in double quotes. If used in a request with method `M-POST`, the `SOAPAction` header name must be qualified with HTTP namespace defined in the `Man` header.

If the action has arguments, each argument is provided with the name of the argument in enclosing tags and the value of the argument within the tags. The data types of the arguments are defined by the UPnP service description.

As discussed in the previous section on SOAP, if a request with a `POST` method is rejected with a `405 Method Not Allowed message`, then the control point must send a second request with the M-POST method and a MAN header, as follows:

```
M-POST controlURL HTTP/1.1
Host: controlURL host:port
Content-Length: length of body in bytes
Content-Type: text/xml; charset="utf-8"
Man: "http://schemas.xmlsoap.org/soap/envelope/"; ns=s
s-SOAPAction: "urn:schemas-upnp-org:service:
  serviceType:v#actionName"

message body same as for POST
```

The request line for this message uses the M- prefix as defined by the HTTP Extension Framework. The headers are the same as the POST method, except that there is now a MAN header that must have the value

```
http://schemas.xmlsoap.org/soap/envelope/
```

The ns directive in the MAN header value defines the namespace for other SOAP headers (SOAPAction in this case). The SOAPAction header (qualified with the namespace defined in the MAN header) must be the service type and version, "#", and the name of the action to invoke, all enclosed in quotes.

The message body for a request using the M-POST method is the same as that for the POST method.

Action Response

A service has 30 seconds to complete the action and respond to the control point, including expected transmission time. According to the UPnP device architecture, actions that are expected to take longer than this should return early and send an event when the action completes. A service responds using the following format:

```
HTTP/1.1 200 OK
Content-Length: length of body in bytes
Content-Type: text/xml; charset="utf-8"
Date: when response was generated
Ext:
Server: OS/version UPnP/1.0 product/version

<s:Envelope
xmlns:s="http://schemas.xmlsoap.org/soap/envelope/"
```

```
s:encodingStyle="http://schemas.xmlsoap.org/soap/
  encoding/">
  <s:Body>
    <u:actionNameResponse xmlns:u="urn:schemas-upnp-org:
      service:serviceType:v">
      <argumentName>output argument value</argumentName>
      other output arguments and values, if any
    </u:actionNameResponse>

  </s:Body>
</s:Envelope>
```

The initial line for the response message is the typical HTTP success response. Headers used for an action response are listed in Table 7.6.

The action response is contained in a typical SOAP <Body> element within a SOAP envelope. By convention, the response to a particular action is named by appending `Response` to the action name. The action response contains any output argument values returned from the action in the same format described previously for input. The first output argument is defined to be the actions return value.

Table 7.6 Action Response Headers

Header	Required	Type	Description
Content-Length	Required	Integer	Length of the body of the message in bytes.
Content-Type	Required	Must be `text/xml`	Should also include the character encoding used (e.g., UTF-8).
Date	Recommended	RFC1123 date	When the response was generated.
Ext	Required	no value	Confirms that the `MAN` header was understood.
Server	Required	String	Concatentation of OS Name, OS version, UpnP/1.0, product name, and product version.

Action Error Response

If the service is not able to successfully complete the action, it sends an error return message to the control point. Error responses are sent in the following format:

```
HTTP/1.1 500 Internal Server Error
Content-Length: length of body in bytes
Content-Type: text/xml; charset="utf-8"
Date: when response was generated
Ext:
Server: OS/version UPnP/1.0 product/version

<s:Envelope
xmlns:s="http://schemas.xmlsoap.org/soap/envelope/"
s:encodingStyle="http://schemas.xmlsoap.org/soap/encoding/">
  <s:Body>
    <s:Fault>
      <faultcode>s:Client</faultcode>
      <faultstring>UPnPError</faultstring>
      <detail>
        <UPnPError xmlns="urn:schemas-upnp-org:control-1-0">
          <errorCode>error code</errorCode>
          <errorDescription>error string</errorDescription>
        </UPnPError>
      </detail>
    </s:Fault>
  </s:Body>
</s:Envelope>
```

The initial response line provides the 500 error code to indicate an unsuccessful request. The headers for an error response are the same as those for a successful response: `Content-Length`, `Content-Type`, and so on.

The body of the message is a SOAP response with the typical `<Envelope>` and `<Body>` elements.

The differences start with the highlighted SOAP `<Fault>` element. An error response for a failed UPnP action includes the required elements of a SOAP fault: `<faultcode>`, `<faultstring>`, and `<detail>`. The `<faultcode>` element must have a value of `Client` qualified with the SOAP namespace. The `<faultstring>` element must be `UPnPError`. The `<detail>` element contains a `<UPnPError>` sub-element that itself has two sub-elements, `<errorCode>` and `<errorDescription>`. Table 7.7 summarizes the possible values for the `<errorCode>` and `<errorDescription>` elements.

Table 7.7 `<errorCode>` and `<errorDescription>` Values for a Failed Action

errorCode	errorDescription	Description
401	Invalid Action	The service has no action of the name provided.
402	Invalid Args	Problem with the input arguments: not enough arguments, too many arguments, wrong name, or wrong type.
403	Out of Sync	Out of synchronization.
501	Action Failed	Current state of service prevents invoking the action.
600–699	UPnP Forum defined	Common action errors. Defined by UPnP Forum Technical Committee.
700–799	Depends on device type	Action-specific errors for standard actions. Defined by UPnP Forum working committees.
800–899	Vendor-defined	Action-specific errors for nonstandard actions. Available to be defined by the UPnP device vendor.

QueryStateVariable

In addition to invoking actions on a device's service, control points may also directly query the service for the value of a state variable. To do this, a control point can use the `QueryStateVariable` action. All services support this action implicitly. A control point can use `QueryStateVariable` to get the value of a single state variable. However, use of this method is discouraged in the Universal Plug and Play Vendor's Implementation Guide (<`http://www.upnp.org/download/UPnP_Vendor_Implementation_Guide_Jan2001.htm`>), a document that contains clarifications to the UPnP Device Architecture specification.

The Implementation Guide recommends that implementers should only invoke actions explicitly defined for the particular service type and should reserve using `QueryStateVariable` for limited testing scenarios. Using explicitly defined functions instead of `QueryStateVariable` has the following benefits:

- *Improved efficiency.* All of a service's state variables can be queried using a single action.
- *Clearer definition of intended use of a service's state variables.* The read and write access patterns are explicit in the service's actions.

- *Improved interoperability.* Control points will use the service only through its standard interface and not in ways unintended by the service designer.
- *Reduced implementation size.* Services do not have to maintain memory for certain types of non-evented state variables.

QueryStateVariable may be removed from future versions of the UPnP standard. Use it with caution.

Summary

This chapter has covered a lot of ground, from RPC basics, to an overview of SOAP, to details about how UPnP control points use SOAP to invoke actions on a device's services. The most important points are:

- SOAP is a messaging and remote procedure call technology that can be used over a variety of transports, but is primarily used over HTTP.
- Along with its use of XML, SOAP is a good choice for a web-based RPC mechanism.
- UPnP control points use SOAP to invoke actions provided by services contained on a device.
- UPnP introduces a few more conventions when using SOAP, such as the `controlURL`, `QueryStateVariable`, and the contents of the `POST` method and `SOAPAction` header.

Chapter 8

Eventing

Knowledge speaks, but wisdom listens.

—Jimi Hendrix

After a control point has discovered a device and retrieved its device and service descriptions, the control point may wish to respond to state changes in the device. UPnP eventing allows control points to register for and receive notifications of device state changes. This chapter explores eventing, starting first with a brief overview of event notification in a distributed system and the publisher/subscriber model. Next, the chapter looks at the General Event Notification Architecture (GENA), the protocol used by UPnP control points and devices to implement eventing. Finally, the chapter covers the details of how GENA is used with the UPnP architecture, including the UPnP template language for events, the subscription process, and the details of each message in the protocol.

Events in a Distributed System

Components of a distributed system generally communicate using two distinct mechanisms—the remote procedure call (discussed in Chapter 7, "Control") and event notification. Event notification is the less common model of the two. With RPC, objects are passively waiting to provide service to clients. However, with event notification, state changes in the system are modeled as events, allowing other objects to dynamically respond, perhaps by invoking services provided by still other objects.

"What is it now?" versus "Let me know when it changes."

To illustrate the difference between the two kinds of systems, consider a stock quote server.

An RPC-based stock quote server might allow clients to call to retrieve the current stock quote for a particular company. Clients can make a call to the server whenever they want to get the value for a particular stock. The client doesn't know when the value changes and must poll the server to keep its value up-to-date.

In contrast, a system based on event notification would allow clients to express interest in monitoring a particular stock and would notify them when the price changed. Upon receiving the notification, the client could act on it by perhaps updating a chart based on the new information. By requiring communication only when needed, event notification can help to create a more efficient system.

Publisher/Subscriber Model

A *publisher/subscriber model* is typically used to implement event notification. In this model, the *publisher* is the source of events and grants a client a subscription when the client registers interest in receiving events provided by the publisher. Upon the occurrence of an event, the publisher delivers an event notification to the client, or *subscriber*. If the subscriber is no longer interested in receiving event notifications, it may elect to unsubscribe for the events, which will cause the publisher to cancel the subscription and discontinue sending events to that client. The subscription may be granted for a particular duration and require a periodic renewal by the client to maintain the subscription.

The publisher/subscriber model is conceptually very simple. It is asynchronous in nature and is very good at modeling systems where asynchronous events need to be propagated from one source component to many other components. One particular protocol for event notification is GENA, the General Event Notification Architecture.

General Event Notification Architecture

General Event Notification Architecture (GENA) is a publisher/subscriber system whereby a subscriber may request, renew, or cancel a subscription. The subscriber first sends a subscription message to a publisher. If the subscription is accepted by the publisher, it responds with a subscription ID and a duration for this particular subscription. Subsequent operations on the subscription, such as renewal and cancellation, use the subscription ID to reference the subscription. To renew the subscription, the subscriber sends a renewal message to the publisher before the subscription expires. When the subscriber is no longer interested in receiving events from the publisher, it may cancel the subscription. Subscriptions may also be cancelled by the publisher.

The Communication Transport

Following the familiar pattern used by other UPnP protocols, GENA brings event notification into the realm of the Web. GENA uses HTTP as the transport for the communication between publishers and subscribers. Figure 8.1 shows GENA's protocol stack.

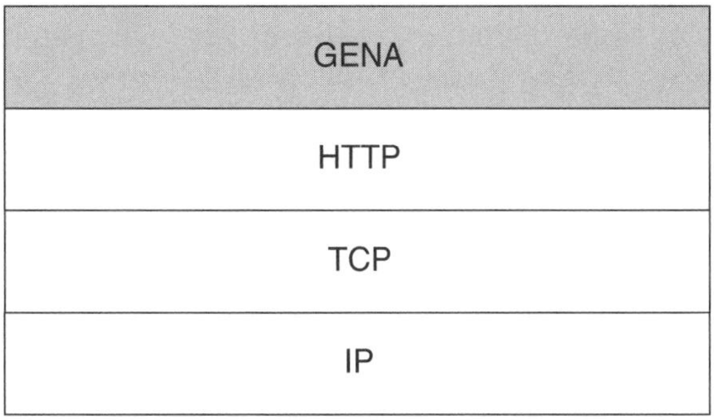

GENA
HTTP
TCP
IP

Figure 8.1 The GENA Protocol Stack

HTTP Methods and Headers

GENA introduces three HTTP methods that are used to manage event subscriptions and deliver messages:

- SUBSCRIBE to subscribe to receive event notifications and to renew an existing subscription. The headers will be different depending on which function is intended.
- UNSUBSCRIBE to terminate a subscription.
- NOTIFY to send an event notification to a subscriber.

GENA introduces the following headers that are used with the new HTTP methods:

- CALLBACK is used to communicate a URL to be used to call back the other entity. For example, the subscriber sends a CALLBACK header when registering to receive events. The publisher uses this URL when sending event notifications.
- NT is the notification type. It is used to tell the subscriber what kind of notification this is.
- NTS is the notification sub-type. It allows further refinement of the notification type.
- SID is the subscription ID. This ID is generated by the publisher to reference a subscription. Both the publisher and subscriber use this ID when communicating with the other and referring to a particular subscription.

GENA messages also use standard HTTP headers such as `Host`, `Timeout`, `Date`, `Server`, `Content-Length`, and `Content-Type`. The meaning of each of these headers when used within GENA messages will be described in following sections that provide the details of the GENA protocol.

Using GENA with UPnP Devices

Conceptually, GENA's simple publisher/subscriber model maps easily to the UPnP object model: UPnP control points are subscribers while UPnP services are publishers. The UPnP device itself is not a source of events, as you might expect, but is just a container for the services.

The UPnP device architecture establishes additional conventions for eventing beyond the basic capabilities provided by GENA:

- *Service description and evented state variables.* As discussed in Chapter 6, the UPnP service description includes a list of actions the service responds to and a list of variables that model the state of the service at run time. Any of these variables can be *evented*, or identified, as capable of sourcing events upon state changes. If one or more of these state variables are evented, then control points may register to receive events from the service and the service publishes event notifications when any of these variables change.
- *XML-based event messages.* The service indicates changes to state variables by sending event messages to control points. Event messages contain the names of one of more state variables and the current value of those variables, expressed using an XML syntax, the UPnP Template Language for eventing.
- *Initial event message.* A special event message is sent when a control point first subscribes to receive events from a service. This special first message includes the names and values for all evented variables provided by the service. This message allows the subscriber to initialize its model of the state of the service.
- *All subscribers get all event messages.* Eventing in the UPnP architecture is designed to keep all subscribers equally informed about the effects of any action. All subscribers are sent all event messages and each event message contains the values for all evented variables. No mechanism is provided to subscribe to event messages on a per-variable basis.
- *Event keys.* As an error detection mechanism to ensure that subscribers have received all event messages sent, the publisher maintains a separate event key for each subscription. For each event message to a subscriber, the publisher increments the event key and includes the value in the notification. To hold this value, the UPnP architecture introduces a SEQ header used in the event notification message.

The following sections go into detail on each of these aspects of UPnP eventing. Figure 8.2 illustrates the basics of eventing between UPnP control points and devices.

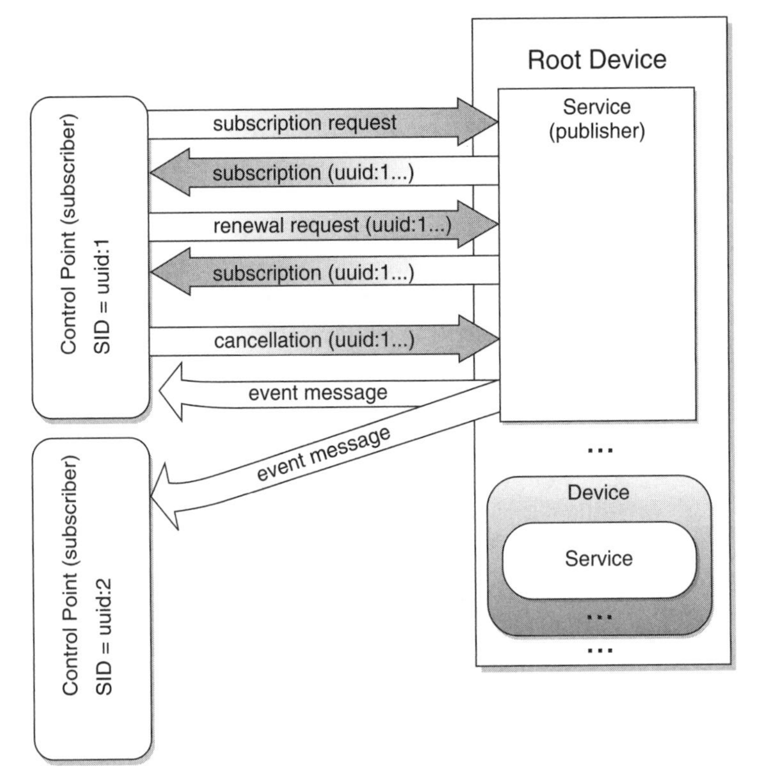

Figure 8.2 UPnP Eventing

Service Description and Evented State Variables

As covered in Chapter 6, "Description," the XML-based UPnP Service Template defines an attribute, `sendEvents`, for state variables. This attribute has two possible values, "`yes`" if the variable is evented, causing the service to send events when it changes value, and "`no`" if it does not cause events to be sent. If the service has one or more state variables marked as sending events, then that service is said to "have eventing." If the service has no evented state variables, the service has nothing to publish and does not process event messages such as subscriptions and renewals.

Which Variables Should Be Evented?

If you are designing a UPnP device, you may be wondering how you determine which variables should be evented. What if you don't want to expose the internal state of your device/service to control points? Whatever happened to object-oriented programming where encapsulation and loose coupling were good things?

The answer is that state variables are part of the abstraction of the device. The state variables, along with the actions supported by the service, define the service's public interface. State variables are not a literal description of how you must implement the service. You may have many variables in your implementation that are not represented in the service description. The bottom line is: You should define and use state variables, evented or not, as it helps to model your service. Decisions about which variables to event are up to the UPnP Forum working committees for standard services and the UPnP device vendor for nonstandard services.

The UPnP Template Language for Eventing

Event notifications are sent in the body of an HTTP message and contain the names of one of more state variables and the current value of those variables, expressed in XML. The notifications are composed according to the XML-based UPnP Template Language. Figure 8.3 shows the part of this language that pertains to eventing.

This schema defines a <propertyset> element that contains 1 to n <property> elements. Each property is one of the evented state

```
<? xml version="1.0"?>

<Schema name="urn:schemas-upnp-org:event-1-0"
    xmlns="urn:schemas-microsoft-com:xml-data"
    xmlns:dt="urn:schemas-microsoft-com:datatypes">
<ElementType name="propertyset" content="eltOnly">
   <element type="property" minOccurs="1" maxOccurs="*"/>
</ElementType>
<ElementType name="property" content="eltOnly" />
</Schema>
```

Figure 8.3 The UPnP Template Language for Eventing

variables and its current value. For example, here's a notification body that contains the current value of a service's three evented state variables:

```
<e:propertyset xmlns:e="urn:schemas-upnp-org:event-1-0">
  <e:property>
    <SomeVariable>this is the value</SomeVariable>
    <AnotherVariable>1028</AnotherVariable>
    <AThirdVariable>some other value</AThirdVariable>
  </e:property>
</e:propertyset>
```

Moderation of Events

It is possible to augment the description of devices and services with attributes that are not part of the UPnP Template Language. One such convention, *moderation*, limits the rate at which events are sent from a publisher to subscribers for state variables that would otherwise change too rapidly for eventing to be useful. Moderation allows the publisher to limit the number of events that are actually sent in response to the rapidly changing state variable. The moderation convention is an exception to the rule requiring all state table changes to evented state variables to result in events. Moderation introduces two optional attributes for evented state variables, `maximumRate`, and `minimumDelta`:

- **maximumRate = *n*.** An integer that specifies the reporting period for the state variable. In other words, the state variable will not be part of an event message more often than every `n` seconds. This attribute is recommended for variables that model continuously changing properties.
- **minimumDelta = *n*.** An integer that specifies by how much the state variable must change since the last time it was included in an event message before it will be included again. This attribute is recommended for variables that model counters. It is only defined for variables with number and real data type.

The publisher can send out any changed moderated variable when an event goes out. The publisher should make its best attempt to meet moderation rules described above, but the publisher can flush recent changes when it sends out events. Moderation affects events only and not state table updates. In other words, calling `QueryStateVariable` may return a more current value than the last update received from an event message.

Decisions about which variables to event and any possible moderation are the responsibility of the appropriate UPnP Forum working committee for standard services and the UPnP device vendor for non-standard services.

Event Keys

Event messages are tagged with an event key. A separate event key is maintained by the publisher for each subscription to facilitate error detection. The event key for a subscription is initialized to 0 when the publisher sends the initial event message. For each subsequent event message, the publisher increments the event key for a subscription and includes that updated key in the event message. Any implementation of event keys should handle overflow and wrap the event key back to 1 (not 0). Subscribers must also handle this special case when the next event key is not an increment of the previous key. The event key should be implemented as a 4-byte (32-bit) integer.

Subscription Processes/Mechanics/Examples

Now take a look at the mechanics of subscribing, canceling, and renewing event subscriptions. For each type of message, you'll look at the format of the message, including HTTP headers used, the format of the response, and possible error return values.

Subscriber List

In order to publish events to subscribers when the events occur, services that publish events keep track of information for each subscriber, as shown in Table 8.1.

The list of subscribers is maintained by the service and is updated upon receiving subscription, renewal, or cancellation messages from subscribers and upon events (when it updates the Event Key field for each subscriber).

Table 8.1 The Subscriber List

Item	Type	Description
Unique Subscription Identifier	URI	The URI must be unique over the lifetime of the subscription. It is generated by publisher in response to subscription message. It is recommended to use universally unique identifiers.
Delivery URL for Event Messages	URI	This URI is provided by the subscriber in the subscription message. It tells the publisher where to deliver the events.
Event Key	Integer	Set to 0 for the initial event message. The event key is incremented for each subsequent event message; subscribers can verify that no event messages have been lost if the subscriber has received sequentially numbered event keys.
Subscription Duration	Integer or keyword `infinite`	Amount of time until the subscription expires.

Subscribing to Events

A control point starts the subscription process by first retrieving the device description document from the device as described in Chapter 6, "Description." The description document contains an event subscription URL and a service identifier for each service provided by the device (the `<eventSubURL>` and `<serviceId>` sub-elements of the `<service>` element, respectively). Then, to subscribe to events from a particular service, the control point sends a subscription request to the service's event subscription URL, in the following format:

```
SUBSCRIBE publisher Path HTTP/1.1
Host: publisher Host:Port
Callback: deliveryURL
NT: upnp:event
Timeout: Second-requested subscription duration
```

The first line is the subscription request. It specifies GENA's `SUBSCRIBE` method, which is used to get or renew a subscription. The *publisher-Path* is the path component of the event subscription URL. The event subscription URL may be relative to the base URL in the device description document. Ending the request line is the required HTTP version, HTTP/1.1.

The request message uses the `Host`, `Callback`, `NT`, and `Timeout` headers as described in the Table 8.2. There is no body required for `SUBSCRIBE` but, as with all HTTP message without a body, there must be a blank line following the last HTTP header.

Table 8.2 Subscription Headers

Header	Required	Type	Description
Host	Required	Domain name or IP address and optional port	The port is from the event subscription URL. If the port is not specified, port 80 is assumed.
Callback	Required	One or more URLs separated by angle brackets	Location to send event messages. Defined by UPnP vendor. Can be more than one URL. If so, the service tries the URLs in order until one succeeds.
NT	Required	Must be `upnp:event`	Notification type for subscription request always upnp:event.
Timeout	Recommended	Keyword `Second-` followed by an integer or keyword `infinite`	Requested duration until subscription expires, either number of seconds or infinite. Recommendation by working committee. Defined by UPnP device vendor.

Accepting Subscriptions

If the service accepts the subscription,[1] the service responds with a unique identifier, called the session ID (SID), and a duration for the subscription. The unique identifier is typically a GUID to ensure uniqueness. The duration is chosen and controlled by the service; the service can select a short duration and cause control points to renew more frequently at the expense of additional network traffic; or, the duration can be long, reducing network traffic, but perhaps requiring the service to expend resources holding subscriptions for control points that have left the network.

[1] According to the UPnP Device Architecture specification, the service should accept as many subscriptions as it can reasonably maintain and deliver.

Subscription Response

To accept a subscription request, a publisher sends a response in the following format:

```
HTTP/1.1 200 OK
Date: when response was generated
Server: OS/version UPnP/1.0 product/version
SID: uuid:subscription-UUID
Timeout: Second-actual subscription duration
```

The response must be sent within 30 seconds, including expected transmission time from the service to the control point. The first line of the response is the typical 200 response to a successful HTTP request. The headers used in the subscription response are summarized in Table 8.3. There is no body for the subscription response, but the message must have a blank line following the last HTTP header.

If a publisher cannot accept the subscription request, or if there is an error with the subscription request itself, the publisher must send a response with one of the errors listed in Table 8.4. Like the successful response, the error response must be sent within 30 seconds, including expected transmission time.

Table 8.3 Subscription Response Headers

Header	Required	Type	Description
Date	Recommended	RFC 1123 date	When response was generated.
Server	Required	String	Concatenation of OS name, OS version, UPnP/1.0, product name, and product version.
SID	Required	Single URI beginning with `uuid:`	Universally unique subscription identifier.
Timeout	Required	Keyword `Second-` followed by an integer, or keyword `infinite`	Length of time until subscription expires, either number of seconds or infinite. Recommendation by a UPnP Forum working committee. Defined by UPnP device vendor. Should be > 1800 seconds (30 minutes).

Table 8.4 Subscription Request Error Values

UPnP Error Type	HTTP Error Return	Sent If
Incompatible Headers	400 Bad Request	SID header and one of `NT` or `Callback` headers are present.
Missing or Invalid Callback	412 Precondition Failed	Callback header is missing or does not contain a valid HTTP URL.
Invalid NT	412 Precondition Failed	`NT` header does not equal upnp:event.
Unable to Accept Subscription	5xx	Publisher is not able to accept the subscription. Publisher responds with an HTTP 500-series error code.

Initial Event Message

As soon as possible after the publisher accepts the subscription, the publisher sends the first or initial event message to the subscriber. This message includes the names and current values for all evented state variables. This is done as a convenience to allow the control point to initialize its representation of the device's state. The control point does not have to explicitly request each variable or wait for an event to occur before it can receive the current value of all of the device's evented state variables.

Subscription Expiration

Subscriptions expire according to the `Timeout` value in the subscription request or renewal. Once subscriptions expire, the subscription is removed from the subscriber list and the publisher stops sending events to that subscription. If the subscriber tries to send any message other than a new subscription message using the SID from the expired subscription, the publisher detects that the SID is invalid and rejects the message.

Renewing a Subscription

Subscriptions last for the duration specified by the publisher in the response to the subscription request. If a control point wants to keep a subscription active beyond this time, it must renew the subscription before it expires.

To renew a subscription, the control point sends a subscription renewal message to the same URL it originally used to subscribe. The subscription renewal message uses the same `SUBSCRIBE` method as the subscription request, but uses different headers. Recall that the subscription request message includes a `Callback` header to specify where to send events and an `NT` header to specify the notification type. These fields are not required in the subscription renewal. Once a subscription is established, the SID is used by the publisher to index into the subscriber list that maintains the information, such as the URI specified in the `Callback` header. For a subscription renewal, the subscriber merely needs to send the `SID` header to indicate which subscription is to be renewed. The message may also include a requested subscription duration to suggest a duration for the renewed subscription. A renewal message that includes the `SID` header and either an `NT` or `Callback` header is in error and will be rejected by the publisher.

The format of the renewal request is as follows:

```
SUBSCRIBE publisher path HTTP/1.1
Host: publisher host:publisher port
SID: uuid:subscription UUID
Timeout: Second-requested subscription duration
(blank line)
```

The first line of the renewal is the same as subscription, providing the `SUBSCRIBE` method, the publisher path, and the HTTP version. The headers for the renewal message are specified in Table 8.5. There is no body for the subscription renewal request, but the message must have a blank line following the last HTTP header.

Table 8.5 Subscription Renewal Headers

Header	Required	Type	Description
HOST	Required	Domain name or IP address and optional port components of eventing URL.	Comes from the `<eventSubURL>` sub-element in the device description. If the port is missing or empty, port 80 is assumed.
SID	Required (defined by GENA)	Single URI. Universally unique subscription identifier. Must begin with uuid:	Must be the subscription identifier assigned by publisher in response to subscription request. Defined by UPnP device vendor.
TIMEOUT	Recommended	Keyword `Second-` followed by an integer (no space) or keyword `infinite`.	Requested duration until subscription expires, either number of seconds or infinite. Recommendation from UPnP Forum working committee. Defined by UPnP device vendor.

Subscription Renewal Response

To accept a renewal, the publisher reassigns a duration for the subscription (perhaps taking into account the duration suggested by the subscriber in the `Timeout` header) and sends a response in the same format as the response to a new subscription request. The response includes the `Date`, `SID`, and `Timeout` headers. The `Date` header shows when the response was generated. The `SID` header is redundant as the subscriber already knows the SID and has used it to renew the subscription. The `Timeout` header is optional and allows the subscriber to suggest a duration for the renewal.

Unlike a subscription request, there is no initial event message sent after a renewal. The initial event message is not needed because the subscriber is already receiving event notifications upon state variables changes and has an accurate representation of the state of the service.

If a publisher cannot accept the renewal, or if there is an error with the renewal request, the publisher must send a response with one of the errors listed in Table 8.6. The response must be sent within 30 seconds, including expected transmission time.

Canceling a Subscription

A subscription remains active until it expires or the control point cancels its subscription. When a control point no longer wishes to receive events from a particular service, it may send a cancellation message to the publisher.

Table 8.6 Subscription Renewal Request Error Values

UPnP Error Type	HTTP Error Return	Sent If
Incompatible Headers	400 Bad Request	`SID` header and one of `NT` or `Callback` headers are present.
Invalid SID	412 Precondition Failed	SID does not correspond to a known, unexpired subscription.
Missing SID	412 Precondition Failed	`SID` header is missing or empty.
Unable to Accept Renewal	5xx	Publisher is not able to accept a renewal; publisher responds with an HTTP 500-series error code.

Normally, a service that is publishing events notices when a subscribed control point leaves the network by issuing a bye-bye message and removes it from its subscription list. However, if a control point terminates abruptly without issuing this message, the service will not know that the control point has been removed from the network and will continue to maintain information about the control point in its subscription list until the subscription expires, consuming resources unnecessarily.

Canceling a subscription when it is no longer needed reduces service, control point, and network load. For example, if the control point didn't cancel an unneeded subscription, control point and service processing and network bandwidth are consumed unnecessarily by sending and receiving these unwanted messages. To cancel a subscription to eventing for a service, a subscriber sends a request with the following format:

```
UNSUBSCRIBE publisher_path HTTP/1.1
Host: publisher_host:port
SID: uuid:subscription_UUID
(blank line)
```

The cancellation message simply contains the UNSUBSCRIBE method, the HOST the cancellation is being sent to, and the subscription identifier for the subscription (the control point received when it originally subscribed to the service) followed by a blank line. There is no body for this message.

Table 8.7 describes the two headers used in the unsubscribe request. All header values are case-sensitive except where noted.

Table 8.7 Subscription Cancellation Headers

Header	Required	Type	Description
HOST	Required	Domain name or IP address and optional port component.	From eventing URL (the `<eventSubURL>` sub-element of the service element in the device description. If the port is missing or empty, port 80 is assumed.
SID	Required (defined by GENA)	Single URI. Universally unique subscription identifier. Must begin with `uuid:`	Must be the subscription identifier assigned by publisher in response to subscription request. Defined by UPnP device vendor.

`Callback`, `NT`, and `Timeout` headers should not appear in a subscription cancellation. The SID is sufficient to indicate which subscription is to be cancelled.

Canceling by the Publisher

Control points should monitor discovery messages from the services to which they have subscribed. If the service cancels its advertisements, it is no longer present to send event notifications, and control points should assume that their subscriptions have been effectively cancelled.

Cancellation Response

If the cancellation message has been successfully received and processed by the service, the service sends the typical HTTP success response to the control point:

```
HTTP/1.1 200 OK
```

If there is an error with the cancellation request, the publisher sends a response with one of the errors listed in Table 8.8.

In either case, success or error response, the response must be received by the control point within 30 seconds, including expected transmission time.

Table 8.8 Subscription Cancellation Error Values

UPnP Error Type	HTTP Error Return	Sent If
Incompatible Headers	400 Bad Request	`NT` or `Callback` headers included along with a `SID` header.
Invalid SID	412 Precondition Failed	SID does not correspond to a known, unexpired subscription.
Missing SID	412 Precondition Failed	`SID` header is missing or empty.

Event Messages

Now that you've seen the mechanics of subscribing, renewing, and canceling a subscription, you are ready to look at the contents of the event notification messages that are sent as a result of the subscription.

A service keeps subscribers informed of changes to its state variables by sending event messages immediately when any of its evented variables changes state.[2] The event message contains the names of all of the service's evented state variables along with their current values. Control points receive the event messages and update their internal representation of the state of the service and, if necessary, reflect these changes to the user—updating a user interface, for example.

As mentioned previously, the publisher sends an initial event message as soon as possible after it accepts a new subscription. This event message is just like event messages to follow, containing the names and values for all evented variables provided by the service, but allows the subscriber to initialize its model of the state of the service, perhaps setting corresponding values for the state variables and using them to populate a user interface.

Event Keys

UPnP eventing introduces a mechanism to ensure that clients can detect whether they have missed one or more event notification messages (and hence have an inaccurate representation of the service).

Each event message has a sequence number, or *event key*. The event key is a 32-bit integer value maintained by the publisher for each subscription. The event key for a subscription is initialized to 0 when the publisher creates the subscription, and the initial event message contains this value. For each subsequent event message, the publisher increments the event key and includes the updated value in the event message.

Overflow of this value must be handled by both publishers and subscribers. The publishing service is responsible for handling overflow by wrapping the event key back to 1 (not 0—the 0 value is reserved for the initial event message), while the subscribers must handle this special case by not interpreting it as an error.

If a subscriber does correctly detect a missed event message, it must unsubscribe and re-subscribe to ensure that it has the current values for the state variables. By re-subscribing, the control point gets all that is associated with a new subscription: a new subscription identifier, a new initial event message, and a new, initialized event key.

If the publisher receives no response from a subscriber, the publisher must optimistically assume that the subscriber is still alive, and it must continue to send event messages to the subscriber until the subscription expires.

---

[2] If the value of more than one variable changes at the same time, the publisher should bundle these changes into a single event message to reduce processing and network traffic.

The NOTIFY Message

To send an event message, a publisher must send a request with the following format:

```
NOTIFY delivery path HTTP/1.1
Host: delivery host:delivery port
Content-Type: text/xml
Content-Length: length of body in bytes
NT: upnp:event
NTS: upnp:propchange
SID: uuid:subscription-UUID
SEQ: event key

<e:propertyset xmlns:e="urn:schemas-upnp-org:event-1-0">
  <e:property>
    <variableName>new Value</variableName>
   other variable names and values (if any) go here...
  </e:property>
</e:propertyset>
```

The request line is a standard request line, including the delivery path and HTTP version, but uses the NOTIFY method, defined by GENA, to indicate that this is an event.

This is the first event-related message that requires a body. The Content-Type and Content-Length headers are used to describe the type and length of the body, respectively. Table 8.9 describes each of the headers used in an event message.

NOTIFY Message Body

The body of the NOTIFY message is composed according to the UPnP Template Language for Eventing. The topmost element in this schema is the <propertyset> element. The <propertyset> element is the container for the current state of the service. The xmlns namespace attribute for the <propertyset> element must be set to urn:schemas-upnp-org:event-1-0. The <propertyset> element, in turn, contains one or more <property> elements.

Each property contains one or more sub-elements used to specify the name and new value of a state variable. The names of the state variables correspond to the <name> sub element of the <stateVariable> element in the service description. All body elements and attributes are case sensitive; body values are not case sensitive except where noted. The order of elements is insignificant. Required elements must occur exactly once (no duplicates), and recommended or optional elements may occur at most once.

Table 8.9 Event Notification Message Headers

Header	Required	Type	Description
Host	Required	Domain name or IP address and optional port	Delivery URL (`CALLBACK` header in subscription message). If the port is missing or empty, port 80 is assumed.
Content-Length	Required	Integer	Length of body in bytes.
Content-Type	Required	`text/xml`	Must be `text/xml`.
NT	Required (defined by GENA)	`upnp:event`	Notification Type. Must be `upnp:event`.
NTS	Required (defined by GENA)	`upnp:propchange`	Notification Sub type. Must be `upnp:propchange`.
SID	Required (defined by GENA)	Single URL. Must be universally unique. Begins with `uuid:`.	Subscription identifier. Defined by UPnP vendor.
SEQ	Required (defined by UPnP)	32-bit integer	Event key. Must be 0 for initial event message. Incremented by 1 for each event message sent to a particular subscriber. To prevent overflow, must be wrapped to 1.

For example, an event message for a UPnP technology-enabled lamp might have the following body:

```
<e:propertyset xmlns:e="urn:schemas-upnp-org:event-1-0">
  <e:property>
    <Power>On</Power>
    <DimmerSetting>8</DimmerSetting>
  </e:property>
</e:propertyset>
```

"Forgiving" XML Processing

Note: For future extensibility, the Flexible XML Processing Profile (FXPP) requires that when processing XML such as the NOTIFY message body described earlier, devices and control points must ignore any unknown elements and their sub-elements or content, and any unknown attributes and their values.

The NOTIFY Message Response

Subscribers must acknowledge receipt of event messages. To do this, they send a typical HTTP success response, as follows:

```
HTTP/1.1 200 OK
```

The subscriber must respond within 30 seconds, including transmission time. If the subscriber does not respond within 30 seconds, the publisher does not continue to try to send the message, but keeps the subscription active and tries to send future event messages to the subscriber until the subscription expires or is cancelled.

If there is an error with the event message, the subscriber responds with one of the error messages in Table 8.10.

Table 8.10 Event Message Errors

UPnP Error Type	HTTP Error Return	Sent If
Invalid SID	412 Precondition Failed	SID does not correspond to a known subscription (Service must terminate this SID when it receives this error response.)
Missing SID	412 Precondition Failed	SID header is missing or empty.
Missing NT or NTS header	400 Bad Request	The `NT` or `NTS` header is missing.
Invalid NT header	412 Precondition Failed	`NT` header does not equal `upnp:event`.
Invalid NTS header	412 Precondition Failed	NTS header does not equal `upnp:propchange`.

Summary

Eventing enables groups of UPnP devices and control points to be a dynamic system, responding automatically to state changes. This chapter has described the following concepts:

- Eventing in a distributed system, contrasting it with synchronous remote procedure call mechanisms such as RPC
- The publisher/subscriber model of eventing
- The GENA protocol

  GENA brings event notification into the realm of the Web, using HTTP as the transport. GENA introduces three new HTTP headers, `SUBSCRIBE`, `UNSUBSCRIBE`, and `NOTIFY`, to handle event subscription and publication. Related headers introduced by GENA include `CALLBACK`, `NT`, `NTS`, and `SID`.
- How the UPnP architecture uses GENA to implement eventing

  The UPnP architecture uses GENA for eventing, adding conventions of its own. In particular, the UPnP architecture uses GENA to publish changes to a service's evented state variables. It uses mechanisms such as an initial event message, event key, and `SEQ` header to communicate service state to control points.

Chapter 9

Presentation

Hobbes: "Well, being a tiger is more than just stripes, you realize."

Calvin: "Kind of a zen thing, huh?"

—Bill Watterson, *The Authoritative Calvin and Hobbes*

UPnP technology enables network devices to present their functionality as programmatic services to be manipulated by control points. The interactions between control points and devices can be entirely automatic, requiring no human intervention. However, it is also possible to manually control UPnP devices using the device's presentation page, a web page provided by the device and loaded by an administrator using a web browser. This chapter covers the UPnP presentation page, the requirements for devices regarding presentation, the details of the UPnP architecture's HTML and HTTP-based presentation, and the mechanics of getting a device's presentation page.

The UPnP Presentation Page

UPnP devices have embedded web servers because most of the communications protocols they use, including XML-based device description, SOAP-based control messages, and GENA's event-related messages, run over HTTP. Besides using the internal web server for programmatic control, devices can also use the embedded web server to provide a web interface for management and control of the device. For example, instead of a control point issuing a SOAP request and getting a response, an administrator using a web browser can load a particular URL and view information about the device or control it using a form submitted to the web server.

The web interface makes it possible for an administrator to ensure the device is operating correctly and to diagnose and fix problems with the device. In particular, an administrator can use the device's web interface to:

- Manipulate the device's operational parameters
- View device statistics
- Manually invoke actions on the device's services

Supplying a web interface for network devices is not something new. Many existing non-UPnP devices do this already. Network print servers, for example, have web pages for configuration and control, allowing the administrator to set operational parameters, print test pages, and so on. But the UPnP architecture does introduce a new name for this administrative interface, calling it a device presentation page.

Like the Control and Eventing phases of the UPnP architecture, a control point can view a device's presentation page only after the control point has discovered the device and has retrieved its device description. If the device is supplying a presentation page, its device description document contains a `<presentationURL>` element as shown in Figure 9.1.

Getting a Device's Presentation Page

To retrieve the presentation page, the control point simply issues an HTTP GET request to the address specified in the presentation URL:

```
GET index.html HTTP 1.1
```

and the device returns a presentation page in the body of the HTTP response.

Presentation Page Requirements

A device vendor is not required to supply a device presentation page. The presentation page is purely an optional administrative interface added to devices that already provide a means for direct programmatic control.

```
<?xml version="1.0"?>
<root xmlns="urn:schemas-upnp-org:device-1-0">
  <specVersion>
    <major>1</major>
    <minor>0</minor>
  </specVersion>
  <device>
    <presentationURL>http://192.168.1.1/index.html
       </presentationURL>
      other device information…
  </device>
</root>
```

Figure 9.1 PresentationURL in a Device Description Document

Even when they do provide presentation pages for their devices, vendors have a lot of leeway in determining the contents of the pages. Unlike device and service templates, presentation pages are not standardized in UPnP Forum working committees. The UPnP Forum does not dictate the required contents, appearance, or capabilities of device presentation pages, but allows these things to be completely determined by the vendor.

However, if a device does supply a URL for a presentation page, the control point must be able to retrieve a page from the URL and load it into a browser. Then, depending upon the capabilities of the page, it must be able to allow a user to control the device and/or view device status. The degree to which each of these can be accomplished depends on the specific capabilities of the presentation page and device.

HTML/HTTP-based Presentation

The UPnP device architecture requires that the HTML page provided by a device must be HTML version 3.0 or later. No other constraints are placed on the presentation page. The device vendor must specify the minimum requirements for browsers to view its device presentation pages, such as which client-side scripting languages it must support and which browser plug-ins are required. Decisions about how the web pages actually interface with the device are left up to the device vendor.

Implementation Choices

As you would expect, there is more than one way for a UPnP developer to implement a device presentation page. In particular, device control has a couple different approaches.

The user interface for the device presentation page is at the browser using HTML. The action is carried out at the device. However, where the input is translated into a command for a device can vary—it can either be at the browser, using client-side scripting, or it can be at the device where, as a result of posting the information gathered from the web page to the device's web server, logic at the device will parse the request and carry out the action. Each method has its benefits and drawbacks.

In the first case, using client-side scripting, the UPnP device vendor can use existing mechanisms already in the device to support control and eventing. This approach does not require additional logic at the device to support presentation—the code is at the browser. For example, a browser, in response to user input, could use client-side scripting to compose and send SOAP control requests to the device. The device would receive these requests and act upon them like any other control point requests; the device wouldn't be able to tell that the request had come from a browser. A single handler is used for both cases. This makes the device simpler, but makes the client more complicated, because the client must have the ability to generate XML and SOAP in order to compose the SOAP message.

With the second approach, a client browser uses POST to send information to the device's internal web server, which then parses the request and controls the device directly though internal APIs rather than through the external SOAP interface. No scripting or composition of SOAP messages at the browser is required. However, this makes the device implementation a bit more complicated, because the device must support both a SOAP handler for standard SOAP messages from control points and another handler for control messages from its device presentation page.

The same holds true for eventing—a presentation page can reuse the GENA interface presented by the device or can make private calls through a web interface.

Figure 9.2 illustrates both approaches. In this diagram, the first browser (top left) has loaded a web page that posts a direct request to the device, passing the function name and parameters in the URL. In this case, the device implementation has a custom handler that parses the URL and makes a call into the device core, perhaps using an internal API.

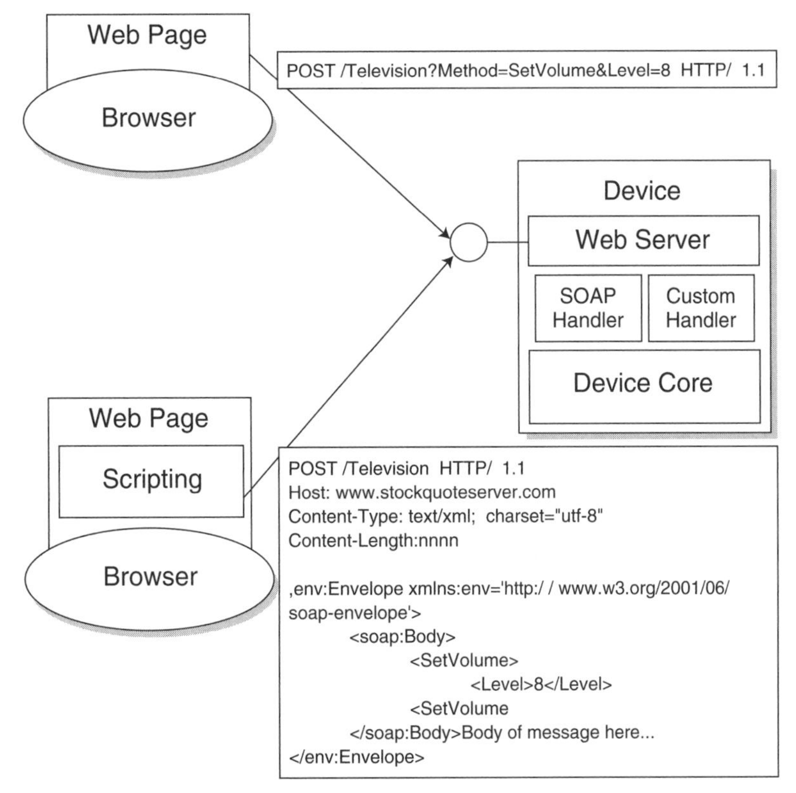

Figure 9.2 Two Ways to Implement Control from a Presentation Page

The second browser has loaded a web page that employs scripting to compose a SOAP request for the device. In this case, the device's normal SOAP handler is invoked. It parses the XML document containing the action name and parameters and makes a call into the device itself, perhaps using the same internal API as the first case.

Localization

UPnP devices will be sold into markets around the world, where many different languages are read and spoken by customers. UPnP device vendors may choose to support multiple languages in the presentation pages provided by their devices. Faced with multiple languages, control points and devices must agree on the language to be used for the presentation page and how the pages will be encoded for transfer from the device to the control point.

The UPnP architecture relies upon the localization mechanisms already included in HTTP and HTML to do this. The localization mechanisms allow the control point/browser to:

- Indicate the language(s) understood by the user
- Indicate the character encodings understood by the control point

and allow the device to:

- Indicate the language(s) of a presentation page sent from the device to the control point
- Indicate the character encoding of a presentation page sent from the device to the control point

Before taking a closer look at how devices and control points agree on the language to use, let's first review how languages are specified using language tags.

Language Tags

A language tag identifies a natural language—spoken, written, or otherwise—that people use to communicate.[1] Language tags are used in HTTP headers to specify the language desired by the client and the language actually provided by the server.

The language tag consists of a primary tag and zero or more sub-tags, each of which is 1 to 8 alphanumeric characters. White space is not allowed within the tag and all tags are case-insensitive.

Language tags can use the ISO-639 and ISO-3166 standards to define languages and countries. The ISO-639 standard defines two-letter language abbreviations that can be used as primary tags to specify the language, while the ISO-3166 standard defines two and three letter country codes that can be used as sub-tags to define the particular variation of the language. For example, the tag en-us specifies English in the United States, while the tag en-ca specifies English as used in Canada.

The name space of language tags is administered by the Internet Assigned Names Authority (IANA).[2] Other tags beyond the standards-based tags are maintained by this organization.

---

[1] Language tags are not used for non-natural languages such as computer programming languages.

[2] See `http://www.iana.org` for more information.

Accept-Language and Content-Language Headers

HTTP has two headers, `Accept-Language` and `Content-Language`, that are used by UPnP control points and devices in the process of requesting, generating, and receiving localized presentation pages.

The HTTP `Accept-Language` request-header specifies the set of languages that are preferred by the control point as a response to the request. The control point includes an HTTP `Accept-Language` header in the request for a presentation page, as in the following request:

```
GET /presentation.html HTTP 1.1
Accept-Language: en-us, en-ca
(blank line)
```

The `Content-Language` header appears in the reply. It specifies the language of the intended audience for the enclosed HTML page. In other words, a request from a control point can specify many possible languages, while a device selects one of those languages and returns the page in that language. If an `Accept-Language` header is present in the request, the response must include a `Content-Language` header.

```
HTTP 1.1 OK
Content-Type: text/html
Content-Language: en-us
Content-Length: xxx

HTML presentation page
```

Character Encodings

Besides specifying which language to use, HTTP clients and servers must also agree on the character encoding—how the content to be sent from the server to the client is to be encoded into a stream of bytes.

The web server (the UPnP device in our case) specifies the character encoding it is using for the returned data. Any character encoding that has been registered with IANA can be used, but encodings are typically limited to

- US-ASCII, the American Standard Code for Information Interchange
- ISO-8859-1, the standard encoding for Western European languages
- UTF-8
- UTF-16

According to the UPnP Device Architecture specification, if the device does not explicitly specify the encoding, the character encoding defaults to UTF-8.

Character encodings can be communicated from the web server to the browser in two ways that are understood by most browsers, the Content-Type and Charset HTTP headers.

Content-Type Header

Documents transmitted with HTTP that are of type text, such as text/xml and text/html, can have a charset parameter to the Content-Type header, which specifies the character encoding of the document. For example, the following HTTP header specifies that the content type is xml and that the document encoding is ISO-8859-1:

```
Content-Type: text/xml; charset=iso-8859-1
```

Headers like this can be specified using HTML's META tag. For example, the following fragment introduces the previous Content-Type header:

```
<META HTTP-EQUIV="Content-Type" CONTENT="text/xml;
  charset=iso-8859-1">
```

The web server takes the value of the HTTP-EQUIV field and makes it a header in the HTTP response. The value of the Content-Type header is the value of the CONTENT field.

Charset Header

Documents transmitted with HTTP can also have an explicit Charset header that names the character encoding used, as follows:

```
Charset: iso-8859-1
```

As in the previous example, the META tag can be used to specify that the web server should include this header in its response back to the browser.

```
<META CHARSET="iso-8859-1">
```

Summary

Presentation is the simplest phase of the UPnP architecture, with only a few points to remember:

- Every UPnP device can provide a web interface for administrative monitoring and control, the device presentation page.
- The device presentation page is an optional feature. Device vendors are free to determine the look, content, and capabilities of the web pages they provide for their devices.
- Vendors must make implementation choices that trade off increased client-side complexity versus increased device-side complexity.
- Localization of presentation pages relies on existing mechanisms present in HTTP and HTML to specify the language for the user and the content encoding.

Now that you've completed this chapter on presentation, you've reached the end the survey of all of the phases and related protocols of the UPnP architecture. It's now time to get busy and implement UPnP support for a real device. The following chapters walk you through this process.

Part 

Developing a UPnP Device

Chapter 10

Introducing the UPnP Super Toaster

A presentation of the UPnP architecture's underlying protocols complete, so now it is time to put that knowledge to use through an example implementation of a real UPnP device. But, as experienced software engineers know, you shouldn't start blindly implementing something without first having a requirements specification. In this chapter you define the feature requirements for the device you will build. The following chapters cover implementation of the device according to the requirements introduced in this chapter.

Who Needs a New Toaster?

You are the lead engineer for a start-up company named InToast Incorporated that is setting out to change the world market for specialty toasters. The basic toaster design hasn't changed much in over 50 years, and your company believes now is the time to unleash upon the world a revolutionary new toaster that will change the way people toast their bread.

Core to the implementation of the Super Toaster is UPnP technology, which your company president considers to be the next big thing. Your job is to use the features of the UPnP architecture to implement the Super Toaster.

Physical Product Description

The talented marketing department at InToast has provided the conceptual drawing in Figure 10.1 of the Super Toaster.

As shown in Figure 10.1, the Super Toaster has the following externally visible features:

- Single bread slot
- Toasting lever
- Darkness dial
- Ethernet port

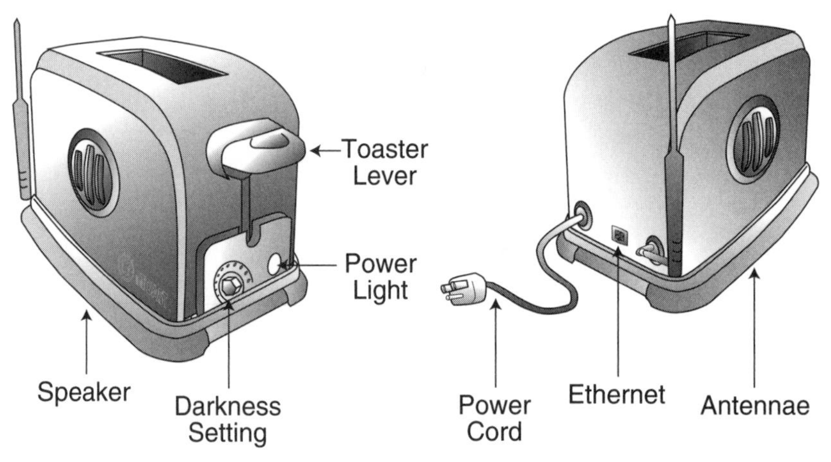

Figure 10.1 Artist's Rendering of the Super Toaster

- Wireless ethernet antenna
- Audio speaker
- Power cord
- Power light

The product management team has also created a no-frills software requirements specification that is presented in the next section.

Software Requirements Specification

The software requirements specification for the Super Toaster, based upon an outline presented in *Software Engineering* (Pressman 2001). The chapters ahead match feature requirements in this specification with features of your device implementation using the UPnP architecture.

Introduction

This document describes the software requirements for InToast's Super Toaster product. The software requirements specification lists the features the software is required to support. It does not specify implementation requirements for the software team, which is free to design the software as it sees fit.

Information Description

This section includes specific internal and external hardware capabilities, interactions with the software, and other software platform requirements.

Target Software Platform

The project's technical lead has chosen Linux as the device's operating system platform for the Super Toaster. Assume all necessary C-libraries are available in the embedded device.

External Hardware

The Super Toaster has the following external hardware components visible by the user and available for the device software to interact with:

- Single bread slot
- Toasting lever

- Darkness dial
- Ethernet port
- Audio speaker

The toasting lever is a binary device: It is either depressed or not depressed at all. When depressed, the lever remains depressed for the duration specified by the darkness dial at the time the lever was depressed.

The darkness dial selects the number of seconds the toasting lever is depressed. It has five predefined toast darkness settings that range from light to dark. The hardware dial itself reports values in the range of 1 to 5, with 1 representing the lightest and 5 representing the darkest. The software can both query and set the current dial setting. Times begin at 20 seconds for dial setting 1 and have a maximum of 100 seconds for a dial setting of 5, incrementing by 20 seconds for each step in between. Adjusting the darkness dial after toasting has begun has no effect on the length of toasting.

Internal Hardware

The SuperToaster has the following internal hardware components:

- Ethernet controller
- AC '97 compliant audio subsystem
- Graphics controller

The Ethernet[†] controller is a standard 10/100 megabits-per-second auto-sensing device. The Ethernet controller has the ability to automatically detect what speed of network it is connected to. The software has read/write access to the Ethernet controller through the standard Linux operating system network drivers.

The audio subsystem supports 44.1 kilohertz stereo audio and is directly accessible to the software through the Linux Open Sound System[†] (OSS) libraries.

In the case of power failure, the SuperToaster, upon resuming power, will immediately lift the lever if it was in the depressed state when power was lost. The software will not receive notification of this change in state in a lost power scenario.

Hardware Interface Library

A hardware interface library is available for the software to use to receive run-time event information from the hardware components.

In addition to defining toaster hardware constants, the library provides interfaces to perform the following:

- Lift the toaster lever
- Depress the toaster lever
- Get/Set the Darkness Dial value
- Get/Set the total pieces of toast toasted
- Get/Set the total time spent toasting
- Callback events when the toaster completes toasting

Notifications are provided by the hardware interface library to client software whenever the toasting lever moves from the depressed (toasting) to the released (not-toasting) state, as well as when moving from the released (non-toasting) to the depressed (toasting) states.

The hardware interface library also provides functions to control all external levers and dials from software. A complete listing of the hardware interface library is provided with this specification. Figure 10.2 provides a high-level block diagram of the device software components.

Referring to Figure 10.2, the shaded UPnP Library is a third-party component that you will select in the next chapter. The Hardware Interface Library is provided by the hardware team, and the Device Software Team is responsible for the Toaster Application Code.

Functional Description

This section includes specific functional requirements of the software. Wherever possible, functional descriptions are given independently of implementation.

IP Network Addressable

The Super Toaster software must support IP network address assignment via DHCP. This allows the Super Toaster to plug into any traditional IP-based home network. It must also support Auto-IP address assignment, a method where network devices can obtain an IP address in the absence of a DHCP server. Auto-IP is used heavily in wireless *ad hoc* networks.

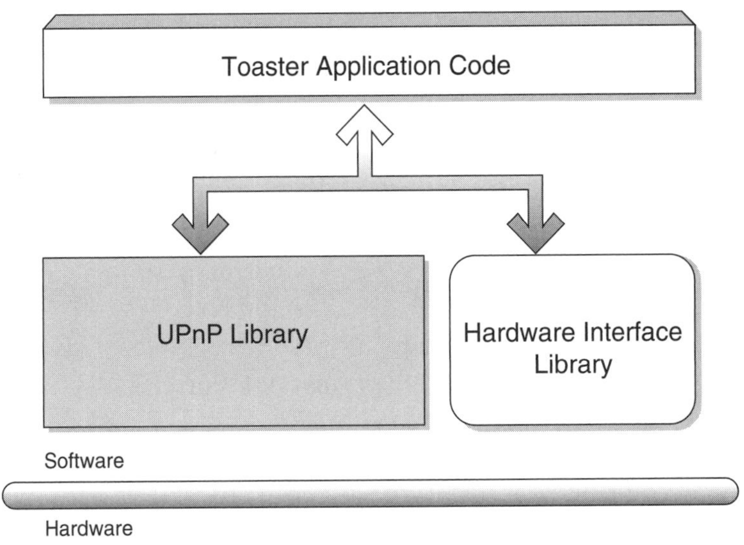

Figure 10.2 High-level Architecture Diagram

Lifetime Statistics

Software must support tracking of the following lifetime statistics over the entire life of the Super Toaster:

- Total slices of bread toasted
- Total length in seconds of toasting

The total-slices-of-bread-toasted value is an integer value representing the total number of bread slices the toaster has toasted over the lifetime of the toaster. It is expected that software will track this value by measuring the number of lever depressions and releases. Partial toasts should be recorded as a complete toast. For example, if a piece of toast was in the process of being toasted and the user prematurely ended the toast cycle by lifting the lever, this would still be counted as a complete toast.

The total number of seconds the device spends toasting is an integer value that simply measures the aggregate length of time the toasting lever is depressed over the lifetime of the toaster.

Network Event Notification

As a node on the home network, the Super Toaster must provide notification to network users about changes in status of the toaster, including error conditions. For example, if a user is logged into his or her workstation and a slice of bread has finished toasting, the software should notify the user of the completion of the toasting cycle.

Toaster status codes are defined as follows:

- TOASTING—the toaster is currently toasting. A toaster is in this state for the length of time the lever is depressed, reverting back to the NOT_TOASTING state only after the lever has lifted.
- NOT_TOASTING—the toaster is currently not toasting.
- ERROR—the toaster is in an error state.

Application-based Control

The Super Toaster must provide software interfaces for user application-based control, including the ability to:

- Raise and lower the Super Toaster lever
- Adjust the darkness setting
- Query the lifetime statistics

The Super Toaster must provide a software interface to obtain run-time event information from the device. This is to allow other nodes on the network to receive notifications of run-time events.

The device software team is not responsible for creating this host application, but is required to provide a sufficient interface on the device for such an application to be created.

Web-based Administration

Much like a network administrator viewing statistics about nodes on the network, owners of the Super Toaster must have the capability to view administrative information via any web browser in the home.

From a central administration page, information about the current status of the toasting slot, the darkness dial, and the toaster's lifetime statistics should be displayed.

InToast's marketing department has created the following mock-up of a sample Web-page for the Super Toaster, as shown in Figure 10.3.

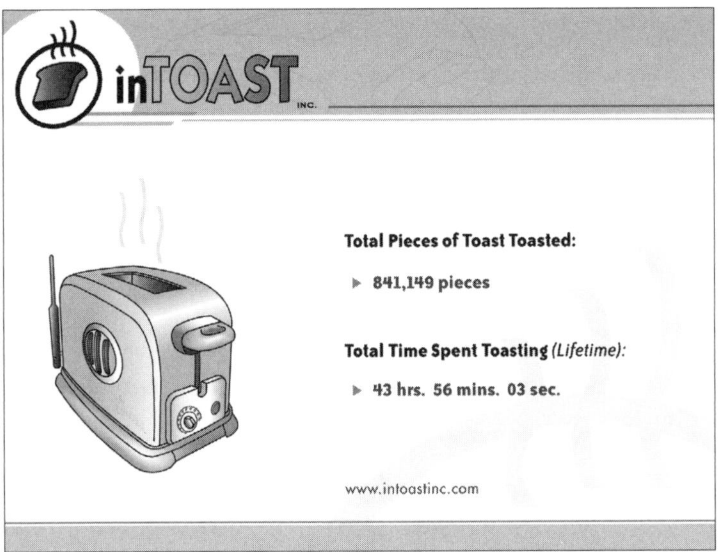

Figure 10.3 Device Web Page

Audio Feedback

To provide a truly unique experience, the Super Toaster must also support the ability to play a single MP3 audio track on the external speaker. The audio is not stored on the device and is streamed to the device using HTTP.

The following audio playback controls must be supported:

- Play—play the specified MP3.
- Pause—pause the currently playing MP3.
- Stop—stop the currently playing MP3.

The audio playback capability must be exposed to other devices on the local network; users have no mechanism to control the audio on the Super Toaster device itself.

Summary

This chapter presented the functional requirements for a UPnP Super Toaster device that you will implement in the chapters ahead. You now have enough information about the device to begin implementation. However, one bit of unfinished business remains: You know the device will be implemented using UPnP technology, but it is your decision to determine how to enable that support in your device. It is this important decision that you tackle in the next chapter.

Chapter 11

Choosing a UPnP SDK

The previous chapter defined the product requirements for the UPnP Super Toaster. Your first task in implementing your device is choosing an SDK for developing UPnP devices. The SDK provides library support for each phase of UPnP device development. This chapter first presents an overview of available SDKs for device development, then focuses on the Intel SDK for UPnP Devices for Linux (Linux SDK) that you'll use for your sample device in the chapters ahead.

What to Look For

As a device implementer you're primarily looking for SDKs for UPnP that support device development. Some SDKs for UPnP support only device or control point development, while others support both. The Super Toaster requires no control point capability, so this is not a requirement for your search.

If you'd like your UPnP device to receive the UPnP Logo and are starting with a predefined device type, such as a UPnP Internet Gateway Device, it is important to choose a device SDK that itself has already passed the logo compliance tests. This will ensure a smoother process when it is time to obtain logo certification for your device.

For some developers, full access to the complete source code is a highly desired benefit that many SDKs for UPnP provide. This complete access to the code offers the ultimate in control and customization, not to mention a firsthand ability to fix bugs in the SDK should they be found.

Often the same SDK code base can support a wide variety of different platforms, ranging from desktop editions of Microsoft Windows to small embedded platforms.

These and many other practical concerns (such as the cost of the SDK) should all be considered by any device implementer when building UPnP devices.

The Implementations

The following is a list of companies with registered SDKs for UPnP device development at the UPnP Forum Web site at the time of writing.

Allegro Software

Allegro Software (`http://www.allegrosoft.com`) offers two different toolkits for developing UPnP devices. Both toolkits are ANSI-C based implementations and delivered as source code. Allegro's Toolkits use a special Allegro Software Abstraction Layer that allows both toolkits to run on a wide variety of embedded platforms, including ATI Nucleus†, Express Logic ThreadX†, Wind River VxWorks†, and all Microsoft Windows platforms.

The RomUPnP Basic toolkit provides complete discovery and presentation capability in less than 10 kilobytes of code (not including a web server). The RomUPnP Basic toolkit interoperates with UPnP 1.0 control points.

The RomUPnP Advanced toolkit adds control and eventing capabilities to Basic toolkit, supporting fully featured UPnP Devices. The Advanced kit also includes XML parsing capabilities as well as compatibility with other Allegro Rom products.

More information about Allegro Software's toolkits for UPnP can be found at `http://www.allegrosoft.com/romupnp.html`.

Atinav Incorporated

Atinav's aveLink† technology supports both C and Java implementations of UPnP devices and control points. Supported versions of Java include Sun's standard (J2SE), Enterprise (J2EE), and Micro (J2ME) Editions.

AveLink's control point capability supports bridging between UPnP and other protocols such as X10.

The aveLink SDK is divided into device and control point libraries for maximum flexibility, and supports the 1.0 version of the UPnP Device Architecture Specification. For more information on aveLink, please refer to `http://www.avelink.com/modules/upnp.htm`.

Lantronix

Lantronix' UPnP Early Adopters Kit† (EAK) provides addressing and discovery capability in a small C-source-based library suitable for integrating into any one of Lantronix' embedded platforms.

The EAK includes sample code and XML that illustrate how to use the EAK with your UPnP-enabled devices. Control point functionality is not supported at the time of writing. For more information on the UPnP EAK, please refer to `http://www.lantronix.com/support/utils/upnp/index.html`.

Metro Link

Metro Link provides four different SDKs for UPnP development. The C Device SDK† is a full-featured C-based library optimized for embedded platforms including Linux, WindRiver's VxWorks, and Metro IPWorks† platforms. The entire implementation can be as small as 55 kilobytes and includes two sample devices.

The Profile SDK for C is an add-on for the C Device SDK that speeds development time of UPnP devices by auto-generating a baseline set of source code for a UPnP device.

Finally, Metro Link offers a Java Control Point SDK and a Java Device SDK for the development of Java-based control points and devices. For more information on any of Metro Link's SDKs, please refer to the following link: `http://www.metrolink.com/products/enable/index.html`.

Microsoft

All current versions of Microsoft Windows XP include support for developing UPnP control point and device applications. XP also includes a native implementation of a UPnP Internet Gateway Device.

For more information about Microsoft UPnP support, please refer to `http://www.microsoft.com/hwdev/tech/nonpc/UPnP/default.asp`.

Siemens

Siemens offers two SDKs for UPnP development, one supporting C++-based devices and control points, and the other supporting development in Java environments. Both SDKs support all phases of UPnP device development and come packaged with a Generic Control Point and test tools for UPnP. Both SDKs can be downloaded from the Siemens web site.

For more information about Siemens' UPnP technology offerings, please refer to `http://www.plug-n-play-technologies.com/`.

Intel

The Intel® SDK for UPnP Devices for Linux is a C-based implementation that supports all phases of UPnP device development. The SDK has been released with full source code under the Berkeley Standard Distribution (BSD) license and is currently hosted by SourceForge as an open source development project for Linux. Under the BSD, device implementers are allowed to use the source code license- and royalty-free, and this license does not place any restrictions on derivative works from the Intel SDK. For complete information, refer to the BSD License included in the SDK.

Intel has made available a version of the Intel SDK for Pocket-PC devices. This SDK supports both device and control point applications on Pocket-PC–based Intel® PCA devices.

For device makers interested in building Internet Gateway Devices, the UPnP Logo certified Intel® UPnP Internet Gateway Device implementation is available. The Intel SDK for UPnP Media Renderers is also available to support implementation of UPnP A/V devices.

For more information on the open source project, please refer to `http://upnp.sourceforge.net`. For more information on the SDK for PCA devices, Intel UPnP Internet Gateway Device, or the Intel SDK for UPnP Media Renderers, please refer to `http://www.intel.com/labs/connectivity/upnp/index.htm`.

The Choice for This Example: The Intel SDK

For the UPnP Super Toaster, you will use the open source Intel SDK. At the time of writing the Intel SDK for UPnP Devices for Linux is at version 1.2.1. Figure 11.1 shows an architectural diagram of the Intel SDK.

The Intel SDK API provides a standard C-function interface for applications to access features of the Intel SDK. The following chapters

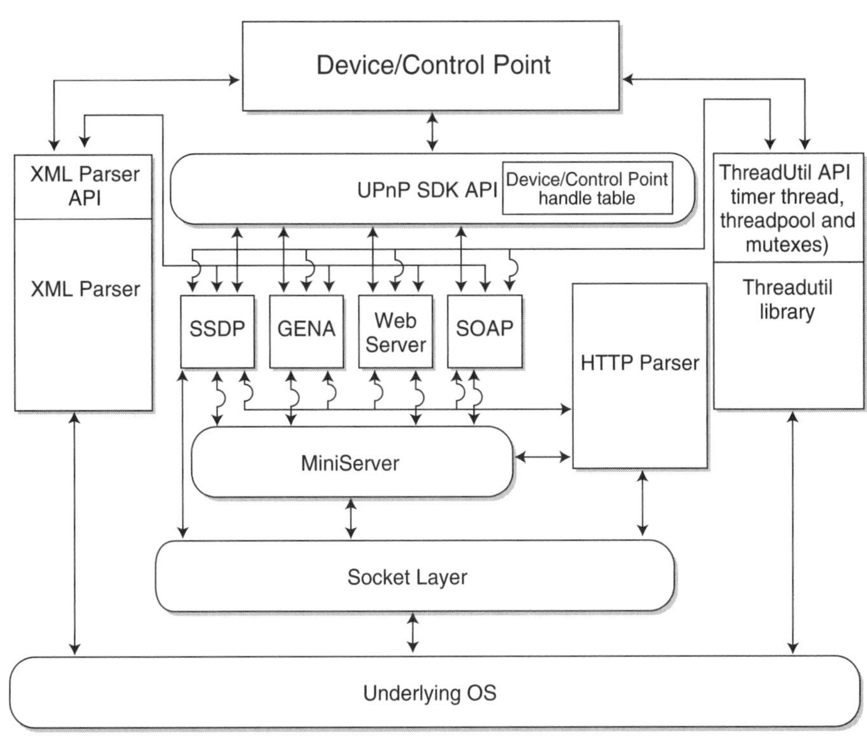

Figure 11.1 Intel SDK Architecture

introduce functions from this API. SSDP, described in Chapter 5, implements support for advertisement and discovery. SOAP, described in Chapter 7, is used in the control phase of the device. GENA, described in Chapter 8, supports eventing in the device. The XML Parser is used to parse all incoming XML documents, and the C-DOM provides programmatic interfaces to a Level 1 DOM representation of the XML. The Threadutil Library provides automatic thread management services for your device, while the integrated Mini-Web Server handles all HTTP-based requests on behalf of our device throughout all phases of device development.

Installation

This section provides a walkthrough of the download, installation, and setup of the Intel SDK. It also provides other tips and useful bits of information that will come in handy when you begin to implement your device.

Note It is highly recommended that you perform UPnP device development on Linux using the Intel SDK logged in as the `root` user. Many of the tasks described in this and future chapters require root privileges on the local machine.

Download

The first task is to download the complete source code for the SDK. It is available in many forms, including pre-built binaries packaged in an installable RPM, or as complete source code for building yourself. This latter option is explored here. First, point your favorite web browser to `http://upnp.sourceforge.net`, shown in Figure 11.2.

Three packages are available:

- upnpsdk: the complete source code for the SDK
- upnpsdk-api-doc: pdf documentation for the SDK
- upnpsdk-rpm: x86 binary installation RPM

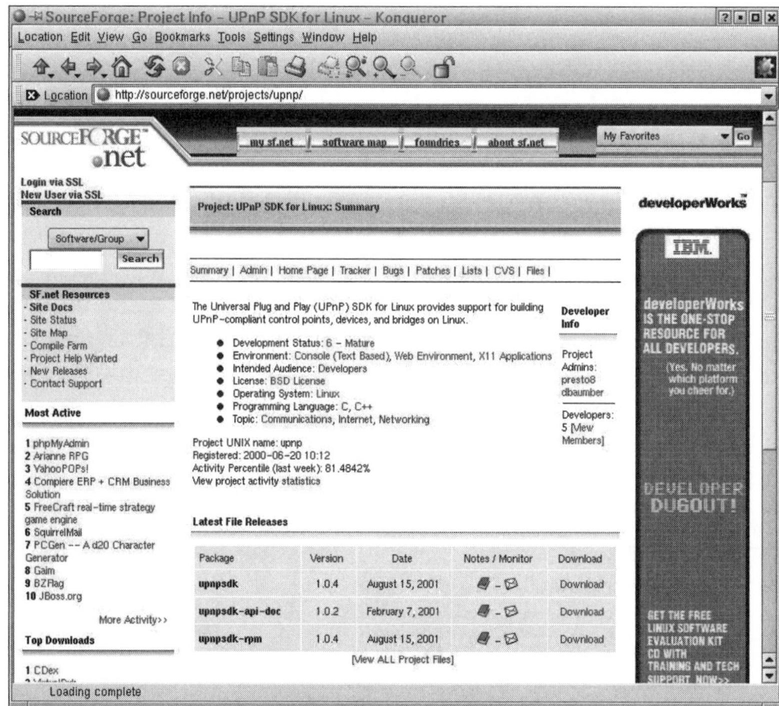

Figure 11.2 Official Source Forge Project Page

Follow the upnpsdk link, download the complete source code, and save the file `libupnp-1.2.1.tar.gz` somewhere on your local machine. First, you must unzip the SDK with the following command:

```
[root@localhost root]# gunzip libupnp-1.2.1.tar.gz
```

Then, you must untar the archive:

```
[root@localhost root]# tar -xvf libupnp-1.2.1.tar
```

This extracts the source files from the tar archive into a directory named after the version of the SDK downloaded, `libupnp-1.2.1` in this case.

Compile

Enter into the newly created directory's upnp subfolder and build the SDK by using the make utility and typing `make` at the command line:

```
[root @localhost root]# cd libupnp-1.2.1/upnp

[root @localhost upnp]# make
```

This builds the entire SDK and results in a three shared object binaries in the `libupnp-1.2.1/bin` directory:

```
[root@localhost bin]# ls -l

-rwxr-xr-x 1 root  root 39584  Jan 18 12:15 libixml.so

-rwxr-xr-x 1 root  root 17484  Jan 18 12:15 libthreadutil.so

-rwxr-xr-x 1 root  root 125704 Jan 18 12:18 libupnp.so
```

You will link these libraries with your UPnP device applications. There are a few additional compilation options, summarized here, that are described completely in the file `libupnp-1.2.1/README`.

The SDK supports four levels of debug information. To build the SDK with debugging information turned on, type the following command:

```
[root@localhost upnp]# make DEBUG=1
```

where the value assigned to the environment variable is one of the following:

- 0—Critical errors only
- 1—Critical and Packet Level errors
- 2—Critical, Packet Level, and Informational debug output
- 3—All levels of debugging information

The default SDK includes a mini web server. If you'd like to use Apache or some other web server to handle your device requests, the optional mini web server can be excluded from the build, with the following command:

```
[root@localhost upnp]# make WEB=0
```

Finally, as a device implementer, you don't need to include the code for control point applications in your device. Fortunately, the library supports building just device or control point capability. To include only device functionality, use the following command:

```
[root@localhost upnp]# make CLIENT=0
```

For additional build and configuration options, please refer to the README file included in the SDK's root folder.

Install

After completing the build process, installing the SDK can be done by typing the following at the command line:

```
[root@localhost upnp]# make install
```

This copies the generated libraries into `/usr/lib` or whatever the appropriate library path is on your system. The UPnP library uses the `LD_LIBRARY_PATH` environment variable to determine where to find the loadable library at run time. If you manually copy `libupnp.so` to some other location, be sure to update `LD_LIBRARY_PATH` to include the new location. For example, if you wanted to include the three libraries generated by the Intel SDK in the same directory as your built application, the following command will ensure that the loader can find the libraries:

```
[root@localhost root]# export LD_LIBRARY_PATH=.
```

Since the UPnP protocol requires the ability to send and receive multicast packets, you must be sure to explicitly enable multicast support, which is disabled by default in Linux. You can do that with the following command:

```
[root@localhost root]# route add -net 239.0.0.0
  netmask 255.0.0.0 eth0
```

where `eth0` is the specific network interface the UPnP library will use. At the time of this writing, the UPnP library only supports operating on a single-network interface. If not explicitly overridden, the library binds to the first active network interface in order of search (`eth0`, `eth1`, and so on). When developing on systems with multiple-network interfaces, keep this in mind. Chapter 12 explains how to override this default binding.

On many systems, it is also necessary to explicitly enable multicast support using `ifconfig`, as shown here:

```
[root@localhost root]# ifconfig allmulti eth0
```

where `eth0` is again the interface with which you want to do UPnP device development. You can verify this by using the `ifconfig` command as shown in Figure 11.3.

Source Tree

After installation, the Intel SDK creates the following top level directories:

- `ixml`—the xml parser
- `threadutil`—thread library
- `upnp`—core upnp library

Beneath each folder is a subdirectory name `bin` that will contain the built shared libraries for each of the modules. Additionally, you'll want to be sure and take a look at the necessary header files for your application, stored in `upnp/inc`.

```
[root@localhost upnp]# ifconfig
eth0 Link encap:Ethernet  HWaddr 00:A0:C9:6E:FA:F4
     inet addr:192.168.0.1  Bcast:192.168.0.255
       mask:255.255.255.0
     UP BROADCAST RUNNING ALLMULTI MULTICAST  MTU:1500
       Metric:1
     RX packets:943866 errors:0 dropped:0 overruns:0
       frame:0
     TX packets:1089610 errors:0 dropped:0 overruns:0
       carrier:0
     collisions:0 txqueuelen:100
     Interrupt:9 Base address:0x4000
lo   Link encap:Local Loopback
     inet addr:127.0.0.1  Mask:255.0.0.0
     UP LOOPBACK RUNNING  MTU:16436  Metric:1
     RX packets:3519 errors:0 dropped:0 overruns:0 frame:0
     TX packets:3519 errors:0 dropped:0 overruns:0
       carrier:0
     collisions:0 txqueuelen:0
```

Figure 11.3 The `ifconfig` Command Verifying ALLMULTI

A sample television device and control point application are included, and are located in the `upnp/sample` directory. The sample television device is a good example of a sample device built with the Intel SDK. For those developers who may also use the Intel SDK to build control point applications, a television control point application is also included.

Using the Intel SDK in Your Applications

Building support for UPnP devices into your applications is fairly straightforward and requires only two steps.

Header Files

The main header file for the Intel SDK is upnp.h, which is located in the `upnpsdk-1.0.4/inc` directory. After adding `#include "upnp.h"` in your application code, simply add the include directory to the compiler flags in your makefile as follows, based upon the installation directory of your SDK:

```
CFLAGS= -I /root/libupnp-1.2.1/upnp/inc
```

Linking With the Library

Similarly, when building your application you need to link it with the `libupnp.so` library generated from the build. Assuming the SDK was installed into `/usr/lib`, the only addition needed to your loader flags in your makefile are:

```
LDFLAGS= -lupnp -ixml -lthreadutil
```

If you installed the libraries into a different location, such as user root's home directory, you'll need to add the following tags to the loader flags:

```
LDFLAGS= -L/root -lupnp -lixml -l threadutil
```

The example `makefile` for your SuperToaster is in Figure 11.4.

It's that easy to include support for the Intel SDK in your device or control point application. Adding device application code is a bit tougher. In the next chapter you'll start that process.

Where to Go for Help

As part of the build process, the UPnP SDK can auto-generate API documentation from the source code. The doc++ tool is required to build

```
#
# Super Toaster Makefile
#
PROG=supertoaster
CFLAGS=-O2 -Wall -I/root/libupnp-1.2.1/upnp/inc \
-I/root/libupnp-1.2.1/upnp/inc/tools/
LDFLAGS=-lupnp -lixml -lthreadutil

# list the Cfiles here
CFILES=main.c upnp.c upnptc.c upnpls.c upnpts.c \
toasterhw.c sample_util.c sample_util2.c
CC = gcc

# List the header files here
CHEADS=toaster.h toasterhw.h sample_util.h sample_util2.h

# the delete command
RM=/bin/rm

# we generate this from the list of C files above
OBJS=$(CFILES:.c=.o)

all: $(PROG)

%.o: %.c $(CHEADS)
	$(CC) $(CFLAGS) -c $(*).c
clean:
	${RM} -f ${OBJS} ${PROG}

${PROG}: ${OBJS}
	${CC} -g -o ${PROG} ${LDFLAGS} ${OBJS}

${PROG}-static: ${OBJS}
	${CC} -static -o ${PROG} ${LDFLAGS} ${OBJS}
```

Figure 11.4 Super Toaster Makefile

the UPnP SDK documentation. Doc++ can be obtained at `http://docpp.sourceforge.net`. After installing doc++, the documentation can be built using the following command:

```
[root@localhost upnpsdk-1.0.4]# make doc
```

There are two mailing lists for the Intel SDK, supported as part of the SourceForge project:

- `upnp-sdk-announce` is used to make project-wide announcements such as bug fixes, updates, and so on.
- `upnp-sdk-discuss` provides developers a forum to ask questions of any kind about the SDK.

You can subscribe to these mailing lists from the SourceForge project page. It is highly recommended that you do so; the lists provide an excellent opportunity to discuss UPnP device development with other engineers using the Intel SDK.

The SDK also includes the capability to generate both html documentation with the following command:

```
[root@localhost upnp]# make doc
```

An API guide in PDF format is also available as part of the Intel SDK package.

Intel® Tools for UPnP Technologies

Developing UPnP devices is not easy. The asynchronous nature of network device interaction inherently makes it difficult to debug code in the synchronous step-by-step fashion of user application development. It's also difficult to figure out exactly why your UPnP device isn't working when you can't get any visibility into what's happening over the network.

Fortunately, Intel has released a set of tools that are useful during UPnP device development. The Intel® Tools for UPnP Technologies assist hardware and software developers in accelerating their development, testing, and deployment of devices that comply with UPnP standards. The tools are available on the included CD-ROM. Be sure to check for the latest version at Intel's UPnP web site, `http://intel.com/labs/connectivity/upnp/`.

Built on Microsoft .NET technologies, the toolkit provides a wide set of useful applications, as described in Table 11.1.

The Intel Tools for UPnP Technologies are invaluable for UPnP device development; it's often impossible to create your device otherwise. Throughout the rest of this book, you'll use some of the tools for your device development. The tools require the Microsoft .NET Runtime

Table 11.1 Intel Tools for UPnP Technologies

Tool Icon	Name	Description
	Device Spy	Perhaps the most useful tool of them all, the Device Spy acts as a universal control point, discovering and enumerating all UPnP devices on the network. With this application, you can view information about each discovered device, retrieve device and service description documents, invoke actions specifying your own parameters, and even subscribe to receive evented state variables.
	Device Sniffer	A network sniffer custom made for UPnP devices. Using this tool you can manually generate searches for UPnP devices and view all UPnP-related packets generated on the network by your device and control points. Often the only way to determine the root cause of a tough problem, the Device Sniffer is a lifesaver for those nasty network-level bugs.
	Device Validator	A useful tool that provides a complete suite of test scenarios to test your UPnP device. Device Validator includes a wide variety of tests for defined device types. It also provides interfaces for adding your own custom device plug-ins for your specific device. The first step toward receiving UPnP Logo certification, Device Validator is widely regarded as the premier test tool for UPnP Logo and interoperability testing.
	Device Author	Allows you to quickly build .NET based UPnP devices without having to write any XML.
	Device Relay	Once your device has been deployed, you'll often find yourself in a different physical location than where your UPnP device is actually running. Device Relay provides the capability to test and debug your device remotely from any location in the world over the Internet by making the device that exists over the WAN interface appear to exist on your own LAN.

Continues

Table 11.1 Intel Tools for UPnP Technologies *(Continued)*

Tool Icon	Name	Description
	Network Light	Everybody needs a new light bulb! This home-automation–based device supports the SwitchPower and Dimmer services. This device can be useful for testing basic action invocation and service subscriptions in control point applications.
	A/V Media Controller	A Device Spy for A/V devices, the A/V Media Controller allows you to discover and setup connections between UPnP A/V Media Renderers and UPnP Media Servers. Also supports browsing content exposed by discovered media servers.
	A/V Media Server	A .NET-based Media Server that can be configured to share local files. The A/V Media Server also parses audio and digital photo metadata for sharing on the network.
	A/V Media Renderer	A .NET-based UPnP A/V Media Renderer that uses the Microsoft Windows Media Player ActiveX control. The A/V Media Renderer supports multiple simultaneous connections and a wide variety of media types, including play lists.
	A/V Wizard	A lightweight control point specially designed for A/V devices, A/V Wizard features both an A/V control point and an integrated Media Server that can generate play lists on the fly.

environment be installed on your PC. The .NET Framework can be obtained from Microsoft at the following address: `http://msdn.microsoft.com/netframework/default.asp`.

Summary

This chapter presented a survey of existing UPnP SDKs available for use in developing UPnP devices and/or control points. Presented were many SDK options for UPnP device development, with the Intel SDK for UPnP Devices for Linux chosen as the SDK you will use as you build your sample devices. As you build the device, the Intel Tools for UPnP Technology will also be featured. In the next chapter you begin the first phase of UPnP device development using the Intel SDK.

Chapter 12

Adding Device Discovery

In the previous chapter the Intel SDK presented itself as the best option for use in building the Super Toaster. In this chapter you begin using the Intel SDK to build your device. First you learn about UPnP device description documents and then map the requirements presented in Chapter 10 to create a device description for the Super Toaster. Finally, the chapter introduces the first set of APIs from the Intel SDK to support the registration and discovery of your device, and you begin writing code to implement your device.

Problem Description

When the UPnP Super Toaster is connected to the network, you'd like the device to automatically announce its presence on the network and for other nodes on the network to receive this announcement without requiring any configuration or setup by the user. UPnP announcement and discovery are the mechanisms designed for this. When a UPnP device joins the network, it sends out an announcement in such a way that other listening nodes on the network can discover the device.

UPnP Device Description

When a UPnP device joins the network, it broadcasts an SSDP announcement. An SSDP announcement contains a URL that references a more detailed device description document. If another node on the network wants to learn more information about an advertised device, it retrieves the devices description document via the specified URL. The device description document contains a wealth of information about the device, including the device name, device type, version, manufacturer, model name, number, and other similar information. More importantly, the device description defines the specific list of services supported by the device. These services, which Chapter 13 covers in detail, provide the heart and soul of the device's functionality.

Device descriptions are XML documents often based on pre-defined templates or schemas adopted by the UPnP Forum. These standard templates provide the basic set of services for a predefined device type, to which implementers can then add vendor-specific extensions. Because your device is not based on a standard UPnP Forum device template, you will need to adhere to some rules in the UPnP Device Architecture specification when naming your device and related services.

Device Implementer Responsibilities

UPnP device implementers have specific conventions to follow when implementing a device. These rules and guidelines exist to ensure the successful interoperability of UPnP devices and are important for all device implementers to respect and follow.

One of the most important things a device implementer must do is to ensure that the device description document is well-formed, meaning that the device description XML is properly formatted, contains no dangling element tags, and follows the UPnP device description document format exactly.

FXPP, discussed in Chapter 5, requires control points and applications that do not recognize a node element or attribute while processing an XML device description document to ignore them and continue. Unfortunately, in practice this rarely occurs. An ill-formed device description could render your device unavailable on the network because a control point refuses to further process the XML after discovering an error.

A device implementer must also ensure that when a device leaves the network, it sends a bye-bye announcement to listening control point applications. If a device does not do this, control point applications may not be able to successfully distinguish between the previously discovered device instance and a newly discovered device when it reappears on the network. The control point application may very well think that the announcement is merely the same device sending its periodic advertisement, rather than a completely new instance of the same device.

UPnP Namespace Requirements

The UPnP Forum requires that device implementers follow namespace guidelines to differentiate between devices that are based on standard device templates and those that are not. This is done using the XML namespace attribute in the device description.

Every UPnP device description document contains a namespace definition that indicates a set of schemas to use for the device. For example, the following namespace declaration will be found for all device types defined by the UPnP Forum:

```
<...urn:schemas-upnp-org...>
```

However, the Super Toaster is a creation of your own company and is not a standard schema defined by the UPnP Forum. You are required then to use your company name in place of the UPnP Forum, as follows:

```
<...urn:schemas-intoast-com...>
```

This declaration indicates that this device is a unique creation of InToast Inc. and is not based on any UPnP standard device template. This ensures that you will have a unique company-specific namespace declaration for the Super Toaster that no other device will share.

Mapping our Requirements

You are now ready to begin the process of mapping your Super Toaster device requirements to the device description document.

Device description documents all follow the same basic format, as shown in Figure 12.1. The device description document is separated into two major sections. The first contains the root device declarator, specification version, and other miscellaneous information. The second contains information about the device, including a list of supported services. In the following sections you fill in this template with information for the Super Toaster.

```
<?xml version="1.0"?>
<root xmlns="...">
...
  <specVersion>
  <device>
    ...
    <serviceList>
      <service>
  ...
      </service>
    </serviceList>
  </device>
</root>
```

Figure 12.1 Device Description Template

Device Namespace

You begin with the namespace definition, which, as just described, you create using the recommended company domain name:

```
<...urn:schemas-intoast-com...>
```

At InToast Inc., you plan to produce a series of UPnP devices. As such, you will append a generic device schema classifier to your existing namespace to indicate the entire class of UPnP version 1.0 devices that your company produces. This gives you the added benefit of having your own vendor-specific device templates that could require, for example, all InToast devices to contain common device services. You extend your namespace as follows:

```
<...urn:schemas-intoast-com:device-1-0...>
```

Now you have a decision to make about how you are going to partition your device. Remember that UPnP devices can be implemented as a set of root devices or as embedded devices under a single root device type.

Looking at the device you're building, there doesn't seem to be a clear separation in functionality that would allow you to create two separate embedded devices. Although a combination TV/VCR might make sense to have separate root devices, clearly for the Super Toaster you have no such requirement, so you'll take the single root device approach.

Having said that, there are certainly examples in which it would be to your advantage to support multiple embedded devices in a single device description document. If you were creating a multi-function toaster-fax machine instead, it very well might make sense to do this, with each function of the product independently represented as a root device.

Multiple Root Devices

The attraction to use multiple, independent logical root devices in a single physical device is often very strong. The architectural separation of the two root devices means you can develop the two device implementations in near isolation from each other.

However, there are some disadvantages when using a multiple root device approach. Because each device is separate from the other, you have to be sure to add support to protect shared data if there is any synchronization needed between the two devices.

Additionally, memory consumption can become a concern for many device makers. In most UPnP library implementations, multiple root devices create many duplicate data structures and processes for each root device.

Furthermore, when you support two root devices in a single physical device, there is no guarantee that the control point application connected to one root device is the same control point application connected to the other.

It is possible to have multiple control points on the same logical network, meaning that as a device implementer you cannot make any assumptions about the number or the identity of the control points connected to your device.

Be careful when considering supporting multiple root devices. The drawbacks and additional complexity it can introduce in your implementation may far outweigh the initial perceived benefits.

You must define the unique device type for your single root device. You continue with the same format as your larger schemas namespace, adding an identifier, `supertoaster:1`, to represent the first version of our device. Putting your schema namespace together with your device name, you now have a complete device type to use in the device description document:

```
<deviceType>urn:schemas-intoast-com:
  supertoaster:1</deviceType>
```

You also know that you're implementing a device compatible with the UPnP 1.0 specification. With this you have enough information to start our XML device description, shown in Figure 12.2.

```
<?xml version="1.0"?>
<root xmlns="urn:intoast-com:device-1-0">
  <specVersion>
    <major>1</major>
    <minor>0</minor>
  </specVersion>
  <URLBase><URLBase>
  <device>
    <deviceType>urn:schemas-intoast-
com:supertoaster:1</deviceType>
    .
    .
    .
  </device>
</root>
```

Figure 12.2 SuperToaster Device Description Document, Part 1

Take note of a few things in Figure 12.2. First, every XML document starts with the XML version identifier. This is done so that XML parsers reading the document know which version of the XML specification they're dealing with.

Supporting Multiple UPnP Specification Versions

Because the major and minor specification versions in a device description document are sub-elements of the root device, and because there is no restriction on the number of root devices advertised from our physical device, you can have two (or more) different root devices that specify different versions of the UPnP Device Architecture specification in the same physical device.

What this means is that with careful use of the UPnP specification version field in the device description document, a single physical device can simultaneously support communication with UPnP version 1 and UPnP version 2 control points with careful use of the spec version field within a single device description document. This is an important capability for forward looking devices that want to be compatible with different versions of the specification.

This is a particularly interesting capability when future versions of the UPnP specification are released. As a device implementer you may want to implement the same functionality for the device to be backward compatible with UPnP specification version 1.0, while also offering an enhanced UPnP specification version 2.0 implementation of the device.

Next, you see the definition of your root device. UPnP device descriptions describe the namespace for a device as an element attribute using the "xmlns" attribute name. The closing element for the root device is at the bottom of the listing; it's often easy to forget this element when writing XML device descriptions by hand. Then you add the UPnP specification version you're implementing (version 1.0 in this case). Finally, the first tag in the device node, the deviceType, contains the unique device type for the SuperToaster.

URLBase

There is one final optional element in the beginning of all device description documents not yet covered: the URLBase element. One of the more interesting elements in the device description, the URLBase element defines an absolute base URL on which all other URLs in the description document will be based. The URLBase is an absolute URL to which all other URLs are appended.

If your device has a machine name on the local network you can specify the port number for all incoming UPnP requests off the local machine name. For example, if my machine name is "jelly," and 5431 is the port number I want to use for incoming UPnP requests, then I would specify the URLBase as follows:

```
<URLBase>http://jelly.intoast.com:5431</URLBase>
```

Or, if I had to use the IP address assigned to my computer I might specify the URLBase as follows:

```
<URLBase>http://192.168.1.10:5431</URLBase>
```

However, how many UPnP devices are going to have either a fully-qualified local domain name or a predetermined static IP address on the local network? Not many, as most devices in a home environment are assigned a DHCP provided IP address from a LAN gateway or similar device.

How to support run-time assigned IP addresses is an interesting topic of a later section in the chapter. For now though, assume that you are fortunate enough to have a fully qualified machine name for your toaster device.

The Super Toaster Device

Now that you're past the introductory elements in the device description, you are ready to describe the meat of our device description—the SuperToaster device itself.

You've already defined your device namespace and the specific device type. The next task is to fill in static information about your device, including the manufacturer, model number, and more, as shown in Figure 12.3.

The `friendlyName` field is most often displayed to users when they look for specific devices. Make sure the value for this field is descriptive enough to distinguish between many different devices on the network. For the most part, it's up to control points how they want to display this information, so as a general rule it's best to be as descriptive as possible.

Next in your device description is the Unique Device Name (UDN), which is a unique identifier for your device that matches only this device instance. The concept is similar to Globally Unique Identifiers (GUIDs), for developers familiar with COM. To create a Super Toaster UDN, you combine unique information such as your corporate domain name, the device type, and the device serial number to get:

```
<UDN>uuid:intoast-com_supertoaster-1_123456789</UDN>
```

This identifier must be truly unique for this or any device, even if you've manufactured thousands of Super Toasters. More importantly, this UDN will be constant for the lifetime of the device. The UPnP Vendor's Implementation Guide requires that UDN's persist over device reboots and other minor software updates. Typically, most UDN's are created at runtime using a combination of the device name and the network interface MAC address. This is a good method to programmatically generate a UDN without having to specify each and every UDN for a set of devices at manufacture time. Chapter 16 illustrates this technique.

Next, you have the option of including a Universal Product Code (UPC) that adorns most consumer products in retail stores. Since your company hasn't received an official UPC for the Super Toaster, you'll just put a placeholder there for now.

```
<friendlyName>InToast's Super Toaster</friendlyName>
<manufacturer>InToast Inc.</manufacturer>
<manufacturerURL>http://www.intoast.com</manufacturerURL>
<modelDescription>Super Toaster 1.0</modelDescription>
<modelName>ST 2002</modelName>
<modelNumber>1.0</modelNumber>
<modelURL>http://www.intoast.com/supertoaster/</modelURL>
<serialNumber>123456789</serialNumber>
```

Figure 12.3 Static Device Description Data

That nearly completes the device description for the Super Toaster device! A summary of what you've created thus far is shown in Figure 12.4.

As shown in Figure 12.4, there is one remaining section of the device description document to complete: services.

Super Toaster Services

Your final task for the device description is to define the services provided by the Super Toaster. This is a process of mapping the functional requirements of your device to specific services that you'd like to provide to control point applications.

For example, a UPnP thermostat could provide a service to get or set the current temperature. A UPnP light bulb could provide a service to

```
<?xml version="1.0"?>
<root xmlns="urn:intoast-com:device-1-0">
  <specVersion>
    <major>1</major>
    <minor>0</minor>
  </specVersion>
  <URLBase>http://jelly.intoast.com:5431/</URLBase>
  <device>
    <deviceType>urn:schemas-intoast-
      com:supertoaster:1</deviceType>
    <friendlyName>InToast's Super Toaster</friendlyName>
    <manufacturer>InToast Inc.</manufacturer>
    <manufacturerURL>http://www.intoast.com</manufacturerURL>
    <modelDescription>Super Toaster 1.0</modelDescription>
    <modelName>ST 2002</modelName>
    <modelNumber>1.0</modelNumber>
    <modelURL>http://www.intoast.com/supertoaster/</modelURL>
    <serialNumber>123456789</serialNumber>
    <UDN>uuid:intoast-com_supertoaster-1_123456789</UDN>
    <UPC>123456789</UPC>
    <serviceList>
      <service>
        ...
      </service>
    </serviceList>
  </device>
</root>
```

Figure 12.4 Super Toaster Device Description Document

turn the light bulb on and off, and another service to receive notifications when the bulb burns out. A UPnP television could provide services to select the channel, control volume properties, and control visual settings such as brightness, tint, or color.

Similarly, you need to map your requirements for your Super Toaster to a set of services. The detailed service description information is covered in the next chapter, but, at this point, you can go ahead and define the high-level services provided by your device.

Typically services can be categorized as follows:

- Informational—provides information about the operational state of the device
- Control—provides interfaces to control the device
- Get and Set—a mixture of both informational and control capabilities

Recall from Chapter 10 the high-level functional requirements for the Super Toaster:

- Lifetime statistics
- Network event notification
- Application-based control
- Web-based administration

There are a couple of different ways you can support these functional requirements. You could have the device support a single UPnP service that implements all of the functional capabilities of the device. Alternatively, you could go to the other extreme and create a separate device service for each individual bit of functionality your device supports.

For this device, you'll take a middle road, and choose a partition that at a high level matches the functional requirement breakdown.

Lifetime Statistics

First, the Super Toaster is required to keep track of lifetime statistics for the device. This sounds like an informational service.

Start the process by adding your first service to the service list for your device. Each service must specify a `serviceType` that is unique only for this device type. The service type follows the same naming conventions and rules set by the UPnP Forum for device types not defined by the UPnP Forum. You define the first service type for your lifetime statistics service as follows:

```
<serviceType>urn:schemas-intoast-

        com:service:lifetimestats:1</serviceType>
```

with the `:1` indicating the first version of this service.

The `serviceId` field is defined in the same way:

```
<serviceId>urn:intoast-

        com:serviceId:lifetimestats1</serviceId>
```

Next, you must specify a Service Control Protocol Definition (SCPD) URL for the service. This is a link to an XML document that describes each of these services you're creating in more detail. Chapter 13 covers the process of defining services for the Super Toaster. For now, just assume the lifetime statistics service is specified in more detail in an SCPD document labeled lifetimeSCPD.xml:

```
<SCPDURL>lifetimeSCPD.xml</SCPDURL>
```

Note that this URL is specified relative to the `URLBase` you defined earlier. Although this is how you have specified the SCPD URL for the lifetime statistics service, instead you could have specified this as an absolute URL, using the complete format `http://device-machine-name.com/lifetimeSPCD.xml` and left out the `URLBase` field.

Finally, the last two elements you need to add to your device service node are the Control and Eventing URLs. These are URLs to which control point applications post requests when sending control information or when subscribing to a device service. Both are relative URLs that simply provide a virtual document for control point applications to post SOAP requests to your device. Chapter 13 examines this behavior in detail. For now, simply define the following URLs for this service:

```
<controlURL>/upnp/control/lifetimestats1</controlURL>
<eventSubURL>/upnp/event/lifetimestats1</eventSubURL>
```

That completes the definition, shown in Figure 12.5, of the Lifetime Statistics service.

Network Event Notification

You're not done yet: You have two more features to support via UPnP Services. The first of these is Network Event Notification. This feature allows your device to report events to other nodes on the network when its status changes. This sounds like an Informational style service.

```
<service>
  <serviceType>
    urn:schemas-intoast-com:service:lifetimestats:1
  </serviceType>
  <serviceId>
    urn:intoast-com:serviceId:lifetimestats1
    </serviceId>
  <controlURL>/upnp/control/lifetimestats1</controlURL>
  <eventSubURL>/upnp/event/lifetimestats1</eventSubURL>
  <SCPDURL>lifetimeSCPD.xml</SCPDURL>
</service>
```

Figure 12.5 Lifetime Stats Service Definition

You add this capability through a UPnP service that provides interfaces to determine the current toasting status of the toaster and send out dynamic events when the device status changes. Taking what you've learned before, you can define this service as shown in Figure 12.6.

Application Based Control Service

The Application Based Control Service allows applications to programmatically control the Super Toaster. This is a control service—something that exposes interfaces to control a UPnP device. The application tells the device to do something, and the device does it. The Toaster Control service is defined in Figure 12.7.

Note that for this service, the `eventSubURL` element is empty. Although the UPnP Device Architecture Specification requires the

```
<service>
  <serviceType>urn:schemas-intoast-
    com:service:toastingstatus:1</serviceType>
  <serviceId>urn:intoast-
    com:serviceId:toastingstatus1</serviceId>
  <controlURL>/upnp/control/toastingstatus1</controlURL>
  <eventSubURL>/upnp/event/toastingstatus11</eventSubURL>
  <SCPDURL>toastingstatusSCPD.xml</SCPDURL>
</service>
```

Figure 12.6 Toasting Status Service

```
<service>
  <serviceType>
    urn:schemas-intoast-com:service:toastercontrol:1
  </serviceType>
  <serviceId>
    urn:intoast-com:serviceId:toastercontrol1
  </serviceId>
  <controlURL>/upnp/control/toastercontrol</controlURL>
  <eventSubURL></eventSubURL>
  <SCPDURL>toastercontrolSCPD.xml</SCPDURL>
</service>
```

Figure 12.7 Toaster Control Service

eventSubURL element to be present in all device service nodes, it is valid to have an empty value for the node. You do this intentionally, because this service will not support dynamic eventing of device information. Device services that support only eventing and do not expose any actions would be allowed the have an empty controlURL.

Web-based Administration

You have one last functional requirement to support in your device: Web-based Administration. Fortunately, the UPnP architecture provides a mechanism for this capability: the Presentation Page. A UPnP device's presentation page is a web page that is viewed with a standard web browser. This web page can provide static capabilities that range from static information to full control of the device. For the purposes of the Super Toaster, you can provide the ability to render the details of the Super Toaster to an administrative user. Chapter 15 covers this fully. For now, in the device description, simply specify a relative URL to the web page that provides this capability.

Here is the last addition:

```
<presentationURL>supertoaster.html</presentationURL>
```

The Complete Device Description Document

The UPnP device description document for the Super Toaster is complete. Figure 12.8 provides the complete listing.

```
<?xml version="1.0"?>
<root xmlns="urn:intoast-com:device-1-0">
  <specVersion>
    <major>1</major>
    <minor>0</minor>
  </specVersion>
  <URLBase>http://192.168.1.10:5431</URLBase>
  <device>
    <deviceType>urn:schemas-intoast-
      com:supertoaster:1</deviceType>
    <friendlyName>InToast's Super Toaster</friendlyName>
    <manufacturer>InToast Inc.</manufacturer>
    <manufacturerURL>http://www.intoast.com</manufacturerURL>
    <modelDescription>Super Toaster 1.0</modelDescription>
    <modelName>ST 2002</modelName>
    <modelNumber>1.0</modelNumber>
    <modelURL>http://www.intoast.com/supertoaster/</modelURL>
    <serialNumber>123456789</serialNumber>
    <UDN>uuid:intoast-com_supertoaster-1_123456789</UDN>
    <UPC>123456789</UPC>
    <serviceList>
      <service>
        <serviceType>
          urn:schemas-intoast-com:service:lifetimestats:1
        </serviceType>
        <serviceId>
          urn:intoast-com:serviceId:lifetimestats1
        </serviceId>
        <controlURL>/upnp/control/lifetimestats1</controlURL>
        <eventSubURL>/upnp/event/lifetimestats1</eventSubURL>
        <SCPDURL>lifetimeSCPD.xml</SCPDURL>
      </service>
      <service>
        <serviceType>
          urn:schemas-intoast-com:service:toastingstatus:1
        </serviceType>
        <serviceId>
          urn:upnp-org:serviceId:toastingstatus1
        </serviceId>
        <controlURL>/upnp/control/toastingstatus1</controlURL>
        <eventSubURL>/upnp/event/toastingstatus11</eventSubURL>
       <SCPDURL>/toastingstatusSCPD.xml</SCPDURL>
      </service>
      <service>
```

Figure 12.8 Complete SuperToaster Device Description Document *(Continues)*

```
        <serviceType>
          urn:schemas-intoast-com:service:toastercontrol:1
        </serviceType>
        <serviceId>
          urn:upnp-org:serviceId:toastercontrol1
        </serviceId>
        <controlURL>/upnp/control/toastercontrol</controlURL>
        <eventSubURL></eventSubURL>
        <SCPDURL>toastercontrolSCPD.xml</SCPDURL>
      </service>
    </serviceList>
    <presentationURL>supertoaster.html</presentationURL>
  </device>
</root>
```

Figure 12.8 Complete SuperToaster Device Description Document

Device Registration

Now that the description document is completed, it's time to register your device using the Intel SDK. This section introduces and demonstrates usage of the API functions needed to complete the definition, registration, and advertisement of your device. First, you need to write the `main()` function for your toaster device. This is the entry point of the application that will launch everything. You'll include this code in a file called `main.c`, listed in Figure 12.9.

```
/*
 * Filename: main.c
 *
 * Description: This file contains the main procedure for
 *              your upnp super toaster device.
 */
/* Include files*/
#include "upnp.h"
#include "toaster.h"
#include "toasterhw.h"
```

Figure 12.9 `main.c` Module Code Listing *(Continues)*

```
/*
 * Function: main
 *
 * Arguments: no command line arguments supported
 *
 * Returns: 0 if successful, -1 if failure
 *
 * Description: This function provides a startup and exit
 *              path for your device. It simply calls an
 *              initialization function for your device, then
 *              waits for some character input, at which
 *              point it calls an un-initialization function
 *              that will clean up your device.
 */
int main()
{
  int ret=0;     /* General purpose error code */
  char c;        /* User input character */

  printf("main: start\n");

  /* Call your UPnP intiialization function */
  ret = upnp_init();
  if(UPNP_E_SUCCESS != ret) {
    printf("main: upnp_init failed\n");
    upnp_cleanup();
    return ret;
  }

  /*
   * Your device initialized, you now want to wait for some
   * user input before you clean up and close the device.
   */
  c = getchar();

  /* You got some user input, go ahead and clean up. */
  ret = upnp_cleanup();
  if(UPNP_E_SUCCESS != ret) {
    printf("main: upnp_cleanup failed\n");
    return ret;
  }

  printf("main: end\n");

  return 0;
}
```

Figure 12.9 `main.c` Module Code Listing

Looking at the code, the entry point to our application simply calls a upnp_init() function that you'll implement shortly. It then waits for some input from the keyboard, and once it receives the input, it calls a upnp_cleanup() function that de-allocates and cleans up your Super Toaster device before exiting.

With that task complete, you can now turn to implementing the upnp_init() function called first by main().

Before you can do anything with the UPnP library, you need to ensure that it is initialized. Remember that unlike a lot of other Linux services (Apache, bind, and so on), the UPnP service itself is not a daemon service running in the background; instead, it is a run-time loadable shared object. As such, you need to initialize the library yourself at run time from your own application using the UpnpInit() function:

```
int UpnpInit (IN const char *HostIP,
              IN unsigned short DestPort);
```

HostIP—Override default binding to specified Host IP Address, specified in dotted quad format. NULL will accept the default address binding to the first available non-loopback Ethernet interface.

DestPort—Override default port binding with specified DestPort. Value 0 will accept default

Returns: UPNP_E_SUCCESS if successful, UPnP specification defined error code if not.

UPnP applications must call this function before any other UPnP library calls. The function initializes the UPnP library and creates a number of threads that run in your application process to support the services and capabilities that the Intel SDK provides.

The two parameters allow the device implementer to override the default IP address binding and port numbers for the UPnP library, although most devices never have a need to use these parameters.

Next, after initializing the library, you must set the root directory for the UPnP web server that is now running. All web requests received by the UPnP library's mini-web server will be serviced from this directory. This is particularly important for your device description document: If you have this directory set incorrectly, then the device and service description documents will not be found. Here is the function that sets the root directory for you:

```
int UpnpSetWebServerRootDir(IN const char *WebDir);
```

`WebDir`—Web server root directory for HTTP web requests

Returns: UPNP_E_SUCCESS if successful.

After calling this function, all web requests that come into your device will be handled from the appropriate directory. Note that the `WebDir` parameter can be either a relative or absolute location in the device file system.

Putting these two APIs together, you have a start to the UPnP initialization routine for your device that you'll include in a file named `upnp.c`, as shown in Figure 12.10.

```
/*
 * Function: upnp_init
 *
 * Description: This function initializes the UPnP library,
 *              sets up the internel web server, registers
 *              your root device, and sends out your initial
 *              device advertisements.
 */
int upnp_init()
{
  int ret = 0;          /* General purpose error code */
  char descpath[512]; /* Path for your description document */

  printf("upnp_init: start\n");

  /* Create your Desc Doc */
  sprintf(descpath, "%s%s", WEB_ROOT_DIR, DEVICE_DESC_DOC);

  /* Generate your device UDN */
  strcpy(g_deviceudn, DEVICE_UDN);

 /*
   * First, initialize the library, with the default
   * HostIP and port numbers.
   */
```

Figure 12.10 Device Initialization Code, Part 1 *(Continues)*

```
  ret = UpnpInit(NULL, 0);
  if(ret != UPNP_E_SUCCESS) {
    printf("upnp_init: UpnpInit failed with code: %d\n", ret);
    return ret;
  }

  /*
   * Next, set your root web server directory.
   */
  ret = UpnpSetWebServerRootDir(WEB_ROOT_DIR);
  if(ret != UPNP_E_SUCCESS) {
    printf("upnp_init: UpnpSetWebServerRootDir failed with code:
%d\n", ret);
    return ret;
  }

  printf("upnp_init: end\n");

  return ret;
}
```

Figure 12.10 Device Initialization Code, Part 1

In the preceding code, you have decided to accept the default Host IP and destination port bindings. In doing so, the UPnP library will bind to the first available Ethernet interface (typically eth0) by default and will randomly generate a port number to use.

When would you ever not do this? Unfortunately, the UPnP library doesn't have the capability to attach to all network interfaces in the system. The `HostIP` parameter allows the device (and control point) application programmer to specify a specific IP address of a specific interface to which the UPnP library should attach. If you accept the default `HostIP` (by specifying NULL for the `HostIP` address), the UPnP library attaches to the first non-loopback interface (that is, eth0) available in the system.

For devices in heavily controlled networks with restricted traffic flow behind a firewall or other node, it can be useful to override the default UPnP port on which the UPnP library will listen. The `DestPort` parameter to `UpnpInit()` allows you to do this. Just provide the alternate port number to use. When zero is specified for the `DestPort` parameter, the UPnP library randomly generates a port number for use. Also, for debugging purposes, if you have multiple devices on the network, it is often easier to filter logged network traffic based on port destination. Be aware though that if either of these parameters are overridden, you must also make sure that the base URL in the device description matches the parameters specified in the call to UpnPInit(). If it doesn't, chances are your device isn't going to appear properly on the network.

With that work done, it is now time to tell the library about your device. You do this through the following function:

```
int UpnpRegisterRootDevice(IN const char *DescUrl,
                           IN Upnp_FunPtr Callback,
                           IN const void *Cookie,
                           OUT UpnpDevice_Handle *Hnd);
```

DescUrl—Pointer to a string for the device description URL

Callback—Function pointer to a function to receive UPnP events

Cookie—Optional user data to be returned on each callback

Hnd—Out parameter that will receive a pointer to the newly created device handle

Returns: UPNP_E_SUCCESS if successful, Intel SDK Defined error code if unsuccessful.

Referring to the function parameter list, note that the DescUrl pointer specified must be an absolute URL that includes the port number specified earlier in the UpnpInit() function. For example, for your example device this would be a DescUrl value of:

```
http://192.168.1.10:5431/supertoaster.xml
```

Typically, the absolute URL needs to be constructed programmatically by your device, especially if you don't have a static IP address for your device.

The Callback function is a pointer to a function with the following signature, as defined in upnp.h:

```
typedef int  (*Upnp_FunPtr) (
    IN Upnp_EventType EventType,
    IN void *Event,
    IN void *Cookie
);
```

The UPnP library calls this function when some event directed toward your device has been received. Chapter 13 covers the implementation and support of this function.

The `Cookie` is a useful mechanism that allows your device registration code to pass information to the UPnP callback handler. This is commonly used to pass device context information without having to declare global variables for your device code.

The `Hnd` parameter returns the handle to the newly created device. You'll want to save this handle, as it will be used for subsequent UPnP library function calls.

Once your device is registered with the UPnP library, you must advertise its presence on the network for any listening control points. This is done using the `UpnpSendAdvertisement()` function:

```
int UpnpSendAdvertisement(IN UpnpDevice_Handle Hnd,
                          IN int Exp);
```

Hnd—Handle to the UPnP device for which we want to post advertisements.

Exp—Expiration time, in seconds, for each announcement, which is also the interval at which announcements are set.

Returns: UPNP_E_SUCCESS if successful, Intel SDK Defined error code if not.

Calling `UpnpSendAdvertisement()` sends SSDP network announcements for the provided UPnP device referenced by the handle provided in `Hnd`.

Through the `Exp` parameter, you can define the lifetime of each advertisement sent, which will also be the interval at which advertisements are sent out for the device. There is a minimum value of 180 seconds for this parameter. Setting it to anything less is not supported and could result in unpredictable behavior.

Take a look at your code in Figure 12.11, with two new functions.

```
/* The callback function for the UPnP Library */
int upnp_callback(Upnp_EventType, void *, void *);

/*
 * Function: upnp_init
 *
```

Figure 12.11 Device Initialization Code, Part 2 *(Continues)*

```
 * Description: This function initializes the UPnP library,
 *              sets up the internal web server, registers
 *              your root device, and sends out your initial
 *              device advertisements.
 */
int upnp_init()
{
  int ret = 0;         /* General purpose error code */
  char descpath[512]; /* Path for your description document */

  printf("upnp_init: start\n");

  ...
  ...
  ...

  /*
   * Register your root device with the Upnp library.
   */
  ret = UpnpRegisterRootDevice(descpath,
                               upnp_callback,
                               &g_device_handle,
                               &g_device_handle);
  if(ret != UPNP_E_SUCCESS) {
    printf("upnp_init: UpnpRegisterRootDevice failed with code:
%d\n", ret);
  }

  /*
   * Send advertisements about your device every 180s.
   */
  ret = UpnpSendAdvertisement(g_device_handle, 180);
  if(ret != UPNP_E_SUCCESS) {
    printf("upnp_init: UpnpSendAdvertisement failed with code:
%d\n", ret);
    return ret;
  }

  printf("upnp_init: end\n");

  return ret;
}
```

Figure 12.11 Device Initialization Code, Part 2

In Figure 12.11, you can see the new function calls. In the UpnpRegisterRootDevice() call, you provide the actual created device handle itself as context in the cookie parameter, even though the device handle isn't officially created until the function call returns.

With device registration and advertisement now completed, your device will now be visible on the network. If any control point applications are running, they will receive these announcements and, if they are interested, will make requests for device and service description information. At this point, your device may also start receiving requests for service action invocation, which you receive through the callback handler provided to UpnpRegisterRootDevice(). Handling of these events is covered in Chapter 13.

Cleaning Up

As every good programmer knows, you must always ensure that any resources allocated during usage of your device are properly released upon exit. The same is true for using the UPnP library. A number of threads and internal data structures are created by the UPnP library that need to be freed up before your UPnP device application terminates.

But, first, there is one other detail you need to be aware of. Other control point applications have discovered your device and expect you to respond to device discovery or service action requests. If your device leaves the network without notifying others that you have done so, control point applications continue to think your device is alive on the network and may attempt to communicate with it. To rectify this and ensure that the network is not left in an inconsistent state, you need to notify the control points on the network when you leave. This is done with the UpnpUnRegisterRootDevice() function:

```
int UpnpUnRegisterRootDevice(IN UpnpDevice_Handle Hnd);
```

Hnd—Handle to the UPnP device we wish to un-register.

Returns: UPNP_E_SUCCESS if successful.

When called, UpnpUnRegisterRootDevice() sends an SSDP bye-bye announcement. The bye-bye announcement ensures that a control point will not be confused about whether or not your device is on the network. Control points receive this message and update their internal representation of the state of the network.

To understand this, think about what happens to a device when it leaves and rejoins the network. The first time the device appears on the network it sends its advertisement. A control point application picks up the announcement and possibly creates an instance representing the device, its service(s), and its state variables. The control point application then configures the device a certain way. For example, if your toaster device has a default value of 3 for its darkness setting, when it first powers up that is the value of the state variable. Then, while using the device, the user may change the setting to a value of 5.

If the device disappears (that is, reboots) unexpectedly from the network without sending a bye-bye notification, the control point application has no idea the device instance it was talking to has left the network. If the device shortly thereafter comes back on the network, the control point will receive an announcement for the new device instance that has a default setting of 3. However, because the device announcements are identical, the control point will not be able to distinguish between this announcement and the one registered previously.

You now have an inconsistent state on the network: Because it is a new instance, the device has reverted back to its default settings and a value of 3, while the control point thinks this is the same device it was talking to earlier, which has a user specified setting of 5.

Sending a bye-bye announcement is a critical task for any device implementer. It is imperative that this step is not forgotten if your device is going to reset or disappear from the network for any reason.

The last step that you must perform is to give the UPnP library a chance to de-allocate memory and clean up worker threads created as part of the library's operation. This can be done with a call to `UpnpFinish()` function:

```
int UpnpFinish( );
```

Returns: UPNP_E_SUCCESS if successful.

After completing this call you can safely exit from our application code. Remember that if you are simply removing your device from the network and plan on adding it back again, it's not necessary to call UpnpFinish().You can simply call the function UpnpUnRegisterRootDevice(), followed again by an UpnpRegisterRootDevice().

The complete source code for your upnp_cleanup() function is listed in Figure 12.12.

```
/*
 * Function: upnp_cleanup
 *
 * Description: This function is called when you want to
 *              clean up all resources associated with your
 *              upnp device. It unregisters your device,
 *              which will cause bye-bye announcements to be
 *              sent for your device.
 */
int upnp_cleanup()
{
  int ret=0;      /* General purpose return */

  printf("upnp_cleanup: start\n");

  /*
   * UnRegister your device
   */
  ret = UpnpUnRegisterRootDevice(g_device_handle);
  if(ret != UPNP_E_SUCCESS) {
   printf("upnp_cleanup: UpnpUnRegisterRootDevice failed with
code: %d\n", ret);
  }

  /*
   * Allow the library to clean-up, even if the unregister
   * failed.
   */
  UpnpFinish();

  printf("upnp_cleanup: end\n");

  return ret;
}
```

Figure 12.12 Device Initialization Code, Part 2

The Inconsistent Device State Problem

UPnP as defined seems to have a problem handling devices that leave the network unexpectedly and aren't able to send bye-bye announcements. As a result, the UPnP network can get in an inconsistent state.

There is no official workaround for this problem; however, there is a trick by which this issue can be resolved. The method is related to the fact that control points that are maintaining state for a given device are typically subscribed to one or more of the device services to receive state variable events.

Control points are required to re-subscribe to a device service on a periodic basis before their subscription expires. The next time the control point attempts to re-subscribe to a device service, the new instance of the device will have no previous record of the subscription that the control point is trying to re-subscribe. In this case, the device can fail the re-subscription request, at which point the control point will then assume that subscription was lost, create a new subscription request, and get the correct values for the subscribed state variables. This brings the network back to a consistent state.

What about the IP Address?

One unique issue in working with the Intel SDK is how to handle dynamically assigned IP addresses in your device. Recall that the `URLBase` in the device description document can specify a base to which all other relative URLs will be appended.

This is fine if the device has a static IP address, but realistically it is very rare for a device to be so fortunate. In most cases the device is going to receive a DHCP-assigned address from a local network gateway.

So what should you do about the static device description? Fortunately, the Intel SDK supports the ability to fill in the URLBase field for you. You can do this with an alternate function for device registration that also provides options for specifying your device description without having to use a static XML file:

```
int UpnpRegisterRootDevice2(IN Upnp_DescType  descriptionType,
                            IN const char *description,
                            IN size_t  bufferLen,
                            IN int config_baseURL,
                            IN Upnp_FunPtr Callback,
                            IN  const void *Cookie,
                            OUT UpnpDevice_Handle *Hnd);
```

descriptionType—Method of device description.

description—Pointer to description doc, in format corresponding to descriptionType.

bufferLen—Length of the buffer pointed to by description, if descriptionType is set to UPNPREG_BUF_DESC.

config_baseURL—If nonzero, automatically configures the URLBase field and serves the device description.

Callback—Function pointer to receive UPnP event callbacks.

Cookie—Optional user data to be returned on each callback.

Hnd—Out parameter that returns the newly created device handle.

Returns: UPNP_E_SUCCESS if successful, other Intel SDK Defined error code if not.

You have a number of interesting parameters to sort through. First, the descriptionType argument supports three different methods, as shown in Table 12.1, that provide more flexibility in registering a device description document.

As useful as these optional device description specification capabilities are, what is perhaps most the useful part of this function is the `config_baseURL` parameter. When set to a value other than zero, the function automatically updates the `URLBase` field of the device description to include current IP address information.

Referring back to your example, if you have a `URLBase` field set as follows in your device description document:

```
<URLBase>http://123.456.789.012:5431/</URLBase>
```

calling the `UpnpRegisterRootDevice2()` function will result in the above `URLBase` address being updated to your current device settings.

Table 12.1 descriptionType Values

Type	Description
UPNPREG_URL_DESC	The device description is specified in an URL, the value of which is specified in the description parameter.
UPNPREG_FILENAME_DESC	The device description is stored in a file, specified in the description parameter.
UPNPREG_BUF_DESC	The device description is contained in a memory buffer pointed to by description, and has a length bufferLen.

Note Although the UpnpRegisterRootDevice2() function's capability to automatically set the URLBase to your current IP address is very useful, this is not a complete solution for many environments. DHCP servers that have addresses that expire and that re-issue different addresses will break the functionality of your device, because the UPnP stack will remain bound to the original IP address. Wherever possible, try to configure your network to issue infinite DHCP lease address.

Figure 12.13 provides a complete listing for upnp_init(), with both the new and old methods of device registration, and the addition of an un-register and re-register cycle to solve the inconsistent device state problem described earlier.

```
/*
 * Function: upnp_init
 *
 * Description: This function initializes the UPnP library,
 *              sets up the internel web server, registers
 *              your root device, and sends out your initial
 *              device advertisements.
 */
int upnp_init()
{
  int ret = 0;        /* General purpose error code */
  char descpath[512]; /* Path for your description document */

  printf("upnp_init: start\n");
```

Figure 12.13 Device Initialization Using UpnpRegisterRootDevice2()
(Continues)

```
  /* Create your Desc Doc */
  sprintf(descpath, "%s%s", WEB_ROOT_DIR, DEVICE_DESC_DOC);

  /* Generate your device UDN */
  strcpy(g_deviceudn, DEVICE_UDN);

  /*
   * First, initialize the library, with the default
   * HostIP and port numbers.
   */
  ret = UpnpInit(NULL, 0);
  if(ret != UPNP_E_SUCCESS) {
    printf("upnp_init: UpnpInit failed with code: %d\n", ret);

    return ret;
  }

  /*
   * Next, set your root web server directory.
   */
  ret = UpnpSetWebServerRootDir(WEB_ROOT_DIR);
  if(ret != UPNP_E_SUCCESS) {
    printf("upnp_init: UpnpSetWebServerRootDir failed with
    code:
%d\n", ret);
    return ret;
  }

#if 0
  /*
   * Register your root device with the Upnp library.
   */
  ret = UpnpRegisterRootDevice(descpath,
                               upnp_callback,
                               &g_device_handle,
                               &g_device_handle);
  if(ret != UPNP_E_SUCCESS) {
    printf("upnp_init: UpnpRegisterRootDevice failed with
    code:
%d\n", ret);
  }
#endif

  /*
   * Register your root device with the Upnp library.
   * This call will automatically set your base url.
   */
```

Figure 12.13 Device Initialization Using UpnpRegisterRootDevice2()
(Continues)

```
  ret = UpnpRegisterRootDevice2(UPNPREG_FILENAME_DESC,
                                descpath,
                                0, 1, upnp_callback,
                                &g_device_handle,
                                &g_device_handle);
  if(ret != UPNP_E_SUCCESS) {
    printf("upnp_init: UpnpRegisterRootDevice2 failed with
    code:
%d\n", ret);
    return ret;
  }

  /*
   * UnRegister your device, which will clean up any records
   * the control points may have of your previous device.
   */
  ret = UpnpUnRegisterRootDevice(g_device_handle);
  if(ret != UPNP_E_SUCCESS) {
   printf("upnp_cleanup: UpnpUnRegisterRootDevice failed with
code: %d\n", ret);
  }

  /*
   * Then, re-register your root device with the Upnp library.
   */
  ret = UpnpRegisterRootDevice2(UPNPREG_FILENAME_DESC,
                                descpath,
                                0, 1, upnp_callback,
                                &g_device_handle,
                                &g_device_handle);
  if(ret != UPNP_E_SUCCESS) {
    printf("upnp_init: UpnpRegisterRootDevice2 failed with
    code:
%d\n", ret);
    return ret;
  }

  /*
   * Send advertisements about your device every 180s.
   */
  ret = UpnpSendAdvertisement(g_device_handle, 180);
  if(ret != UPNP_E_SUCCESS) {
   printf("upnp_init: UpnpSendAdvertisement failed with code:
%d\n", ret);
    return ret;
  }
```

Figure 12.13 Device Initialization Using `UpnpRegisterRootDevice2()`
(Continues)

```
  printf("upnp_init: end\n");

  return ret;
}
```

Figure 12.13 Device Initialization Using UpnpRegisterRootDevice2()

This is a very useful capability that significantly reduces the workload for the device and allows you much greater flexibility in creating device description documents.

Programmatic Description Document Creation

One of the most powerful features UpnpRegisterRootDevice2 provides is the ability to programmatically create your device description through the use of the UPNPREG_BUF_DESC description type. This has significant advantages as it frees the device implementer from having to store static device description documents on the device. With this capability the adventurous device maker could choose to dynamically generate the device description document at run time.

Intel Tools for UPnP Technologies

Having completed the device description document for your device and written code to bring it up on the network, how can you make sure that the Super Toaster is working properly? You can use the Intel Tools for UPnP Technologies. Although your first guess might be to use the Device Spy tool to determine whether you can discover your device, you cannot do so because your device service description documents are not complete. When a device announces itself on the network, Device Spy attempts to parse all device and service description documents. Since you have not yet completed your service description documents, Device Spy does not list your device.

Fortunately, you can use Device Sniffer to test whether your Super Toaster device is properly sending out advertisements on the network for your device. Think of Device Sniffer as a network monitor exclusively for UPnP devices. Figure 12.14 shows the basic user interface for Device Sniffer.

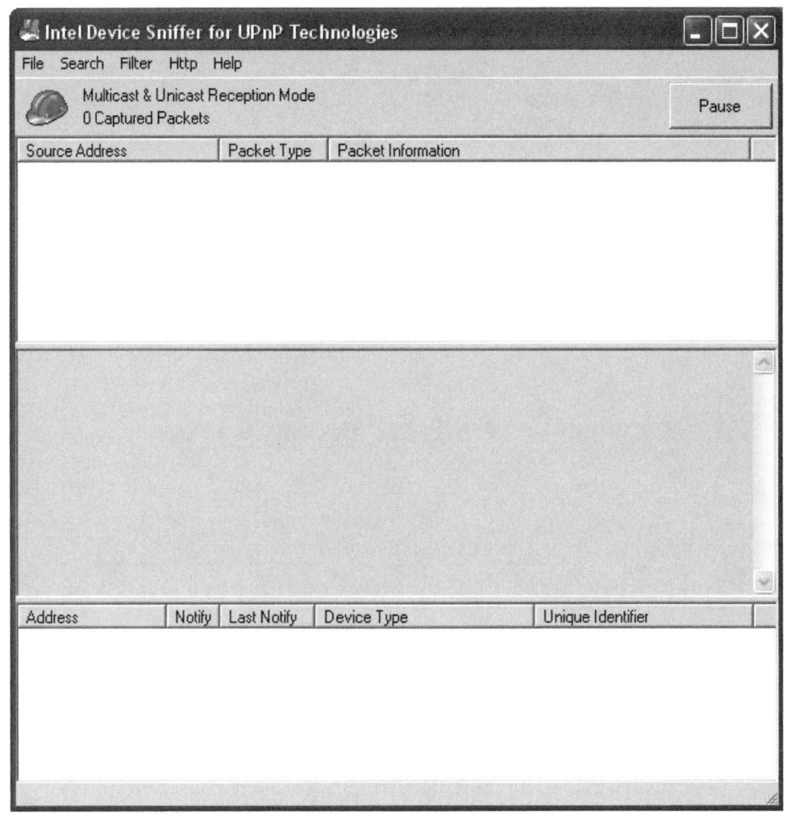

Figure 12.14 Device Sniffer

There are three primary sections of the Device Sniffer user interface: The top pane lists UPnP related packets sniffed off the network. The middle pane displays information about a selected packet, and the bottom pane lists specific discovered devices, like your Super Toaster.

First, a brief introduction to the various options in the menus for Device Sniffer:

- File Menu—Options to modify the display
  - — Clear Packet Capture clears the captured packets displayed in the top pane.
  - — Show Packet Details hides or displays the top pane.
  - — Show Device Tracking hides or displays the bottom pane.

- Search—Search options
  - Search All Devices sends out a discovery request to find all devices.
  - Search Root Devices sends out a `upnp:rootdevice` request to find all root UPnP devices.
  - Search Specific Type searches for specific UPnP Forum defined device types.
- Filter—Modify filter options
  - Enable Packet Capture toggles the capturing of packets.
  - Capture Multicasts toggles the capture of multicast packets.
- Http—Modify HTTP request options
  - Show HTTP Requestor opens a child window that allows you to make HTTP requests.
  - Use Requestor for HTTP requests when selected, uses the integrated HTTP Requestor window to make HTTP requests.
  - Use Browser for HTTP requests when selected, uses the default Web browser to issue HTTP requests.

Device Sniffer can be used to test the functionality of your device. First, be sure Device Sniffer is up and running. When you start your Super Toaster device, you'll see a series of packets captured. Figure 12.15 shows sniffed packets in the packet pane. Clicking on one of the packets lists its contents in the middle packet pane. The first packet your device sends out is a generic `upnp:rootdevice` announcement. In the packet, you can see useful information about your device, such as your device's UDN and the location of the device description document you created earlier in this chapter.

If for some reason you don't see any announcements in the packet capture window, be sure to check your system firewall settings. This is the most common culprit. Following the `upnp:rootdevice` announcement, your device sends out announcements for your specific device type, shown in Figure 12.16.

The second set of announcements contains your complete device namespace and information about the specific Intel SDK you're using to develop your device. The last set of announcements, shown in Figure 12.17, are for each of the device services supported by your device.

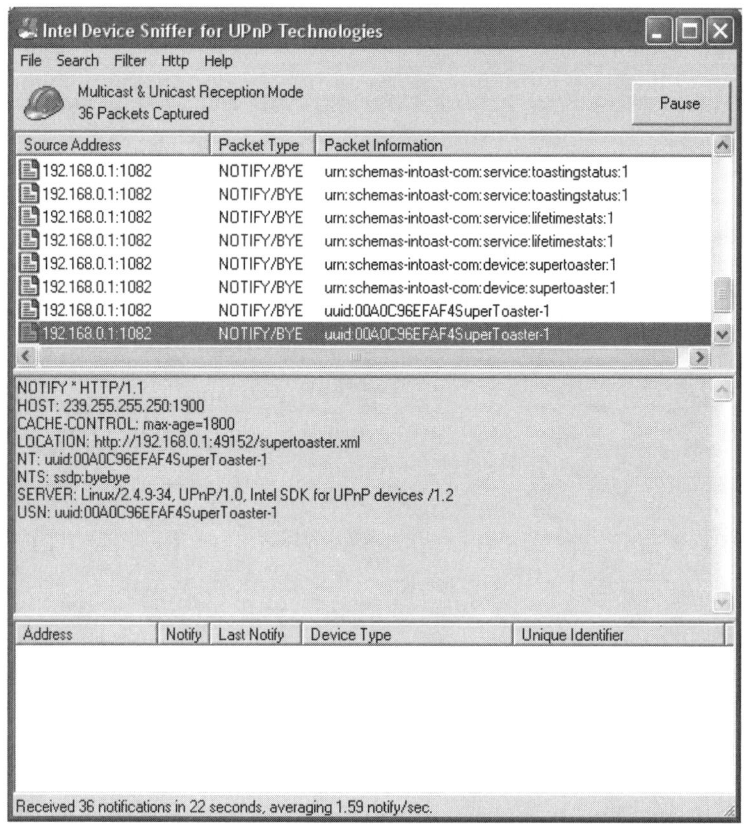

Figure 12.15 Device Sniffer, after Super Toaster Has Started

Having so many announcements may seem a bit excessive, but they're all very important. Each of the announcements support a specific method of discovering your device: by generic root device, by specific device type, by your device UDN, or by one of the named services your device supports.

So far so good! Your Super Toaster is properly sending out the required announcements, and the information in them appears to be valid. When a real control point on the network receives these announcements, the first thing it's going to do is to try to retrieve your detailed device description document. You can simulate this behavior

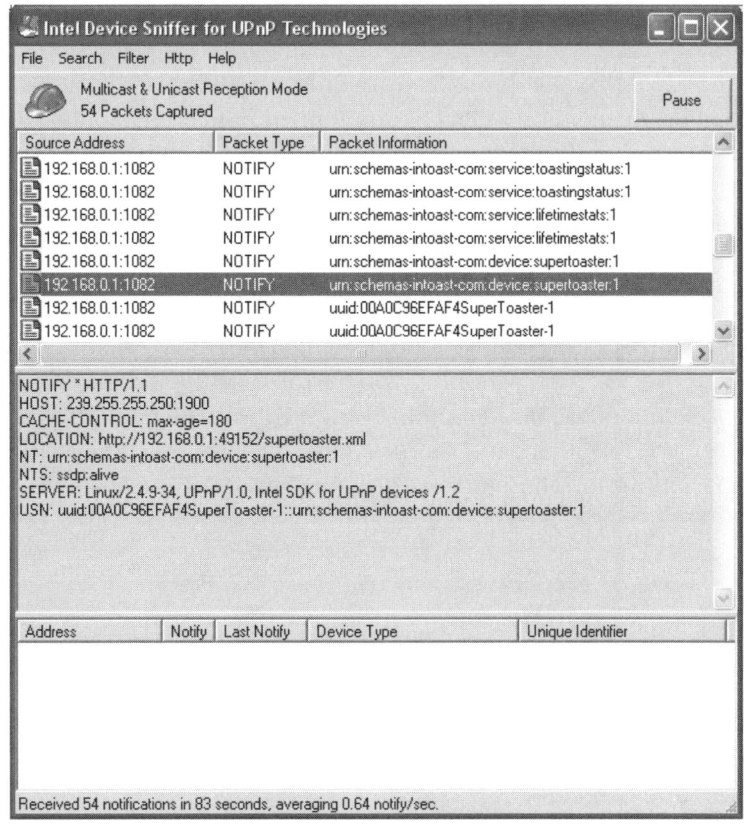

Figure 12.16 Super Toaster Device Announcement

with Device Sniffer by selecting one of your device announcements that contains a LOCATION field, and selecting and right-clicking the mouse to bring up a context menu, shown in Figure 12.18.

Selecting Open issues an HTTP request to your device using the currently enabled web viewer (in this case, the integrated HTTP Requestor). Figure 12.19 shows that the HTTP requestor was able to successfully retrieve your device description document.

The HTTP Requestor window shows not only the issued HTTP request, but also the response received from your device. In fact, you can put anything in the address bar of the HTTP Requestor, including your

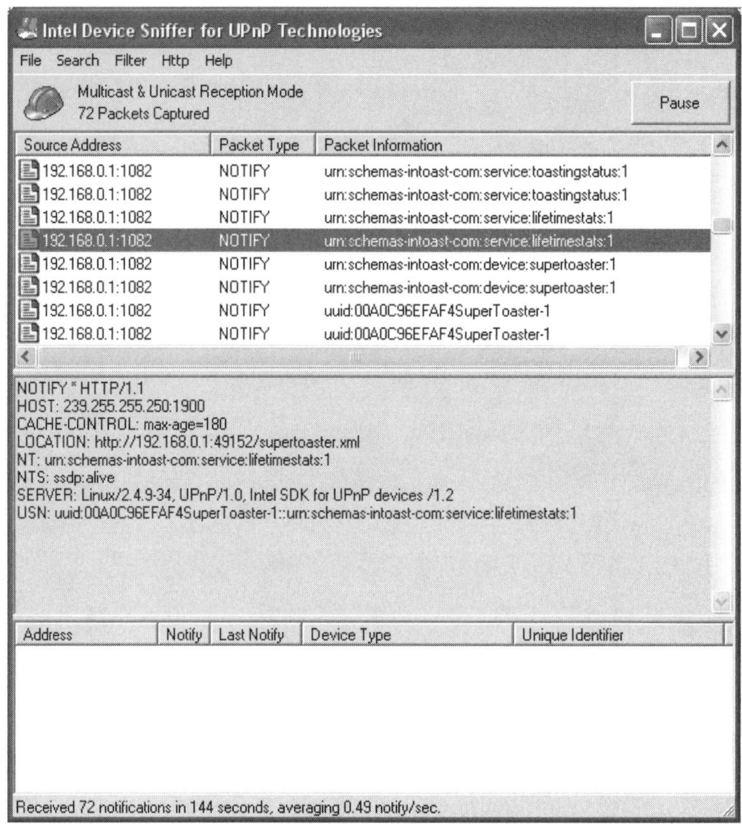

Figure 12.17 SuperToaster Service Announcements

SCPDURLs if you'd like. Doing so at this point returns a "HTTP 404 not found" error though, because you've not written those documents yet.

By using Device Sniffer you've successfully verified that your device is properly announcing itself on the network and that it is capable of responding to control points.

If for some reason your device announcements aren't appearing on the network, don't worry, it happens to the best of us. Recall that in your code you've added a series of printf statements to assist in debugging. In the console window, you can see a call stack of sorts for device startup and shutdown sequences, shown in Figure 12.20.

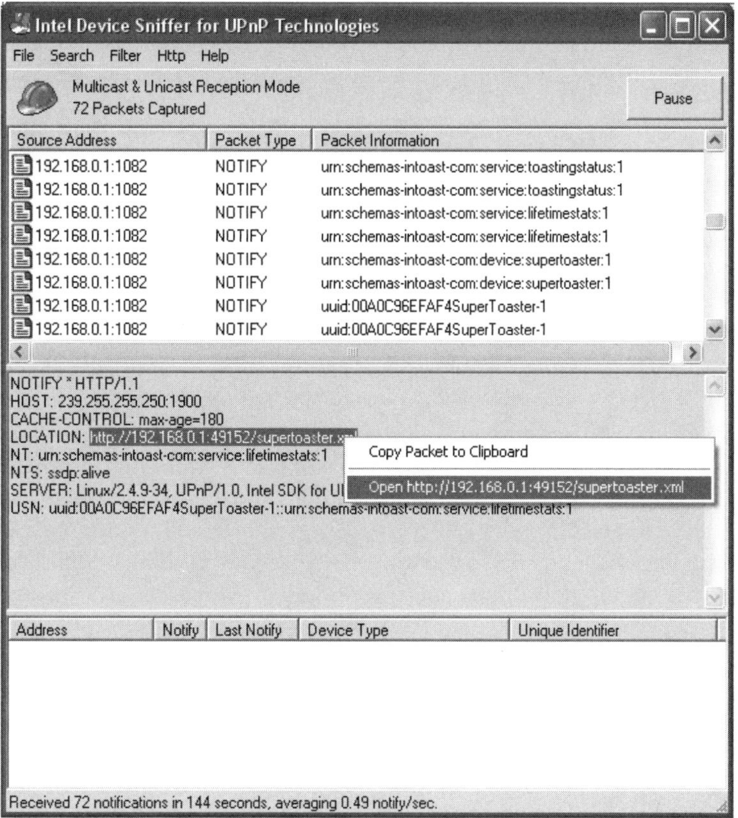

Figure 12.18 Right-click Context Menu

Look at this startup sequence first when trying to determine what is wrong with your device. Chapter 16 discusses some additional tips and tricks to follow if you are having trouble verifying your device functionality at this stage.

Figure 12.19 HTTP Requestor Window

```
[root@ns1 upnp]# ./supertoaster main: start
upnp_init: start
hw_init start
hw_init stop
upnp_init: end

upnp_cleanup: start
hw_cleanup: start
hw_cleanup: stop
upnp_cleanup: end
main: end
```

Figure 12.20 Console Startup Sequence

Summary

This chapter introduced the concept of UPnP device description documents, mapped the Super Toaster device product requirements to a real device description document, and covered all the necessary Intel SDK APIs needed for initializing, configuring, registering, announcing, unregistering, and finishing your UPnP device session. You have made significant progress toward a functional UPnP device. In fact, you now have a complete framework for everything you need for the device to show up on the network and respond to device description requests.

Device Sniffer can be extremely useful in verifying a device's functionality at this early stage of device development. The following chapters will fill in the gaps of the framework with additional functionality to complete your device.

Chapter 13

Defining Device Services

In the last chapter you learned how to create a device description document for your device and how to implement support for this important capability. In this chapter you continue with a related description activity for your device: service descriptions. You will learn how UPnP service descriptions fit into the description model, walk through the creation of some simple service description documents for your device, and finally learn how to programmatically handle service action invocation on your device using the Intel SDK.

Introduction

UPnP devices are only as useful as the capabilities they provide. A device that only provides a device description document is not terribly exciting or useful to control points. You need a mechanism by which to expose capabilities, interfaces, and properties of your device to control points.

Recall from Chapter 12 that UPnP uses two kinds of description documents. Device description documents describe the device and its static properties such as manufacturer, serial number, and other static information. However, that information isn't enough to actually communicate with or make use of the device. For this you need UPnP service descriptions.

UPnP service descriptions describe remote function calls on the device. These remote function calls are called *actions*. Actions are defined in the service description document, along with the action arguments and any associated state variables. Actions can be invoked by a UPnP control point. Actions can cause specific events to happen on the device, can return information back to the control point, or can have no response at all. Figure 13.1 shows the message flow when a control point invokes an action on a device service.

The control point application uses the device description to determine the service definitions and then retrieves the corresponding service description documents for the discovered device. Only after performing these steps does the control point application know enough about the device to make the proper service action invocation(s).

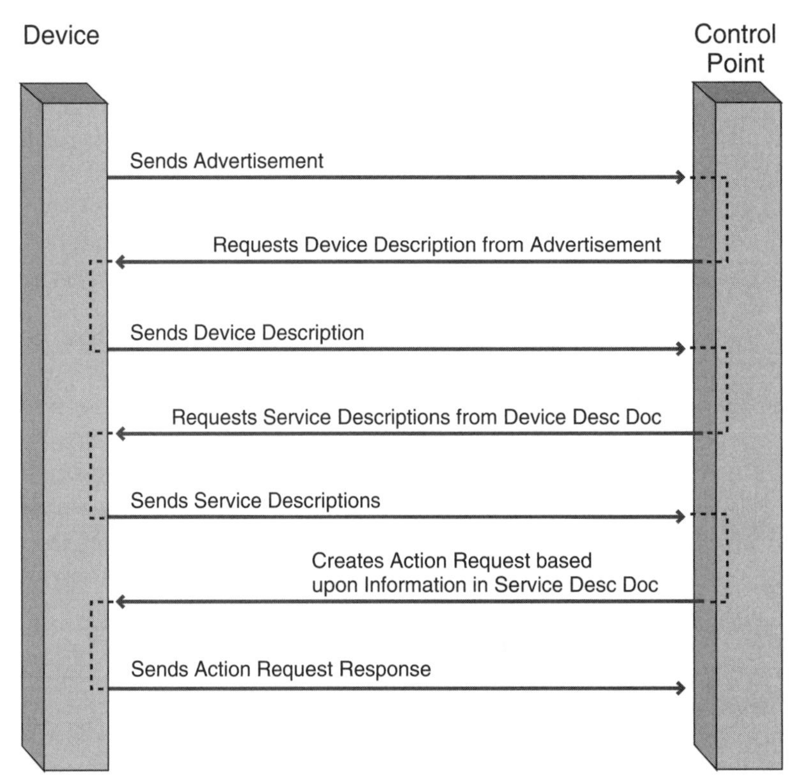

Figure 13.1 Control Point Invoking an Action

In an ideal world, control points would simply trust the device and service types reported, and assume all services are properly implemented. Unfortunately, this is rarely the case in the real world. Required services and actions for a given device type may not always exist, and calling an action that doesn't exist could, in the worst case, cause a segmentation fault in the device.

Service Characteristics

Every UPnP service may have zero or more actions. Each action may then have zero or more arguments, which themselves are marked with an in or out direction. If there exists at least one output argument, this argument can alternatively be marked as a return value for the action. Finally, each action argument must correspond to a defined state variable in the service.

Service actions typically come in the following forms:

- Get—query specific state variable values or receive notifications when the values change.
- Set—set a device state variable, often resulting in some associated action on the device.
- Get and Set—combination of the previous two service forms.
- Do Something—tell the device to perform some kind of task.

For example, a UPnP thermostat could expose a "Get" action to retrieve the current temperature and a "Set" action to set the time when the thermostat should come on; a "Get and Set" action could combine the last two actions, while a "Do Something" action may tell the thermostat to adjust the current temperature immediately.

Although every UPnP service is required to have one or more associated state variables, services aren't required to support any actions. Consider an "Error" service for the UPnP thermostat that asynchronously sends an error event back to the control point. There are no actions for a control point to call; however, in this case the "Error" state variable could be evented back to all subscribed control points. The next chapter covers service subscriptions and evented state variables more fully.

Service Description Documents

Much like the device description document introduced in the last chapter, service description documents are also XML-based and follow many of the same conventions as the device description.

UPnP service description documents specify the supported actions for the service, the parameters and associated state variable for the action, and the state variables contained in the service. They have the basic format shown in Figure 13.2.

The `actionList` contains the definition of any number of actions, their parameters, and return values, while the `serviceStateTable` provides information about the state variables used in this service.

UPnP Data Types

UPnP devices and control points are strongly typed. For each action argument, you are required to specify a specific data type. Because the UPnP architecture is platform independent, an integer on one platform may not be the same as an integer on another. To resolve this issue, the UPnP Forum has defined a specific set of data types for all devices and control points to interpret in the same way.[1]

```
<?xml version="1.0"?>
<scpd xmlns=" ... ">
  <specVersion>
  </specVersion>
  <actionList>
    <action>
      ...
    </action>
  </actionList>
  <serviceStateTable>
    <stateVariable ..>
      ...
    </stateVariable>
  </serviceStateTable>
</scpd>
```

Figure 13.2 Service Description Document Template

---

[1] XML experts will note some similarity between these data types and those defined in the XML Schema specification.

Table 13.1, taken from the UPnP Device Architecture specification, summarizes the data types available for use in UPnP devices:

Table 13.1 UPnP Data Types

Data Type	Description
ui1	Unsigned 1-byte integer
ui2	Unsigned 2-byte integer
ui4	Unsigned 4-byte integer
i1	Signed 1-byte integer
i2	Signed 2-byte integer
i4	Signed 4-byte integer, same format as int
int	4-byte fixed point integer, between –2147483648 and 2147483647, may have leading zeros, no commas
r4	4-byte floating point, same format as float
r8	8-byte floating point, same format as float
number	Same as r8
fixed.14.4	Same as r8, but a maximum of 14 digits to the left of the decimal, and a maximum of 4 to the right
float	Floating-point number. Mantissa and/or exponent may have leading sign or leading zeros
char	Unicode string, one character in length
string	Unicode string, unlimited length
date	Month, day, year conforming to ISO 8601, without time data
dateTime	ISO8601 date with time, but no time zone
dateTime.tz	ISO8601 date with optional time and time zone
time	Time as specified in ISO8601 with no date and time zone
time.tz	Time as specified in ISO8601 with optional time zone, but no date

Continues

Table 13.1 UPnP Data Types *(Continued)*

Data Type	Description
boolean	0 for false, 1 for true
bin.base64	Base64 encoded binary data
bin.hex	Hexadecimal digits, as octects
uri	Universal Resource Identifier
uuid	Universally Unique ID, specified as hexadecimal octets

It is imperative that you follow these strict data type guidelines when implementing your device. Control points are notoriously sensitive to improperly typed data. For example, don't return a NULL or empty value for the URI, as by definition URIs aren't allowed to be empty.

Super Toaster SCPDs

The previous chapter identified three services that your Super Toaster device supports:

- Lifetime Statistics
- Toaster Status
- Toaster Control

This chapter limits itself to those services that do not have any asynchronous event-based information, covering only the Lifetime Statistics and Toaster Control Services. The next chapter covers Toaster Status.

As in the previous chapter, you must use the unique namespace identifier made up of a combination of your company name and the version of the UPnP specification to which you'll conform. Thus, you can start each of your service description documents with the XML shown in Figure 13.3.

Lifetime Statistics Service

For the Lifetime Statistics service you must define the list of supported actions. Recall that a service may have zero or more actions. Each of these actions may have zero or more parameters, each of which can be either input or output parameters.

```
<?xml version="1.0"?>
<scpd xmlns="urn:schemas-intoast-com:supertoaster-service-1-0">
  <specVersion>
    <major>1</major>
    <minor>0</minor>
    </specVersion>
  ...
</scpd>
```

Figure 13.3 Service Description Document, Part 1

According to your original product requirements in Chapter 10, you must implement lifetime statistics for two properties:

- Total slices of bread toasted
- Length in seconds of toasting

These properties translate nicely into a few actions on the device. You want to provide the opportunity to retrieve values for control point applications and have the ability to reset each statistic to some user-defined value.

Before you define the actions you'll support, take a moment and identify the state variables in the Lifetime Statistics service. First, you need an unsigned integer representing the total slices of bread toasted and another unsigned integer representing the total number of seconds of active toasting.

For each state variable, you must define the following:

- name—the required service unique name of the state variable.
- dataType—a required UPnP data type (from Table 13.1) for the state variable.
- defaultValue—an optional default value, in the proper data type format for this state variable.
- allowedValueRange—an optional range the state variable supports.

For each state variable, only the name and dataType fields are required; the others are optional but highly recommended. In addition, the stateVariable sendEvents attribute for each state variable must also state whether the state variable is evented or not. For the services you define in this chapter, none of your state variables will be evented. The next chapter covers eventing.

With this information, you can go ahead and define your state variables as shown in Figure 13.4.

That completes the definition of the state variables in the Lifetime Statistics service. Next you define the actions in the service.

You already know that you need to provide access to the just-defined state variables. You'll implement a few actions to support these state variables. You'll provide a "get" style action to retrieve each lifetime statistic, and then you'll provide a set action for each as well, just in case you'd like to reset the values. You'll call these functions simply:

- `getTotalSlices`—gets the totalSlices value
- `getTotalTime`—gets the totalTime value
- `setTotalSlices`—sets the totalSlices value to the argument provided
- `setTotalTime`—sets the totalTime value to the argument provided

```
<?xml version="1.0"?>
<scpd xmlns=
  "urn:schemas-intoast-com:supertoaster-service-1-0>
  <specVersion>
  <major>1</major>
  <minor>0</minor>
  </specVersion>
  <actionList>
    ...
  </actionList>
  <serviceStateTable>
    <stateVariable sendEvents="no">
      <name>totalSlices</name>
      <dataType>ui4</dataType>
      <defaultValue>0</defaultValue>
    </stateVariable>
    <stateVariable sendEvents="no">
      <name>totalTime</name>
      <dataType>time</dataType>
      <defaultValue>0</defaultValue>
    </stateVariable>
  </serviceStateTable>
</scpd>
```

Figure 13.4 Lifetime Stats Service State Variables

Each of these actions must be included in your service description document. For each action, you must define the following:

- name—required name of the action; this is, in effect, the function call name.
- argumentList—required list of arguments for the action, and for each:
  - — `name` is the required argument (parameter) name
  - — `direction` is the required direction of the parameter, in or out
  - — `retval` is an optional specification that one (and only one) out argument is a return value; must be the first defined out argument in the argumentList
  - — `requiredStateVariable` is a required specification of an associated service state variable for the argument

For these properties, all are required with the exception of the retval specification for each argument, which is optional. Referring to Figure 13.5, you can see the definition of the `getTotalSlices` action, which takes no parameters, but does return the unsigned integer value of the total slices:

```
<?xml version="1.0"?>
<scpd xmlns="urn:schemas-intoast-com:supertoaster-service-1-0">
  ...
  <actionList>
    <action>
      <name>getTotalSlices</name>
      <argumentList>
        <argument>
          <name>totalSlices</name>
          <direction>out</direction>
          <retval />
          <relatedStateVariable>totalSlices
            </relatedStateVariable>
        </argument>
      </argumentList>
    </action>
  </actionList>
  <serviceStateTable>
...
  </serviceStateTable>
</scpd>
```

Figure 13.5 Lifetime Statistics, getTotalSlices Action

For this action, you have specified an out direction for the single argument and have added the `retval` declarator to specify that this is the return value for the action. You have also made sure to relate it to the corresponding state variable in the `serviceStateTable`, `totalSlices`. This is an important step that's easy to forget.

But I Don't Want to Specify a State Variable!

Most people new to the UPnP architecture wonder why it's required to specify an associated state variable for each action parameter. It often seems wasteful to create a state variable that you'll never use just so you can accept a parameter or two.

The parallel in structured programming would be a requirement that every parameter into a function must also have a corresponding global variable to match the parameter. Clearly this seems wasteful, so why the requirement?

This is a very good question to which a clear answer doesn't exist. The best explanation for this is that this requirement is a legacy leftover from the early days of UPnP, when early designers felt actions would only be used to update device state variables.

Since that time actions and other advanced features have been added to the UPnP architecture, but the requirement to have an associated state variable for each action parameter remains.

With one action completed, you can now define the `getTotalTime` action for the Lifetime Statistics service, shown in Figure 13.6.

All that remains is to define the two set actions for your two state variables. The definition of these actions is very similar to their "get" counterparts with two small differences: The direction of the parameter is reversed to the "in" direction, and you no longer have a return value for the function.

Figure 13.7 shows the complete lifetime statistics service description.

```
<?xml version="1.0"?>
<scpd xmlns=
"urn:schemas-intoast-com:supertoaster-service-1-0">
    ...
    <action>
      <name>getTotalTime</name>
      <argumentList>
      <argument>
        <name>totalTime</name>
        <direction>out</direction>
        <retval />
        <relatedStateVariable>totalTime
          </relatedStateVariable>
        </argument>
      </argumentList>
    </action>
  </actionList>
  <serviceStateTable>
...
  </serviceStateTable>
</scpd>
```

Figure 13.6 Lifetime Stats `getTotalTime` Action

```
<?xml version="1.0"?>
<scpd xmlns=
"urn:schemas-intoast-com:supertoaster-service-1-0">
  <specVersion>
  <major>1</major>
  <minor>0</minor>
  </specVersion>
  <actionList>
    <action>
      <name>getTotalSlices</name>
      <argumentList>
        <argument>
          <name>totalSlices</name>
          <direction>out</direction>
          <retval />
          <relatedStateVariable>totalSlices
            </relatedStateVariable>
        </argument>
      </argumentList>
    </action>
```

Figure 13.7 Complete Lifetime Statistics Service Description *(Continues)*

```
    <action>
      <name>getTotalTime</name>
      <argumentList>
        <argument>
          <name>totalTime</name>
          <direction>out</direction>
          <retval />
          <relatedStateVariable>totalTime
            </relatedStateVariable>
        </argument>
      </argumentList>
    </action>
    <action>
      <name>setTotalSlices</name>
      <argumentList>
        <argument>
          <name>totalSlices</name>
          <direction>in</direction>
          <relatedStateVariable>totalSlices
            </relatedStateVariable>
        </argument>
      </argumentList>
    </action>
    <action>
      <name>setTotalTime</name>
      <argumentList>
        <argument>
          <name>totalTime</name>
          <direction>in</direction>
          <relatedStateVariable>totalTime
            </relatedStateVariable>
        </argument>
      </argumentList>
    </action>
  </actionList>
  <serviceStateTable>
    <stateVariable sendEvents="no">
      <name>totalSlices</name>
      <dataType>ui4</dataType>
      <defaultValue>0</defaultValue>
    </stateVariable>
    <stateVariable sendEvents="no">
      <name>totalTime</name>
```

Figure 13.7 Complete Lifetime Statistics Service Description *(Continues)*

```
      <dataType>time</dataType>
      <defaultValue>0</defaultValue>
    </stateVariable>
  </serviceStateTable>
</scpd>
```

Figure 13.7 Complete Lifetime Statistics Service Description

To Retval or Not to Retval

With so many different ways to return a value from a UPnP action, you may be wondering why retval is required at all if you can just specify a parameter with an out direction; both values will make it back to the calling control point.

The answer lies simply in the correlation between UPnP actions and traditional structured programming syntax. For example, if you have implemented a function in C that performs the same function as your getTotalSlices action, you could define the function like this:

```
int getTotalSlices();
```

where the return value is the value of totalSlices. This is how you defined your action, specifying the retval property for the output parameter. However, you could also just as well define this function as follows:

```
void getTotalSlices(int *slices);
```

In this case, the function doesn't explicitly return anything, but through a integer pointer you can send "out" the same value for the total number of slices. Both functions serve the same purpose and both would have out parameters designated for the action. But, for the latter definition, you would omit the retval declarator and define the action to simply have an out argument.

So, in the end it comes down to style. Just as some engineers would implement functions with integer return values, others would insist on void return values, providing the result through by-reference parameters. The same flexibility exists in the UPnP architecture.

That completes the definition of the Lifetime Statistics service. Later you'll see how to handle these actions in your device implementation, but first you have one more service to define.

Toaster Control Service

Recall from Chapter 12 that the Toaster Control service was defined to allow a control point to change the physical properties of the device. This includes the following:

- Raise or lower the toast lever
- Adjust the darkness setting

These two capabilities fit nicely into a few control-style actions. You'll create three new actions with the following functions:

- Raise Lever
- Depress Lever
- Adjust Darkness Setting

Start first with the Raise Lever and Depress Lever actions. The hardware engineers at InToast are so confident in their design that they have told us that the toaster will never fail to raise or lower the lever when controlled by software. You'll assume they are correct and take that into consideration when defining your action. Since the action is not returning anything back to the calling control point, you can define this action as shown in Figure 13.8.

```
<?xml version="1.0"?>
<scpd xmlns=
"urn:intoast-com:supertoaster-service-1-0">
  <specVersion>
    <major>1</major>
    <minor>0</minor>
  </specVersion>
  <actionList>
    <action>
      <name>liftLever</name>
    </action>
    <action>
      <name>depressLever</name>
    </action>
  </actionList>
  <serviceStateTable>
  </serviceStateTable>
</scpd>
```

Figure 13.8 Toaster Control Service Description, Part 1

There are a few interesting things to note about this service description. First, the Raise Lever and Depress Lever actions have no arguments or return values. Although their definition in the service description document certainly looks like it is missing something, it is nonetheless a perfectly valid action description.

Furthermore, you have not defined any state variables for these actions in the `serviceStateTable`. This may seem strange, but is perfectly acceptable. Because you do not have any arguments for these actions, you are free from defining any state variables as well.

For the remaining action, `adjustDarkness`, you know that you'll have one input argument to specify the desired darkness setting. In this case you have not received a strict guarantee from the hardware team that this dial will perform as expected, so you should return to the calling control point the new value of the darkness state variable just to make sure.

You also know that from your product requirements in Chapter 10, the dial has a defined range of 1 to 5, with 5 being the darkest setting and 1 being the lightest. So, what if the control point application provides you with a value outside of that range? Fortunately, UPnP provides a built-in capability to inform control points about parameter ranges. You can take advantage of the allowed range specifiers for the darkness state variable, as you see in Figure 13.9.

Adding ranges for your state variables is not always a guarantee that control points will respect the range and not invoke actions with data outside the specified range. For this reason, device implementers should still be sure to check all incoming values before assuming they're within an acceptable range.

This XML service description satisfies all requirements from the functional requirements in Chapter 10. Yet as many experienced software engineers know, that doesn't always mean your job is done. There is one problem with the service description you have created: How can a control point know what current state the device is in when it connects? Although you can get the darkness value by trying to set it, you don't want to override what the user has already configured. Furthermore, you have no capability to understand what state the toasting lever is in.

You could certainly specify default values in the service description, but that may not always be enough. Just because a control point connects to a device doesn't mean that the device will revert back to its factory default state. More likely, the device has been running for quite some time and you have no idea what current state the device is in.

```
<?xml version="1.0"?>
<scpd xmlns=
"urn:intoast-com:supertoaster-service-1-0">
  ...
  <actionList>
     ...
    <action>
       <name>adjustDial</name>
       <argumentList>
         <argument>
           <name>dialSetting</name>
           <direction>in</name>
           <relatedStateVariable>darkness
             </relatedStateVariable>
         </argument>
         <argument>
           <name>newDarkness</name>
           <direction>out</direction>
           <relatedStateVariable>darkness
             </relatedStateVariable>
         </argument>
       </argumentList>
    </action>
  </actionList>
  <serviceStateTable>
    <stateVariable sendEvents="no"</stateVariable>
      <name>darkness</name>
      <dataType>ui1</dataType>
      <defaultValue>3</defaultValue>
      <allowedValueRange>
        <minimum>1</minimum>
        <maximum>5</maximum>
        <step>1</step>
      </allowedValueRange>
    </stateVariable>
  </serviceStateTable>
</scpd>
```

Figure 13.9 Toaster Control Service Description, Part 2

For your toaster, think of the last user of the device. They may have previously adjusted the toast darkness settings. For this reason, you need to provide some mechanism by which the control point can determine the current state of the device.

The easiest way to accomplish this is to provide a fourth action that returns the current status of the device. You'll call this action GetDeviceStatus, and it will return the boolean state of the lever and the integer state of the darkness dial. The definition of GetDeviceStatus is shown in Figure 13.10.

```
<?xml version="1.0"?>
<scpd xmlns=
"urn:intoast-com:supertoaster-service-1-0">
  ...
  <actionList>
    <action>
      <name>GetDeviceStatus</name>
      <argumentList>
        <argument>
          <name>leverState</name>
          <direction>out</direction>
          <relatedStateVariable>leverState
            </relatedStateVariable>
        </argument>
        <argument>
          <name>darkness</name>
          <direction>out</direction>
          <relatedStateVariable>darkness
            </relatedStateVariable>
        </argument>
      </argumentList>
    </action>
  </actionList>
  <serviceStateTable>
    <stateVariable sendEvents="no"</stateVariable>
      <name>leverState</name>
      <dataType>boolean</dataType>
      <defaultValue>false</defaultValue>
    </stateVariable>
    <stateVariable sendEvents="no"</stateVariable>
      <name>darkness</name>
      <dataType>ui1</dataType>
      <defaultValue>5</defaultValue>
      <allowedValueRange>
        <minimum>1</minimum>
        <maximum>5</maximum>
        <step>1</step>
```

Figure 13.10 Toaster Control Service, Part 3 *(Continues)*

```
      </allowedValueRante>
    </stateVariable>
  </serviceStateTable>
</scpd>
```

Figure 13.10 Toaster Control Service, Part 3

Note that in order to support this action, you had to add a state variable for the lever state because you specified it as an out argument.

This service provides a simple interface that polls the device to determine its status. Traditionally, polling-style interfaces are not the most efficient. In the next chapter, you learn how you can improve this interface to support dynamic events.

This brings to a close your design for the control service. Next you learn how to handle the remote invocation of these actions in your code.

Supporting Service Action Invocation

You're making pretty good progress on your device. You have successfully completed the description phase and now have two out of three service description documents completed. The UPnP library will be listening on your interfaces for incoming action requests. When these requests are received, they are dispatched to your application code. How? Good question.

Recall that in the previous chapter, you made a call to `UpnpRegisterRootDevice()` to register your device with the UPnP library. One of the parameters to this function call was a pointer to a callback handler. To refresh your memory, Figure 13.11 shows the bit of code that did that from your device initialization function.

You pass in the device callback function in the second parameter, which has the following defined type:

```
typedef int  (*Upnp_FunPtr) (
    IN Upnp_EventType EventType,
    IN void *Event,
    IN void *Cookie );
```

Whenever the UPnP library receives network communication directed toward your registered device that is not automatically handled by the library, it calls your device callback function.

```
/*
 * Register your root device with the UpnP library.
 * This call will automatically set your base URL.
 */
ret = UpnpRegisterRootDevice2(UPNPREG_FILENAME_DESC,
                              descpath,
                              0, 1, upnp_callback,
                              &g_device_handle,
                              &g_device_handle);
if(ret != UPNP_E_SUCCESS) {
  printf("upnp_init: UpnpRegisterRootDevice2 failed with
    code: %d\n", ret);
  return ret;
}
```

Figure 13.11 Root Device Registration

The type of events that you're concerned with in this chapter are action requests for the services that you've defined. You add support to the `upnp.c` module, for a `upnp_callback()` function as shown in Figure 13.12.

```
/*
 * Function: upnp_callback
 *
 * Parameters: Upnp_Event type indicating the specific
 *             callback event, pointer to the event itself,
 *             and cookie information.
 *
 * Returns: UPNP_E_SUCCESS if everything worked,
 *          UPNP_E_INVALID_ARGS if the event is NULL,
 *          and your cookie.
 *
 * Description: This function handles all callback events
 *              from the UPnP Library. It dispatches events
 *              to their specific event handlers.
 */
int upnp_callback(Upnp_EventType eventtype, void *event,
void *cookie)
{
  int ret=0;      /* General purpose return code */
```

Figure 13.12 Device Callback *(Continues)*

```
  printf("upnp_callback: start\n");

  /* Check your parameters */
  if(event == NULL) {
    printf("upnp_callback: NULL event structure\n");
    return UPNP_E_BAD_REQUEST;
  }

  /* Dispatch the event based on event type. */
  switch(eventtype) {
    case UPNP_CONTROL_ACTION_REQUEST:
      /* A control point is invoking an action. */
      printf("upnp_callback: UPNP_CONTROL_ACTION_REQUEST\n");
      ret = upnp_actions((struct Upnp_Action_Request *)event);
      break;
    default:
      /* An unhandled event type */
      printf("upnp_callback: unsupported event type: %d\n",
             eventtype);
      ret = UPNP_E_BAD_REQUEST;
      break;
  }

  printf("upnp_callback: end\n");

  return ret;
}
```

Figure 13.12 Device Callback

You implement this function with a switch statement because as you continue to add capabilities to your device in future chapters you'll simply add new cases.The implementation of the `upnp_actions()` function is covered below.

Once in your device handler, you can handle the specific action as you see fit. But how do you know what specific action on what service was invoked? Thankfully, the UPnP library provides a `Upnp_Action_Request` structure that contains useful information for handling action requests. You pass this structure, defined in `upnp.h`, and shown in Figure 13.13, into your `action_request()` handler.

There are a couple of fields in this structure that are particularly useful and important. The `ActionRequest` member is a DOM document representation of the actual SOAP request your device received. If you need to get specific parameters from the SOAP request packet, or feel

```
struct Upnp_Action_Request
{
  /** The result of the operation. */
  int ErrCode;

  int Socket;

  /** The error string in case of error. */
  char ErrStr[LINE_SIZE];

  /** The Action Name. */
  char ActionName[NAME_SIZE];

  /** The unique device ID. */
  char DevUDN[NAME_SIZE];

  /** The service ID. */
  char ServiceID[NAME_SIZE];

  /** The DOM document describing the action. */
  IXML_Document ActionRequest;

  /** The DOM document describing the result of the
      action. */
  IXML_Document ActionResult;

  /** IP Address of the control point requesting
      this action. */
  struct in_addr CtrlPtIPAddr;

  /** The DOM document containing the information
      from the SOAP header. */
  IXML_Document *SoapHeader;

};
```

Figure 13.13 UPnP Action Request Structure

like parsing the request packet yourself, this is the member that provides you with the necessary information.

Fortunately, the Intel SDK automatically extracts a few of the most useful fields of the SOAP request packet. The first is the `ActionName`, which matches one of the ActionName fields that you defined in your original service description document. Speaking of services, this structure also contains a `ServiceID` and a `DeviceUDN`, that should match, respectively, the service ID and device UDN you specified in your device description document.

These two fields have important uses in your implementation. You should always check to see that the DevUDN matches your device. For devices with multiple root devices, a single callback handler could actually support all devices, by first looking at the DevUDN to determine which device the callback is targeted for.

The ServiceID field is also very useful, because it is the only way to determine what the service for the invoked action is. The service action names only need to be unique for that given service, meaning that you could easily have two services with identically named actions. Without the ServiceID to match them against, you would never be able to tell what service the action is for.

The next two members of the structure are ErrCode and ActionResult. If an action completes successfully, it is your responsibility to set the ErrCode to UPNP_E_SUCCESS. Otherwise, the UPnP library sends an error response back to the calling device after calling your handler. The ActionResult member is a DOM document that represents the SOAP action response without parameters, return values, and other useful information. Later, you'll find out how to create the action response.

The final two members of the structure are useful when the device absolutely must know all information about the request being made. Via the CtrlPtIPAddr and SoapHeader information you can determine exactly which control point invoked your action and review SOAP header information that packaged the action request.

You now have enough information to begin to implement a UPnP action handler. You'll start by making sure the call is to your device, and then try to match the serviceId field with the service IDs for the defined Super Toaster services; then, if matched, you'll pass the Upnp_Action_Request structure to the appropriate service handler, as shown in Figure 13.14.

```
/*
 * Funtion: upnp_actions
 *
 * Paramters: pointer to a Upnp_Action_Request structure
 *
 * Returns: UPNP_E_SUCCESS if successful, service handler error
 *          code if not.
 *
```

Figure 13.14 Action Request Handler *(Continues)*

```
 * Description: This function dispatches an action invocation
 *              request to the specific service handler by
 *              matching up the serviceId of the requested
 *              action.
 */
int upnp_actions(struct Upnp_Action_Request *request)
{
  int ret=0;      /* General purpose return code */

  printf("upnp_actions: start\n");

  /* First check if the request structure is valid */
  if(request == NULL) {
    printf("upnp_actions: request pointer is NULL\n");
    return UPNP_E_BAD_REQUEST;
  }

  /* Make sure this request is for your device. */
  if(strcmp(request->DevUDN, g_deviceudn) != 0) {
    /* It's not for us. */
    printf("upnp_actions: request not for your device\n");
    return UPNP_E_BAD_REQUEST;
  }

  /* You need to match the serviceID to one of your services. */
  if(strcmp(request->ServiceID, LIFETIME_STATS_SERVICEID)==0){
  {
    /* It's a call for the Lifetime Stats Service. */
    printf("upnp_actions: request for Lifetime Status
             Service\n");
    ret = upnp_lsactions(request);
  } else if(strcmp(request->ServiceID,
             TOASTER_CONTROL_SERVICEID) == 0) {
    /* It's a call for the Toaster Control Service. */
    printf("upnp_actions: request for Toaster Control
             Service\n");
    ret = upnp_tcactions(request);
  } else {
     /*
      * The control point is asking for a service that doesn't
      * exist, or a service that doesn't support any actions.
      */
    ret = UPNP_E_BAD_REQUEST;
  }

  return ret;
}
```

Figure 13.14 Action Request Handler

Things are starting to look pretty good. You have a good chunk of framework code that allows you to easily add implementation code for each of the supported actions, based on the service identifier. Before you get to that, there some important things to know about this code.

First, if you are unable to match the `ServiceID` with one that your device supports, you set the error code to `UPNP_E_BAD_REQUEST`. Although it may seem you have drawn this constant out of thin air, it does have special meaning for UPnP devices. The UPnP Device Architecture specification defines a set of error codes that device implementers may return. The value 401 indicates that an invalid action name was given. Table 13.2 summarizes the most frequently used error codes.

Constant definitions of some of these error codes are included in toaster.h, with the rest already defined in upnp.h. Before you begin to implement your actions, you must first look at the format of a SOAP response packet. Recall that all action invocations are sent to your device in the form of a SOAP request packet. At the completion of every action, you must send back a properly formatted SOAP response to the control point. Specifically, you must create a SOAP packet with the format shown in Figure 13.15, as specified by the UPnP Device Architecture specification.

The UPnP library automatically creates an envelope for you, but you need to craft a string representing the body of the SOAP packet. You must fill in the actionName, serviceType, and argumentName with the values appropriate to your device.

Table 13.2 UPnP Device Architecture Error Codes*

Error Code Value	Description
401	Invalid Action: Not able to match an action by the given name at this service
402	Invalid Args: Something was wrong with the arguments provided
403	Out of synchronization
501	Action Failed

* For the complete list of error codes, refer to the UPnP Device Architecture Specification.

```
<s:Envelope
  xmlns:s="http://schemas.xmlsoap.org/soap/envelope/"
  s:encodingStyle="http://schemas.xmlsoap.org/soap/encoding/">
  <s:Body>
    <u:actionNameResponse xmlns:u="serviceType">
<argumentName>out arg value</argumentName>
  ...
</u:actionNameResponse>
  </s:Body>
</s:Envelope>
```

Figure 13.15 SOAP Envelope for Action Responses

It is not enough to just create this SOAP response string, however. Recall from the definition of the `Upnp_Action_Response` structure, that the `ActionResponse` member was a DOM Document. You must convert your string into a DOM Document using the following function:

```
IXML_Document *ixmlParseBuffer(IN const char *dom_str)
```

`dom_str`—XML string that can be parsed into a DOM document.

Returns: DOM Document representing the XML string passed in.

With that understood, you are now ready to implement support for your actions. You begin with the most basic of all actions, those in the Toaster Control service that accept no arguments and have no out arguments. All functions relating to the Toaster Control service are implemented in the file `upnptc.c`. You'll also prefix the letters "`tc`", for toaster control, to all functions in this module. In this way, the casual reader of the code can always tell what service module is supporting that function. Figure 13.16 shows a listing of the function `upnp_tcactions()`, which supports all action invocation for the Toaster Control service.

In `upnp_tcactions()`, you first check the validity of the request structure (just in case) and then simply try to match up the requested action name with those actions supported in the Toaster Control service.

```
/*
 * Function: upnp_tcactions
 *
 * Paramters: pointer to a Upnp_Action_Request structure
 *
 * Returns: UPNP_E_SUCCESS if everything worked, UPnP
 *          specification defined error code if not.
 *
 * Description: This function dispatches actions within the
 *              Toaster Control Service.
 */
int upnp_tcactions(struct Upnp_Action_Request *request)
{
  int ret = UPNP_E_SUCCESS;  /* General purpose return code */

  printf("upnp_tcactions: start\n");

  /* Make sure your pointer isn't null. */
  if(request == NULL) {
    printf("upnp_tcactions: request pointer is NULL\n");
    return UPNP_E_BAD_REQUEST;
  }

  /* Match up the action name with those you support. */
  if(strcmp(request->ActionName, "liftLever") == 0) {
    /* Call the handler for the liftLever action. */
    ret = upnp_liftlever(request);
  } else if(strcmp(request->ActionName, "depressLever") == 0)
{
    /* Call the handler for the depressLever action. */
    ret = upnp_depresslever(request);
  } else if(strcmp(request->ActionName, "adjustDial") == 0) {
    /* Call the handler for the adjustDial action. */
    ret = upnp_adjustdial(request);
  } else if(strcmp(request->ActionName, "getDeviceStatus")
          == 0) {
    /* Call the handler for the getDeviceStatus action. */
    ret = upnp_getdevicestatus(request);
  } else {
    /* Unrecognized action */
    printf("upnp_tcactions: unrecognized action: %s\n",
          request->ActionName);
    request->ErrCode = UPNP_E_INVALID_ACTION;
    ret = UPNP_E_INVALID_ACTION;
  }

  return ret;
}
```

Figure 13.16 upnp_tcactions() Code Listing

You'll first consider the depressLever and liftLever actions. Since all the work for these actions is done internally to your device (to lift or depress the lever), all you need to do is make sure that has been done without error before setting ErrCode to UPNP_E_SUCCESS and crafting your action response. Figure 13.17 lists code to support these actions in the upnptc.c module.

```
/*
 * Function: upnp_liftlever
 *
 * Parameters: pointer to a Upnp_Action_Request structure
 *
 * Returns: UPNP_E_SUCCESS if successful, UPnP specification
 *          defined error code if not
 *
 * Description: This function handles the "liftLever" action
 *              for the Toaster Control Service.
 */
int upnp_liftlever(struct Upnp_Action_Request *request)
{
  int ret=0;                /* General purpose return code */
  char result_str[512];     /* Our soap response packet */

  printf("upnp_liftlever: start\n");

  /* First call the HW interface library function. */
  ret = hw_liftlever();
  if(ret == TOASTER_SUCCESS) {
    printf("upnp_liftlever: hw_liftlever succeded\n");

    /* It worked Craft the SOAP body. */
    sprintf(result_str, "<u:%sResponse xmlns:u=\"%s\"> \
                          </u:%sResponse>",
                         request->ActionName,
                         TOASTER_CONTROL_SERVICETYPE,
                         request->ActionName);

    /* Convert it into a DOM. */
    request->ActionResult = ixmlParseBuffer(result_str);

    /* Set the error code. */
    request->ErrCode = UPNP_E_SUCCESS;
  } else {
```

Figure 13.17 liftLever and depressLever Actions *(Continues)*

```
    printf("upnp_liftlever: hw_liftlever failed\n");

    /* It failed, so fail the action. */
    request->ErrCode = UPNP_E_ACTION_FAILED;
  }

  printf("upnp_liftlever: end\n");

  return request->ErrCode;
}


/*
 * Function: upnp_depresslever
 *
 * Parameters: pointer to a Upnp_Action_Request structure
 *
 * Returns: UPNP_E_SUCCESS if successful, UPnP specification
 *          defined error code if not
 *
 * Description: This function handles the "depressLever"
 *              action for the Toaster Control Service.
 */
int upnp_depresslever(struct Upnp_Action_Request *request)
{
  int ret=0;              /* General purpose error code */
  char result_str[512];   /* SOAP packet body response */

  printf("upnp_depresslever: start\n");

  /* First call the HW interface library function. */
  ret = hw_depresslever();
  if(ret == TOASTER_SUCCESS) {
    printf("upnp_depresslever: hw_depresslever succeded\n");

    /* It worked Craft the SOAP body. */
    sprintf(result_str, "<u:%sResponse xmlns:u=\"%s\"> \
                         </u:%sResponse>",
                        request->ActionName,
                        TOASTER_CONTROL_SERVICETYPE,
                        request->ActionName);

    /* Convert it into a DOM. */
    request->ActionResult = ixmlParseBuffer(result_str);
```

Figure 13.17 liftLever and depressLever Actions *(Continues)*

```
    /* Set the error code. */
    request->ErrCode = UPNP_E_SUCCESS;
  } else {
    printf("upnp_depresslever: hw_liftlever failed\n");

    /* It failed, so fail the action. */
    request->ErrCode = UPNP_E_ACTION_FAILED;
  }

  printf("upnp_depresslever: end\n");

  return request->ErrCode;
}
```

Figure 13.17 `liftLever` and `depressLever` Actions

Now carefully review this code. For the first time, you're seeing an invocation of a function in your hardware library. All functions in the hardware library are implemented in toasterhw.c, and have the characters "hw_" prefacing them.

After calling the appropriate "hw" interface library function to perform the requested task, you must craft the body of the SOAP response packet:

```
/* It worked Craft the SOAP body */
sprintf(result_str, "<u:%sResponse xmlns:u=\"%s\"> \
                     </u:%sResponse>",
                    request->ActionName,
                    TOASTER_CONTROL_SERVICETYPE,
                    request->ActionName);
```

This matches exactly the format for the Body specified in the UPnP Device Architecture specification. This string must be properly formed, otherwise control point parsers may not be able to read the response. Then finally, you convert the string into a DOM document using the newly introduced `Upnp_ParseBuffer()` function and set the `ErrCode` field to `UPNP_E_SUCCESS`.

You have now finished writing two of your actions! You have introduced quite a bit of additional complexity and structure to your code. Make sure you understand what you've completed thus far before continuing. You will be using the basic framework created here to support all future work.

The DOM

If you're new to XML you've probably never heard of the Document Object Model, also known as DOM. DOM is a World Wide Web Consortium (W3C) recommendation to represent XML and other similar document styles in a well-defined object model.

The idea behind DOM is that each UPnP XML device has a clear concept of parent and child nodes, starting with the <root> node, and each sub-node underneath root, such as your UPnP <device>. These nodes, in a DOM document, get stored in a tree-like format with a concept of parent, child, and sibling nodes. Leaf values at a node are the text between two tags in an XML document.

If you have an XML document represented as a DOM document, then you can search it just like it was a tree, starting at the root, looking for children, and finally finding the value you're looking for at a leaf node.

The Intel SDK uses the DOM to store XML documents ranging from your original device description document to the SOAP action requests and responses you're using in this chapter. The Intel SDK supports the complete Level 2 DOM specification, and the SDK API documentation contains a complete list of interfaces for managing DOM documents.

For your device development, this book attempts to shield you as much as possible from the complexities of DOM; however, it will come up every so often, so it's important to understand the concept and how it works. For more information on DOM, please refer to `http://www.w3.org/DOM/`.

Now you'll mix things up a bit by adding support for the `AdjustDial` action. This action is different from the previous two in that it has an out argument specified as a return value that you need to include in the SOAP response string. For out arguments tagged as return values, you must frame the value of the out argument in the SOAP response packet with:

```
<ReturnValue> </ReturnValue>
```

Recall from your service description that the `AdjustDial` action accepts a single input argument for the new dial setting. You need to get this parameter somehow so you can adjust the dial to that setting. Although the UPnP library doesn't support this capability natively, the utility files included in the SDK samples do. Look for the files `sample_util.c` and `sample_util.h` in the `upnpsdk-1.0.4/samples/tvdevice` folder to add this support to your device. You'll recognize functions from these files, because they'll be prefaced with `SampleUtil_`.

The Upnp_Action_Request structure you introduced earlier has a member called ActionRequest that is a UPnP DOM document of the actual SOAP action request. Everything—from the name of the action invoked, to the service id, to the parameters provided by the calling control point—is included in this DOM document. This is where the SampleUtil_GetFirstDocumentItem() utility function comes in. Parsing DOM documents by hand is a surprisingly difficult chore. Thankfully, the following function does this dirty work for you, returning only the value you're interested in:

```
char* SampleUtil_GetFirstDocumentItem(
                    IN IXML_Document ActionRequest,
                    IN char *NodeName)
```

ActionRequest—The name of the action request you're processing.

NodeName—The specific node name that you want to get the value for.

Returns: Pointer to a string of the value that you're looking for.

With this function at your disposal, you're now ready to add support for the AdjustDial action, complete with retrieving a parameter value and providing a return value in your XML response as shown in Figure 13.18.

```
/*
 * Function: upnp_adjustdial
 *
 * Parameters: pointer to a Upnp_Action_Request structure
 *
 * Returns: UPNP_E_SUCCESS if successful, UPnP specification
 *          defined error code if not
 *
 * Description: This function handles the "adjustDial" action
 *              for the Toaster Control Service.
 */
int upnp_adjustdial(struct Upnp_Action_Request *request)
{
  int ret=0;             /* General purpose error code */
  char result_str[512]; /* SOAP packet body response */
  char *value=NULL;      /* SOAP parameter */
```

Figure 13.18 Code Listing for adjustDial Action *(Continues)*

```
int dialvalue=0;      /* The value you want to set your dial*/

printf("upnp_adjustdial: start\n");

/* First, you need to extract the new dial value parameter. */
value = SampleUtil_GetFirstDocumentItem(
              request->ActionRequest,
              "dialSetting");

/* Make sure it worked. */
if(value == NULL) {
  printf("upnp_adjustdial: couldn't retrieve dialSetting
          value\n");
  request->ErrCode = UPNP_E_ACTION_FAILED;
  return request->ErrCode;
}

/* Convert it to an integer. */
dialvalue = atoi(value);

/* Now, call the HW interface library function. */
ret = hw_setdialvalue(dialvalue);
if(ret == TOASTER_SUCCESS) {
  printf("upnp_liftlever: hw_liftlever succeded\n");

  /* It worked Craft the SOAP body. */
  sprintf(result_str, "<u:%sResponse xmlns:u=\"%s\"> \
                       <ReturnValue>%d</ReturnValue> \
                       </u:%sResponse>",
                      request->ActionName,
                      TOASTER_CONTROL_SERVICETYPE,
                      dialvalue,
                      request->ActionName);

  /* Convert it into a DOM. */
  request->ActionResult = ixmlParseBuffer(result_str);

  /* Set the error code. */
  request->ErrCode = UPNP_E_SUCCESS;
} else {
  printf("upnp_liftlever: hw_liftlever failed\n");

  /* It failed, so fail the action. */
  request->ErrCode = UPNP_E_ACTION_FAILED;
}
```

Figure 13.18 Code Listing for adjustDial Action *(Continues)*

```
  printf("upnp_adjustdial: end\n");

  return request->ErrCode;
}
```

Figure 13.18 Code Listing for adjustDial Action

Pay careful attention to the slightly different formatting of the action response to support the return value.

So far so good! With these basic tools, you can now add support for nearly every kind of action. Yet there remains one slight variation on the action support you have implemented thus far: actions with multiple out parameters.

Multiple Out Parameters

There is one action left to implement that is different from all previous actions you've implemented thus far. The getDeviceStatus action has two output parameters instead of one and does not explicitly specify one to be the return value.

Strange as this may seem, it's perfectly acceptable. Recall the earlier discussion of C programming techniques and UPnP actions. Chances are you have written functions that had a return value with very little use but that had multiple pass-by-reference parameters that returned useful information.

UPnP actions are the same way. There is no requirement to have a return value at all, and devices are free to support as many output parameters as they want. The significant difference for you as a device implementer is how you construct the return SOAP packet.

For actions that have a single output value that is specified as a return value, the value (as you saw in the implementations just shown) is framed by <ReturnValue> tags.

So what should you do in the case of multiple out arguments? It's really quite simple: Just continue to list them one after the other using the argument name as the tag:

```
<var1name>var1value</var1name>
<var2name>var2value</var2name>
...
```

The same method also applies to the case where a return value is specified (Remember that it can only be on the first out parameter), and then the rest of the out parameters follow:

```
<ReturnValue>var1value</ReturnValue>
<var2name>var2value</var2name>
<var3name>var3value</var3name>
```

When listing multiple parameters, the order must be the same as listed in the service description because that's how the control point application is going to expect them.

The following implementation of the `getDeviceStatus` action shown in Figure 13.19 illustrates this technique.

```
/*
 * Function: upnp_getdevicestatus
 *
 * Parameters: pointer to a Upnp_Action_Request structure
 *
 * Returns: UPNP_E_SUCCESS if successful, UPnP specification
 *          defined error code if not.
 *
 * Description: This function handles the "getDeviceInfo"
 *              action for the Toaster Control Service.
 */
int upnp_getdevicestatus(struct Upnp_Action_Request *request)
{
  char result_str[512];  /* SOAP packet body response */
  int dialvalue=0;       /* The current values of your dial */
  int leverstate=0;      /* The current state of your lever */

  printf("upnp_getdevicestatus: start\n");

  /* First, you need to get the values from your HW library. */
  dialvalue = hw_getdialvalue();
  leverstate = hw_getleverstate();

  /* Now, you need to craft the SOAP body. */
  sprintf(result_str, "<u:%sResponse xmlns:u=\"%s\"> \
                       <%s>%d</%s> \
```

Figure 13.19 Multiple Out Parameters *(Continues)*

```
                                <%s>%d</%s> \
                                </u:%sResponse>",
                                request->ActionName,
                                TOASTER_CONTROL_SERVICETYPE,
                                "leverState",
                                leverstate,
                                "leverState",
                                "darkness",
                                dialvalue,
                                "darkness",
                                request->ActionName);

    /* Convert it into a DOM. */
    request->ActionResult = ixmlParseBuffer(result_str);

    /* Set the error code. */
    request->ErrCode = UPNP_E_SUCCESS;

    printf("upnp_getdevicestatus: end\n");

    return request->ErrCode;
}
```

Figure 13.19 Multiple Out Parameters

Simple as that! You have now covered every possible variation of return values and output arguments in a device service action implementation. With this knowledge you can also easily finish your implementation of action support for the Lifetime Statistics service, included in the code listing shown in Figure 13.20. Following the naming conventions you've been using, all functions relating to the Lifetime Statistics service are contained in a file `upnpls.c`, and all functions in that module include the letters `ls` for Lifetime Statistics.

The Complete Service Action Handlers

Figure 13.20 shows the complete code listing for the Toaster Control service.

```
/*
 * Filename: upnptc.c
 *
 * Description: This file implements support for the Toaster
 *              Control Service actions.
 */

#include <stdlib.h>
#include <unistd.h>
#include <string.h>
#include "toaster.h"
#include "toasterhw.h"

/*
 * Function: upnp_tcactions
 *
 * Paramters: pointer to a Upnp_Action_Request structure
 *
 * Returns: UPNP_E_SUCCESS if everything worked, UPnP
 *          specification defined error code if not.
 *
 * Description: This function dispatches actions within the
 *              Toaster Control Service.
 */
int upnp_tcactions(struct Upnp_Action_Request *request)
{
  int ret = UPNP_E_SUCCESS;     /* General purpose return code */

  printf("upnp_tcactions: start\n");

  /* Make sure your pointer isn't null. */
  if(request == NULL) {
    printf("upnp_tcactions: request pointer is NULL\n");
    return UPNP_E_BAD_REQUEST;
  }

  /* Match up the action name with those you support. */
  if(strcmp(request->ActionName, "liftLever") == 0) {
    /* Call the handler for the liftLever action. */
    ret = upnp_liftlever(request);
  } else if(strcmp(request->ActionName, "depressLever") == 0) {
    /* Call the handler for the depressLever action. */
    ret = upnp_depresslever(request);
  } else if(strcmp(request->ActionName, "adjustDial") == 0) {
    /* Call the handler for the adjustDial action. */
    ret = upnp_adjustdial(request);
```

Figure 13.20 Complete Listing of Toaster Control Module *(Continues)*

```
  } else if(strcmp(request->ActionName, "getDeviceStatus")
          == 0) {
    /* Call the handler for the getDeviceStatus action. */
    ret = upnp_getdevicestatus(request);
  } else {
    /* Unrecognized action */
    printf("upnp_tcactions: unrecognized action: %s\n",
      request->ActionName);
    request->ErrCode = UPNP_E_INVALID_ACTION;
    ret = UPNP_E_INVALID_ACTION;
  }

  return ret;
}

/*
 * Function: upnp_liftlever
 *
 * Parameters: pointer to a Upnp_Action_Request structure
 *
 * Returns: UPNP_E_SUCCESS if successful, UPnP specification
 *          defined error code if not.
 *
 * Description: This function handles the "liftLever" action
 *              for the Toaster Control Service.
 */
int upnp_liftlever(struct Upnp_Action_Request *request)
{
  int ret=0;              /* General purpose return code */
  char result_str[512];   /* Our soap response packet */

  printf("upnp_liftlever: start\n");

  /* First call the HW interface library function. */
  ret = hw_liftlever();
  if(ret == TOASTER_SUCCESS) {
    printf("upnp_liftlever: hw_liftlever succeded\n");

    /* It worked Craft the SOAP body. */
    sprintf(result_str, "<u:%sResponse xmlns:u=\"%s\"> \
                          </u:%sResponse>",
                         request->ActionName,
                         TOASTER_CONTROL_SERVICETYPE,
                         request->ActionName);
```

Figure 13.20 Complete Listing of Toaster Control Module *(Continues)*

```
    /* Convert it into a DOM. */
    request->ActionResult = ixmlParseBuffer(result_str);


    /* Set the error code. */
    request->ErrCode = UPNP_E_SUCCESS;
  } else {
    printf("upnp_liftlever: hw_liftlever failed\n");

    /* It failed, so fail the action. */
    request->ErrCode = UPNP_E_ACTION_FAILED;
  }

  printf("upnp_liftlever: end\n");

  return request->ErrCode;
}


/*
 * Function: upnp_depresslever
 *
 * Parameters: pointer to a Upnp_Action_Request structure
 *
 * Returns: UPNP_E_SUCCESS if successful, UPnP specification
 *          defined error code if not.
 *
 * Description: This function handles the "depressLever" action
 *              for the Toaster Control Service.
 */
int upnp_depresslever(struct Upnp_Action_Request *request)
{
  int ret=0;                /* General purpose error code */
  char result_str[512];     /* SOAP packet body response */

  printf("upnp_depresslever: start\n");

  /* First call the HW interface library function. */
  ret = hw_depresslever();
  if(ret == TOASTER_SUCCESS) {
    printf("upnp_depresslever: hw_depresslever succeded\n");

    /* It worked Craft the SOAP body. */
    sprintf(result_str, "<u:%sResponse xmlns:u=\"%s\"> \
                         </u:%sResponse>",
```

Figure 13.20 Complete Listing of Toaster Control Module *(Continues)*

```
                          request->ActionName,
                          TOASTER_CONTROL_SERVICETYPE,
                          request->ActionName);

    /* Convert it into a DOM. */
    request->ActionResult = ixmlParseBuffer(result_str);

    /* Set the error code. */
    request->ErrCode = UPNP_E_SUCCESS;
  } else {
    printf("upnp_depresslever: hw_liftlever failed\n");

    /* It failed, so fail the action. */
    request->ErrCode = UPNP_E_ACTION_FAILED;
  }

  printf("upnp_depresslever: end\n");

  return request->ErrCode;
}

/*
 * Function: upnp_adjustdial
 *
 * Parameters: pointer to a Upnp_Action_Request structure
 *
 * Returns: UPNP_E_SUCCESS if successful, UPnP specification
 *          defined error code if not.
 *
 * Description: This function handles the "adjustDial" action
 *              for the Toaster Control Service.
 */
int upnp_adjustdial(struct Upnp_Action_Request *request)
{
  int ret=0;              /* General purpose error code */
  char result_str[512];   /* SOAP packet body response */
  char *value=NULL;       /* SOAP parameter */
  int dialvalue=0;    /* The value you want to set your dial */

  printf("upnp_adjustdial: start\n");

  /* First, you need to extract the new dial value parameter. */
  value = SampleUtil_GetFirstDocumentItem(
              request->ActionRequest,
              "dialSetting");
```

Figure 13.20 Complete Listing of Toaster Control Module *(Continues)*

```
  /* Make sure it worked. */
  if(value == NULL) {
    printf("upnp_adjustdial: couldn't retrieve dialSetting
            value\n");
    request->ErrCode = UPNP_E_ACTION_FAILED;
    return request->ErrCode;
  }

  /* Convert it to an integer. */
  dialvalue = atoi(value);

  /* Now, call the HW interface library function. */
  ret = hw_setdialvalue(dialvalue);
  if(ret == TOASTER_SUCCESS) {
    printf("upnp_liftlever: hw_liftlever succeded\n");

    /* It worked Craft the SOAP body. */
    sprintf(result_str, "<u:%sResponse xmlns:u=\"%s\"> \
                         <ReturnValue>%d</ReturnValue> \
                         </u:%sResponse>",
                        request->ActionName,
                        TOASTER_CONTROL_SERVICETYPE,
                        dialvalue,
                        request->ActionName);

    /* Convert it into a DOM. */
    request->ActionResult = ixmlParseBuffer(result_str);

    /* Set the error code. */
    request->ErrCode = UPNP_E_SUCCESS;
  } else {
    printf("upnp_liftlever: hw_liftlever failed\n");

    /* It failed, so fail the action. */
    request->ErrCode = UPNP_E_ACTION_FAILED;
  }
  printf("upnp_adjustdial: end\n");

  return request->ErrCode;
}

/*
 * Function: upnp_getdevicestatus
 *
```

Figure 13.20 Complete Listing of Toaster Control Module *(Continues)*

```
 * Parameters: pointer to a Upnp_Action_Request structure
 *
 * Returns: UPNP_E_SUCCESS if successful, UPnP specification
 *          defined error code if not.
 *

 * Description: This function handles the "getDeviceInfo"
 *              action for the Toaster Control Service.
 */
int upnp_getdevicestatus(struct Upnp_Action_Request *request)
{
  char result_str[512];    /* SOAP packet body response */
  int dialvalue=0;         /* The current values of your dial */
  int leverstate=0;        /* The current state of your lever */

  printf("upnp_getdevicestatus: start\n");

  /* First, you need to get the values from your HW library. */
  dialvalue = hw_getdialvalue();
  leverstate = hw_getleverstate();

  /* Now, you need to craft the SOAP body. */
  sprintf(result_str, "<u:%sResponse xmlns:u=\"%s\"> \
                      <%s>%d</%s> \
                      <%s>%d</%s> \
                      </u:%sResponse>",
                      request->ActionName,
                      TOASTER_CONTROL_SERVICETYPE,
                      "leverState",
                      leverstate,
                      "leverState",
                      "darkness",
                      dialvalue,
                      "darkness",
                      request->ActionName);

  /* Convert it into a DOM. */
  request->ActionResult = ixmlParseBuffer(result_str);

  /* Set the error code. */
  request->ErrCode = UPNP_E_SUCCESS;

  printf("upnp_getdevicestatus: end\n");

  return request->ErrCode;
}
```

Figure 13.20 Complete Listing of Toaster Control Module

Figure 13.21 lists the complete source code for the Lifetime Statistics module.

```
/*
 * Filename: upnpls.c
 *
 * Description: This file implements support for the Lifetime
 *              Stats Service actions.
 */

#include <stdlib.h>
#include <unistd.h>
#include <string.h>
#include "toaster.h"
#include "toasterhw.h"

/*
 * Function: upnp_lsactions
 *
 * Paramters: pointer to a Upnp_Action_Request structure
 *
 * Returns: UPNP_E_SUCCESS if everything worked, UPnP
 *          specification defined error code if not.
 *
 * Description: This function dispatches actions within the
 *              Lifetime Stats Service.
 */
int upnp_lsactions(struct Upnp_Action_Request *request)
{
  int ret = UPNP_E_SUCCESS;   /* General purpose return code */

  printf("upnp_lsactions: start\n");

  /* Make sure your pointer isn't null. */
  if(request == NULL) {
    printf("upnp_lsactions: request pointer is NULL\n");
    return UPNP_E_BAD_REQUEST;
  }

  /* Match up the action name with those you support. */
  if(strcmp(request->ActionName, "getTotalSlices") == 0) {
    /* Call the handler for the getTotalSlices action. */
    ret = upnp_gettotalslices(request);
  } else if(strcmp(request->ActionName, "getTotalTime") == 0) {
```

Figure 13.21 Complete Listing of Lifetime Statistics Module *(Continues)*

```
    /* Call the handler for the getTotalTime action. */
    ret = upnp_gettotaltime(request);
  } else if(strcmp(request->ActionName, "setTotalSlices")==0) {
    /* Call the handler for the setTotalSlices action. */
    ret = upnp_settotalslices(request);
  } else if(strcmp(request->ActionName, "setTotalTime") == 0) {
    /* Call the handler for the setTotalTime action. */
    ret = upnp_settotaltime(request);
  } else {
    /* Unrecognized action */
    printf("upnp_lsactions: unrecognized action: %s\n",
          request->ActionName);
    request->ErrCode = UPNP_E_INVALID_ACTION;
    ret = UPNP_E_INVALID_ACTION;
  }

  printf("upnp_lsactions: end\n");

  return ret;
}


/*
 * Function: upnp_gettotalslices
 *
 * Parameters: pointer to a Upnp_Action_Request structure
 *
 * Returns: UPNP_E_SUCCESS if successful, UPnP specification
 *          defined error code if not.
 *
 * Description: This function handles the "getTotalSlices"
 *              action for the Toaster Control Service.
 */
int upnp_gettotalslices(struct Upnp_Action_Request *request)
{
  char result_str[512];   /* SOAP packet body response */
  int totalslices=0;      /* The value of total slices */

  printf("upnp_gettotalslices: start\n");

  /* Now, call the HW interface library function. */
  totalslices = hw_gettotaltoasts();

  /* It worked Craft the SOAP body. */
```

Figure 13.21 Complete Listing of Lifetime Statistics Module *(Continues)*

```
  sprintf(result_str, "<u:%sResponse xmlns:u=\"%s\"> \
                       <%s>%d</%s> </u:%sResponse>",
                       request->ActionName,
                       LIFETIME_STATS_SERVICETYPE,
                       "totalSlices",
                       totalslices,
                       "totalSlices",
                       request->ActionName);

  /* Convert it into a DOM. */
  request->ActionResult = ixmlParseBuffer(result_str);
  if(request->ActionResult == NULL) {
    printf("NULL Parse Buffer!\n");
  }

  /* Set the error code. */
  request->ErrCode = UPNP_E_SUCCESS;

  printf("upnp_gettotalslices: end\n");

  return request->ErrCode;
}

/*
 * Function: upnp_gettotaltime
 *
 * Parameters: pointer to a Upnp_Action_Request structure
 *
 * Returns: UPNP_E_SUCCESS if successful, UPnP defined error
 *          code if not.
 *
 * Description: This function handles the "getTotalTime" action
 *              for the Toaster Control Service.
 */
int upnp_gettotaltime(struct Upnp_Action_Request *request)
{
  char result_str[512];    /* SOAP packet body response */
  int totaltime=0;         /* The value of total slices */

  printf("upnp_gettotaltime: start\n");

  /* Now, call the HW interface library function. */
  totaltime = hw_gettotaltime();

  /* It worked Craft the SOAP body. */
```

Figure 13.21 Complete Listing of Lifetime Statistics Module *(Continues)*

```
  sprintf(result_str, "<u:%sResponse xmlns:u=\"%s\"> \
                        <%s>%d</%s> \
                        </u:%sResponse>",
                       request->ActionName,
                       LIFETIME_STATS_SERVICETYPE,
                       "totalTime",
                       totaltime,
                       "totalTime",
                       request->ActionName);

  /* Convert it into a DOM. */
  request->ActionResult = ixmlParseBuffer(result_str);

  /* Set the error code. */
  request->ErrCode = UPNP_E_SUCCESS;

  printf("upnp_gettotaltime: end\n");

  return request->ErrCode;
}

/*
 * Function: upnp_settotalslices
 *
 * Parameters: pointer to a Upnp_Action_Request structure
 *
 * Returns: UPNP_E_SUCCESS if successful, UPnP defined error
 *          code if not.
 *
 * Description: This function handles the "setTotalSlices"
 *              action for the Toaster Control Service.
 */
int upnp_settotalslices(struct Upnp_Action_Request *request)
{
  int ret=0;               /* General purpose error code */
  char result_str[512];    /* SOAP packet body response */
  char *value=NULL;        /* The SOAP parameter */
  int totalslices=0;       /* The value of total slices */

  printf("upnp_settotalslices: start\n");

  /* First, you need to extract the new dial value parameter. */
  value = SampleUtil_GetFirstDocumentItem(
              request->ActionRequest,
              "totalSlices");
```

Figure 13.21 Complete Listing of Lifetime Statistics Module *(Continues)*

```
  /* Make sure it worked. */
  if(value == NULL) {
    printf("upnp_settotalslices: couldn't retrieve totalSlices\
            value\n");
    request->ErrCode = UPNP_E_ACTION_FAILED;
    return request->ErrCode;
  }

  /* Convert it to an integer. */
  totalslices = atoi(value);

  /* Now, call the HW interface library function. */
  ret = hw_settotaltoasts(totalslices);
  if(ret == TOASTER_SUCCESS) {
    printf("upnp_settotalslices: hw_settotaltoasts \
succeded\n");

    /* It worked Craft the SOAP body. */
    sprintf(result_str, "<u:%sResponse xmlns:u=\"%s\"> \
                         </u:%sResponse>",
                        request->ActionName,
                        TOASTER_CONTROL_SERVICETYPE,
                        request->ActionName);

    /* Convert it into a DOM. */
    request->ActionResult = ixmlParseBuffer(result_str);

    /* Set the error code. */
    request->ErrCode = UPNP_E_SUCCESS;

  } else {
    printf("upnp_settotalslices: hw_settotaltoasts failed\n");

    /* It failed, so fail the action. */
    request->ErrCode = UPNP_E_ACTION_FAILED;
  }
  printf("upnp_settotalslices: end\n");

  return request->ErrCode;
}

/*
 * Function: upnp_settotaltime
 *
```

Figure 13.21 Complete Listing of Lifetime Statistics Module *(Continues)*

```
 * Parameters: pointer to a Upnp_Action_Request structure
 *
 * Returns: UPNP_E_SUCCESS if successful, UPnP defined error
 *          code if not.
 *
 * Description: This function handles the "setTotalTime" action
 *              for the Toaster Control Service.
 */
int upnp_settotaltime(struct Upnp_Action_Request *request)
{
  int ret=0;              /* General purpose error code */
  char result_str[512];   /* SOAP packet body response */
  char *value=NULL;       /* The SOAP parameter */
  int totaltime=0;        /* The value of total slices */

  printf("upnp_settotaltime: start\n");

  /* First, you need to extract the new dial value parameter. */
  value = SampleUtil_GetFirstDocumentItem(
              request->ActionRequest,
              "totalTime");

  /* Make sure it worked. */
  if(value == NULL) {
    printf("upnp_settotaltime: couldn't retrieve totalSlices value\n");
    request->ErrCode = UPNP_E_ACTION_FAILED;
    return request->ErrCode;
  }

  /* Convert it to an integer. */
  totaltime = atoi(value);

  /* Now, call the HW interface library function. */
  ret = hw_settotaltime(totaltime);
  if(ret == TOASTER_SUCCESS) {
    printf("upnp_settotalslices: hw_settotaltime succeded\n");

    /* It worked Craft the SOAP body. */
    sprintf(result_str, "<u:%sResponse xmlns:u=\"%s\"> \
                          </u:%sResponse>",
                         request->ActionName,
                         TOASTER_CONTROL_SERVICETYPE,
                         request->ActionName);

    /* Convert it into a DOM. */
    request->ActionResult = ixmlParseBuffer(result_str);
```

Figure 13.21 Complete Listing of Lifetime Statistics Module *(Continues)*

```
    /* Set the error code */
    request->ErrCode = UPNP_E_SUCCESS;

  } else {
    printf("upnp_settotalslices: hw_settotaltime failed\n");

    /* It failed, so fail the action. */
    request->ErrCode = UPNP_E_ACTION_FAILED;
  }
  printf("upnp_settotaltime: end\n");

  return request->ErrCode;
}
```

Figure 13.21 Complete Listing of Lifetime Statistics Module

Intel Tools for UPnP Technology

Now that you've completed the service description documents for your device, as well as implemented action invocation support for those services, you can now use the Device Spy to test the functionality of your device.

Device Spy is probably the most useful tool you'll find for UPnP device development. It acts as a universal control point application with the capability to discover devices of any type and also supports the ability to invoke any defined service action. As discussed in Chapter 12, when Device Spy receives the initial device announcements, it retrieves and parses the device description document, and also tries to retrieve and parse each of the specified service description documents.

Because you still haven't implemented the Toaster Status service, Device Spy will fail when it tries to retrieve that service description document. So you can use Device Spy by simply changing the SCPDURL field in your device description to be the same as one of the other service description documents you have completed. Doing this satisfies Device Spy that a real service description document does exist for the Toaster Status service, even if it is the same as one of the other services; Device Spy is so generic in the kinds of devices it supports, it doesn't care.

Figure 13.22 shows Device Spy at startup. There are two primary panes to Device Spy. The left pane is a Windows Explorer style tree structure that is populated with discovered devices. The pane on the right side displays contextual information about the item selected on the left.

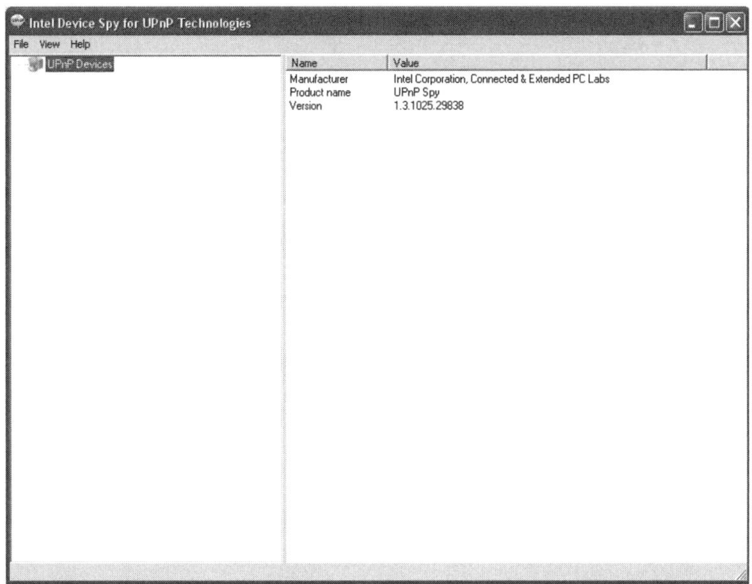

Figure 13.22 Device Spy at Startup

Device Spy's menu system includes the following items:

- File—manages Device Spy data
  - — Copy Information Table To Clipboard copies all text in the right information table pane to the clipboard.
- View—performs tasks that will update the user interface
  - — Rescan Network sends out a `upnp:rootdevice` request to discover all available nodes on the network.
  - — Expand All Devices expands each node in the left pane to its fullest.
  - — Collapse All Devices is the opposite of Expand All Devices.

Make sure Device Spy is up and running, and start the Super Toaster Device. You'll automatically see it appear in the left pane of Device Spy, shown in Figure 13.23.

In the left pane, you see your device. On the right pane, you see some information about your device, most of which should look familiar from your device description document. One piece of information

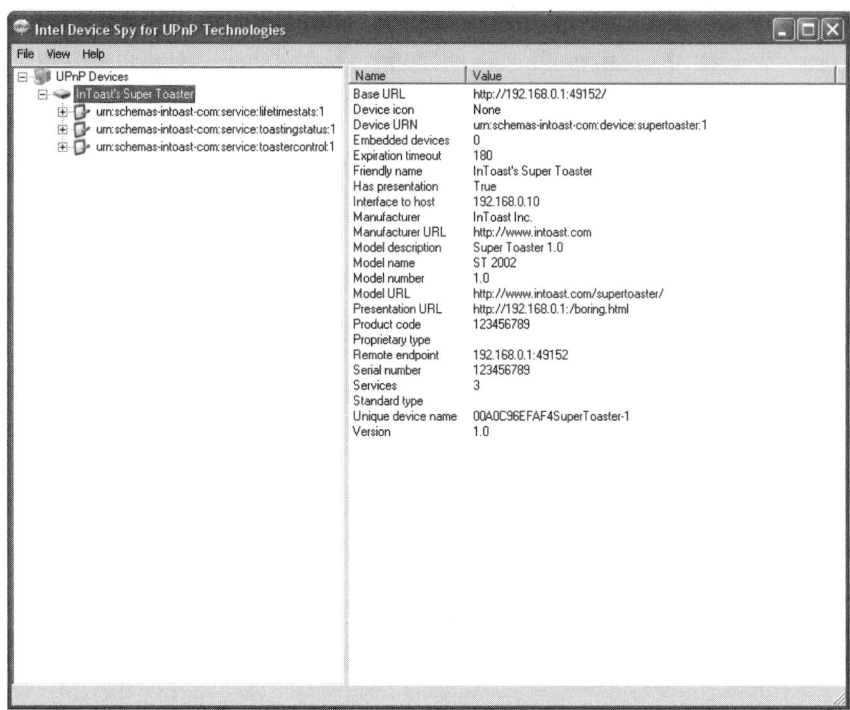

Figure 13.23 SuperToaster in Device Spy

available to you in the right pane now is the specific port number the UPnP library selected for your device. This is particularly helpful to match up an IP Address:Port Number combination when scanning through potentially hundreds of packets in the Device Sniffer. Use this information to filter out other packets coming from nodes that you don't care about.

Expanding your device out one level gives the three services supported by your device. Clicking on one of the services provides additional information shown in Figure 13.24.

Clicking on the Lifetime Statistics service, you see in the right pane that there are four actions (Methods) implemented in this service, there are two state variables, and the SCPDURL is also there for your information. In fact, if you right-click any of the device or device service names in the left pane, you'll get the option of viewing the XML document that describes the selected component, as seen in Figure 13.25.

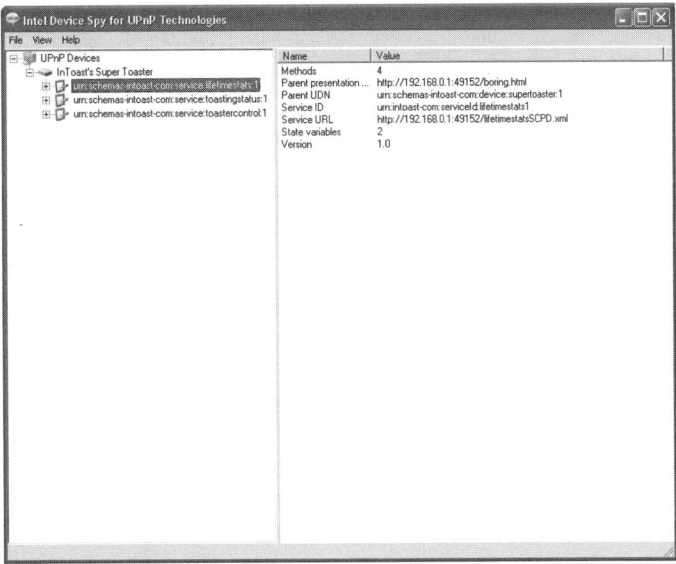

Figure 13.24 Device Spy Service Information

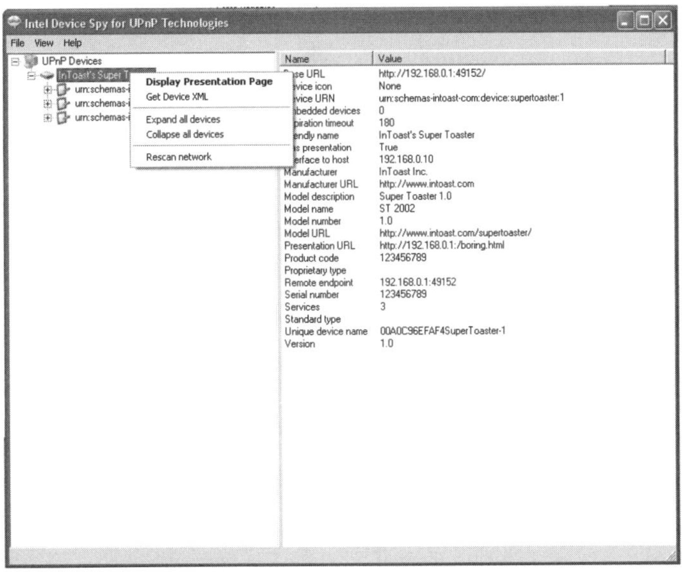

Figure 13.25 Device Right-click Context Menu

Note that you are also given the option of displaying your device presentation page. Unfortunately, selecting this option will result in a `404 bad request`, because you haven't implemented it yet. You'll do so in Chapter 15. Device Spy also presents useful information about each of the state variables supported by the service. Figure 13.26 shows your device completely expanded out.

In the right hand pane, you see information about the `totalSlices` state variable. This is very useful—especially when you forget the exact type of a state variable. Note also that there is a field to display the last known value of the state variable. This field is only updated when the state variable is evented, which you'll read about in the next chapter.

By far, the most useful capability of Device Spy is being able to invoke any of your device actions. Simply double-click one of the service actions in the left pane and a child window opens up, as shown in Figure 13.27.

Figure 13.27 shows the `adjustDial` action. The first three pieces of information in the top left corner of the window are the device name,

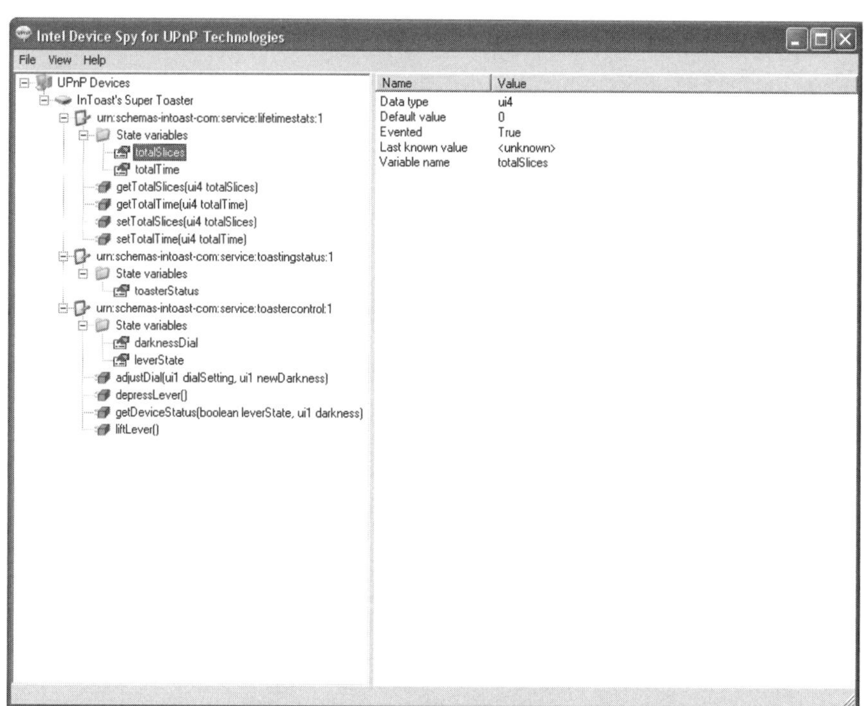

Figure 13.26 Device Spy State Variable Information

service name, and service action name that you're invoking. You can clearly see there are two parameters for this action: one in parameter (`dialSetting`) indicated by the left-to-right arrow icon, of type ui1, and one out parameter (`newDarkness`) indicated by the right-to-left arrow icon, also of type ui1.

Using this window, you can plug in your desired input parameter value and click invoke, as you see in Figure 13.28.

You can see in the status bar of Figure 13.28 that the action invocation of your device is now complete, and it took a measured time of 130 milliseconds to complete the action. You also see in the out parameter field the returned value from the action.

Note that for all actions with in parameters, Device Spy automatically validates the provided parameter before actually invoking the action on the device. For example, the dialSetting in parameter for `adjustDial` is defined to be a ui1. If you put some letters (for example "abc") in the text field, Device Spy complains about invalid data. Be careful not to

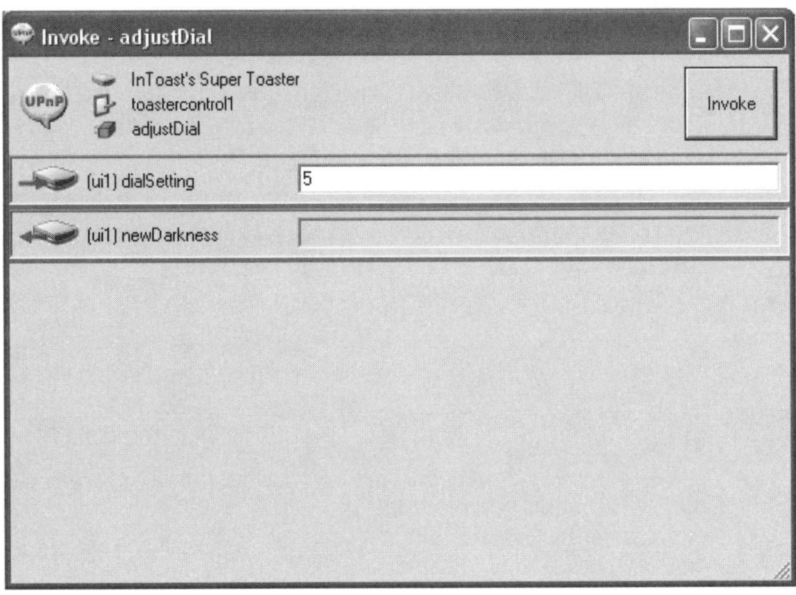

Figure 13.27 Device Spy `adjustDial` Action

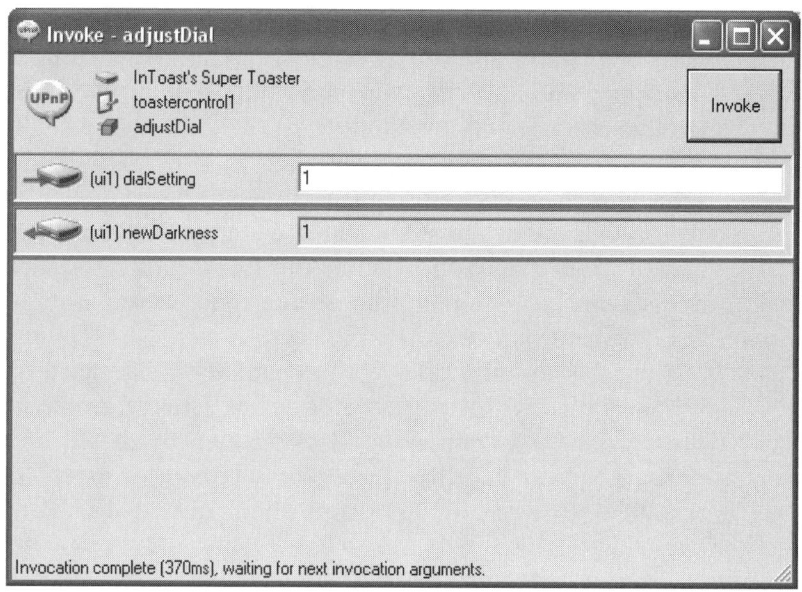

Figure 13.28 `adjustDial` Invocation Complete

rely on this in all cases. You have no guarantee that all control points will be as nice. Make sure your action invocation can gracefully handle invalid data or incorrect parameter types.

You can also verify the action invocation by looking at your console window output shown in Figure 13.29, where you see the control flow through your code for an action invocation.

```
upnp_callback: start
upnp_callback: UPNP_CONTROL_ACTION_REQUEST
upnp_actions: start
upnp_actions: request for Toaster Control Service
upnp_tcactions: start
upnp_adjustdial: start
hw_setdialvalue: start
hw_setdialvalue: end
upnp_adjustdial: end
upnp_callback: end
```

Figure 13.29 Console Window Call Sequence

As discussed earlier, behind the scenes of each action invocation are SOAP requests and SOAP responses. Although Device Spy hides much of the gory details, if you'd like to see the actual invocation requests and responses, hit the F12 key for any action invocation window and you'll see the XML behind the window, as shown in Figure 13.30.

This capability is particularly useful when you're not seeing the expected response after hitting "Invoke." Chances are there is something wrong with the XML your device is sending back. This gives you an opportunity to see the actual response, as received by Device Spy.

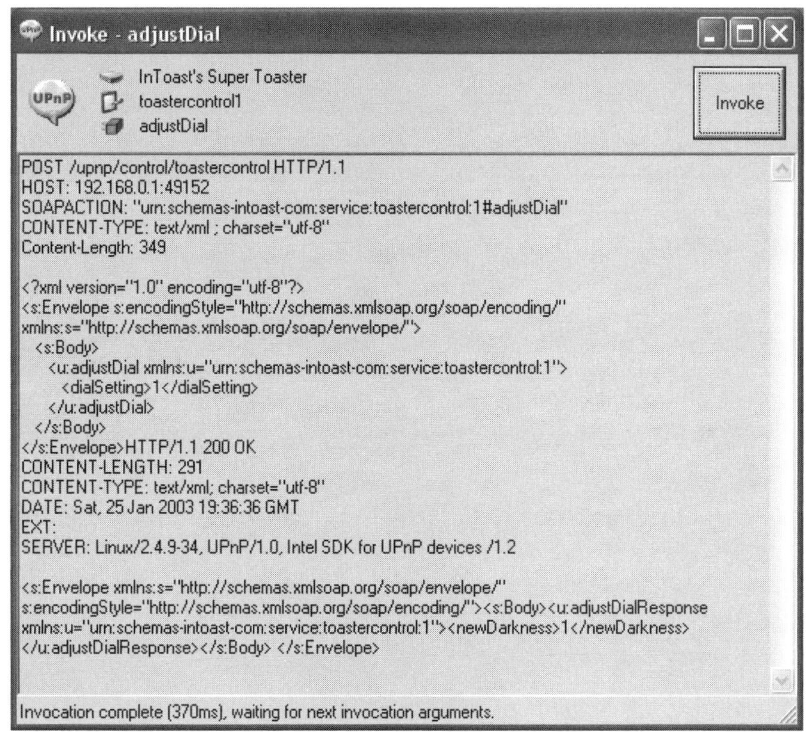

Figure 13.30 Device Spy Action Invocation XML

Summary

In this chapter you have explored the concept of device services and actions. You successfully mapped your product feature requirements to UPnP service description documents and implemented programmatic support in your Super Toaster to support these services and actions.

Then you were introduced to Device Spy, and you saw how it could be used during device development to view information about a device and to invoke its actions.

The next chapter covers service subscriptions, eventing, and implementing support for the last service of your device.

Chapter 14

Handling Subscriptions and Events

In the previous chapter you learned how to define service description documents and add control support to your device through the definition and support of UPnP service actions. Each defined action that has input or output parameters for your Super Toaster also had a list of associated state variables. In this chapter you learn what it means for a state variable to be evented, understand how to manage service subscriptions, and implement support for subscriptions and eventing in your sample device.

Problem Description

UPnP devices like your Super Toaster have a wealth of information that control point applications would like to get their hands on. One way to retrieve this information is to call an explicit action exposed on the device that returns the value of the associated state variable. Yet polling is inefficient and puts unnecessary burden on your device and on available network bandwidth. Instead, the control point application would prefer a mechanism to receive instant asynchronous notification when a state variable in a service changes. For this you have UPnP service subscriptions and the eventing of service state variables.

UPnP Service Subscriptions

Simply put, UPnP service subscriptions are a method for subscribing to asynchronous events on the device. The UPnP device architecture uses a subscriber/publisher relationship to define eventing. The subscriber is a control point application interested in receiving information from a device, called the publisher. For the remainder of this chapter the term *control point* may be used interchangeably with *subscriber* and *device* may be used interchangeably with *publisher*.

Internally changing the value of an evented state variable causes a device to publish information to registered subscribers. State variables can change for any number of reasons. For example, the invocation of some action or some unprovoked event on the device itself may cause the value of a state variable to change. In either case, both cause the state variable to change and therefore could cause an event.

Although there is no restriction on the number or types of an evented state variable, this state variable eventing must be explicitly designated in the service description document. Figure 14.1 shows the definitions of your state variables in the Lifetime Stats service, defined in the previous chapter.

Referring to the XML, you'll note that each `stateVariable` node has an attribute named `sendEvents`. If this value is set to "yes," then this

```
<?xml version="1.0"?>
<scpd xmlns=
  "urn:schemas-intoast-com:supertoaster-service-1-0>
    ...
  <serviceStateTable>
    <stateVariable sendEvents="no">
      <name>totalSlices</name>
      <dataType>ui4</dataType>
      <defaultValue>0</defaultValue>
    </stateVariable>
    <stateVariable sendEvents="no">
      <name>totalTime</name>
      <dataType>time</dataType>
      <defaultValue>0</defaultValue>
    </stateVariable>
  </serviceStateTable>
</scpd>
```

Figure 14.1 Service Description Template

state variable is to be evented or published to all registered subscribers when its value changes. State variables whose `sendEvents` attribute are set to "no" are not capable of being evented to anyone.

Here's a practical example for this capability: If a user of your Super Toaster was in the middle of reading their e-mail when they suddenly got the urge for a great piece of toast, they'd very much like to return to reading their e-mail while the toast is toasting. Using subscriptions, a control point application on the PC could subscribe to a service that provided status on the state of the toaster. When the toaster finishes toasting, the value of its toasting status would be evented to the subscribed control point, providing the user at the computer with a notification of the change in status of your device.

Event Subscription URL

An excellent question to consider is how your device receives these subscription requests. If you think all the way back to Chapter 12, when you defined your device, you defined each service in the fashion shown in Figure 14.2.

The field that provides the control point with the information it needs to make subscription requests is the `eventSubURL`. This field combined with the base URL provides a location for control points to post all subscription-related requests. The `controlURL` serves the same purpose for service actions. These URLs are used by the UPnP library's internal web server to recognize and properly route incoming requests of your device.

```
<service>
  <serviceType>
    urn:schemas-intoast-com:service:lifetimestats:1
  </serviceType>
  <serviceId>
    urn:intoast-com:serviceId:lifetimestats1
    </serviceId>
  <controlURL>/upnp/control/lifetimestats1</controlURL>
  <eventSubURL>/upnp/event/lifetimestats1</eventSubURL>
  <SCPDURL>lifetimeSCPD.xml</SCPDURL>
</service>
```

Figure 14.2 Device Service Description

Subscription Semantics

A UPnP device has a one-to-many relationship with its service subscriptions. Any number of different control points can subscribe to events for a given service, meaning the device can support multiple subscriptions per service. When an event occurs, information about that event (described in XML) is published to all control points who have previously subscribed to the service.

Subscription granularity is at a service level: There is no mechanism to subscribe to a specific evented state variable in a service. Subscriptions to a service result in all evented state variables in that service being published to all subscribers.

Every subscription has an explicit expiration time, specified by the device when accepting a subscription. Control points that wish to continue their subscription past the expiration time must re-subscribe with the device.

When a subscription is first accepted by the device, it must send an initial event to the subscriber providing the current state of all evented state variables. This allows the subscriber to initialize its representation of the device's state variables with their current values. From that point on, events are published to that control point only when the value of a state variable has changed.

Some state variables may change so rapidly that it doesn't make sense to event them each time they change, lest the network get flooded with event messages. In this special case, the UPnP specification allows devices to use their discretion and publish the event at a reasonable, moderated rate. There is no requirement that the device send event updates immediately when they happen, although as a general rule devices should do so as soon as reasonably possible.

The publisher of events is responsible for keeping track of all subscribed nodes. This does incur some overhead on a device, so although the device is not required to accept all subscription requests, it is expected that each device handle as many subscriptions as it reasonably can.

There are three types of subscription requests made of the device: Subscription Request, Subscription Renewal Request, and Subscription Cancellation Request.

Subscription Request

A subscription request is received by the device when a control point is interested in obtaining a subscription to one of the device's services.

The device has two options: It can accept or reject the subscription. If it accepts the subscription, it must maintain the following information about the subscriber:

- Unique Subscription Identifier
- Delivery URL for events
- Event Key
- Subscription Duration

The Unique Subscription Identifier is generated by your device in response to a subscription request and should be globally unique. The Delivery URL provides a location at the subscriber for your device to publish events. The Event Key is used to incrementally number each event message published to a subscriber. In this way a subscriber can detect if it missed an event. Finally, the Subscription Duration is the length of time (in seconds) that indicates how long the accepted subscription will be valid. Your device can choose any value it wishes, even using the keyword "infinite" to designate that the subscription never expires. Internally, the UPnP library keeps track of these subscription durations for you. If control points don't re-subscribe to the service before this duration expires, the subscription is lost.

Using this information, the device has all it needs to maintain a subscription. In fact, should the device have persistent storage capability, subscriptions to control points could even be maintained in the case of brief power failure or other interruption.

Subscription Renewal Request

Just like your favorite magazine, sooner or later you'll need to request a subscription renewal. Since most subscriptions have a defined duration or expiration, control points that wish to remain subscribed to a device service's events must send periodic renewal requests to the device. Renewal requests contain only the previously assigned SID and a requested subscription expiration value. The device uses the subscription identifier to look up the subscription record and accepts or rejects the request in the same fashion as a first-time subscription request. When a device is accepting a renewal, it is not required to send the special initial event information.

Devices are free to decline a renewal request, in which case the original subscription expires and the device no longer publishes events to that subscriber. Any requests made of the device using the now-expired subscription identifier will fail.

Subscription Cancellation Request

When a subscriber has no desire to continue receiving published events from the device it should send a subscription cancellation request to the publishing device. This helps reduce the amount of unnecessary network traffic between a device and its subscribers.

Cancellation requests, like renewal requests, contain only the previously assigned SID. With the exception of an invalid SID or malformed request packet, devices do not have any choice but to accept cancellation requests.

Upon acceptance of a cancellation request, the device should immediately stop publishing events to that subscriber.

Subscription Events

Specifically, an event occurs whenever the value of a UPnP state variable changes. Devices are not required to send the event in any minimum amount of time after the state variable change, but they are expected to do so as soon as reasonably possible for the device.

The longer the device waits to publish the state variable change event, the less responsive your device will seem. Remember that events are going to be used by control point applications to display information to users, often in the form of a user interface. If an event that causes an evented state variable to change occurs on the device and the device waits a long time before sending the event, then from the perspective of the user of the control point application, the device appears unresponsive, or at best very slow.

Each published event must contain the name of all evented state variables for the subscribed service and their current values. If something happens on the device that causes more than one state variable to change at the same time, the UPnP Device Architecture specification recommends that the device aggregate these changes into a single published event, to avoid unnecessarily flooding the network with events.

Just like action request responses, subscription events are packaged into an XML document and published to listening subscribers. Subscriptions use a construct called a property set that has the format shown in Figure 14.3.

Property sets contain each state variable's name and value listed in the body of the property set. Note that the *stateVariableValue* field is a string; so just like action request responses, non-string-based state variables must be converted into strings when creating the property set.

```
<e:propertyset xmlns:e="urn:schemas-namespace:event-1-0>
  <e:property>
   <stateVariableName>stateVariableValue</stateVariableName>
       ...
  </e:property>
</e:propset>
```

Figure 14.3 Property Set Format

Advertisement and Subscription Lengths

One of the first things a UPnP device implementer considers is how long to make the periodic advertisement interval and subscription duration values.

The answer is both simple and complex. A strict reading of the UPnP Device Architecture specification says the minimum advertisement and subscription period should be 1800 seconds, or 30 minutes. Many devices will simply use this suggested value, but most device implementers should consider the pros and cons of doing so.

Every time a device sends an SSDP announcement, it consumes network traffic. By making the advertisement periods long, you reduce the amount of unnecessary network traffic. However, a long interval between advertisements may result in a long waiting period before devices are found on the network. Although control points can certainly search regularly for devices, this is an active process that may not be repeated regularly. The act of reducing the advertisement interval increases the chance that control point applications will discover your device sooner rather than later. Just how small to make this period is a difficult choice best left for the specific device and its expected usage scenarios.

What about the subscription length? For a control point, more frequent subscription renewals mean more work, but can also provide the earliest indications that a device has gone off the network. When a control point attempts to re-subscribe and either receives no response or an invalid SID response, this indicates that either the device has left the network or has had a power cycling event.

Fortunately for you, the Intel SDK provides a flexible set of functions to support subscription and eventing. In the remainder of the chapter, you implement support for subscriptions and eventing in your Super Toaster device.

UPnP Super Toaster

Now turn your attention to your sample device, the UPnP Super Toaster, and see where evented state variables and service subscriptions could be useful. Referring back to Chapter 12, you partitioned your functional requirements into three UPnP services:

- Lifetime Statistics
- Toaster Control
- Toaster Status

You handled the first two services in the previous chapter, and now you have to implement the Toaster Status service. Here again are the functional requirements from Chapter 10, which led to the creation of this service.

Network Event Notification

As a node on the home network, the Super Toaster must provide notification to network users in the home when a slice of bread has finished toasting. For example, if a user is logged into a workstation, and a slice of bread has finished toasting, the software should notify the user of the completion of the toasting cycle.

Toaster Status codes are defined as follows:

- TOASTING—the toaster is currently toasting.
- NOT_TOASTING—the toaster is currently not toasting.

Now that you know about UPnP Eventing, this functional requirement for your Super Toaster seems a perfect match for UPnP Eventing. From the functional requirements, you need to determine the number and type of state variables to include for this service. Define the following evented state variable:

> `toasterStatus`—a string that indicates what the toaster is currently doing.

That covers the functional requirements for state variables for the toasting status service. At this point, you may be thinking that you need to add a few actions to provide interfaces into the service, either to provide access to the state variables or perform some other duty on the device.

Surprisingly, this single state variable is all that you need in the toasting status service. Recall that UPnP has no requirements to have a minimum number of actions for a given service, so just having a single state variable in a service is sufficient.

Furthermore, because you'll take advantage of the UPnP architecture's subscription and eventing capabilities, there's no need to provide action-based interfaces into the device to return values of the evented state variable; instead, you'll rely on control points subscribing to this service to receive events for the state variable.

Toaster Status SCPD

With the design of your service complete, as in the previous chapter, you must write the SCPD for this service. Figure 14.4 provides such a definition.

The primary difference between this SCPD and those you defined for your other device services is the lack of any defined actions, and also that the state variable defined in this service has the `stateVariable` attribute `sendEvents` set to "yes." This informs control points that read this service description that if they have a valid subscription to this device service, they will receive events for those state variables whose `sendEvents` attribute is set to "yes."

```
<?xml version="1.0"?>
<scpd xmlns=
  "urn:schemas-intoast-com:supertoaster-service-1-0>
  <specVersion>
    <major>1</major>
    <minor>0</minor>
  </specVersion>
  <actionList>
  </actionList>
  <serviceStateTable>
    <stateVariable sendEvents="yes">
      <name>toasterStatus</name>
      <dataType>string</dataType>
    </stateVariable>
  </serviceStateTable>
</scpd>
```

Figure 14.4 Toaster Status SCPD

With your service description document now complete, you can turn your attention to adding code in your device implementation to support subscriptions and eventing of your state variable.

To Event or Not To Event

A difficult question facing all device implementers is how to decide when to event a state variable and when not to. Fortunately, there are some guidelines to follow that can help.

The first characteristic to consider is how control point applications will use the state variable. If, like your sample device, information about state variable changes is best received as soon as possible after the change, then certainly eventing the state variable is the right choice.

On the other hand, if control point applications will only need the value of the state variable infrequently, it is best not to flood the local network with a bunch of unwanted state variable change notifications, but instead to offer actions that support the querying of the state variable.

Interestingly, you could certainly provide both an action-based interface and eventing support for the same state variable. Although this may seem redundant, it certainly offers the most flexibility. Supporting actions is certainly the less expensive of the two options, as the device (or control point) need not maintain state and other information for a subscription; actions can simply be called without incurring any overhead.

Implementation

Just like actions, subscription-related requests are distributed to your UPnP device application through the callback function you specified in the call to `UpnPRegisterRootDevice()` back in Chapter 12. Recall that in this callback function, shown in Figure 14.5, you switched on the event type.

Adding support for subscriptions starts here, with a new case for events of type `UPNP_EVENT_SUBSCRIPTION_REQUEST` and a new function, shown in Figure 14.6, that will handle all subscription-related requests.

```
/*
 * Function: upnp_callback
 *
 * Parameters: Upnp_Event type indicating the specific
 *             callback event, pointer to the event itself,
 *             and cookie information
 *
 * Returns: UPNP_E_SUCCESS if everything worked,
 *          UPNP_E_INVALID_ARGS if the event is NULL, and
 *          your cookie.
 *
 * Description: This function handles all callback events from
 *              the UPnP Library. It dispatches events to
 *              their specific event handlers.
 */
int upnp_callback(Upnp_EventType eventtype, void *event,
                  void *cookie)
{
  int ret=0;       /* General purpose return code */

  printf("upnp_callback: start\n");

  /* Check your parameters. */
  if(event == NULL) {
    printf("upnp_callback: NULL event structure\n");
    return UPNP_E_BAD_REQUEST;
  }

  /* Dispatch the event based on event type. */
  switch(eventtype) {
    case UPNP_CONTROL_ACTION_REQUEST:
      /* A control point is invoking an action. */
      printf("upnp_callback: UPNP_CONTROL_ACTION_REQUEST\n");
      ret = upnp_actions((struct Upnp_Action_Request *)event);
      break;
    default:
      /* An unhandled event type */
      printf("upnp_callback: unsupported event type: %d\n",
             eventtype);
      ret = UPNP_E_BAD_REQUEST;
      break;
  }

  printf("upnp_callback: end\n");

  return ret;
}
```

Figure 14.5 Device Callback Handler

```
/*
 * Function: upnp_callback
 *
 * Parameters: Upnp_Event type indicating the specific callback
 *             event, pointer to the event itself, and cookie
 *             information
 *
 * Returns: UPNP_E_SUCCESS if everything worked,
 *          UPNP_E_INVALID_ARGS if the event is NULL, and
 *          your cookie.
 *
 * Description: This function handles all callback events from
 *              the UPnP Library. It dispatches events to
 *              their specific event handlers.
 */
int upnp_callback(Upnp_EventType eventtype, void *event,
void *cookie)
{
  int ret=0;      /* General purpose return code */

  printf("upnp_callback: start\n");

  /* Check your parameters. */
  if(event == NULL) {
    printf("upnp_callback: NULL event structure\n");
    return UPNP_E_BAD_REQUEST;
  }

  /* Dispatch the event based on event type. */
  switch(eventtype) {
    case UPNP_CONTROL_ACTION_REQUEST:
      /* A control point is invoking an action. */
      printf("upnp_callback: UPNP_CONTROL_ACTION_REQUEST\n");
      ret = upnp_actions((struct Upnp_Action_Request *)event);
      break;
    case UPNP_EVENT_SUBSCRIPTION_REQUEST:
      /* A control point wants a subscription. */
      printf("upnp_callback: UPNP_EVENT_SUBSCRIPTION_REQUEST\n");
      ret = upnp_subscriptions(
            (struct Upnp_Subscription_Request *)event);
      break;
    default:
      /* An unhandled event type. */
      printf("upnp_callback: unsupported event type: %d\n",
            eventtype);
```

Figure 14.6 Device Callback with Subscription Support *(Continues)*

```
        ret = UPNP_E_BAD_REQUEST;
        break;
    }

    printf("upnp_callback: end\n");

    return ret;
}
```

Figure 14.6 Device Callback with Subscription Support

Upnp_Subscription_Request

Much like action requests in the last chapter, subscription requests also come with a special structure containing a wealth of useful information to help you to handle the requests. You can see the definition of this structure in Figure 14.7.

Referring to the `Upnp_Subscription_Request` structure, the first two members are used to ensure that the subscription is not only targeted to your device (by matching the `UDN` field), but also to match the subscription request with a specific service on the device using the `ServiceId`. Even though the Toaster Status service defined in this chapter is the only service with evented state variables, this does not prevent control points from trying to subscribe to all of the Super Toaster services. Fortunately, you can use the `ServiceId` field to filter out and reject subscription requests to device services that don't support the eventing of any state variables.

```
struct Upnp_Subscription_Request
{
  /** The identifier for the service being subscribed to.*/
  char *ServiceId;

  /** Universal device name. */
  char *UDN;

  /** The assigned subscription ID for this subscription. */
  Upnp_SID Sid;

};
```

Figure 14.7 UPnP Subscription Request Structure

The final field in this structure, the subscription ID, is automatically created and filled in for you by the UPnP library. This subscription ID is valid only if you accept the subscription. If you would like to use your own SID numbering scheme, there's nothing preventing you from doing so by simply overwriting the Sid field in this structure before accepting the subscription.

Note that, for some reason, the Upnp_Subscription_Request structure has slightly modified the names of the service ID and device UDN fields. In Upnp_Action_Request, the service ID member is serviceID, while in the Upnp_Subscription_Request structure it is serviceId. Similarly, in the Upnp_Action_Request structure, the device UDN field is DevUDN, but in the Upnp_Subscription_Request structure it is simply UDN. Be aware of these differences when you are writing your device code!

Armed with this information, you are now ready to start your upnp_subscriptions handler, listed in Figure 14.8.

```
/*
 * Function: upnp_subscriptions
 *
 * Parameters: pointer to a Upnp_Subscription_Request structure
 *
 * Returns: UPNP_E_SUCCESS if successful, service subscription
 *          handler error code if not.
 *
 * Description: This function dispatches a subscription request
 *              to the specific service handler by matching up
 *              the serviceId of the subscription request.
 */
int upnp_subscriptions(struct Upnp_Subscription_Request *request)
{
  int ret=0;      /* General purpose error code */

  /* First check if the request structure is valid. */
  if(request == NULL) {
    printf("upnp_subscriptions: request pointer is NULL\n");
    return UPNP_E_BAD_REQUEST;
  }
```

Figure 14.8 Subscription Request Handler, Part 1 *(Continues)*

```
/* Then, you need to make sure this request is for your device.*/
if(strcmp(request->UDN, g_deviceudn) != 0) {
  /* It's not for you. */
  printf("upnp_actions: request not for your device\n");
  return UPNP_E_BAD_REQUEST;
}

/* You need to match the serviceID to one of your services. */
if(strcmp(request->ServiceId, TOASTING_STATUS_SERVICEID)
         == 0) {
  /* It's a call for the Toasting Status Service. */
  printf("upnp_actions: request for Toasting Status Service\n");
  ret = upnp_tssubscriptions(request);
} else {
  /*
   * The control point is asking for a service that doesn't
   * exist, or a service that doesn't support subscriptions.
   */
  ret = UPNP_E_BAD_REQUEST;
}

return UPNP_E_SUCCESS;
```

Figure 14.8 Subscription Request Handler, Part 1

Looking at the code, you first ensure that this request is for your device by matching the device UDN in the request with what you know your UDN to be. Next, you try to match your new Toaster Status service with the service specified in the subscription request. If you don't find a match, you return an error code stating that the arguments provided in the subscription request were invalid.

You'll continue your standard naming conventions by placing all code relating to the Toasting Status service in the file name `upnptc.c`. All functions in this module have the letters "`tc`" as a prefix to their name to indicate module membership, as the function `upnp_tssubscriptions()` illustrates.

The API

After recognizing that a subscription request is for your toaster status service, you must first accept the subscription and then send out the initial values of the evented state variables in the subscribed service. This section introduces the necessary functions to perform this task.

You begin by introducing a function that allows you to create all the important property sets for use in accepting subscriptions:

```
int UpnpAddToPropertySet(IN OUT IXML_Document **PropSet,
                         IN char *ArgName,
                         IN char *ArgVal)
```

`PropSet`—Double pointer to a DOM Document to store the XML Property Set. If NULL, creates a new document.

`ArgName`—Pointer to a character string of the name of the state variable argument to add to the `PropSet`.

`ArgVal`—Pointer to a character string value of the named state variable.

Returns: UPNP_E_SUCCESS when successful, Intel SDK defined error code if not.

This function creates a DOM representation of the XML property set introduced earlier in this chapter. Calling this function with a NULL DOM document for the first argument automatically creates the document, which can then be used in future calls. Calling this function repeatedly with the same `PropSet` gradually builds a property set by adding the specified argument and value with each call.

This useful function will save you significant time and effort when building property sets for event notifications to subscribed control points. Fortunately, the Intel SDK also contains a function that, when given a property set, sends out the notification to all registered control points:

```
int UpnpNotifyExt(IN UpnpDeviceHandle Hnd,
                  IN const char *DevID,
                  IN const char *ServID,
                  IN IXML_Document *PropSet)
```

`Hnd`—Handle to your UPnP device, obtained from a previous call to `UpnPRegisterRootDevice()`.

`DevID`—Pointer to a character string of your device ID, specified in your device description document.

`ServID`—Pointer to a character string of the serviceID for which you are publishing this event.

Continues

`PropSet`—DOM Document representing the property set to publish.

Returns: UPNP_E_SUCCESS when successful, Intel SDK defined error code if not.

Parameters to this function include everything the UPnP library needs to automatically publish property sets to all subscribed control points. This is a big timesaver because you don't have to call this function multiple times for each subscribed control point. These functions are defined in `upnptools.h`. You are encouraged to check out the remaining useful utility functions defined in `upnptools.h`.

How does the UPnP library know about these subscribed control points? It knows based upon previous calls to `UpnpAcceptSubscriptionExt()` when you receive a subscription request:

```
int UpnpAcceptSubscriptionExt( IN UpnpDeviceHandle Hnd,
                               IN const char *DevID,
                               IN const char *ServID,
                               IN IXML_Document PropSet,
                               IN Upnp_SID SubsId)
```

`Hnd`—Handle to your UPnP Device, obtained from a previous call to `UpnpRegisterRootDevice`.

`DevID`—Pointer to a character string of your device ID, specified in your device description document.

`ServID`—Pointer to a character string of the service ID for which you are publishing this event.

`PropSet`—DOM Document representing the property set to publish.

`SubsId`—The subscription ID for the newly registered control point.

Returns: UPNP_E_SUCCESS when successful.

Every time you receive a subscription request, you can call this function to accept it. By providing your deviceId, serviceId, the property set of evented variables for this service, and the subscription ID for the subscribing control point, you provide the UPnP library with enough information to manage many of the small details of subscription management.

For example, you don't have to explicitly handle subscription renewal requests; the UPnP library automatically grants those renewal requests on your behalf. You don't have to do anything when receiving a subscription cancellation either; the UPnP library performs any cleanup and approves the cancellation request.

If you'd like to refuse the subscription request or renewal, simply do not call UpnpAcceptSubscriptionExt() in your subscription handler.

As you'll see in the next section, this makes it easier to support subscription acceptance and the publishing of events to subscribed control points.

The Code

Armed with a set of useful functions, you can now fully implement your subscription handler. Because both UpnpAcceptSubscriptionExt() and UpnpNotifyExt() need a property set, you first work on creating your property set for this service. Once you have created the property set, you formally accept the subscription with a call to UpnpAcceptSubscriptionExt()

```
/*
 * Function: upnp_tssusbscriptions
 *
 * Parameters: pointer to a Upnp_Subscription_Request structure
 *
 * Description: This function handles subscription requests
 *              for the toasting status service.
 */
int upnp_tssubscriptions(struct Upnp_Subscription_Request
                         *request)
{
  IXML_Document *propset = NULL; /* Your property set */
  char toasterstatusstr[64];     /* Toaster Status state var */

  printf("upnp_tssubscriptions: start\n");

  /*
   * For each state variable in this service that you event,
   * you need to add it to the property set.
   */
```

Figure 14.9 Subscription Request Handler, Part 2 *(Continues)*

```
  /* First, let's figure out what your current state is. */
  if(hw_getleverstate() == LEVER_UP) {
    strcpy(toasterstatusstr, "NOT_TOASTING");
  } else {
    strcpy(toasterstatusstr, "TOASTING");
  }

  /* Now add it to the set. */
  UpnpAddToPropertySet(&propset, "toasterStatus",
                       toasterstatusstr);

  /* Now accept the subscription. */
  UpnpAcceptSubscriptionExt(g_device_handle, g_deviceudn,
                            TOASTING_STATUS_SERVICEID,
                            propset,
                            request->Sid);

  /* Free the propset. */
  ixmlDocument_free(propset);

  printf("upnp_tssubscriptions: end\n");

  return UPNP_E_SUCCESS;
}
```

Figure 14.9 Subscription Request Handler, Part 2

Referring to the code, you add each of your evented state variables one by one through repeated calls to `UpnpAddToPropertySet()`. Because `propset` was initialized to NULL, the first call to `UpnpAddToPropertySet()` creates the property set. You make sure to free it before you exit this function. After accepting the subscription, the UPnP library is now capable of handling subscription renewals and cancellations on your behalf.

With your subscription now accepted, you have a responsibility to update the subscribed control point with the new value of your evented state variable whenever it changes. You create a special function for this, called `upnp_tsupdate()`, that simply sends out update notifications for the Toaster Status service, using `UpnpNotifyExt()`, shown in Figure 14.10.

This function is actually very similar to accepting a subscription. In both cases you must create a property set that contains the name and current value of the state variable you're eventing. The parameters to

```
/*
 * Function: upnp_tsupdate
 *
 * Description: This function sends event updates for all
 *              evented state variables in this service.
 */
void upnp_tsupdate()
{
  IXML_Document propset=NULL;  /* Property set for your service */
  char toasterstatusstr[64];   /* Toaster status state var */

  printf("upnp_tsupdate: start\n");

  /*
   * First, build your property set of evented state variables.
   */

  /* Get your current state. */
  if(hw_getleverstate() == LEVER_UP) {
    strcpy(toasterstatusstr, "NOT_TOASTING");
  } else {
    strcpy(toasterstatusstr, "TOASTING");
  }

  /* Add the state variable to the property set. */
  UpnpAddToPropertySet(&propset, "toasterStatus",
                       toasterstatusstr);

  /*
   * Now, you send out the notify.
   */
  UpnpNotifyExt(g_device_handle,
                g_deviceudn,
                TOASTING_STATUS_SERVICEID,
                propset);

  /* Free your property set. */
  ixmlDocument_free(propset);

  printf("upnp_tsupdate: end\n");

  return;
}
```

Figure 14.10 Code Listing for upnp_tsupdate()

UpnpNotifyExt() are the same as the first four parameters to UpnpAcceptSubscriptionExt(). These give the UPnP library everything it needs to know about the specific control points that have subscribed to receive the property set. Note that unlike accepting a subscription, you do not specify a specific SID. This is because you could have multiple control points subscribed to the same device service. Fortunately, you can let the UPnP library handle those details for you.

That completes the code for your subscription handler! You now fully support accepting subscription requests, while the UPnP library completes support for handling subscription renewals and cancellations on your behalf. Figure 14.11 presents the complete code for the Toaster Status Service, including the new upnp_tscallback() function that is called by the Hardware Interface Library when the toaster status changes.

```
/*
 * Filename: upnpts.c
 *
 * Description: This file implements support for the Toasting
 *              Status Service.
 */

#include <stdlib.h>
#include <unistd.h>
#include <string.h>
#include "toaster.h"
#include "toasterhw.h"

/*
 * Function: upnp_tssusbscriptions
 *
 * Parameters: pointer to a Upnp_Subscription_Request structure
 *
 * Description: This function handles subscription requests
 *              for the toasting status service.
 */
int upnp_tssubscriptions(struct Upnp_Subscription_Request
                         *request)
{
  IXML_Document propset = NULL;  /* Your property set */
  char toasterstatusstr[64];     /* Toaster Status var */
```

Figure 14.11 Complete Subscription Request Handler *(Continues)*

```
  printf("upnp_tssubscriptions: start\n");

  /*
   * For each state variable in this service that you event,
   * you need to add it to the property set.
   */

  /* First you need to figure out what your current state is. */
  if(hw_getleverstate() == LEVER_UP) {
    strcpy(toasterstatusstr, "NOT_TOASTING");
  } else {
    strcpy(toasterstatusstr, "TOASTING");
  }

  /* Now add it to the property set. */
  UpnpAddToPropertySet(&propset, "toasterStatus",
toasterstatusstr);

  /* Now accept the subscription. */
  UpnpAcceptSubscriptionExt(g_device_handle, g_deviceudn,
                            TOASTING_STATUS_SERVICEID,
                            propset,
                            request->Sid);

  /* Free the propset. */
  ixmlDocument_free(propset);

  printf("upnp_tssubscriptions: end\n");

  return UPNP_E_SUCCESS;
}

/*
 * Function: upnp_tsupdate
 *
 * Description: This function sends event updates for all
 *              evented state variables in this service.
 */
void upnp_tsupdate()
{
  IXML_Document propset=NULL;  /* Property set for your service */
  char toasterstatusstr[64];   /* Toaster Status state var */

  printf("upnp_tsupdate: start\n");
```

Figure 14.11 Complete Subscription Request Handler *(Continues)*

```
  /*
   * First, build your property set of evented state variables.
   */

  /* Get your current state. */
  if(hw_getleverstate() == LEVER_UP) {
    strcpy(toasterstatusstr, "NOT_TOASTING");
  } else {
    strcpy(toasterstatusstr, "TOASTING");
  }

  /* Add the state variable to the property set. */
  UpnpAddToPropertySet(&propset, "toasterStatus",
                       toasterstatusstr);

  /*
   * Now, you send out the notify.
   */
  UpnpNotifyExt(g_device_handle,
                g_deviceudn,
                TOASTING_STATUS_SERVICEID,
                propset);

  /* Free your property set. */
  ixmlDocument_free(propset);

  printf("upnp_tsupdate: end\n");

  return;
}

/*
 * Function: upnp_tscallback
 *
 * Description: This function is called to tell you
 *              that something has changed with the toaster.
 */
void upnp_tscallback()
{
  printf("upnp_tscallback: start\n");

  /* Event your updates. */
  upnp_tsupdate();

  printf("upnp_tscallback: end\n");
}
```

Figure 14.11 Complete Subscription Request Handler

You have completed subscription and eventing support for the Toaster Status service. This also marks the completion of the final service you will support on the Super Toaster.

Super Toaster Improvements

Subscriptions and evented state variables can be powerful for devices. They provide an excellent way for devices to asynchronously publish immediate updates of device state variables to subscribed control points. Because of this, you should take another look at the two services you implemented in the previous chapter and determine whether either of those could similarly benefit from subscription and evented state variables support.

Lifetime Statistics

In this service, you have state variables that represent the total slices of toast your toaster has toasted and the total time your toaster has spent toasting. In your current implementation you provide actions to get the values of these state variables. Could control point applications benefit from the eventing of these state variables?

The answer to this question lies in the usage of these statistics. If control point applications would like to display real-time information about your device and its lifetime statistics, then eventing these state variables certainly provides the earliest and easiest opportunity for control point applications to get at this data. It also means that control points wouldn't need to continuously poll your device by calling the get-style actions you've implemented.

In fact, it's easy to imagine this service being implemented just as the Toaster Status service was, with no actions of any kind—that is, providing only evented state variables.

To make this change in your implementation, you would first need to change the SCPD for the Lifetime Statistics service, updating the state variable `sendEvents` attribute for each state variable to the value of "yes." This change has been made in the updated Lifetime Statistics SCPD shown in Figure 14.12.

Then you need to add programmatic support to not only accept subscriptions, but also to receive and send out updates when notified from the Hardware Interface Library, just as you did with the Toaster Status service. You create similar functions to support this in the Lifetime Statistics module, listed in Figure 14.13.

```
<?xml version="1.0"?>
<scpd xmlns=
  "urn:schemas-intoast-com:supertoaster-service-1-0">
  <specVersion>
  <major>1</major>
  <minor>0</minor>
  </specVersion>
  <actionList>
    .
    .
    .
  </actionList>
  <serviceStateTable>
    <stateVariable sendEvents="yes">
      <name>totalSlices</name>
      <dataType>ui4</dataType>
      <defaultValue>0</defaultValue>
    </stateVariable>
    <stateVariable sendEvents="yes">
      <name>totalTime</name>
      <dataType>time</dataType>
      <defaultValue>0</defaultValue>
    </stateVariable>
  </serviceStateTable>
</scpd>
```


Figure 14.12 Updated Lifetime Statistics SCPD

```
/*
 * Function: upnp_lssusbscriptions
 *
 * Parameters: pointer to a Upnp_Subscription_Request structure
 *
 * Description: This function handles subscription requests
 *              for the Lifetime Stats service.
 */
int upnp_lssubscriptions(struct Upnp_Subscription_Request
                         *request)
{
  IXML_Document propset = NULL;   /* Your property set */
  char totaltimestr[64];          /* Total Time string */
  char totaltoastsstr[64];        /* Total Toasts string */
```

Figure 14.13 New Lifetime Statistics Functions to Support Subscriptions *(Continues)*

```
  printf("upnp_lssubscriptions: start\n");

  /*
   * For each state variable in this service that you event,
   * you need to add it to the property set. Calling
   * UpnpAddToPropertySet with a NULL property set will
   * create one for you.
   */
  sprintf(totaltoastsstr, "%d", hw_gettotaltoasts());
  UpnpAddToPropertySet(&propset, "totalSlices", totaltoastsstr);

  sprintf(totaltimestr, "%d", hw_gettotaltime());
  UpnpAddToPropertySet(&propset, "totalTime", totaltimestr);

  /* Now accept the subscription. */
  UpnpAcceptSubscriptionExt(g_device_handle, g_deviceudn,
                            LIFETIME_STATS_SERVICEID,
                            propset,
                            request->Sid);

  /* Free the propset. */
  ixmlDocument_free(propset);

  printf("upnp_lssubscriptions: end\n");

  return UPNP_E_SUCCESS;
}

/*
 * Function: upnp_lsupdate
 *
 * Description: This function sends event updates for all
 *              evented state variables in this service.
 */
void upnp_lsupdate()
{
  IXML_Document propset=NULL; /* Property set for your service */
  char totaltimestr[64];      /* Total Time string */
  char totalslicesstr[64];    /* Total Slices string */

  printf("upnp_lsupdate: start\n");

  /*
   * First, build your property set of evented state variables.
   */
```

Figure 14.13 New Lifetime Statistics Functions to Support Subscriptions *(Continues)*

```
  sprintf(totalslicesstr, "%d", hw_gettotaltoasts());
  UpnpAddToPropertySet(&propset, "totalSlices", totalslicesstr);

  sprintf(totaltimestr, "%d", hw_gettotaltime());
  UpnpAddToPropertySet(&propset, "totalTime", totaltimestr);

  /*
   * Now, send the notify for your evented state variables.
   */
  UpnpNotifyExt(g_device_handle,
                g_deviceudn,
                LIFETIME_STATS_SERVICEID,
                propset);

  /* Free your property set. */
  ixmlDocument_free(propset);

  printf("upnp_lsupdate: start\n");

  return;
}

/*
 * Function: upnp_lscallback
 *
 * Description: This function is called to tell you
 *              that something has changed with the toaster
 */
void upnp_lscallback()
{
  printf("upnp_lscallaback: start\n");

  /* Event your updates. */
  upnp_lsupdate();

  printf("upnp_lscallaback: end\n");
}
```

Figure 14.13 New Lifetime Statistics Functions to Support Subscriptions

There are a few interesting things to note about the Lifetime Statistics service implementation of subscriptions that are slightly different than the Toasting Status service.

First, the Lifetime Statistics service has multiple evented state variables. You need to be sure to add all evented state variables to the property set, even if only one of the two has actually changed. Recall that this is a limitation of the UPnP Device Architecture, because subscriptions apply equally to all evented state variables in the service. Technically, it is possible to send events for the state variables one by one, but in practice it usually works better to event them in a single property set as implemented in this chapter.

Second, the most important difference is how the `totalToasts` and `totalTime` state variable values are added to the property set. `UpnpAddToPropertySet()` requires the current value of the state variable be represented as character strings. This was no problem in the Toasting Status service, where the state variable you were eventing was a string, but in this case you must convert the integer values to their string representations before adding to the property set. The simple reason for this is that, just like SOAP responses to actions, everything gets converted to a big string representing an XML document.

Finally, you need to decide whether or not to keep the get-style actions in the Lifetime Statistics service. From a device implementer perspective, actions can at times be preferred over subscriptions due to the reduced overhead in not having to maintain subscription information. On the other hand, leaving the actions in certainly provides the greatest flexibility to control point applications. This is what you'll do here.

In most cases, it's a design decision specific to a device implementation. If information and state variable changes are going to be generated infrequently, then it's probably best to event them. If the information is going to be updated rapidly (like once per second), then it would be inefficient to have the device make a TCP connection to each subscribed control point to notify about the event each and every time; it may be more efficient for control points to poll an action every few seconds on the persistent control connection to get the same information.

Toaster Control Service

Turning your attention to the Toaster Control service, consider whether it could be updated to support subscriptions and eventing. The Toaster Control service contains only two state variables: one that represents the current lever state and another that represents the darkness dial setting.

At first glance, eventing the lever state might seem like a good idea; but is it really? Whenever considering making a state variable evented, a device implementer should always consider whether the information that would be communicated to subscribed control points is actually useful *and* unique. Since you already event the current toaster state in the Toaster Status service, the lever state information is redundant. If the `toasterStatus` state variable is "TOASTING," this means the lever is depressed, and vice versa. So there is no need to event the lever state.

Why have the lever state at all then? An excellent question! Remember that for every action parameter (either in or out) the UPnP Device Architecture specification requires that you have an associated state variable; so alas, you must leave this state variable in for the `GetDeviceStatus` action, although internally you may not actually have a state variable representing the lever state. And, having this information also available through an action is certainly the most flexible solution for control point application developers.

The `darknessDial` state variable, on the other hand, has no such redundancy with other state variables on the device. Should you event it? Probably not. It turns out that this state variable is actually a bad candidate for eventing, specifically because of the rate of change of the state variable. A device should never event a state variable that changes frequently, because publishing events for each state change would flood the network with notification messages, not to mention that the cost of setting up and tearing down a TCP connection for every event can certainly put a sizable burden on a device. Because a user could turn the `darknessDial` and generate a large number of unique state events, the worst-case scenario would require a large number of event notifications be sent out over the network. This is clearly inefficient and unnecessary for control points.

This closer review of the state variables in the Toaster Control service has yielded no changes, so you'll leave it alone.

Alternate APIs

Earlier this chapter demonstrated how to accept subscriptions and sent events using the Intel SDK. Although it is the opinion of the authors that these are the easiest functions to use for accepting subscriptions and eventing, they are not the only functions provided by the Intel SDK for use in your device.

The alternate APIs presented in this section expect device service state variable's names and corresponding values of state variables to be stored in matching single-dimension arrays. For example, the ith

position in the array of state variable names array matches the ith position in the array of state variable values. This method of storing state variables can be more efficient for device with a large number of state variables to maintain.

Using this storage method, subscriptions can alternatively be accepted by the following function:

```
int UpnpAcceptSubscription(IN UpnpDeviceHandle Hnd,
                           IN const char *DevID,
                           IN const char *ServID,
                           IN char **VarName,
                           IN const char **NewVal,
                           IN int cVariables,
                           IN Upnp_SID SubsId)
```

Hnd—Handle to your UPnP Device, obtained from a previous call to UpnpRegisterRootDevice().

DevID—Pointer to a character string of your device ID, specified in your device description document.

ServID—Pointer to a character string of the service ID for which you are publishing this event.

VarName—Pointer to an array of state variable names.

NewVal—Pointer to an array of state variable values.

cVariables—Integer value representing the total number of evented state variables described by the arrays pointed to by VarName and NewVal.

SubsId—The Subscription ID for this accepted subscription.

Returns: UPNP_E_SUCCESS when successful, Intel SDK error code if not.

You see the array-storage method in the `VarName` and `NewVal` parameters. The `cVariables` parameter provides a maximum boundary for access to the state variable arrays.

There is a matching notify function that uses the same array storage method:

```
int UpnpNotify(IN UpnpDeviceHandle Hnd,
               IN const char *DevID,
               IN const char *ServID,
               IN char **VarName,
               IN const char **NewVal,
               IN int cVariables)
```

Hnd—Handle to your UPnP Device, obtained from a previous call to `UpnpRegisterRootDevice()`.

DevID—Pointer to a character string of your device ID, specified in your device description document.

ServID—Pointer to a character string of the service ID for which you are publishing this event.

VarName—Pointer to an array of state variable names.

NewVal—Pointer to an array of state variable values.

cVariables—Integer value representing the total number of evented state variables described by the arrays pointed to by VarName and NewVal.

Returns: UPNP_E_SUCCESS when successful, Intel SDK error code if not.

Again, this version of `UpnpNotify()` expects an array of state variable names, with a matching array of state variable values. To see a UPnP device implementation that uses this method of state variable storage and uses these alternate APIs, please refer to the sample TV device included in the Intel SDK.

Intel Tools for UPnP Technology

Testing subscriptions and eventing is difficult unless you have a control point application for your device. Fortunately, Device Spy comes in handy here, because in addition to supporting the invocation of actions, it also supports subscribing to device services and receiving events for evented state variables.

Let's introduce the few menu options left out of the last chapter that deal directly with subscriptions and eventing:

- File—manage Device Spy data
  - — Copy Event Log To Clipboard copies the entire Event Log to the clipboard.
  - — Clear Event Log clears all currently displayed events in the Event Log pane.
- View—adjust properties of the user interface
  - — Event Log toggles the display of the Event Log.

As shown in Figure 14.14, when you right-click a service and click "Subscribe to Events," an Event pane is added to the user interface.

The Event Log pane lists all received events by Device Spy. For your Super Toaster, when you right-click and ask to be subscribed to that service, the subscription accept handlers for each service are called, where you provide your initial property set. You can see this firsthand in the Event Log pane shown in Figure 14.15.

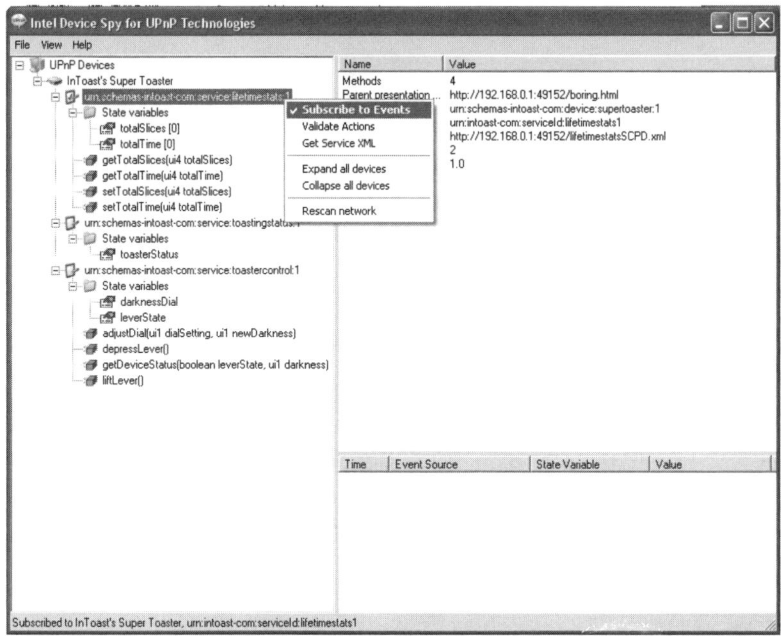

Figure 14.14 Device Spy Service Subscriptions

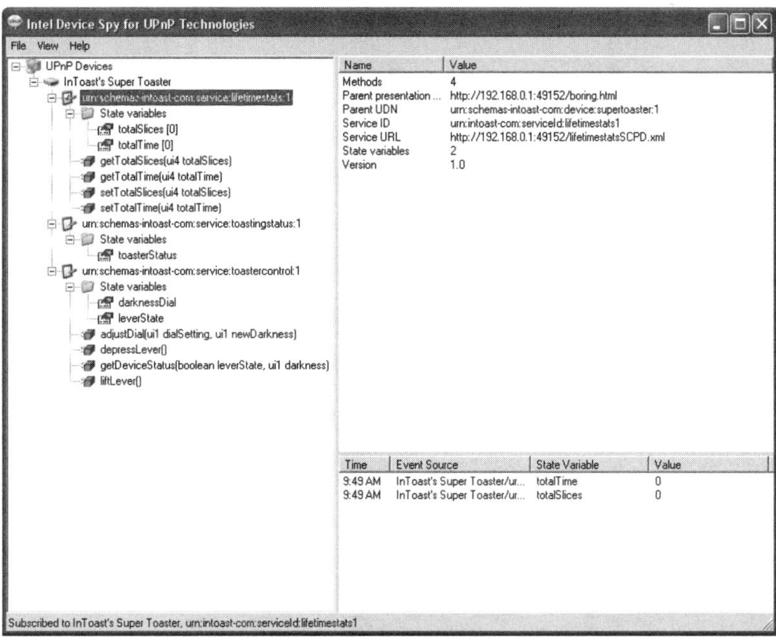

Figure 14.15 Device Spy Initial Events

Now, when you invoke actions that affect the state of the device, the Hardware Interface Library calls your callback handlers, which sends events to Device Spy. You can see this firsthand by manually invoking `setTotalTime` and viewing the result in the Event Log pane shown in Figure 14.16.

Like the device pane, the Event Log pane also has a right-click contextual menu that allows you to copy the event to the clipboard for viewing in notepad or other similar text editor.

Using Device Spy to subscribe to subscriptions and receive events is very useful. In fact, if it wasn't for Device Spy, you'd have no idea whether your Super Toaster did what it was supposed to do. With subscription and eventing support complete, you can test all the capabilities of your Super Toaster.

In the last example, you'll invoke `depressLever` and let the toaster go through a toasting cycle to see the events that should come back when the device finishes toasting. You can see this in Figure 14.17.

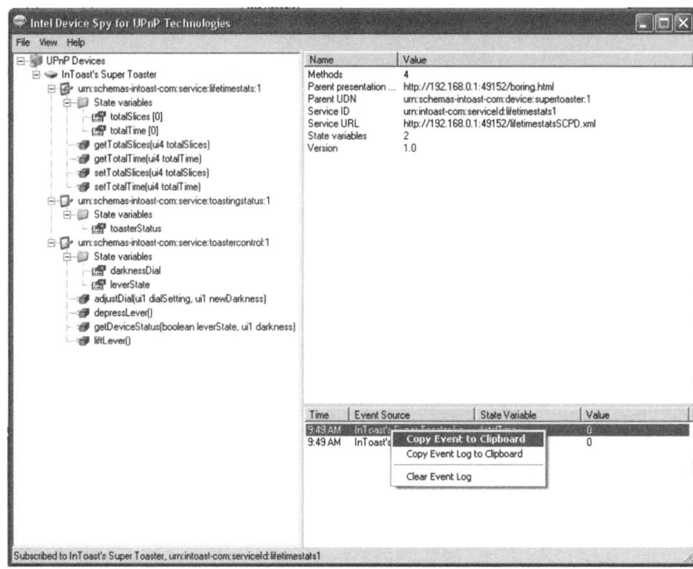

Figure 14.16 Run-time Event Log Notifications

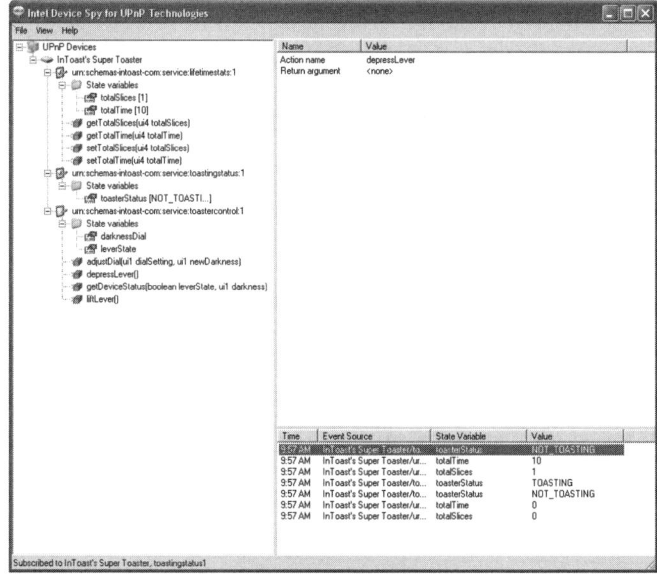

Figure 14.17 The Super Toaster Works!

The Super Toaster works! This is exciting stuff. In the Event Log pane, you can actually see your device change state from NOT_TOASTING to TOASTING, and when toasting completes, you see the `totalTime` and totalSlices state variables also updated with their new values.

This completes verifying the functionality of your Super Toaster. You have only one task remaining: the device presentation page covered in Chapter 15.

Summary

This chapter introduced you to the concept of UPnP subscriptions and their relationship to evented state variables. You covered the basic publisher/subscriber model of eventing in UPnP and provided semantic details of its operation. In the second half of the chapter you added subscription support to your sample device using the Intel SDK and used Device Spy to test the functionality of your device. With the completion of subscription support, your sample device is nearly complete. However, there is one last phase of the UPnP device model for you to support: Presentation, covered in the next chapter.

Chapter 15

Creating Device Presentation Pages

In the previous chapter you learned how to add subscription and eventing support to your device. There is only one final piece of functionality to add: Presentation. In this chapter you learn what it means for a device to support presentation and how you can create a presentation page.

Problem Description

At any given point in time, there are going to be a number of UPnP devices on the network. Up until now, the only way to find out more information about a device is to have a control point application discover it and invoke a series of service actions. But what if a custom-designed control point application isn't available? It would still be nice to find out information about the device. This is the purpose of presentation pages.

UPnP Presentation Pages

Simply put, UPnP presentation pages are HTML-based Web pages, hosted by a device that can be viewed in any web browser on the network. Instead of having a complex control point application, users can view information about a device by simply pulling up its presentation page in a web browser.

Presentation pages can provide many different types of information, ranging from static information held in the device description document (manufacturer, model, version, and so on) to dynamic information about current state variable values. Enterprising devices can even offer the ability to invoke actions from a presentation page, although this is uncommon.

The level of support in a device presentation page is entirely up to the capabilities of the device. In fact, the UPnP architecture specifies no specific functional requirements for the presentation page. Support for presentation is entirely optional and can contain as little or as much information or control capabilities as the device manufacturer chooses.

The UPnP Device Architecture specification requires only that presentation pages conform to HTML 3.0 or later.

Presentation URL

The presentation page is specified in the device description document. Recall from Chapter 12 that you simply specified an HTML filename for the presentation URL.

```
<?xml version="1.0"?>
<root xmlns="urn:intoast-com:device-1-0">
  <specVersion>
    <major>1</major>
    <minor>0</minor>
  </specVersion>
  <URLBase>http://jelly.intoast.com:5431</URLBase>
  <device>
    <deviceType>urn:schemas-intoast-
      com:supertoaster:1</deviceType>
    <friendlyName>InToast's Super Toaster</friendlyName>
    <manufacturer>InToast Inc.</manufacturer>
    ...
    <serviceList>
      ...
    </serviceList>
    <presentationURL>/supertoaster.html</presentationURL>
  </device>
</root>
```

Figure 15.1 Complete SuperToaster Device Description Document

Like the service description documents, the presentation page is retrieved using the URLBase also specified in the device description document.

Localization

One of the more interesting capabilities of HTML 3.0-compliant presentation pages is providing localization support for the device. Remember that all other device interactions are done programmatically and are invisible to the user. Because a presentation page is the only immediately visible display of a device, it is the only piece that needs to be localized for specific markets.

Fortunately, HTML provides simple mechanisms to enable this kind of support. Devices can use the META tag with the CHARSET attribute to designate specific character sets supported by the device, as shown here for Russian language:

```
<HTML LANG="ru">

<META CONTENT=CHARSET="ISO-8859-5">
```

When a client's web browser is also set to look for a specific character set, it will find the appropriate page on the device.

Control points and browsers can also make the device's job easier by specifying the language they will accept from a request. This is done using the ACCEPT-LANGUAGE field in the HTTP header. Say that a web browser makes a request as follows:

```
GET supertoaster.html HTTP/1.0

ACCEPT-LANGUAGE=ru

ACCEPT-CHARSET=iso-8859-5
```

When the device receives such a request, it can match the requested language and character set by including the CONTENT-LANGUAGE field in the response:

```
GET supertoaster.html HTTP/1.0

CONTENT-LANGUAGE=ru

CONTENT-CHARSET=iso-8859-5

[Response Body]
```

Using these capabilities of HTTP, a single device can simultaneously support a wide variety of world markets.

Creating a Presentation Page

You'll begin your support of presentation pages for the Super Toaster by creating a simple static web page that displays some information about the device. Figure 15.2 lists the source code for your web page.

Viewing the Presentation Page

With the presentation page added to the device, you now need a way to bring it up in a Web browser. Obviously, if you know the exact IP address and port number of the device, entering this into a web browser achieves the desired effect. But for most users this is a technical detail they'd just as soon ignore.

Fortunately, with the Intel Tools for UPnP Technologies, this is easy. Using Device Spy, simply right-click any device listed in the device pane, and select "View Presentation Page," as shown in Figure 15.3.

The devices presentation page loads in your currently selected web browser, as can be seen in Figure 15.4.

This successfully completes the creation and support of a static presentation page for your UPnP Super Toaster. It's a relatively painless process that doesn't require any new code to be added to your device, but also doesn't add anything interesting to your device. In the next section, you'll see how you can make a device presentation page a bit more interesting.

```
<HTML>
<TITLE>Super Toaster Presentation Page!</TITLE>
<BODY>
  <H1>Thank you for buying the Super Toaster!</H1>
  <P> <H2>This is a boring static Presentation Page</H2>
</BODY>
</HTML>
```

Figure 15.2 Super Toaster Presentation Page Source Code

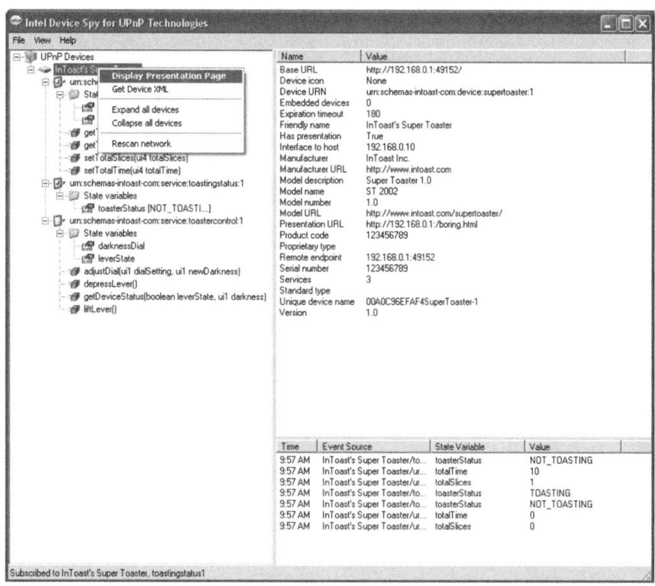

Figure 15.3 Using Device Spy to View Presentation Page

Figure 15.4 Device Presentation Page

Dynamic Presentation Page Creation

For many device makers, creating a presentation page in advance may not be acceptable or have much value. It's easy to imagine a presentation page that displays accurate run-time information about the device, including values of state variables. This capability can certainly be provided by a device presentation page but does require a bit of heavy lifting by the device.

In this section, you'll see two ways to dynamically update an existing web page when device state changes, so that a user will be given the most up-to-date information when viewing the presentation page. For your SuperToaster, you will add the real-time display of lifetime statistics on the presentation page.

Using the DOM

The basic idea behind updating the device presentation page at run time is to update the HTML that you presented to the web browser client that is viewing the page. To do this, you need to somehow update the HTML when your state information changes so that the next time a web client retrieves the presentation page, the content is different. In short, you must parse the HTML, and update it appropriately.

There are a number of different ways to parse HTML. Because it is similar to XML and can usually be represented in a tree format such as DOM, many XML parsers may also support HTML parsing. In this case, the supporting dynamic presentation page creation involves the following steps:

1. Represent the HTML document as a DOM (or equivalent tree representation).
2. When you'd like to update the text of a string in the document, find the corresponding node, and update its node value.
3. Generate a new HTML document (replacing the old copy) from the tree representation.

After these steps, each time a web client requests the document, the document will contain the updated values. Figure 15.5 shows a slightly updated version of your previous presentation page.

Note that you've added text to the web page to display the values of the two state variables from the Lifetime Statistics service. What you'd like to do is update the values in the HTML source code when they change in the device.

```
<HTML>
<TITLE>Super Toaster Presentation Page!</TITLE>
<BODY>
  <H1>Lifetime Statistics</H1>
  <H2>TotalToasts: </H2><I>0</I>
  <H2>Total Time: </H2><B>0</B>
</BODY>
</HTML>
```

Figure 15.5 Updated Simple HTML Source Code

Writing the Code

The most difficult part about this method of supporting dynamic page updates is using the DOM parser and its associated function calls to traverse the tree. Before you tackle that problem, you need to first load the HTML page into a DOM Document using the `ixmlLoadDocument()` function.

```
IXML_Document *ixmlLoadDocument(IN char *xmlFile);
```

`xmlFile`—Path on disk to an XML-like file.

Returns: Pointer to a DOM document that represents the specified xmlFile, NULL if document creation was unsuccessful.

Although the Intel SDK documentation suggests that this function only takes XML files, the requirement is that the files be XML-like. In particular, they must be well formed, with clear starting and closing tags, as in your simple HTML web page. There is a complementary function, `ixmlPrintDocument()`, that takes any DOM document and converts it back into a string.

```
DOMString ixmlPrintDocument
            IN IXML_Node *OperationNode);
```

`OperationNode`—UPnP Node that you want to print.

Returns: Pointer to a string that represents the document, NULL if string creation was unsuccessful.

DOM types are not strict, in the sense that a pointer to an IXML_Document is really just a pointer to a root node in the document, so it can be used interchangeably with IXML_Node. Similarly, a DOMString is just a normal character string, and can be used wherever you'd normally use char *.

Recall that you want to convert your HTML page into DOM, update the DOM, and then write the updated DOM back out to disk, so that the next time a client web browser requests the presentation page, it will contain the updated information.

You have enough information to begin the upnp_updatepresentation() function, shown in Figure 15.6.

With this complete, you now must perform the heavy lifting. To parse a DOM tree, you need to find a specific tag to look for, and then perform some kind of tree search, replacing the current value with the new value. What this involves is starting at the root node of a document and performing a breadth-depth search of the tree looking for the specific node you'd like to update. Once found, you need to update the text attribute of that node with the new value you'd like in its place. This book includes code written to perform this task, and it is included in the sample_util2.c file. First, here is some information about the function:

```
int SampleUtil_getAndSetNodeValue(
            IN OUT IXML_Document *RootNode,
            IN const char *ParentName,
            IN const char *ElementName,
            IN const char *NewValue);
```

RootNode—Root node of a DOM document to Search. The DOM document will be updated on return.

ParentName—Name of the immediate parent of the ElementName.

ElementName—Name of the element whose value will be changed.

NewValue—Requested new value for the specified Element.

Returns: UPNP_E_SUCCESS if successful, -1 if not.

The source code for this function is contained in sample_util2.c and is listed in Figure 15.7. Understanding this function is useful if you use the DOM to perform other tasks, but is otherwise not germane to Presentation Page creation.

```
/*
 * Function: update_presentation
 *
 * Description: This function update your presentation page
 *              using the DOM method.
 */
void upnp_updatepresentationDOM()
{
  char page[256];             /* File Path to your page */
  IXML_Document *doc=NULL;    /* Your DOM document */
  DOMString *str=NULL;        /* Dom String for your updated doc */
  char toasts[16];            /* Total toasts */
  char time[16];              /* Total Time */
  int fd=0;                   /* File Descriptor */
  int ret=0;                  /* General purpose error code */

  printf("upnp_updatepresentation: start\n");

  /* Create your path. */
  sprintf(page, "%s%s", WEB_ROOT_DIR, PRESENTATION_PAGE);

  /*
   * The DOM Method. First, convert the web page to a DOM
   * Document. Then, update the node values, and write
   * it back out to disk as the new web page.
   */
  doc = ixmlLoadDocument(page);
  if(doc == NULL) {
    printf("upnp_updatepresentation: Couldn't parse doc\n");
    return;
  }

  /* Now, get your updated values. */
  sprintf(toasts, "%d", hw_gettotaltoasts());
  sprintf(time, "%d", hw_gettotaltime());

  /*
   * TODO: Update the DOM Document with your new values.
   */

  /*
   * TODO: Convert DOM back into a string and write to file.
   */
```

Figure 15.6 upnp_updatepresentation(), Part 1 *(Continues)*

```
  printf("upnp_updatepresentation: end\n");

  return;
}
```

Figure 15.6 upnp_updatepresentation(), Part 1

```
/*
 * Function: SampleUtil_getAndSetNodeValue
 *
 * Arguments: The node from which to start the search, the parent
 *            node name for the element, name to begin the
 *            search, requested value to set the child text
 *            node. This function can only be used for
 *            modifying nodes of the format:
 *              <ParentNodeName>
 *                <ElementName>value</ElementName>
 *              </ParentNodeName>
 *
 * Returns: 0 if success, nonzero otherwise
 *
 * Description: This function is useful when trying to modify
 *              certain values in a DOM, which typically was
 *              created from an XML doc, and will eventually be
 *              converted back into XML. After specifying the
 *              root node from which you wish to begin the
 *              search, this function performs a breadth-depth
 *              search of the tree looking for the specified
 *              parent_node_name. Once found, all children of
 *              the parent_node_name are matched with the
 *              provided element_name. Once the first matching
 *              element_name has been found, that element's value
 *              is updated with the provided value.
 *
 *              Note that this function does have a few
 *              limitations: namely, if there are multiple nodes
 *              in the system with the same parent_node_name at
 *              different levels of hierarchy, this function will
 *              simply use the first found in its search.
 */
int SampleUtil_getAndSetNodeValue(Upnp_Node *upnp_root_node,
char *parent_node_name, char *element_name, char *value)
```

Figure 15.7 Code Listing for SampleUtil_getAndSetNodeValue() *(Continues)*

```
{
  IXML_Node *tmp_node=NULL;        /* Temporary node to cycle
                                      through node lists */
  IXML_Node *upnp_node=NULL;       /* Node that matches
                                      root_node_name */
  IXML_NodeList *node_list=NULL;   /* Node list of children or
                                      siblings */
  int i;                           /* General purpose counter */

  printf("SampleUtil_getAndSetNodeValue: start\n");

  /*
   * First check if you don't have any child nodes. If you don't,
   * then you've exhausted this path.
   */
  if(!ixmlNode_hasChildNodes(upnp_root_node)) {
    printf("SampleUtil_getAndSetNodeValue: No child nodes, it's a
          leaf, EXIT\n");
    return 1;
  }

  /*
   * Cycle through this level of nodes and try to find the node
   * that matches the parent node name. This needs to be a
   * recursive search. If the node you're currently at has a
   * child, you need to call yourself again and look at all the
   * nodes at the child's level.
   */
  upnp_node = upnp_root_node;

  while((upnp_node != NULL) &&
       (0 != strcmp(ixmlNode_getNodeName(upnp_node),
       parent_node_name))) {
    /* Recursively search if there is a child. */
    if(ixmlNode_hasChildNodes(upnp_node)) {
      /* Get it and call ourselves again. */
      if(0 == SampleUtil_getAndSetNodeValue(
        ixmlNode_getFirstChild(upnp_node),
        parent_node_name,
        element_name, value)) {
      return 0;
      }
    }

    /* Otherwise, this node had no children, so just go to the
       next sibling in the list. */
```

Figure 15.7 Code Listing for `SampleUtil_getAndSetNodeValue()` *(Continues)*

```
    upnp_node = ixmlNode_getNextSibling(upnp_node);
  }

  if(upnp_node == NULL) {
    /* You didn't find the node & there was an error. */
    printf("SampleUtil_getAndSetNodeValue: couldn't find specified
          root_node_name\n");
    return 1;
  }

  /* Get a list of child nodes for the specified root node. */
  node_list = ixmlNode_getChildNodes(upnp_node);
  if(NULL == node_list) {
    printf("SampleUtil_getAndSetNodeValue: get child nodes
          failed\n");
    return 1;
  }

  /* Now, you need to cycle through the children looking for the
     specific element node specified. */
  i=0;
  tmp_node = ixmlNodeList_item(node_list, i);
  ixmlNode_getNodeName(tmp_node));

  while((tmp_node != NULL) &&
(strcmp(ixmlNode_getNodeName(tmp_node),
       element_name) != 0)) {
    i++;
    tmp_node = ixmlNodeList_item(node_list, i);
  }

  if(tmp_node == NULL) {
    /* couldn't find element node. */
    ixmlNodeList_free(node_list);
    return 1;
  }

  /* Now that you have the element node, you need to get its text
     node, which is the first child. */
  tmp_node = ixmlNode_getFirstChild(tmp_node);
  if(tmp_node == NULL) {
    /* Error condition */
    ixmlNodeList_free(node_list);
    return 1;
  }
```

Figure 15.7 Code Listing for `SampleUtil_getAndSetNodeValue()` *(Continues)*

```
  /* Now, set it to what you want. */
  ixmlNode_getNodeValue(tmp_node));
  ixmlNode_setNodeValue(tmp_node, value);

  /* All done! Cleanup. */
  ixmlNodeList_free(node_list);

  return 0;
}
```

Figure 15.7 Code Listing for `SampleUtil_getAndSetNodeValue()`

Referring to Figure 15.7, the code follows a straightforward algorithm. It recursively follows each branch to the end, looking for a node with the specified name. Once found, the node's text value is updated to the parameter passed in, and the recursive call stack folds up.

Using this function, you can now update your simple HTML presentation page. Referring to Figure 15.5, the `ParentNodeName` is "BODY", and the `ElementName` is "I" and "B" respectively for the two values. Using this information, you can complete your function `upnp_update-presentation()`, listed in Figure 15.8.

```
/*
 * Function: update_presentation
 *
 * Description: This function will update your presentation page
 *              using the DOM method.
 */
void upnp_updatepresentationDOM()
{
  char page[256];             /* File Path to your page */
  IXML_Document *doc=NULL;    /* Your DOM document */
  IXML_DOMString *str=NULL;   /* Dom String for your updated doc */
  char toasts[16];            /* Total toasts */
  char time[16];              /* Total Time */
  int fd=0;                   /* File Descriptor */
  int ret=0;                  /* General purpose error code */
```

Figure 15.8 Complete Code Listing for `upnp_updatepresentation()`
(Continues)

```
printf("upnp_updatepresentation: start\n");

/* Create your path. */
sprintf(page, "%s%s", WEB_ROOT_DIR, PRESENTATION_PAGE);

/*
 * The DOM Method. First, convert the web page to a DOM
 * Document. Then, update the node values, and write
 * it back out to disk as the new web page.
 */
doc = ixmlLoadDocument(page);
if(doc == NULL) {
  printf("upnp_updatepresentation: Couldn't parse doc\n");
  return;
}

/* Now, get your updated values. */
sprintf(toasts, "%d", hw_gettotaltoasts());
sprintf(time, "%d", hw_gettotaltime());

/* Set them in the DOM. */
ret = SampleUtil_getAndSetNodeValue(doc, "BODY", "B", toasts);
ret = SampleUtil_getAndSetNodeValue(doc, "BODY", "I", time);

/* Write it back out to file. */
fd = open(page, O_RDWR | O_TRUNC);
if(fd == -1) {
  printf("upnp_updatedpresentation: open failed\n");
  return;
}

/* Convert to String. */
str = ixmlPrintDocument((IXML_Node *)doc);
if(str == NULL) {
  printf("upnp_updatepresentation: new print document
        failed\n");
  return;
}

/* Write the string to file. */
ret = write(fd, str, strlen(str));
```

Figure 15.8 Complete Code Listing for upnp_updatepresentation()
(Continues)

```
  if(ret == -1) {
    printf("upnp_updatepresentation: write failed\n");
    return;
  }

  /* All Done! Free up memory. */
  close(fd);
  ixmlFreeDOMString(str);

  printf("upnp_updatepresentation: end\n");

  return;
}
```

Figure 15.8 Complete Code Listing for `upnp_updatepresentation()`

The last thing you'll do (not shown) is to simply add a call to `upnp_updatepresenation()` every time your device gets a callback from the hardware library. The next time someone requests the HTML presentation page, it will call this function to update the html page. You can see this firsthand in Figure 15.9 after completing a toast cycle.

An Imperfect Solution

Although it works, there are a few problems with this approach. As you've already seen, it's a tad complex. Manipulating and understanding DOM documents is something most engineers would rather never have to do.

Furthermore, processing and manipulating DOM documents incurs measurable overhead; many embedded devices may not have sufficient processing or memory overhead to perform such tasks.

Finally, the biggest problem with representing HTML as DOM is that most HTML web pages are not always strictly formatted like XML documents, so this makes it very difficult to guarantee that they'd be readable by a DOM parser. HTML documents that have tags like <META> that do not have closing tags cannot be parsed by the DOM parser.

The next section introduces you to a quick-and-dirty method for dynamically updating a device presentation page without worrying about DOM.

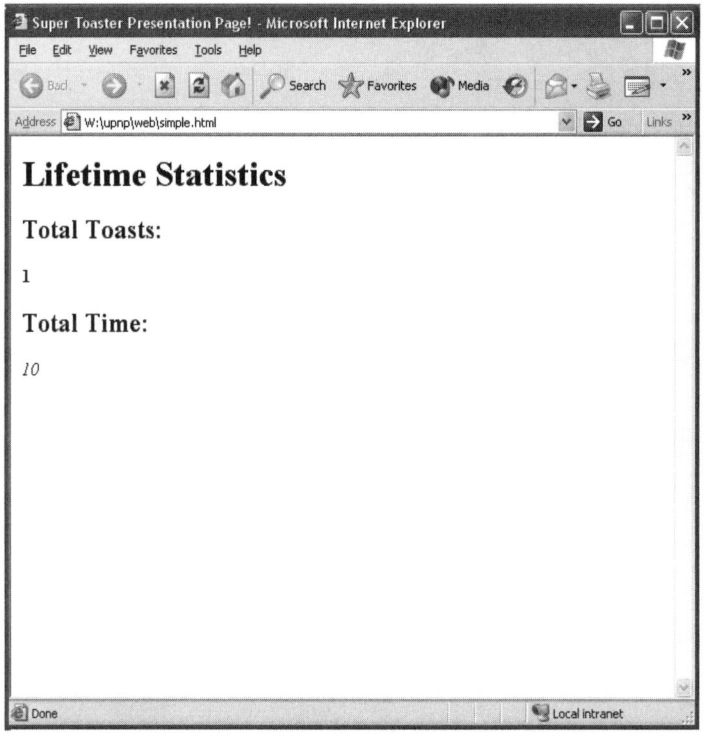

Figure 15.9 Updated Presentation Page

Copy and Paste

The second method for updating values in a device presentation page is fairly reminiscent of the copy-and-paste operation. It's a bit of a hack, but as you'll see, it's actually quite effective. The idea behind this approach is that you can divide up any given presentation page into three distinct parts:

- Prologue is the portion of the HTML document that exists before the text you want to update.
- The body is the text you actually want to update at run time.
- Epilogue is the remainder of the HTML document that occurs after the text you want to update.

What you'll do is keep the prologues and epilogues in memory and dynamically generate the HTML page every time you need to update the text in question. Obviously, for HTML documents that have multiple portions of text, you repeat the prologue and body sections until you have no remaining text to update in the document:

As before, you can reduce this process into a few tasks that should seem a bit easier to manage than the DOM method:

1. Partition your HTML into the three (or more) sections identified above.
2. Update the body as needed.
3. Concatenate the three (or more) sections together to form the complete HTML document.

Before you write any code, you must first divide your HTML web page into the three sections identified above. To make things more interesting, you're going to use a professionally designed web page for your Super Toaster. This is a normal HTML web page, unmodified from its original source. Figure 15.10 lists the HTML source code for the new Presentation Page, with the two small bits of code that you'd like to update shaded for clarity.

```
<html>
<head>
<title>InToast, Inc.</title>
<meta http-equiv="Content-Type" content="text/html;
charset=iso-8859-1">
</head>

<body bgcolor="#FFFFFF" text="#000000" marginheight=0,
marginwidth=0, topmargin=0, leftmargin=0
background="images/background.gif">
<table width="750" border="0" cellspacing="0" cellpadding="0">
  <tr>
    <td height="118"><img src="images/top_header.gif" width="750"
height="118"></td>
  </tr>
  <tr>
    <td height="402" valign="top">
      <table width="750" border="0" cellspacing="0"
```

Figure 15.10 Fancy HTML Presentation Page *(Continues)*

```
cellpadding="0" height="402">
        <tr>
          <td width="50"> </td>
          <td width="350"><img src="images/toaster.gif"
width="203" height="300"></td>
          <td width="350" valign="top">
            <table width="350" border="0" cellspacing="0"
cellpadding="4">
              <tr>
                <td height="100"> </td>
              </tr>
              <tr>
                <td><img src="images/title_toast_numbers.gif"
width="268" height="16"></td>
              </tr>
              <tr>
                <td>
                  <table width="350" border="0" cellspacing="0"
cellpadding="0">
                    <tr>
                      <td width="15"> </td>
                      <td width="30">
<img src="images/orange_arrow.gif"
width="10" height="12"></td>
                        <td><font face="Verdana, Arial, Helvetica,
sans-serif" size="1"><font size="2"
color="#3366CC">
                        ####
</font></font></td></tr>
                  </table>
                </td>
              </tr>
              <tr>
                <td height="50"> </td>
              </tr>
              <tr>
                <td><img src="images/title_toast_time.gif"
width="313" height="20"></td>
              </tr>
              <tr>
                <td>
                  <table width="350" border="0" cellspacing="0"
cellpadding="0">
                    <tr>
                      <td width="15"> </td>
                      <td width="30">
```

Figure 15.10 Fancy HTML Presentation Page *(Continues)*

```
<img src="images/orange_arrow.gif"
width="10" height="12"></td>
                      <td><font face="Verdana, Arial, Helvetica,
sans-serif" size="1"><font size="2"
color="#3366CC">
                        ####
                      </font></font></td>
                    </tr>
                  </table>
                </td>
              </tr>
              <tr>
                <td> </td>
              </tr>
              <tr>
                <td> </td>
              </tr>
              <tr>
                <td> </td>
              </tr>
              <tr>
                <td><font face="Verdana, Arial, Helvetica,
sans-serif" size="1"><font size="2" color="#666666">Visit
                  us on the web!</font></font></td>
              </tr>
              <tr>
                <td><font face="Verdana, Arial, Helvetica, sans-
serif" size="1"><font size="2" color="#3366CC">
<a href="http://www.intoast.com">
www.intoast.com</a></font></font></td>
              </tr>
            </table>
          </td>
        </tr>
      </table>
    </td>
  </tr>
  <tr>
    <td height="30"><img src="images/bottom_footer.gif"
width="750" height="30"></td>
  </tr>
</table>
</body>
</html>
```

Figure 15.10 Fancy HTML Presentation Page

Viewed as a whole, the code in Figure 15.10 can be intimidating. But, when viewed in terms of a prologue (the section before the first shaded line), the body (the section between the two shaded lines), and a prologue (the last part of the document), the complicated HTML code can be clearly divided into different sections.

The plan is to create constants in your device source code for the identified sections and then concatenate the updated values that you care about together with the constant portions of the HTML code to create updated HTML code for your device. In the next section, you'll learn how to do this.

Writing the Code

With your web page sufficiently partitioned, you now add programmatic code support for this method of dynamically updating your device presentation page. You'll statically store the contents of the prologue and epilogue sections in memory. Whenever the state variable changes, you simply construct the complete web page by concatenating the three (or more) sections together. Figure 15.11 lists the new `upnp_updatepresentation()` function that uses this method.

```
/*
 * Function: update_presentation
 *
 * Description: This function updates your presentation page
 *              using the in memory HTML store method.
 */
void upnp_updatepresentation()
{
  char page[256];       /* File path to your web page */
  int fd=0;             /* File descriptor */
  char toasts[16];      /* Total toasts */
  char time[16];        /* Total Time */

  printf("upnp_updatepresentation: start\n");

  /* Create your path. */
  sprintf(page, "%s%s", WEB_ROOT_DIR, PRESENTATION_PAGE);
```

Figure 15.11 New `upnp_updatepresentation()` Listing *(Continues)*

```
  /* Now, get your updated values. */
  sprintf(toasts, "%d", hw_gettotaltoasts());
  sprintf(time, "%d", hw_gettotaltime());

  /* Open your web page. */
  fd = open(page, O_RDWR | O_TRUNC);
  if(fd == -1) {
    printf("upnp_updatepresentation: open failed\n");
    return;
  }

  /* Write back. */
  write(fd, PROLOGUE, strlen(PROLOGUE));
  write(fd, toasts, strlen(toasts));
  write(fd, PROLOGUE2, strlen(PROLOGUE2));
  write(fd, time, strlen(time));
  write(fd, EPILOGUE, strlen(EPILOGUE));

  /* Done! Close file. */
  close(fd);

  printf("upnp_updatepresentation: end\n");

  return;
}
```

Figure 15.11 New `upnp_updatepresentation()` Listing

And, with that you're done! Clearly this method is easier than the DOM approach you tried earlier, and, best of all, it's much more flexible, because you can now take HTML of any kind and apply the partitioning technique described. This frees you from the simple HTML you used in the beginning of the chapter to get more complex and far better looking presentation pages such as the one shown in Figure 15.12.

You'd have a difficult time doing this using any other method but the Copy and Paste techniques outlined in this chapter.

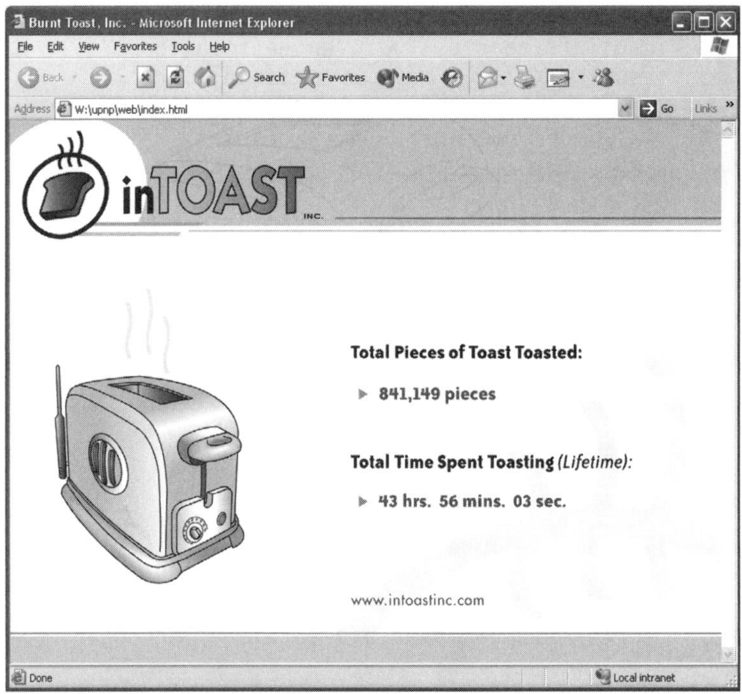

Figure 15.12 Professional Presentation Page

Advanced Topics

For those particularly adventuresome device makers, the land of web scripts offers nearly limitless possibilities for what a presentation page supports.

Invoking Actions

Although the Intel SDK does not support the direct invocation of actions from web pages, using scripts written in VBScript in the HTML presentation page on a Windows-based PC can invoke actions on the device. The TV Sample devices included in the Intel SDK contains VBScript code demonstrating this technique.

Server Scripts

There's no reason why the web server on the device couldn't also execute scripts on behalf of the user. Although the integrated web server in the Intel SDK doesn't support this capability, there's nothing preventing a device manufacturer from adding another more fully featured web server that could support the execution of CGI and other web scripts.

Summary

This chapter introduced the final stage of UPnP device development: Presentation. It began with an overview of presentation pages and the capabilities they can offer. Next, you created a simple presentation page for your device that displayed static information. Then you learned two methods for supporting dynamic creation of presentation pages that display accurate run-time information: the first using the integrated DOM parser; the second, a crude-yet-effective Copy and Paste technique. This completes the creation of your UPnP device! You've gone through each of the five phases of a UPnP Device. In the next chapter you look back at what you've created, and discuss some advanced device-creation topics.

Chapter 16

Putting It All Together

In the previous chapter, you completed your UPnP Super Toaster. From Chapter 12, you've added support for the five phases of the UPnP Device Architecture specification. This chapter takes a look back at where you've been and offers advanced tips for each phase of UPnP device development.

The Four Steps of Device Development

The following four sections briefly review activities at each phase of device development, highlighting the primary activities involved in each stage with the work products produced. The following sections can be used as an initial road map and checklist for device development. They also offer some tips and best-known methods at each stage for validating a correctly operating device and trying to figure out what to do when things don't work as expected.

Device Description

In Chapter 12, you began the quest for the perfect toaster by focusing on the device description documents that described information about your device. Key issues you faced here were how to partition the functionality of your device into different services or even multiple separate embedded devices. Work products in the phase of development included your device description document and code to initialize the Intel SDK libraries, register your root device, and send periodic announcements for your device and its services.

The only option for testing your device at this stage is to use Device Sniffer. Make sure that when your device is started, you can see the initial SSDP announcements sent on the network. Make sure also that your device can respond to `upnp:rootdevice` queries and that you can retrieve the device description document.

If you do not see any packets in Device Sniffer, make sure that the multicast route has been added to the route table (see Chapter 11), and if your development machine has multiple network interfaces, make sure that you've properly initialized the UPnP stack to the correct interface.

Device Services

Chapter 13 focused on filling out the service description documents for each of your device services, identifying individual actions and state variables for each service. Then you added basic service action response to your device, providing the framework for all future work on your device.

Using Device Spy is the best way to test functionality of your device at this stage. Test to see whether your device shows up in Device Spy. Invoke every action, and try as many different combinations of parameters, or sequences of actions, you can think of. Chances are there is one more you didn't try that will break your device.

If your device doesn't show up in Device Spy, try to manually retrieve every XML device and service description document using Device Sniffer. If you can't retrieve one using the data provided in the SSDP announce and SCPDURLs, then you've found your problem.

Another good technique when you're having problems at this stage is to selectively remove services and action definitions from your device and service description documents. Often you'll have a malformed bit of XML that Device Spy is not able to parse. Once you start removing chunks of XML it usually gets pretty easy to isolate the problem.

Also, as simple as it may sound, Internet Explorer also happens to be an excellent XML parser. Try opening your XML documents in Internet Explorer and see what happens. If you've got bad XML, it does a nice job of telling you exactly where the problem is, as seen in Figure 16.1.

In addition, if you have multiple devices running on the same machine that are using the same IP address and port number, Device Spy can't tell the difference between them. If you are on a busy network

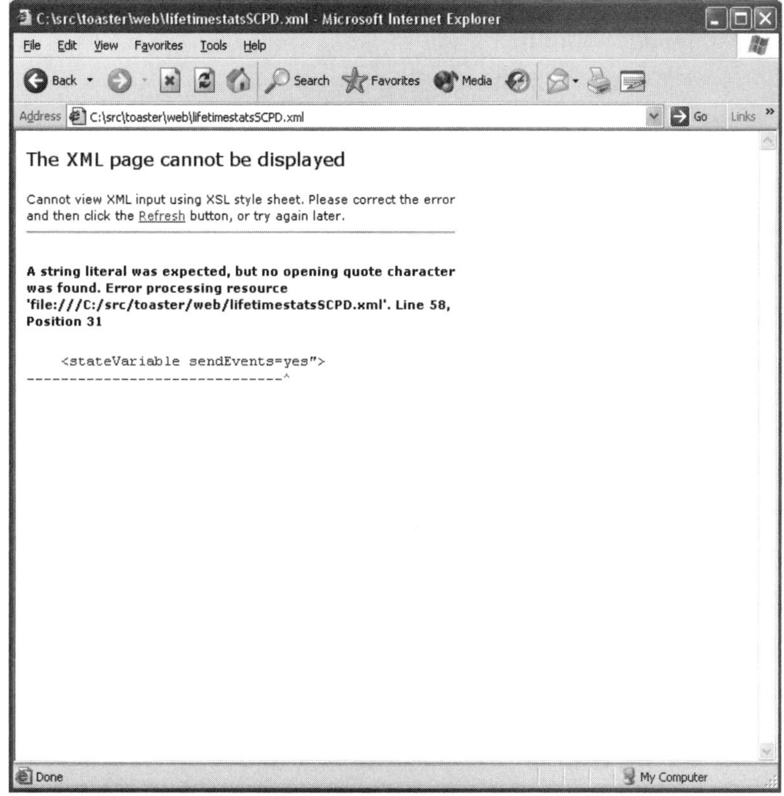

Figure 16.1 Using a Web Browser to Debug XML

with a lot of UPnP devices, make sure that none of the other devices are also using the same device UDN as your device. Both of these scenarios prevent a device from being discovered by Device Spy.

Another great idea at any stage is to start up a known device, such as the Network Light that comes with the Intel tools package. If your network is properly configured, you should see the Network Light just fine. If you can't, then the problem may not be with your device after all—double-check your network configuration, or try restarting Device Spy and your UPnP device.

Subscriptions and Eventing

Chapter 14 introduced the concept of service subscriptions and their relationship to evented state variables. You added support to your device for accepting service subscriptions and added code to event state variables when they were updated to subscribed control points, completing the functional programming of your SuperToaster.

To test the ability of your device to accept subscriptions, Device Spy is the tool of choice. And, since at this stage all device functionality is basically complete, you can test the complete device by calling actions, subscribing to services, and looking for evented state variables.

If your event notifications aren't showing up properly in Device Spy, make sure you're formatting the notify envelope properly and are putting the state variables in a known order (usually the same order listed in the service description document).

Presentation

Finally, in Chapter 15 you added a bit of flash and excitement to your device with the creation of a device presentation page. Then with a bit of inventive coding you improved the presentation page for your device to dynamically update the displayed values for your evented state variables.

To debug device presentation, Device Sniffer is once again your friend. Try retrieving the presentation page using Device Sniffer. Again, using a web browser to try and parse the HTML is a good idea here, but be aware that most modern Web browsers are extremely lenient when it comes to improperly formatted HTML.

Advanced Topics

Even though you've successfully created a fully functional device, there is still much to learn when developing UPnP devices. The following sections discuss a few advanced topics of UPnP device design and implementation.

Embedded Devices

Embedded device developers know all too well the constraints that exist on embedded platforms. Now imagine a fully functional UPnP device with integrated XML parsers and HTTP web servers. Building embedded UPnP devices is not easy, but, fortunately, there are a few tricks to improve the performance of your UPnP device on an embedded platform.

Thread Count

The Intel SDK contains a custom thread manager that uses a thread pool to complete the many different tasks of the SDK. In an embedded system, where resources are limited, it's often helpful to reduce or limit the number of threads currently running in the system. This helps to ensure the processor load never gets out of hand, while also keeping memory consumption low.

The `config.h` file found in the `upnp/inc/tools` contains a constant called MAX_THREADS where the number of threads can be set. Generally, this number should be kept around a minimum of 10, but that is certainly better than letting the number of threads grow unbounded.

Memory Consumption

Wherever possible, reducing and restricting memory consumption is also a primary goal of embedded device makers. Fortunately, the Intel SDK also allows a few opportunities to control memory consumption. In addition to the MAX_THREADS count just discussed, you can also specify the maximum size for an HTTP read request. This prevents a malicious HTTP server from sending an unbounded size HTTP response, causing buffers on the device to overflow. Also, in the `config.h` file located in `upnp/inc/tools`, the HTTP_READ_BYTES constant allows this value to be specified.

Code Size

Often the most precious resource on an embedded device is memory storage. Without the benefit of large hard drives, only code that is absolutely required can be allowed to reside in flash memory. Fortunately, the Intel SDK allows specific functional blocks to be excluded if they are not needed.

For example, if your device doesn't use the DOM parser, you can exclude it. Or, if your device doesn't have any evented state variables, then there's certainly no reason to include the GENA module. To do this, look for entries titled EXCLUDE_XXXX[0,1], where "XXXX" is the specific module you intend to replace. By changing both values to zero, that module will not be built into the generated UPnP library.

Multiple Interfaces

Many embedded devices have multiple interfaces—typically, one wired and one wireless. When the embedded device starts up, an active interface is selected, and the rest of the application code is started.

This presents a problem for a UPnP device that must bind to a specific interface. At any given time, how does the UPnP device application know which is the active interface (that is, eth0 or eth1)?

A best known method to handle this problem is for the kernel and the DHCP client to make sure that before any user applications (like your UPnP device) are started, an active interface is identified and all other interfaces are disabled. In this way, when the UPnP device starts, only one Ethernet interface is active, and the UPnP library automatically binds to the first (and only) interface found.

Other Stuff

The Intel SDK also includes a few other configuration options interesting to all UPnP device developers, not just those developing embedded devices.

Duplicate Announcements

Wireless networks with frequent interference and busy wired networks can experience the occasional lost packet. For UPnP devices, a lost announcement can mean the difference between a functional device and a device that appears dead to the user.

Fortunately, the Intel SDK allows the number of SSDP announcements sent out on behalf of the device to be customized. By default this value is set to 2, meaning that every time the device sends an SSDP NOTIFY, two copies are sent out. For greater confidence that control points will hear about your device, the SSDP_COPY constant in `config.h` can be increased.

Advertisement Interval

UPnP devices are required to re-advertise themselves within the advertisement interval specified at device registration. Control points use this information to monitor the state of the network and have devices expire that do not send their re-NOTIFY within the advertisement interval. But what if the device is busy and the re-advertisement is sent out late? Most control points are not going to be forgiving of the tardy advertisement and will assume the device has left the network, freeing up any stored state or other resources pertaining to the device. When the late advertisement is finally received by the control point, it will think the advertisement is for a new device instance, because it was received after the designated advertisement interval.

The Intel SDK uses a value called the AUTO_ADVERTISEMENT_TIME; that is, the number of seconds *before* the end of the advertisement interval that the UPnP library tries to send out the SSDP NOTIFY packets. This helps ensure they are received by any listening control points before the end of the advertised interval. Although the default value is 30 seconds, firsthand experience indicates that this is often not long enough. A value of at least 60 seconds performs better than the default. There is nothing wrong with a control point receiving the periodic advertisement a little early.

Hidden Presentation Pages

Often, as a device developer, you'd like the convenience of a UPnP presentation page to get at detailed run-time information about your device, but you don't necessarily want this capability exposed to the end user. If you explicitly specify a presentation URL in your device description document, anyone with a Windows XP-based PC sees the device and can view the presentation page.

The trick is to not specify the presentation page in the device description document. You, the developer (or the customer support person), will know the exact name of the file in the device's web server root directory, so you can access it by manually typing the address of the device description document.

In this way you get the best of both worlds—the convenience of a device presentation page without the exposure of administrative information to your users.

Device Reentrancy Protection

One of the easy things to forget about UPnP device development is that you have absolutely no control over how frequently or in what order actions within your device are called. This means that shared data between different services, or even within different actions in the same service, must be protected.

You all know about the many different ways to protect synchronized data. However, instead of implementing methods for each and every piece of data, and then having to worry about deadlock scenarios, quite often the easiest thing to do when developing a UPnP device is to add a single mutex that protects the `upnp_callback()` function.

It's actually quite simple if you think about it. For your UPnP device, there is only one single point of entry for everything that could be requested of it—the callback function registered when calling `UpnpRegisterRootDevice()`. In this function, adding a mutex lock call right before switching on the event type and dispatching to the appropriate service, with a matching unlock call after the specific service handler has finished, is guaranteed to protect your device.

Obviously, the one drawback to this approach is performance. Many devices might be able to handle multiple different actions at the same time, while others may only need to protect access to individual services or actions. Whatever the granularity that works for your device, be sure not to forget this very important step in UPnP device development.

Using the MAC Address for the Device UDN

As introduced in Chapter 12, the Device UDN is a static field that is supposed to represent a globally unique value to identify a specific device. Often the easiest way to create a guaranteed unique UDN at run time, without having to pre-program a device with a static UDN at manufacture, is to simply use the MAC address of the Ethernet interface to which the device is bound. There are two major tasks involved in doing this. The first is to simply get the MAC address and create your device UDN. The second is to programmatically insert the MAC address into your device description document.

Code is included in the sample_util2.c file that retrieves a MAC address from the current interface. Once you have that information, you need to update your device description document *at run time*, *before* you register your root device.

```
int SampleUtil_GetMacAddress(IN char *InterfaceName,
                             IN int len,
                             OUT char *macAddress);
```

`InterfaceName`—Interface from which you retrieve the MAC address.

`len`—Length of the string pointed to by MacAddress.

`MacAddress`—String in which the MAC address for the interface specified by Interface Name is returned.

Returns: UPNP_E_SUCCESS if successful, -1 if not.

Updating the Device Description Document

Fortunately, UpnpRegisterRootDevice2() supports an option to pass in an in-memory device description document. The difficult part is getting your description document properly formed in memory to use for that function call. The process you'll use is as follows: First, take your statically stored device description document and load it into a DOM. Then, parse the DOM looking for the UDN field, replacing the value with your MAC address-generated UDN. Finally, convert the DOM back into a string, and use it to register your root device. Fortunately, Chapter 15 introduced a function that does the DOM processing for you: SampleUtil_getAndSetNodeValue().

Your updated upnp_init() procedure is listed in Figure 16.2.

```
/*
 * Function: upnp_init
 *
 * Description: This function initializes the UPnP library,
 *              sets up the internel web server, registers
 *              your root device, and sends out your initial
 *              device advertisements.
 */
int upnp_init()
{
  int ret = 0;           /* General purpose error code */
  char descpath[512];    /* Path for your description document */
  char macaddr[64];      /* MAC address for your device */
  IXML_Document upnp_doc=NULL;    /* DOM Document */
  DOMString str=NULL;  /* Our in-memory description doc */

  printf("upnp_init: start\n");

  /* Create your Desc Doc. */
  sprintf(descpath, "%s%s", WEB_ROOT_DIR, DEVICE_DESC_DOC);

  /* Generate your device UDN from your MAC address.*/
  ret = SampleUtil_GetMacAddress("eth0", 64, macaddr);
  if(ret != 0) {
    printf("upnp_init: unable to get MAC address\n");
    strcpy(macaddr, DEVICE_UDN);
  } else {
    /* Append your device name in case there are multiple
       devices on the same machine. */
```

Figure 16.2 Updated upnp_init() Using MAC Address for the Device UDN *(Continues)*

```
    strcat(macaddr, "SuperToaster-1");
  }

  /*
   * Set the UDN in the description doc with your
   * MAC Address.
   */

  /* Make a DOM out of your starter doc. */
  upnp_doc = ixmlLoadDocument(devicedescdoc);
  if(upnp_doc == NULL) {
    /* Something didn't work. */
    debug_printf("upnp_initservices: failed to create DOM\n");
    /* Set some errors. */
    return -1;
  }

  /* Get the root node of the document. */
  upnp_node = ixmlNode_getFirstChild((IXML_Node *)upnp_doc);

  /* Update the mac address. */
  strcpy(g_deviceudn, "uuid:");
  strcat(macaddress, "SuperToaster");
  strcat(g_deviceudn, macaddress);

  /* Set the UDN field in the DOM document. */
  ret = SampleUtil_getAndSetNodeValue(upnp_node, "device", "UDN",
                                      g_deviceudn);
  if(ret != 0) {
    /* Some kind of error. */
    printf("upnp_init: Upnp_getAndSetNodeValue UDN failed\n");
    ixmlDocument_free(upnp_doc);
    return -1;
  }

  /*
   * You're done making your dynamic modifications. Put the DOM
   * back into an XML doc for sending back to the control point.
   */
  str = ixmlPrintDocument((IXML_Node *)upnp_node);
  if(str == NULL) {
    /* Problems */
    printf("upnp_init: unable to convert into string\n");
    ixmlDocument_free(upnp_doc);
    return -1;
  }
```

Figure 16.2 Updated `upnp_init()` Using MAC Address for the Device UDN *(Continues)*

```
  /* Initialize your mutex. */
  pthread_mutex_init(&g_upnpmutex, NULL);
  ixmlDocument_free(upnp_doc);

/*
  * First, initialize the library with the default
  * HostIP and port numbers.
  */
  ret = UpnpInit(NULL, 0);
  if(ret != UPNP_E_SUCCESS) {
    printf("upnp_init: UpnpInit failed with code: %d\n", ret);
    return ret;
  }

  /*
   * Next, set your root web server directory.
   */
  ret = UpnpSetWebServerRootDir(WEB_ROOT_DIR);
  if(ret != UPNP_E_SUCCESS) {
   printf("upnp_init: UpnpSetWebServerRootDir failed with code: %d\n",
          ret);
    return ret;
  }

  /*
   * Register the root device, using your in-memory buffer.
   * This call automatically fills in the BaseURL field.
   */
  ret = UpnpRegisterRootDevice2(UPNPREG_BUF_DESC,
                                g_devicedescdoc,
  strlen(g_devicedescdoc), 1,
                                upnp_callback, &g_device_handle,
                                &g_device_handle);
  if(ret != UPNP_E_SUCCESS) {
    printf("upnp_init: UpnpRegisterRootDevice2 failed with ret
            %d\n", ret);
    UpnpFinish();
    return -1;
  }

  /*
   * UnRegister your device, which cleans up any records the
   * control points may have of your previous device.
   */
  ret = UpnpUnRegisterRootDevice(g_device_handle);
```

Figure 16.2 Updated `upnp_init()` Using MAC Address for the Device UDN *(Continues)*

```
  if(ret != UPNP_E_SUCCESS) {
    printf("upnp_cleanup: UpnpUnRegisterRootDevice failed with
            code: %d\n", ret);
  }


  /*
   * Register the root device, using your in-memory buffer.
   * This call automatically fills in the BaseURL field.
   */
  ret = UpnpRegisterRootDevice2(UPNPREG_BUF_DESC,
                                g_devicedescdoc,
  strlen(g_devicedescdoc), 1,
                                upnp_callback, &g_device_handle,
                                &g_device_handle);
  if(ret != UPNP_E_SUCCESS) {
    printf("upnp_init: UpnpRegisterRootDevice2 failed with ret
           %d\n", ret);
    UpnpFinish();
    return -1;
  }

  /*
   * Send advertisements about your device every 180s.
   */
  ret = UpnpSendAdvertisement(g_device_handle, 180);
  if(ret != UPNP_E_SUCCESS) {
    printf("upnp_init: UpnpSendAdvertisement failed with code:
           %d\n", ret);
    return ret;
  }

  /*
   * Register your callback handlers with the HW interface
   * library.
   */
  ret = hw_init(toaster_callback);
  if(ret != TOASTER_SUCCESS) {
    printf("upnp_init: hw_init failed\n");
    return ret;
  }

 printf("upnp_init: end\n");

  return ret;
}
```

Figure 16.2 Updated upnp_init() Using MAC Address for the Device UDN

Testing with Device Validator

Included as part of the Intel Tools for UPnP technologies is an extremely useful test tool called Device Validator. The purpose of Device Validator is to help ensure that your device (and the UPnP stack it is built on) properly supports all the requirements of the UPnP Device Achitecture version 1.0. Device Validator also tests the responsiveness of your device to see how well it can handle a storm of subscription or action invocations. Device Validator is shown in Figure 16.3.

Device Validator has two primary parts to its user interface. On the left side is a tree structure that lists the available tests that can be performed on your device. Some are device-specific (such as those in the UPnP A/V branch), while others are generic for all devices, such as the Discovery branch.

Select the branch of tests you'd like to run, click on the Select Target button to choose your device (in this case you've chosen the Super Toaster), and click "Execute" to begin performing the tests.

As shown in Figure 16.3, as each test is performed, statistics on the right pane are updated along with a status bar showing progress. When tests are passed, the node in the tree turns from gray to green. When tests fail, the node turns red.

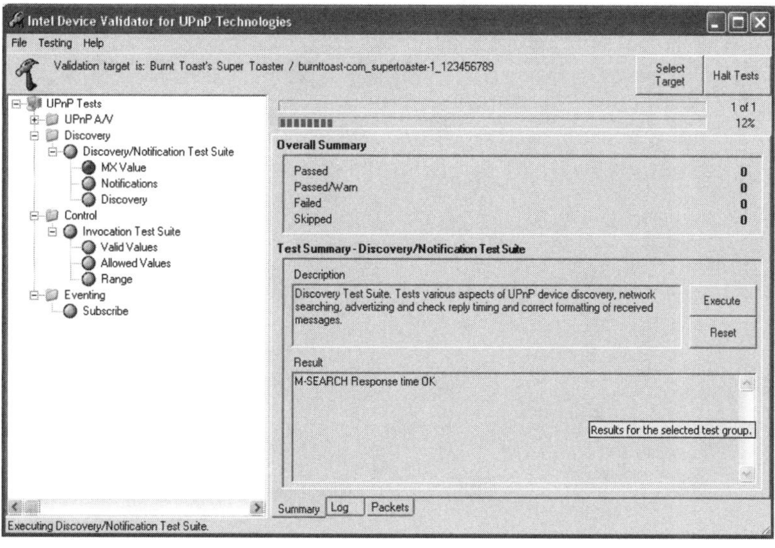

Figure 16.3 Device Validator

Device Validator is an extremely powerful tool that has become the de facto standard for validating device performance and improving interoperability at UPnP Plug Fests.

Device Spy Trick

As you've probably noticed, when you click "Invoke" in Device Spy, a child window is opened for the action invocation. When the device disappears from the network (either by sending normal bye-bye messages or because it crashed), the child windows stay even though the device has left the device pane.

What may seem like a bug is actually a feature. Setting up all your action windows with the proper parameters for easy and frequent invocation is no easy process. If you can make sure your device reappears each time on the same IPAddress:Port as it did before, you don't need to reopen your action windows—they'll automatically work for the new device instances. This is very useful when you're debugging a frequently crashing device.

Summary

In this chapter you reviewed the four steps to UPnP device development, focusing on the work products produced at each stage. The chapter ended with a discussion of more advanced topics facing UPnP device developers. This chapter officially brings to a close your journey of UPnP device development, where you started back in Chapter 10 with a requirements document. In the next section of the book you'll take a look at the UPnP A/V specification, and even consider adding audio playback to your Super Toaster.

Part IV

Advanced Topics

Chapter 17

UPnP Audio/Video

This chapter introduces one of the most popular areas of UPnP device development: UPnP Audio/Video, or UPnP A/V for short. The UPnP A/V working committee has defined an architecture for distributing digital audio and video using UPnP. You'll learn the specific device types supported in UPnP A/V, what services and actions those devices are required to support, and how they work together to support UPnP technology-based media distribution in the home.

Problem Statement

In today's home, a wide variety of disparate devices exist that support the storage, playback, and rendering of content. DVD players, VCRs, and televisions are a staple of the consumer home. Yet these devices are typically tied to a specific format type and don't present the same network-based discovery, configuration, and control that UPnP devices can offer. The goal would be to bring the benefits of UPnP into the audio/video world, making the management of content and control of rendering that content format agnostic, while making the technology even easier to use.

It is precisely this problem that UPnP A/V can solve. This chapter introduces UPnP A/V and describes the major functional components and their interactions.

UPnP A/V Architecture Overview

Following the standard UPnP technology model, UPnP A/V uses multiple logical devices with a single control point to coordinate activities between them. This frees the user from having to interact with and configure many distinct devices to make them talk together. Instead, users communicate only with the UPnP A/V control point, which performs the work of discovering and configuring the other UPnP A/V devices on the network.

The basic UPnP A/V architecture uses a triangle of interacting devices, as shown in Figure 17.1.

As shown in Figure 17.1, UPnP A/V defines two device types: the Media Server and the Media Renderer. Simply, the Media Server is a device that is storing the content, while the Media Renderer is the device that renders the content. The UPnP A/V Control Point discovers Media Servers and Media Renders on the network. Using defined UPnP actions, the control point connects a Media Server to the Media Renderer, at which point the two devices can stream the content directly from each other without the UPnP A/V control point getting in the way.

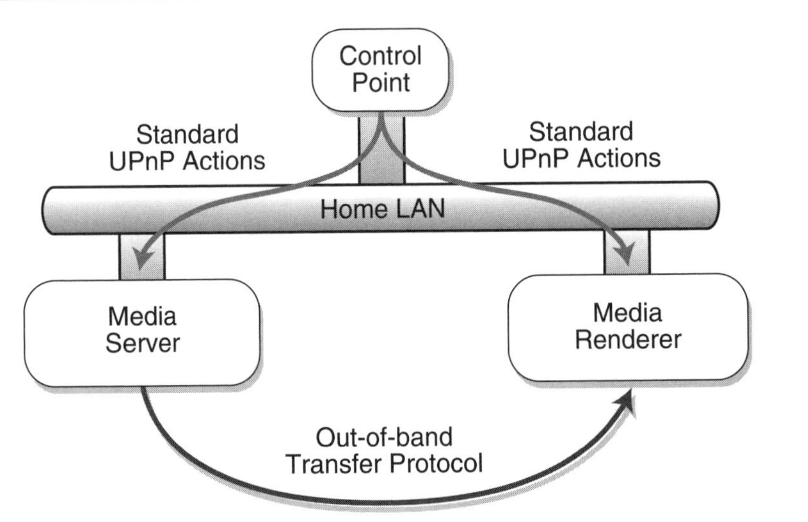

Figure 17.1 UPnP A/V architecture

UPnP A/V was designed to support the following goals:

- Media and transfer protocol agnostic
- Direct source-to-sink transfer of content
- Ability to support A/V devices of all complexities

The first of these goals is satisfied by defining the standard UPnP A/V actions in Media Server and Media Renderer devices that allow the control point to simply act as a matchmaker of sorts between the Media Server and Media Renderer devices, completely independent of the media format or eventual out-of-band transport protocol the devices will use. The three-way architecture of UPnP A/V also allows renderers of content to connect directly to the source of the content, whether that source is in the home network or somewhere on the Internet. The control point, and user for that matter, doesn't need to be bothered with such details. Finally, UPnP A/V supports the third goal of scalable devices of all levels of complexity by defining a minimal set of services and actions that each device must support, which ensures basic interoperability and functionality while also defining a set of optional services and actions that would support an extensive set of advanced device capabilities.

Finally, it's important to note that UPnP A/V supports both the "push" and the "pull" models of streaming content. This means that MediaServers can actively push content to the sink where it will be rendered, or MediaRenderers can actively pull the content from the actual source of the content.

The set of UPnP A/V Specifications available from `http://www.upnp.org` includes:

- UPnP AV Architecture
- Media Server Device Template
- Media Renderer Device Template
- Rendering Control Service Template
- Connection Manager Service Template
- AV Transport Service Template
- Content Directory Service Template

Each specification defines a set of required and optional state variables and actions. The following sections formally introduce the Media Renderer and Media Server device types, along with the set of services and actions each supports.

A_ARG_TYPE

One of the first things you'll notice looking through the A/V specifications is the naming of service state variables with the text "A_ARG_TYPE_" appended to the beginning of the name. Recall that Chapter 13 discussed the requirement that each service action have a corresponding state variable. Yet some device services don't actually need to maintain state for those state variables and, instead, need the defined state variable simply to specify the parameter type.

UPnP A/V solves this problem by distinguishing those state variables that exist only for the purpose of argument typing, with the text "A_ARG_TYPE_" appended to the beginning of the state variable name.

LastChange

UPnP assumes that each device has one set of state variables. When a state variable is defined to support eventing, control points expect to receive event notifications for one instance of that state variable.

Unfortunately, UPnP A/V devices can have multiple instances of the same state variable. Imagine a Media Renderer playing multiple simultaneous audio streams. In this case a set of state variables for each independent stream exists and needs to be evented.

The solution to this problem is a unique state variable called "LastChange." When the value of a state variable changes, information about the change is evented as part of a "LastChange" state variable event. The LastChange state variable events all evented state variables that changed since the last LastChange event was sent.

The format of the event allows devices (and the control points that receive the event) to differentiate between different sets of state variables. Each MediaRenderer has a defined InstanceID for each connection instance that is currently being supported. If a Media Renderer has multiple current connections, it has multiple Instance IDs, each with their own set of state variables describing the current state of that connection.

Figure 17.2 lists the XML for a LastChange event from a device that currently has two instances: one playing video, the other playing audio. Both instances support Volume, but each instance has a different value for Volume.

```
<Event xmlns="urn:schemas-upnp-org:metadata-1-0/AVT_RCS">
  <InstanceID val="0">
    <Brightness val="36">
    <Contranst val="74">
    <Volume val="0">
    ...
  </InstanceID>
  <InstanceID val="1">
    <Mute channel="Master" val="0">
    <Volume val="74">
    ...
  </InstanceID>
</Event>
```

Figure 17.2 LastChange Event XML

UPnP A/V Media Server

The UPnP A/V Media Server device is used by UPnP A/V control points to search for and locate content that is available for playback. Media Servers could support devices such as VCRs, DVD players, CD players, or even live TV tuners. The primary function of a Media Server is to provide a mechanism for UPnP A/V control points to discover what content in the Media Server is available for rendering.

A CD player would enumerate the current CDs inserted in the player, along with the track numbers and other information about the CD. A TV tuner would describe the current list of channels available for viewing, along with detailed program information for each. Finally, a PC could act as a Media Server, advertising all the digital media (MP3s, MPEG videos, and so on) stored on the PC.

Every UPnP A/V Media Server contains a ContentDirectory service, a ConnectionManager service, and an optional AVTransport service. Each of these services is covered in the following sections.

ContentDirectory Service

The ContentDirectory service is probably the most frequently used service in the Media Server. Through the actions defined in the ContentDirectory service, a UPnP A/V control point can browse the list of content available in the Media Server. Content is described in Content Items and Containers that includes available meta-data and other information about the content.

For example, an MP3 file might have a Container that includes not only a reference to the file itself but all the ID3 tag information as well (Artist, Album, Track Number), or even album cover art or song lyrics.

When advertising content, the ContentDirectory service also describes the specific transport protocols available to get the content. These may include HTTP, FTP, RTP, and so on. In this way, when a UPnP A/V control point is trying to match up a Media Server and a Media Renderer, it can make sure there is a common transfer protocol between them that would allow the transferring and rendering of the enumerated content.

The Content Directory Service uses a XML Metadata format called the Digital Item Declaration Language (DIDL). The DIDL defines a standard way to package and describe digital media, such as digital photos. In fact, many digital cameras automatically include DIDL information in the generated photos. Table 17.1 lists the supported state variables for the Content Directory service. Table 17.2 lists required actions for the Content Directory service.

Table 17.1 Content Directory Service State Variables

Name	Required or Optional	Evented	Data Type	Description
TransferID's	O	Yes	string	A CSV list of the currently active Transfers
A_ARG_TYPE_ObjectID	R	No	string	Used with actions that include an ObjectID parameter, it uniquely identifies an individual object within the Content Directory service
A_ARG_TYPE_Result	R	No	string	Used with actions that include a Result parameter, Result returns a DIDL-formatted result string
A_ARG_TYPE_Search Criteria	O	No	string	Used with actions that include a SearchCriteria parameter; provides one or more criteria to be used when querying the Content Directory

Continues

Table 17.1 Content Directory Service State Variables *(Continued)*

Name	Required or Optional	Evented	Data Type	Description
A_ARG_TYPE_Browse Flag	R	No	string	Used with Browse actions, the BrowseFlag parameter specifies options for browsing.
A_ARG_TYPE_Filter	R	No	string	Used with actions that include a Filter parameter; indicates which metadata properties should be returned from a browse or search.
A_ARG_TYPE_Sort Criteria	R	No	string	Used with actions that include a SortCriteria parameter; provides an ordered list of properties to search for
A_ARG_TYPE_Index	R	No	ui4	Used with actions that include an Index parameter; specifies an offset into an arbitrary list of objects
A_ARG_TYPE_Count	R	No	ui4	Used with actions that include a Count parameter; specifies a number of objects
A_ARG_TYPE_UpdateID	R	No	ui4	Used with actions that include an UpdateID parameter; return value is either the SystemUpdateID or the No ContainerUpdateID
A_ARG_TYPE_TransferID	O	No	ui4	Used with actions that include a TransferID parameter; uniquely identifies a specific instantiated file transfer

Continues

Table 17.1 Content Directory Service State Variables *(Continued)*

Name	Required or Optional	Evented	Data Type	Description
A_ARG_TYPE_Transfer Status	O	No	string	Used with actions that include a TransferStatus parameter; provides information about the current status of an instantiated file transfer
A_ARG_TYPE_Transfer Length	O	No	string	Used with actions that include a TransferLength parameter; represents the total length of transfer for a file
A_ARG_TYPE_Transfer Total	O	No	string	Used with actions that include a TransferTotal parameter; represents the total amount of data transferred
A_ARG_TYPE_TagValue List	O	No	string	Contains a CSV list of pairs of XML fragments
A_ARG_TYPE_URI	O	No	URI	Used in actions that include a URI parameter, describes a URI
Search-Capabilities	R	No	string	CSV list of property names used in a search query
Sort-Capabilities	R	No	string	CSV list of tags that can be used to order search or browse results
System-UpdateID	R	Yes	ui4	Changes whenever any object in the Content Directory changes. Used to notify control points when something in the Content Directory has changed
Container-UpdateID's	O	Yes	string	Unordered CSV list of (ContainerID, Containter-UpdateID) pairs used to notify Control Points when containers are updated

Table 17.2 Content Directory Service Actions

Name	Required or Optional	Description
GetSearchCapabilities	R	Returns the supported search capabilities of the Content Directory
GetSortCapabilities	R	Returns a CSV list of meta-data tags that can be used in specifying sort criteria
GetSystemUpdateIDs	R	Returns the current value of the SystemUpdateID state variable
Browse	R	Allows the caller to incrementally browse the native hierarchy of Content Directory Objects.
Search	O	Allows the caller to search the Content Directory for specific objects that match a provided search criteria
CreateObject	O	Creates a new container object
DestroyObject	O	Destroys a previously created container object, including all existing children of the specified container
UpdateObject	O	Modifies, deletes, or inserts metadata into an existing object container
ImportResource	O	Transfers a file from a specified remote source to a specified local destination in the Content Directory service
ExportResource	O	Transfers a file from a local source to a specified remote destination.
StopTransferResource	O	Stops a currently active file transfer
GetTransferProgress	O	Returns the current status of a file transfer
DeleteResource	O	Deletes all elements in the Content Directory Service that match a specified URI
CreateReference	O	Creates a new reference to an existing container object

ConnectionManager Service

The ConnectionManager service is used to create and manage sets of MediaRenderer connections to the MediaServer. Without the ConnectionManager service, a Media Server would be able to support only one active connection at a time. The primary action supported by the ConnectionManager service, `GetProtocolInfo()`, allows an A/V control point to retrieve information about what protocols the device supports sending or receiving.

The optional `PrepareForConnection()` action returns a unique connection InstanceID that UPnP A/V control points can use to reference the created connection when adjusting properties of the connection in the optional AVTransport service, which is defined in the next section. `PrepareForConnection()` also allows an A/V control point to instantiate multiple simultaneous connections to the device. Devices that do not support `PrepareForConnection()` by definition support at most one Connection ID.

The ConnectionManager service is a prime example of how UPnP A/V supports a scalable set of devices, from those simple MediaServers that support only one connection at a time to the fully featured MediaServer that can simultaneously support and manage multiple independent connections.

Table 17.3 lists required state variables for the Connection Manager service. Table 17.4 lists required actions for the Connection Manager Service.

Table 17.3 Connection Manager Service State Variables

Name	Required or Optional	Evented	Data Type	Description
SourceProtocol-Info	R	Yes	string	Contains a CSV list of information about what protocols the Connection Manager supports for sourcing data
SinkProtocol-Info	R	Yes	string	Contains a CSV list of information about what protocols the Connection Manager supports for sinking (rendering)

Continues

Table 17.3 Connection Manager Service State Variables *(Continued)*

Name	Required or Optional	Evented	Data Type	Description
CurrentConnectionIDs	R	Yes	string	CSV list of current active connections, specified by ConnectionID
A_ARG_TYPE_ Connection-Status	O	No	string	Used in actions to provide Connection Status information for a specified ConnectionID
A_ARG_TYPE_ Connection-Manager	R	No	string	Used with actions that wish to specify a "Peer-ConnectionManager"
A_ARG_TYPEDirection	R	No	string	Used with actions that include a Direction parameter, to indicate push vs. pull data transfer
A_ARG_TYPE_ProtocolInfo	R	No	string	Used with actions that include a ProtocolInfo parameter; specifies what protocols the Connection Manager supports
A_ARG_TYPE_ ConnectionID	R	No	i4	Used with actions that include a ConnectionID parameter; indicates a specific Connection ID
A_ARG_TYPE_AV TransportID		No	i4	Used with actions that include a AVTransportID parameter; indicates a specific AVTransportID
A_ARG_TYPE_RcsID	R	No	i4	Used with actions that include a RcsID parameter; specifies a Resource Id

Table 17.4 Connection Manager Service Actions

Name	Required or Optional	Description
GetProtocolInfo	R	Returns information on what protocols the Connection Manager supports
PrepareForConnection	O	Used to allow the device to prepare for and instantiate a new ConnectionID for the purposes of sending or receiving content
ConnectionComplete	O	Used to inform the device that the specified ConnectionID is no longer in use and can be closed
GetCurrentConnectionIDs	R	Returns a CSV list of currently active Connection IDs
GetCurrentConnectionInfo	O	Returns information about a specific Connection ID

AVTransport Service

The optional AVTransport service provides the UPnP A/V control point with the ability to adjust and control the playback of the content stored in the MediaServer. Actions in this optional service include standard VCR-like operations of Play, Pause, Stop, Seek, and so on. Note that the existence of these actions indicates that the MediaServer supports the "pushing" of content to a MediaRenderer, as the control actions are adjusting properties of the stream at its source, not in the Renderer.

For MediaServers that support multiple connections, although only one AVTransport service is advertised, using the different InstanceIDs when invoking actions in effect accesses a different logical instance of the advertised AVTransport service for each different InstanceID.

Table 17.5 lists required state variables for the AVTransport Service. Note that none of the state variables in the AVTransport are evented. Information about all state variable change events are transmitted in the LastChange state variable indexed by the InstanceID.

Table 17.6 lists required actions for the AVTransport Service. All AVTransport actions take an InstanceID as a parameter that determines to which AVTransportInstance the action is applied.

Table 17.5 AVTransport Service State Variables

Name	Required or Optional	Evented	Data Type	Description
TransportState	R	No	string	The current state of the Transport Service; e.g., PLAYING, STOPPED, etc.
TransportStatus	R	No	string	The current error status of the service
PlaybackStorageMedium	R	No	string	Indicates the storage medium of the media specified by the AVTransportURI state variable
RecordStorage-Medium	R	No	string	Indicates the storage medium where the resource specified by AVTrnasportURI is recorded
PossiblePlaybackStorage Media	R	No	string	CSV list of supported storage media that the device can support for playback
PossibleRecord-Storage Media	R	No	string	CSV list of storage media onto which the device can record
CurrentPlay-Mode	R	No	string	Indicates the current play mode (e.g., random, repeat, etc.) of the device.
TransportPlay-Speed	R	No	ui4	Indicates the speed relative to normal speed. (e.g., ∫, π, etc.)
RecordMediumWriteStatus	R	No	ui4	Write protection status of the currently loaded media

Continues

Table 17.5 AVTransport Service State Variables *(Continued)*

Name	Required or Optional	Evented	Data Type	Description
CurrentRecordQualityMode	R	No	ui4	Indicates the current record quality setting
PossibleRecordQuality Modes	R	No	ui4	CSV list of supported record quality modes
NumberOf-Tracks	R	No	string	Current number of tracks available to the AVTrans-port instance
CurrentTrack	R	No	string	The current track number being played
CurrentTrack-Duration	R	No	string	Duration of the current track
CurrentMedia-Duration	R	No	string	Duration of the current media specified by AVTransportURI
CurrentTrack-MetaData	O	No	URI	DIDL-Lite formatted metadata for the current AVTransportURI
CurrentTrack-URI	R	No	string	URI reference to the cur-rent track
AVTransport-URI	R	No	string	URI reference to the cur-rent resource controlled by the AVTransport instance
AVTransport-URIMetaData	R	No	string	DIDL-Lite metadata for the resource pointed to by the AVTransportURI state variable
NextAV-TransportURI	R	No	string	Specifies the AVTrans-portURI to be played when the current AVTransportURI finishes

Continues

Table 17.5 AVTransport Service State Variables *(Continued)*

Name	Required or Optional	Evented	Data Type	Description
NextAV-TransportURI-MetaData	R	No	string	DIDL-Lite metadata for the resource pointed to by the NextAVTransport-URI state variable
RelativeTime-Position	R	No	string	Current time position from the beginning of the current track
AbsoluteTime-Position	R	No	string	Current time position from the beginning of the current specified media
RelativeCounterPosition	R	No	i4	Current position of a counter from the beginning of the current track
AbsoluteCounterPosition	R	No	i4	Current position of a counter from the beginning of the current media
Current-Transport-Actions	O	No	string	CSV list of the current supported control actions in the AVTransport service
A_ARG_TYPE_SeekMode	R	No	string	Used in actions that have a SeekMode parameter; indicates the allowed units to seek
A_ARG_TYPE_SeekTarget	R	No	string	Used in actions that have a SeekTarget parameter; indicates a target track number to which the disk can seek
A_ARG_TYPE_InstanceID	R	No	ui4	Used in actions that have a InstanceID parameter; indicates the specific InstanceID to which the action should apply

Table 17.6 AVTransport Service Actions

Name	Required or Optional	Description
SetAVTransportURI	R	Sets the AVTransportURI state variable
SetNextAVTransportURI	O	Sets the NextAVTransportURI state variable
GetMediaInfo	R	Returns information associated with the current media
GetTransportInfo	R	Returns information associated with the current transport state
GetPositionInfo	R	Returns information about the current position of the resource specified by the AVTransportURI state variable
GetDeviceCapabilities	R	Returns information about device capabilities for the current resource specified by the AVTransportURI state variable
GetTransportSettings	R	Returns information on AVTransport settings for the specified InstanceID, (current play mode, recording quality mode, etc.)
Stop	R	Stop the current resource specified by the AVTransportURI state variable
Play	R	Play the current resource specified by the AVTransportURI state variable
Pause	O	Pause the current resource specified by the AVTransportURI state variable
Record	O	Start recording on the specified transport instance
Seek	R	Seek forward or reverse to the specified seek target on the current resource
Next	R	Advance to the next track in the resource specified by the AVTransportURI.; only applies to playlists
Previous	R	Advance to the previous track in the resource specified by the AVTransportURI; only applies to playlists

Continues

Table 17.6 AVTransport Service Actions *(Continued)*

Name	Required or Optional	Description
SetPlayMode	O	Set the desired play mode (random, repeat, etc.) of the device
SetRecordQualityMode	O	Set the desired record quality mode for the device
GetCurrentTransport Actions	O	CSV list of current list of supported required and optional actions in the AVTransport Service instance

UPnP A/V Media Renderer

The other UPnP device that makes up the UPnP A/V triangle, a UPnP A/V Media Renderer, is used to play back, or render, content from the network. Media Renderers could include televisions, stereos, in-home speakers, or even a wild piece of digital art that reacts to music. The Media Renderer is the end-point device that the user has selected to render some content. As such, it has services and actions that support controlling properties of how the content is rendered, controlled, and set up. The next few sections introduce the required ConnectionManager, RenderingControl, and optional AVTransport services.

ConnectionManager Service

Similar to the Connection Manager service provided by the Media Server, the Media Renderers Connection Manager service allows UPnP A/V control points the opportunity to query the device and find out what types of media and transport protocols the device supports when rendering content.

Similar to Media Servers that support multiple simultaneous connections, Media Renderers can also support such a capability through the Connection Manager service. Think of an A/V receiver with many different output channels for different rooms in the house. Certainly this kind of Media Renderer would benefit from the creation of different independent connection instances. The InstanceID returned from the `PrepareForConnection()` call is used in future action invocations in the other services supported by the Media Renderer. The Connection Manager service also provides actions for control points to discover how many InstanceIDs are active, as well as retrieving properties of each active connection.

Like Media Servers that support only one connection, Media Renderers that are capable of rendering only one stream at a time return an InstanceID of 0. State variables and actions supported in the Connection Manager service are listed in Tables 17.3 and 17.4 respectively.

RenderingControl Service

The heart and soul of the Media Renderer, the RenderingContol service provides UPnP A/V control points the ability to adjust properties of how content is being rendered. Using the actions of the RenderingControl service, properties such as Volume level, Brightness, Loudness, Tint, Color Contrast, and so on can be controlled by users of the Media Renderer. Note that not all of these actions are required. Certainly it doesn't make sense for a audio-only Renderer to support adjusting the brightness levels of a display.

Table 17.7 lists required state variables for the RenderingControl service. Like the AVTransport service, the RenderingControl service does not individually event any of the supported state variables. It instead relies upon the LastChange state variable to package evented state variables ordered by InstanceID. Table 17.8 lists required actions for the RenderingControl service.

Table 17.7 Rendering Control Service State Variables

Name	Required or Optional	Evented	Data Type	Description
PresetNameList	R	No	string	CSV list of valid present names currently supported by the device
Brightness	O	No	ui2	Current brightness setting of the display device
Contrast	O	No	ui2	Current contrast setting of the display device
Sharpness	O	No	ui2	Current sharpness setting of the display device
RedVideoGain	O	No	ui2	Current setting of the red gain control for the display device

Continues

Table 17.7 Rendering Control Service State Variables *(Continued)*

Name	Required or Optional	Evented	Data Type	Description
GreenVideo-Gain	O	No	ui2	Current setting of the green gain control for the display device
BlueVideoGain	O	No	ui2	Current setting of the blue gain control for the display device
RedVideoBlackLevel	O	No	ui2	Current setting for the minimum output intensity of red for the display device
GreenVideo-BlackLevel	O	No	ui2	Current setting for the minimum output intensity of green for the display device
BlueVideoBlackLevel	O	No	ui2	Current setting for the minimum output intensity of blue for the display device
Color-Temperature	O	No	ui2	Current setting for the color quality of white for the display device
Horizontal-Keystone	O	No	i2	Current level of compensation for horizontal distortion in the display image
Vertical-Keystone	O	No	i2	Current level of compensation for vertical distortion in the display image
Mute	O	No	boolean	Boolean value designating whether the device is currently muted
Volume	O	No	ui2	Current volume setting of the audio channel

Continues

Table 17.7 Rendering Control Service State Variables *(Continued)*

Name	Required or Optional	Evented	Data Type	Description
VolumeDB	O	No	i2	Current volume setting of the audio channel in 1/256 of a decibel (dB)
Loudness	O	No	boolean	Boolean value designating whether loudness is active
A_ARG_TYPE_Channel	R	No	string	Used in actions to specify a specific audio or video channel
A_ARG_TYPE_Instance ID	R	No	ui4	Used in actions to specify a InstanceID for the action to apply to
A_ARG_TYPE_Preset Name	R	No	string	Used in actions to specify the name of a device preset

Table 17.8 Rendering Control Service Actions

Name	Required or Optional	Description
ListPresets	R	Returns the list of currently defined presets
SelectPreset	R	Restores Rendering Control state variables to a defined preset set of values
GetBrightness	O	Returns the current value of the Brightness state variable
SetBrightness	O	Sets the value of the Brightness state variable
GetContrast	O	Returns the current value of the Contrast state variable
SetContrast	O	Sets the value of the Contrast state variable
GetSharpness	O	Returns the current value of the Sharpness state variable

Continues

Table 17.8 Rendering Control Service Actions *(Continued)*

Name	Required or Optional	Description
SetSharpness	O	Set the value of the Sharpness state variable
GetRedVideoGain	O	Returns the current value of the Red-VideoGain state variable
SetRedVideoGain	O	Set the value of the RedVideoGain state variable
GetGreenVideoGain	O	Returns the current value of the Green-VideoGain state variable
SetGreenVideoGain	O	Set the value of the GreenVideoGain state variable
GetBlueVideoGain	O	Returns the current value of the Blue-VideoGain state variable
SetBlueVideoGain	O	Set the value of the BlueVideoGain state variable
GetRedVideoBlackLevel	O	Returns the current value of the RedVideo-BlackLevel state variable
SetRedVideoBlackLevel	O	Set the value of the RedVideoBlackLevel state variable
GetGreenVideoBlackLevel	O	Returns the current value of the Green-VideoBlackLevel state variable
SetGreenVideoBlackLevel	O	Set the value of the GreenVideoBlackLevel state variable
GetBlueVideoBlackLevel	O	Returns the current value of the BlueVideo-BlackLevel state variable
SetBlueVideoBlackLevel	O	Set the value of the BlueVideoBlackLevel state variable
GetColorTemperature	O	Returns the current value of the ColorTem-perature state variable
SetColorTemperature	O	Set the value of the ColorTemperature state variable

Continues

Table 17.8 Rendering Control Service Actions *(Continued)*

Name	Required or Optional	Description
GetHorizontalKeystone	O	Returns the current value of the HorizontalKeystone state variable
SetHorizontalKeystone	O	Set the value of the HorizontalKeystone state variable
GetMute	O	Returns the current value of the Mute state variable
SetMute	O	Sets the value of the Mute state variable
GetVolume	O	Returns the current value of the Volume state variable
SetVolume	O	Set the value of the Volume state variable
GetVolumeDB	O	Returns the current value of the VolumeDB state variable
SetVolumeDB	O	Set the value of the VolumeDB state variable
GetVolumeDBRange	O	Returns the valid range for the VolumeDB state variable
GetLoudness	O	Returns the current value of the Loudness state variable
SetLoudness	O	Set the value of the Loudness state variable

AVTransport Service

Just like the UPnP A/V Media Server, the Media Renderer can also optionally support the AVTransport service. The AVTransport service provides control points with the ability to use VCR-like operations (Play, Pause, Stop, and so on) to control the playback of content on the Renderer.

Supporting the AVTransport service on a Media Renderer device typically means that the Renderer does most of the active streaming from the source of the content, in a "pull" method. In this way, calling actions in the AVTransport service on the Media Renderer device would cause it to adjust the rate or specific manner in which it is pulling, or streaming, the content from its source.

Service state variables and actions for the AVTransport service are defined in Tables 17.5 and 17.6 respectively.

UPnP A/V Control Point

Perhaps the most important node on the UPnP A/V network, the UPnP A/V Control Point, performs all discovery and coordination between Media Servers and Media Renderers. Recall that the UPnP architecture provides no mechanism for UPnP devices to communicate directly with each other. This is the role that the A/V control point plays. When the user wants the Renderer to pause playing an audio stream, it is the A/V control point that invokes the action on the user's behalf.

Typically, the application the user is interacting directly with is the A/V control point. When users want to search for content, it is the A/V control point that discovers all the Media Servers on the network and invokes actions in each, providing the search criteria specified by the user.

Often the unsung hero in a UPnP A/V network, all the intelligence to use Media Servers and Media Renderers is in the A/V control point. Recall that there may be multiple different Media Servers and Renderers on the network. A common feature for A/V control points is to aggregate the list of available content in the dozen or so Media Servers that may exist on the network into a single list viewable by the user. In this way, the A/V control point can take much of the complexity of the home network's topology out of the picture. Users don't care exactly where on what device content is stored, they're interested simply in what is available for them to view.

Similar to setting up a graph of nodes, the A/V control point must work to find an appropriate renderer (often based on user input if there are several renderers in the home) to play back the content the user has selected based upon what format types and transfer protocols are supported by each Media Server and Media Renderer.

The power of UPnP A/V is that all of this complicated activity is completely abstracted to the end user. No longer does the user have to manually configure a playback device or figure out what format of video may exist on a given CD, and which of the playback devices in the home can support it.

A home of UPnP A/V devices is where users can conveniently and quickly access all of their digital media without having to worry about complicated setup and configuration of Renderer devices.

End User Scenario: Audio Playback

In this section, you'll go through the process of selecting some content to play on a given Media Renderer, highlighting the specific UPnP device actions invoked at each step. You'll assume that you have a single Media Server and a single Media Renderer, that the Media Renderer supports the "pull" model of distribution using HTTP, and that it supports the playback of MP3 audio files.

To discover content, the A/V control point must discover and invoke a `Browse()` or `Search()` action in the Media Server's Content Directory service to retrieve a container object for the content you'd like to play back. Next, the A/V control point must discover and invoke a `GetProtocolInfo()` action in the Media Renderer to match appropriate protocol formats between the content you want to play and what the Media Renderer supports.

Then the A/V control point calls `PrepareForConnection()` in both the Media Server and Media Renderer (if implemented) storing the returned InstanceIDs. At this point the A/V control point can invoke `Play()` on the Media Renderer, which causes the Renderer to initiate an out-of-band connection to the device to begin streaming the content to the Media Rendering device. Once playing, the A/V control point can now invoke actions in the Rendering Control service to adjust the properties of the rendering stream, such as volume, brightness, and so on. Figure 17.3 is a sequence diagram of this process.

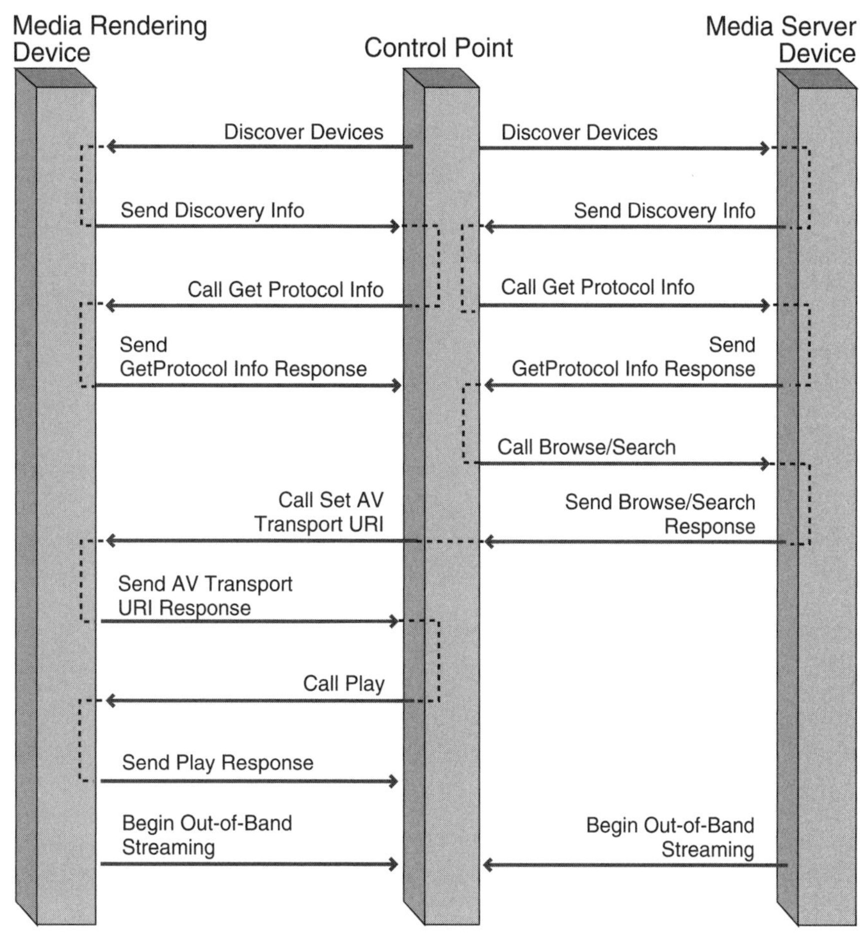

Figure 17.3 Playback Message Sequence Diagram

Summary

This chapter introduced a powerful new architecture for supporting the management and playback of media using UPnP. It began with an overview of UPnP A/V's unique three-way interaction model and continued with coverage of each of the distinct device types in a UPnP A/V network. It finished with a detailed discussion of the real-world scenario of playing back audio on a Media Rendering device. In the next chapter you'll use the information you learned in this chapter to actually implement basic support for a UPnP A/V Media Rendering device in your Super Toaster.

Chapter 18

Adding UPnP A/V Support to the Super Toaster

The previous chapter introduced UPnP A/V, the set of defined UPnP A/V devices, and the services that those devices must support. In this chapter you'll put that knowledge to good use by adding basic Media Rendering support to your Super Toaster device.

Super Duper Toaster

What could be better than a toaster that talked? The executive staff at InToast Incorporated has come to the engineering team and requested that audio playback capabilities be added to the Super Toaster. With this capability users will no longer have to stand and watch for the toast to pop up; instead, they will hear a voice.

This capability is a perfect match for UPnP A/V, and fortunately you can build on the support you already have. A/V Rendering control points search for Media Rendering devices by the specific supported service types. What this means is that even though your Super Toaster does not have a device type of a Media Renderer, because it supports the appropriate defined services, a UPnP A/V control point will be able to discover it and take advantage of its services.

Ground Rules

The previous chapter listed the set of defined services and the required state variables and actions needed for minimal UPnP A/V support. You're going to cheat and implement only the services and actions sufficient to support the basic playback of media.

You will add support to each of the three service definitions, so the control point will be able to recognize your device as an A/V-capable device. To do this, you'll need to add these services to your device description document and include SCPD description documents for these services as well.

Figure 18.1 lists the updated device description document for your SuperToaster that includes the new UPnP A/V services.

```
<?xml version="1.0"?>
<root xmlns="urn:intoast-com:device-1-0">
  <specVersion>
    <major>1</major>
    <minor>0</minor>
  </specVersion>
  <URLBase>http://192.168.1.10:5431</URLBase>
  <device>
    <deviceType>urn:schemas-intoast-
            com:device:supertoaster:1</deviceType>
    <friendlyName>InToast's Super Toaster</friendlyName>
    <manufacturer>InToast Inc.</manufacturer>
    <manufacturerURL>http://www.intoast.com</manufacturerURL>
    <modelDescription>Super Toaster 1.0</modelDescription>
    <modelName>ST 2002</modelName>
    <modelNumber>1.0</modelNumber>
    <modelURL>http://www.intoast.com/supertoaster/</modelURL>
    <serialNumber>123456789</serialNumber>
    <UDN>uuid:intoast-com_supertoaster-1_123456789</UDN>
    <UPC>123456789</UPC>
    <serviceList>
      <service>
        <serviceType>urn:schemas-intoast-
          com:service:lifetimestats:1</serviceType>
        <serviceId>urn:intoast-
          com:serviceId:lifetimestats1</serviceId>
        <SCPDURL>lifetimestatsSCPD.xml</SCPDURL>
        <controlURL>/upnp/control/lifetimestats1</controlURL>
```

Figure 18.1 Updated SuperToaster Device Description Document *(Continues)*

```
    <eventSubURL>/upnp/event/lifetimestats1</eventSubURL>
  </service>
  <service>
    <serviceType>urn:schemas-intoast-
        com:service:toastingstatus:1</serviceType>
    <serviceId>urn:upnp-
        org:serviceId:toastingstatus1</serviceId>
    <SCPDURL>toastingstatusSCPD.xml</SCPDURL>
    <controlURL>/upnp/control/toastingstatus1</controlURL>
    <eventSubURL>/upnp/event/toastingstatus11</eventSubURL>
  </service>
  <service>
    <serviceType>urn:schemas-intoast-
         com:service:toastercontrol:1</serviceType>
    <serviceId>urn:upnp-
         org:serviceId:toastercontrol1</serviceId>
    <SCPDURL>toastercontrolSCPD.xml</SCPDURL>
    <controlURL>/upnp/control/toastercontrol</controlURL>
    <eventSubURL></eventSubURL>
  </service>
  <service>
    <serviceType>urn:schemas-upnp-
         org:service:RenderingControl:1</serviceType>
    <serviceId>urn:upnp-
         org:serviceId:RenderingControl1</serviceId>
    <SCPDURL>rcscpd.xml</SCPDURL>
    <controlURL>/upnp/control/RenderingControl</controlURL>
    <eventSubURL>/upnp/event/RenderingControl</eventSubURL>
  </service>
  <service>
    <serviceType>urn:schemas-upnp-
         org:service:AVTransport:1</serviceType>
    <serviceId>urn:upnp-org:serviceId:AVTransport1</serviceId>
    <SCPDURL>avtscpd.xml</SCPDURL>
    <controlURL>/upnp/control/AVTransport</controlURL>
    <eventSubURL>/upnp/event/AVTransport</eventSubURL>
 </service>
 <service>
    <serviceType>urn:schemas-upnp-
         org:service:ConnectionManager:1</serviceType>
    <serviceId>urn:upnp-
         org:serviceId:ConnectionManager1</serviceId>
    <SCPDURL>cmscpd.xml</SCPDURL>
    <controlURL>/upnp/control/ConnectionManager</controlURL>
    <eventSubURL>/upnp/event/ConnectionManager</eventSubURL>
  </service>
```

Figure 18.1 Updated SuperToaster Device Description Document *(Continues)*

```
    </serviceList>
   <presentationURL>/boring.html</presentationURL>
</device>
</root>
```

Figure 18.1 Updated SuperToaster Device Description Document

Note that the service types for the three added UPnP A/V services use a `upnp-org` namespace instead of your `intoast-com` namespace. This is because these services are defined by the UPnP Forum and must be identified as such. If you left the service types as `intoast-com`, UPnP A/V control points would not have been able to properly recognize these services.

For the three services, you will provide complete service description documents that include all required and optional services. Although you will implement support for only a few actions and state variables, the documents will act as a to-do list of additional actions to complete UPnP A/V support. Figure 18.2 lists the first service description document for the Connection Manager service.

```
<?xml version="1.0" encoding="utf-8"?>
<scpd xmlns="urn:schemas-upnp-org:service-1-0">
   <specVersion>
      <major>1</major>
      <minor>0</minor>
   </specVersion>
   <actionList>
      <action>
         <name>GetCurrentConnectionInfo</name>
         <argumentList>
            <argument>
               <name>ConnectionID</name>
               <direction>in</direction>
               <relatedStateVariable>A_ARG_TYPE_ConnectionID
</relatedStateVariable>
            </argument>
            <argument>
               <name>RcsID</name>
               <direction>out</direction>
               <relatedStateVariable>A_ARG_TYPE_RcsID
```

Figure 18.2 Connection Manager SCPD *(Continues)*

```
</relatedStateVariable>
            </argument>
            <argument>
               <name>AVTransportID</name>
               <direction>out</direction>
               <relatedStateVariable>A_ARG_TYPE_AVTransportID
</relatedStateVariable>
            </argument>
            <argument>
               <name>ProtocolInfo</name>
               <direction>out</direction>
               <relatedStateVariable>A_ARG_TYPE_ProtocolInfo
</relatedStateVariable>
            </argument>
            <argument>
               <name>PeerConnectionManager</name>
               <direction>out</direction>
               <relatedStateVari-
able>A_ARG_TYPE_ConnectionManager
</relatedStateVariable>
            </argument>
            <argument>
               <name>PeerConnectionID</name>
               <direction>out</direction>
               <relatedStateVariable>A_ARG_TYPE_ConnectionID
</relatedStateVariable>
            </argument>
            <argument>
               <name>Direction</name>
               <direction>out</direction>
               <relatedStateVariable>A_ARG_TYPE_Direction
</relatedStateVariable>
            </argument>
            <argument>
               <name>Status</name>
               <direction>out</direction>
               <relatedStateVari-
able>A_ARG_TYPE_ConnectionStatus
</relatedStateVariable>
            </argument>
         </argumentList>
      </action>
      <action>
         <name>ConnectionComplete</name>
         <argumentList>
```

Figure 18.2 Connection Manager SCPD *(Continues)*

```
            <argument>
               <name>ConnectionID</name>
               <direction>in</direction>
               <relatedStateVariable>A_ARG_TYPE_ConnectionID
</relatedStateVariable>
            </argument>
         </argumentList>
      </action>
      <action>
         <name>PrepareForConnection</name>
         <argumentList>
            <argument>
               <name>RemoteProtocolInfo</name>
               <direction>in</direction>
               <relatedStateVariable>A_ARG_TYPE_ProtocolInfo
</relatedStateVariable>
            </argument>
            <argument>
               <name>PeerConnectionManager</name>
               <direction>in</direction>
               <relatedStateVari-
able>A_ARG_TYPE_ConnectionManager
</relatedStateVariable>
            </argument>
            <argument>
               <name>PeerConnectionID</name>
               <direction>in</direction>
               <relatedStateVariable>A_ARG_TYPE_ConnectionID
</relatedStateVariable>
            </argument>
            <argument>
               <name>Direction</name>
               <direction>in</direction>
               <relatedStateVariable>A_ARG_TYPE_Direction
</relatedStateVariable>
            </argument>
            <argument>
               <name>ConnectionID</name>
               <direction>out</direction>
               <relatedStateVariable>A_ARG_TYPE_ConnectionID
</relatedStateVariable>
            </argument>
            <argument>
               <name>AVTransportID</name>
               <direction>out</direction>
               <relatedStateVariable>A_ARG_TYPE_AVTransportID
```

Figure 18.2 Connection Manager SCPD *(Continues)*

```
</relatedStateVariable>
            </argument>
            <argument>
               <name>RcsID</name>
               <direction>out</direction>
               <relatedStateVariable>A_ARG_TYPE_RcsID
</relatedStateVariable>
            </argument>
         </argumentList>
      </action>
      <action>
         <name>GetProtocolInfo</name>
         <argumentList>
            <argument>
               <name>Source</name>
               <direction>out</direction>
               <relatedStateVariable>SourceProtocolInfo
</relatedStateVariable>
            </argument>
            <argument>
               <name>Sink</name>
               <direction>out</direction>
               <relatedStateVariable>SinkProtocolInfo
</relatedStateVariable>
            </argument>
         </argumentList>
      </action>
      <action>
         <name>GetCurrentConnectionIDs</name>
         <argumentList>
            <argument>
               <name>ConnectionIDs</name>
               <direction>out</direction>
               <relatedStateVariable>CurrentConnectionIDs
</relatedStateVariable>
            </argument>
         </argumentList>
      </action>
   </actionList>
   <serviceStateTable>
      <stateVariable sendEvents="no">
         <name>A_ARG_TYPE_ProtocolInfo</name>
         <dataType>string</dataType>
      </stateVariable>
```

Figure 18.2 Connection Manager SCPD *(Continues)*

```
<stateVariable sendEvents="no">
   <name>A_ARG_TYPE_ConnectionStatus</name>
   <dataType>string</dataType>
   <allowedValueList>
      <allowedValue>OK</allowedValue>
      <allowedValue>ContentFormatMismatch</allowedValue>
      <allowedValue>InsufficientBandwidth</allowedValue>
      <allowedValue>UnreliableChannel</allowedValue>
      <allowedValue>Unknown</allowedValue>
   </allowedValueList>
</stateVariable>
<stateVariable sendEvents="no">
   <name>A_ARG_TYPE_AVTransportID</name>
   <dataType>i4</dataType>
</stateVariable>
<stateVariable sendEvents="no">
   <name>A_ARG_TYPE_RcsID</name>
   <dataType>i4</dataType>
</stateVariable>
<stateVariable sendEvents="no">
   <name>A_ARG_TYPE_ConnectionID</name>
   <dataType>i4</dataType>
</stateVariable>
<stateVariable sendEvents="no">
   <name>A_ARG_TYPE_ConnectionManager</name>
   <dataType>string</dataType>
</stateVariable>
<stateVariable sendEvents="yes">
   <name>SourceProtocolInfo</name>
   <dataType>string</dataType>
</stateVariable>
<stateVariable sendEvents="yes">
   <name>SinkProtocolInfo</name>
   <dataType>string</dataType>
</stateVariable>
<stateVariable sendEvents="no">
   <name>A_ARG_TYPE_Direction</name>
   <dataType>string</dataType>
   <allowedValueList>
      <allowedValue>Input</allowedValue>
      <allowedValue>Output</allowedValue>
   </allowedValueList>
</stateVariable>
<stateVariable sendEvents="yes">
   <name>CurrentConnectionIDs</name>
```

Figure 18.2 Connection Manager SCPD *(Continues)*

```
            <dataType>string</dataType>
        </stateVariable>
    </serviceStateTable>
</scpd>
```

Figure 18.2 Connection Manager SCPD

This is first exposure to the A_ARG_TYPE state variable convention introduced in the previous chapter. This convention is used in actions such as `PrepareForConnection()` whose parameters do not have a one-to-one mapping with a state variable. Since renderers can support multiple connections, the associated state variable in the action definition must be just the type of the parameter, not the actual state variable itself.

The AVTransport and Rendering Control SCPD documents are included on the CD-ROM, but are not listed here due to their length.

The AVTransport service description document makes use of the LastChange state variable introduced in the previous chapter. Note that no state variables in the AVTransport SCPD have the `sendEvents` attribute set to yes. This is because all state variable change event information is sent via the `LastChange` state variable in that service. This completes the definition of the additional services your device must support.

Writing the Code

To support the minimal playback of audio in your Super Toaster, you'll need to add support for the three actions you defined earlier in this chapter. This means including support in your action and subscription dispatchers to handle the new service types. You also add three new files, one for each of the additional services, named `upnpavt.c`, `upnprc.c`, and `upnpcm.c` for the three UPnP A/V services.

First, the listing shown in Figure 18.3 gives the updated `upnp_actions()` and `upnp_subscriptions()` handlers in `upnp.c`.

```
/*
 * Function: upnp_actions
 *
 * Parameters: pointer to a Upnp_Action_Request structure
 *
 * Returns: UPNP_E_SUCCESS if successful, service handler error
 *          codeif not.
 *
 * Description: This function dispatches an action invocation
 *              request to the specific service handler by
 *              matching up the serviceId of the requested
 *              action.
 */
int upnp_actions(struct Upnp_Action_Request *request)
{
  int ret=0;      /* General purpose return code */

  printf("upnp_actions: start\n");

  /* First check if the request structure is valid. */
  if(request == NULL) {
    printf("upnp_actions: request pointer is NULL\n");
    return UPNP_E_BAD_REQUEST;
  }

  /* Then, you need to make sure this request is for your device.*/
  if(strcmp(request->DevUDN, g_deviceudn) != 0) {
    /* It's not for you */
    printf("upnp_actions: request not for your device\n");
    return UPNP_E_BAD_REQUEST;
  }

  /* You need to match the serviceID to one of your services. */
  if(strcmp(request->ServiceID, LIFETIME_STATS_SERVICEID) == 0) {
    /* It's a call for the Lifetime Stats Service. */
    printf("upnp_actions: request for Lifetime Status Service\n");
    ret = upnp_lsactions(request);
  } else if(strcmp(request->ServiceID, TOASTER_CONTROL_SERVICEID)
           == 0) {
    /* It's a call for the Toaster Control Service. */
    printf("upnp_actions: request for Toaster Control Service\n");
    ret = upnp_tcactions(request);
  } else if(strcmp(request->ServiceID,
           RENDERING_CONTROL_SERVICEID) == 0) {
```

Figure 18.3 Updated upnp_actions() and upnp_subscriptions() Handlers *(Continues)*

```
    /* It's a call for the A/V Rendering Control Service. */
    printf("upnp_actions: request for Rendering Control
           Service\n");
    ret = upnp_rcactions(request);
  } else if(strcmp(request->ServiceID,
CONNECTION_MANAGER_SERVICEID) == 0) {
    /* It's a call for the A/V Connection Manager Service. */
    printf("upnp_actions: request for Connection Manager
           Service\n");
    ret = upnp_cmactions(request);
  } else if(strcmp(request->ServiceID, AVTRANSPORT_SERVICEID) ==
            0) {
    /* It's a call for the A/V Transport Service. */
    printf("upnp_actions: request for AVTransport Service\n");
    ret = upnp_avtactions(request);
  } else {
     /*
     * The control point is asking for a service that doesn't
     * exist, or a service that doesn't support any actions.
     */
    ret = UPNP_E_BAD_REQUEST;
  }

  printf("upnp_actions: end\n");

  return ret;
}

/*
 * Function: upnp_subscriptions
 *
 * Parameters: pointer to a Upnp_Subscription_Request structure
 *
 * Returns: UPNP_E_SUCCESS if successful, service subscription
 *          handler error code if not.
 *
 * Description: This function dispatches a subscription request
 *              to the specific service handler by matching up
 *              the serviceId of the subscription request.
 */
int upnp_subscriptions(struct Upnp_Subscription_Request *request)
{
  int ret=0;      /* General purpose error code */

  printf("upnp_subscriptions: start\n");
```

Figure 18.3 Updated `upnp_actions()` and `upnp_subscriptions()` Handlers *(Continues)*

```
/* First, check if the request structure is valid. */
if(request == NULL) {
  printf("upnp_subscriptions: request pointer is NULL\n");
  return UPNP_E_BAD_REQUEST;
}

/* Then, you need to make sure this request is for your device.*/
if(strcmp(request->UDN, g_deviceudn) != 0) {
  /* It's not for you */
  printf("upnp_actions: request not for your device\n");
  return UPNP_E_BAD_REQUEST;
}

/* You need to match the serviceID to one of your services. */
if(strcmp(request->ServiceId, LIFETIME_STATS_SERVICEID) == 0) {
  /* It's a call for the Lifetime Stats Service. */
  printf("upnp_subscriptions: request for Lifetime Status /
        Service\n");
  ret = upnp_lssubscriptions(request);
} else if(strcmp(request->ServiceId, TOASTING_STATUS_SERVICEID)
         == 0) {
  /* It's a call for the Toasting Status Service. */
  printf("upnp_subscriptions: request for Toasting Status /
        Service\n");
  ret = upnp_tssubscriptions(request);
} else if(strcmp(request->ServiceId,
         RENDERING_CONTROL_SERVICEID) == 0) {
  /* It's a call for the A/V Rendering Control Service. */
  printf("upnp_subscriptions: request for Rendering Control /
        Service\n");
  ret = upnp_rcsubscriptions(request);
} else if(strcmp(request->ServiceId,
         CONNECTION_MANAGER_SERVICEID) == 0) {
  /* It's a call for the A/V Connection Manager Service. */
  printf("upnp_subscriptions: request for Connection Manager /
        Service\n");
  ret = upnp_cmsubscriptions(request);
} else if(strcmp(request->ServiceId, AVTRANSPORT_SERVICEID) ==
         0) {
  /* It's a call for the A/V Transport Service. */
  printf("upnp_subscriptions: request for AVTransport
        Service\n");
  ret = upnp_avtsubscriptions(request);
} else {
```

Figure 18.3 Updated upnp_actions() and upnp_subscriptions() Handlers *(Continues)*

```
        /*
         * The control point is asking for a service that doesn't
         * exist, or a service that doesn't support subscriptions.
         */
        ret = UPNP_E_BAD_REQUEST;
    }

    printf("upnp_subscriptions: end\n");

    return UPNP_E_SUCCESS;
}
```

Figure 18.3 Updated `upnp_actions()` and `upnp_subscriptions()` Handlers

Connection Manager Service

When determining whether a renderer has the ability to play media, the first thing a UPnP A/V control point does is invoke the Connection Manager's `GetProtocolInfo()` action. This tells the control point what types of media the renderer can support with playback.

Two out parameters are returned from a call to `GetProtocolInfo`. The first, associated with the `SourceProtocolInfo` state variable, tells the caller what kinds of media types this device supports when sourcing content. Obviously, your Super Toaster does not source any content, so this state variable will be blank.

The second parameter is associated with the `SinkProtocolInfo` state variable and tells UPnP A/V control points what kinds of media the device supports for playback. Here you want to specify the appropriate MIME-types for MP3 audio. The format for the `SinkProtocolInfo` string state variable is as follows:

sink-transport:source-transport:sink-mediatype:source-mediatype

where each of the fields between the colons is replaced with your desired value. The special character '*' is used to indicate no support. For a sink device that supports the playback of MP3 audio over the HTTP transport protocol, the `SinkProtocolInfo` state variable would look like this:

```
http-get:*:audio/mp3:*
```

This is a good first attempt, but is incomplete. The reason is that MIME types are an informal, uncontrolled type specification system. MP3 audio files can actually be specified a number of different ways. If you don't specify every possible MIME type for MP3 audio, you risk not interoperating successfully with a control point that is trying to match up a different MP3 MIME type from the one you've advertised. To solve this, you simply create a comma separated list of SinkProtocolInfo strings that includes all possible MP3 MIME types:

```
http-get:*:audio/mp3:*,http-get:*:audio/mpeg:*,
  http-get:*:audio/mpeg3:*
```

Now you're ready to add some code! Figure 18.4 lists the source code for the Connection Manager module, with support for the GetProtocolInfo() action.

```
/*
 * Filename: upnpcm.c
 *
 * Description: This file implements support for the UPnP A/V
 *              Connection Mananger Service
 */

#include <stdlib.h>
#include <unistd.h>
#include <string.h>
#include "toaster.h"
#include "toasterhw.h"

#define SOURCE_PROTOCOL_INFO " "
#define SINK_PROTOCOL_INFO "http-get:*:audio/mp3:*,http-get:*:audio/
mpeg:*,http-get:*:audio/mpeg3:*"

/*
 * Function: upnp_cmtactions
 *
 * Parameters: pointer to a Upnp_Action_Request structure
 *
 * Returns: UPNP_E_SUCCESS if everything worked, UPnP
 *          specification defined error code if not.
 *
 * Description: This function dispatches actions within the
 *              UPnP A/V Connection Manager Service.
 */
int upnp_cmactions(struct Upnp_Action_Request *request)
```

Figure 18.4 Connection Manager Module Source Listing *(Continues)*

```
{
  int ret = UPNP_E_SUCCESS;      /* General purpose return code */

  printf("upnp_cmactions: start\n");

  /* Make sure your pointer isn't null. */
  if(request == NULL) {
    printf("upnp_cmactions: request pointer is NULL\n");
    return UPNP_E_BAD_REQUEST;
  }

  /* Match up the requested action with one you support. */
  if(strcmp(request->ActionName, "GetProtocolInfo") == 0) {
    /* Call the handler for the liftLever action. */
    ret = upnpav_getprotocolinfo(request);
  } else {
    /* Unrecognized action */
    printf("upnp_cmactions: unrecognized action: %s\n",
           request->ActionName);
    request->ErrCode = UPNP_E_INVALID_ACTION;
    ret = UPNP_E_INVALID_ACTION;
  }

  printf("upnp_cmactions: end\n");

  return ret;
}

/*
 * Function: upnpav_getprotocolinfo
 *
 * Parameters: pointer to a Upnp_Action_Request structure
 *
 * Returns: UPNP_E_SUCCESS if successful, UPnP specification
 *          defined error code if not.
 *
 * Description: This function handles the UPnP A/V
 *              GetProtocolInfo function. It simply returns
 *              the value of your protocol info state variable.
 */
int upnpav_getprotocolinfo(struct Upnp_Action_Request *request)
{
  char result_str[512];      /* Soap resposne string */
```

Figure 18.4 Connection Manager Module Source Listing *(Continues)*

```
  printf("upnpav_getprotocolinfo: start\n");

  /* Package up your protocol info strings. */
  sprintf(result_str, "<u:%sResponse xmlns:u=\"%s\"> \
                      <%s>%s</%s> \
                      <%s>%s</%s> \
                      </u:%sResponse>",
                      request->ActionName,
                      CONNECTION_MANAGER_SERVICETYPE,
                      "Source",
                      SOURCE_PROTOCOL_INFO,
                      "Source",
                      "Sink",
                      SINK_PROTOCOL_INFO,
                      "Sink",
                      request->ActionName);

  /* Convert it into a DOM. */
  request->ActionResult = ixmlParseBuffer(result_str);

  /* Set the error code. */
  request->ErrCode = UPNP_E_SUCCESS;

  printf("upnpav_getprotocolinfo: end\n");

  return request->ErrCode;
}
```

Figure 18.4 Connection Manager Module Source Listing

You have one task remaining for the Connection Manager service: subscriptions. Unlike the AVTransport and Rendering Control services, the Connection Manager service does not support a LastChange style eventing system. It simply events the values for the three evented state variables: `SourceProtocolInfo`, `SinkProtocolInfo`, and `CurrentConnectionIDs`. You've statically defined the values of the first two state variables, and can do so for the third as well. Because your device will only ever support one connection (that is, you do not support `PrepareForConnection`), the `CurrentConnectionIDs` will only ever have one value: `0`.

The side effect of this is that these values never change for the lifetime of your device. This does not allow you to skip out on implementing subscription of this service, however. Instead, you send an initial event only at subscription.

With this information, you can complete your support for the Connection Manager service with a function to handle subscriptions, listed in Figure 18.5.

```
/*
 * Function: upnp_cmsusbscriptions
 *
 * Parameters: pointer to a Upnp_Subscription_Request structure
 *
 * Description: This function handles subscription requests for
 *              the UPnP A/V Connection Manager service.
 */
int upnp_cmsubscriptions(struct Upnp_Subscription_Request *request)
{
  IXML_Document *propset = NULL;    /* Your property set */

  printf("upnp_cmsubscriptions: start\n");

  /* Add your three evented state variables to the property set. */
  UpnpAddToPropertySet(&propset, "SourceProtocolInfo",
                       SOURCE_PROTOCOL_INFO);
  UpnpAddToPropertySet(&propset, "SinkProtocolInfo",
                       SOURCE_PROTOCOL_INFO);
  UpnpAddToPropertySet(&propset, "CurrentConnectionIDs",
                       g_currentconnectionids);


  /* Now accept the subscription. */
  UpnpAcceptSubscriptionExt(g_device_handle, g_deviceudn,
                             CONNECTION_MANAGER_SERVICEID,
                             propset,
                             request->Sid);

  /* Free the propset. */
  ixmlDocument_free(propset);

  printf("upnp_cmsubscriptions: end\n");

  return UPNP_E_SUCCESS;
}
```

Figure 18.5 Connection Manager Subscription Handler

That completes support for the Connection Manager service. When an A/V control point discovers your device, it will now be able to determine what media types you support.

AVTransport Service

After making sure a discovered A/V device can support a desired media type, the control point needs to tell the device the URI for the media itself. The AVTransport service provides this capability through the `SetAVTransportURI()` action. `SetAVTransportURI` takes an in parameter associated with the `AVTransportURI` state variable of type URI that you need to save for later use.

Figure 18.6 lists the code to support this action in the AVTransport service.

```
/*
 * Filename: upnpavt.c
 *
 * Description: This file implements support for the UPnP A/V
 *              Transport Service.
 */

#include <stdlib.h>
#include <unistd.h>
#include <string.h>
#include "toaster.h"
#include "toasterhw.h"

/*
 * Function: upnp_avtactions
 *
 * Parameters: pointer to a Upnp_Action_Request structure
 *
 * Returns: UPNP_E_SUCCESS if everything worked, UPnP
 *          specification defined error code if not.
 *
 * Description: This function dispatches actions within the
 *              UPnP A/V Transport Service.
 */
int upnp_avtactions(struct Upnp_Action_Request *request)
{
  int ret = UPNP_E_SUCCESS;     /* General purpose return code */
```

Figure 18.6 AVTransport Module Code Listing *(Continues)*

```
  printf("upnp_avtactions: start\n");

  /* Make sure your pointer isn't null. */
  if(request == NULL) {
    printf("upnp_avtactions: request pointer is NULL\n");
    return UPNP_E_BAD_REQUEST;
  }

  /* Match the action name with what you support. */
  if(strcmp(request->ActionName, "SetAVTransportURI") == 0) {
    /* Call the handler for the liftLever action */
    ret = upnpav_setavtransporturi(request);
  } else {
    /* Unrecognized action */
    printf("upnp_avtactions: unrecognized action: %s\n",
           request->ActionName);
    request->ErrCode = UPNP_E_INVALID_ACTION;
    ret = UPNP_E_INVALID_ACTION;
  }

  printf("upnp_avtactions: end\n");

  return ret;
}

/*
 * Function: upnp_setavtransporturi
 *
 * Parameters: pointer to a Upnp_Action_Request structure
 *
 * Description: This function handles the SetAVTransportURI
 *              action, and extracts and saves the URI.
 */
int upnpav_setavtransporturi(struct Upnp_Action_Request *request)
{
  char *value=NULL;     /* Your extracted parameter value */
  char result_str[512]; /* SOAP response packet */

  printf("upnpav_setavtransporturi: start\n");

  /* First, you need to extract the new dial value parameter. */
  value = SampleUtil_GetFirstDocumentItem(
              request->ActionRequest,
              "totalSlices");
```

Figure 18.6 AVTransport Module Code Listing *(Continues)*

```
  /* Make sure it worked. */
  if(value == NULL) {
    printf("upnpav_setavtransporturi: couldn't retrieve
           totalSlices value\n");
    request->ErrCode = UPNP_E_ACTION_FAILED;
    return request->ErrCode;
  }

  /* Set your global state variable. */
  strcpy(g_avtransporturi, value);

  /* It worked Craft the SOAP body response. */
  sprintf(result_str, "<u:%sResponse xmlns:u=\"%s\"> \
                        </u:%sResponse>",
                       request->ActionName,
                       AVTRANSPORT_SERVICETYPE,
                       request->ActionName);

  /* Convert it into a DOM. */
  request->ActionResult = UpnpParse_Buffer(result_str);

  /* Set the error code. */
  request->ErrCode = UPNP_E_SUCCESS;

  free(value);

  /*
   * Send a state variable change event.
   */

  printf("upnpav_setavtransporturi: end\n");

  return request->ErrCode;
}
```

Figure 18.6 AVTransport Module Code Listing

As you can see, this has been a pretty standard implementation so far. You have some unfinished business in the AVTransport module. When the `AVTransportURI` state variable is updated, you need to send out an event indicating it has been changed. However, you cannot send an event in the traditional way because this state variable does not have its `sendEvents` attributes set to yes. The AVTransport service does have a `LastChange` state variable, and it is through this state variable that you must send your notification.

Recall that the format of a LastChange state variable looks like the the listing shown in Figure 18.7.

For your device, you have only one current connection, so there is only one InstanceID with a value zero. With this information, you can now provide interfaces to package up and send a LastChange event for the AVTransportURI state variable. You construct the LastChange event in a similar method to dynamically updating your presentation page in Chapter 15. You define a prologue and a epilogue for the event, and then allow the specific action (SetAVTransportURI in this case) to provide the body of the event.

Figure 18.8 lists this updated code to support subscriptions and eventing for the AVTransport module.

```
<Event xmlns="urn:schemas-upnp-org:metadata-1-0/AVT_RCS">
  <InstanceID val="0">
    <Brightness val="36">
    <Contranst val="74">
    <Volume val="0">
    ...
  </InstanceID>
  <InstanceID val="1">
    <Mute channel="Master" val="0">
    <Volume val="74">
    ...
  </InstanceID>
</Event>
```

Figure 18.7 LastChange Event

```
#define AVT_PREFACE "<Event xmlns=\"urn:schemas-upnp-org:metadata-1-0/
AVT\">"
#define AVT_END "</Event>"

/*
 * Function: upnp_avtsusbscriptions
 *
 * Parameters: pointer to a Upnp_Subscription_Request structure
 *
```

Figure 18.8 AVTransport Subscription and LastChange *(Continues)*

```
 * Description: This function handles subscription requests for
 *              the UPnP A/V Transport service.
 */
int upnp_avtsubscriptions(struct Upnp_Subscription_Request *request)
{
  IXML_Document *propset = NULL;    /* Your property set */

  printf("upnp_avtsubscriptions: start\n");

  /* Add Last Change to the property set. */
  UpnpAddToPropertySet(&propset, "LastChange", g_avtlastchange);

  /* Now accept the subscription. */
  UpnpAcceptSubscriptionExt(g_device_handle, g_deviceudn,
                            AVTRANSPORT_SERVICEID,
                            propset,
                            request->Sid);

  printf("upnp_avtsubscriptions: end\n");

  return UPNP_E_SUCCESS;
}

/*
 * Function: upnp_avtupdate
 *
 * Parameters: SOAP formatted update
 *
 * Description: This function will update the LastChange state
 *              variable.
 */
void upnp_avtupdate(char *update)
{
  strcpy(g_avtlastchange, AVT_PREFACE);
  strcat(g_avtlastchange, update);
  strcat(g_avtlastchange, AVT_END);
}
```

Figure 18.8 AVTransport Subscription and `LastChange`

Recall from Chapter 17 that the AVTransport service also supports CD-Player style capabilities to control the playback of the media. To complete the basic playback of MP3 audio, you'll add support for the `Play()`, `Pause()`, and `Stop()` actions.

For each of these actions you'll call an appropriate interface in an audio decoder library. The specific implementation of the audio decoder is not important; as long as it supports similar interfaces, you could use any audio or video library.

The Play, Pause, and Stop actions are fairly straightforward. They're going to simply call the appropriate function in the audio module. What makes their implementation interesting is the LastChange event. When you change from the STOPPED to the PLAYING state, or the PLAYING to the PAUSED state, you must notify control points that you have done so, as represented by the `TransportState` state variable. This is done through the `LastChange` event.

Figure 18.9 lists the implementation of the remaining actions for the AVTransport service.

```
/*
 * Function: upnpav_play
 *
 * Parameters: pointer to a Upnp_Action_Request structure
 *
 * Returns: UPNP_E_SUCCESS if everything worked, other UPnP
 *          defined error code if not.
 *
 * Description: This function implements the Rendering Control
 *              play action by attempting to play the current
 *              avtransport uri.
 */
int upnpav_play(struct Upnp_Action_Request *request)
{
  int ret=0;              /* General purpose error code */
  char result_str[512];   /* SOAP Response Packet */

  printf("upnpav_play: start\n");

  /*
   * Start playing!
   */
  audio_play();

  /* It worked Craft the SOAP body response. */
  sprintf(result_str, "<u:%sResponse xmlns:u=\"%s\"> \
                       </u:%sResponse>",
                      request->ActionName,
```

Figure 18.9 AVTransport Actions *(Continues)*

```
                            RENDERING_CONTROL_SERVICETYPE,
                            request->ActionName);

  /* Convert it into a DOM. */
  request->ActionResult = ixmlParseBuffer(result_str);

  /* Set the error code. */
  request->ErrCode = UPNP_E_SUCCESS;

  /* Update your Last Change event. */
  upnp_avtupdate("<InstanceID val=\"0\"><TransportState \
                 val=\"PLAYING\"/></InstanceID>");

  printf("upnpav_play: end\n");

  return request->ErrCode;
}

/*
 * Function: upnpav_pause
 *
 * Parameters: pointer to a Upnp_Action_Request structure
 *
 * Returns: UPNP_E_SUCCESS if everything worked, other UPnP
 *          defined error code if not.
 *
 * Description: This function implements the Rendering Control
 *              Pause action by attempting to pause the currently
 *              playing avtransport uri.
 */
int upnpav_pause(struct Upnp_Action_Request *request)
{
  int ret=0;    /* General purpose error code */
  char result_str[512];   /* SOAP Response Packet */

  printf("upnpav_pause: start\n");

  /* Pause the playback. */
  audio_pause();

  /* It worked Craft the SOAP body response. */
  sprintf(result_str, "<u:%sResponse xmlns:u=\"%s\"> \
                        </u:%sResponse>",
                       request->ActionName,
```

Figure 18.9 AVTransport Actions *(Continues)*

```
                        RENDERING_CONTROL_SERVICETYPE,
                        request->ActionName);

  /* Convert it into a DOM. */
  request->ActionResult = ixmlParseBuffer(result_str);

  /* Set the error code. */
  request->ErrCode = UPNP_E_SUCCESS;

  /* Update your Last Change event. */
  upnp_avtupdate("<InstanceID val=\"0\"><TransportState \
              val=\"PAUSED\"/></InstanceID>");

  printf("upnpav_pause: end\n");

  return request->ErrCode;
}

/*
 * Function: upnpav_stop
 *
 * Parameters: pointer to a Upnp_Action_Request structure
 *
 * Returns: UPNP_E_SUCCESS if everything worked, other UPnP
 *          defined error code if not.
 *
 * Description: This function implements the Rendering Control
 *              play action by attempting to stop the current
 *              avtransport uri.
 */
int upnpav_stop(struct Upnp_Action_Request *request)
{
  int ret=0;    /* General purpose error code */
  char result_str[512];   /* SOAP Response Packet */

  printf("upnpav_stop: start\n");

  /* Stop the track! */
  audio_stop();

  /* It worked Craft the SOAP body response. */
  sprintf(result_str, "<u:%sResponse xmlns:u=\"%s\"> \
                         </u:%sResponse>",
                        request->ActionName,
```

Figure 18.9 AVTransport Actions *(Continues)*

```
                         RENDERING_CONTROL_SERVICETYPE,
                         request->ActionName);

  /* Convert it into a DOM. */
  request->ActionResult = ixmlParseBuffer(result_str);

  /* Set the error code. */
  request->ErrCode = UPNP_E_SUCCESS;

  /* Update your Last Change event. */
  upnp_avtupdate("<InstanceID val=\"0\"><TransportState \
             val=\"STOPPED\"/></InstanceID>");

  printf("upnpav_stop: end\n");

  return request->ErrCode;
}
```

Figure 18.9 AVTransport Actions

That's it! You have successfully implemented support for a UPnP A/V control point to discover your device, determine its supported transport and media protocols, tell your device about a specific URI, and then control the playback of the URI. Note that we have chosen not to implement any of the optional RenderingControl actions for our device; however, in the real world we certainly would have liked to provide volume control and other features for our customers. A stub implementation of this service is provided on the CD-ROM.

Although your implementation is far from complete (there are many additional required actions to support), this exercise should demonstrate that implementing A/V support in a device is really no different than adding support for any other service. There are actions to implement, state variables to maintain, and subscriptions to event, just like the SuperToaster services you implemented in Chapters 12 through 14. In fact, the same could be said for any of the UPnP Forum Working Committee specifications: They all defined a standard set of services and actions to support if you want to be compatible with the specification.

Intel Tools for UPnP Technology

You can verify the successful implementation of UPnP A/V services by using another useful tool included in the Intel Tools for UPnP Technology package. Intel® AV Wizard is a user-friendly front end to a UPnP A/V control point that works just like a typical PC media player. The only difference, of course, is that the device to which content is being rendered could exist anywhere on the network.

Figure 18.10 shows the Intel A/V Wizard finding our Super Toaster now enabled with UPnP A/V Services.

After integrating rendering playback support with your favorite media codec libraries, the Intel A/V Wizard will be a valuable tool to test and debug.

Figure 18.10 Intel A/V Wizard

Summary

In this chapter you used the information presented in Chapter 17 to add basic Media Rendering support for your Super Toaster. Although the support is far from complete, it provides enough of a framework for future development should you decide to finish it. This concludes the coverage of UPnP A/V. In the remaining chapters you'll look at additional UPnP technologies that are gaining in popularity.

Chapter 19

Developing Control Point Applications

After completing development of a UPnP Device, it is often necessary to also develop a control point application with the capability to programmatically discover and control devices of a specific type. Although any compatible UPnP library can be used for the development of a control point application, in addition to supporting device development, the Intel SDK also supports interfaces for the development of control point applications. This chapter briefly introduces the API that enables your application to search for devices, invoke actions, and subscribe to services.

Problem Description

A device is only as useful as the applications that can control and access its capabilities. In UPnP terminology, these control point applications have the capability to programmatically discover, control, invoke actions, subscribe to services, and receive events. Although general-purpose tools like the Intel Device Spy can be used to provide this capability, their use is intended for development purposes only. Ultimately, an application that provides this capability to the end user is needed.

UPnP Control Point Applications

Control point applications are programs with the capability to programmatically discover, control, and communicate with specific UPnP device types. Writing a control point application can range from a simple one-day task to a complicated and involved multiple man-month project. Development is typically divided into multiple phases:

- Discovery—Discovering the UPnP devices you're interested in
- Control—Invoking actions to control the behavior of the device
- Subscriptions—Subscribing to services and handling events

The following sections introduce you to interfaces to support the development of a control point application and show you how to write a very simple program to discover, invoke actions, and subscribe to services. For a more complete example, please refer to the sample TV control point application included in the Intel SDK.

Before you begin discovering devices, the task of initialization and registration with the UPnP library must be done. Just as when you write devices, before any other interfaces can be called, the device must be initialized by a call to `UpnpInit()`. Then, instead of registering a device with the library, you register the control point as a UPnP client using the following interface:

```
int UpnpRegisterClient (IN Upnp_FunPtr Callback,
                        IN const void *Cookie,
                        OUT UpnpClient_Handle *Hnd);
```

Callback—Function pointer to a callback function that is invoked when the UPnP library has client-related information for the control point application.

Cookie—User-provided cookie that is given as a parameter to the callback function when invoked.

Hnd—Pointer to a variable that designates the control point client handle for future calls to the UPnP library.

Returns: UPNP_E_SUCCESS if successful, UPnP specification defined error code if not.

After calling `UpnpRegisterClient()`, any other client interfaces may be invoked using the returned handle. When the control point application exists, just like a device, it is necessary to unregister any previously registered client handles. The following interface provides this capability:

```
int UpnpUnRegisterClient (IN UpnpClient_Handle *Hnd);
```

Hnd—Pointer to a control point client handle to unregister UPnP library.

Returns: UPNP_E_SUCCESS if successful, UPnP specification defined error code if not.

After a successful call to `UpnpUnRegisterClient()`, you may finish cleaning up resources in the UPnP library with a final call to `UpnpFinish()`, in the same fashion as developing a device. With these interfaces, you can create a skeleton for your control point application, listed in Figure 19.1.

```
int main()
{
  int ret=0;

  /* First initialize the UPnP Library. */
  ret = UpnpInit(NULL, 0);
  if(ret != UPNP_E_SUCCESS) {
    printf("UpnpInit failed\n");
    return ret;
  }

  /* Next, register yourself as a Client. */
  ret = UpnpRegisterClient(upnp_callback, &g_handle, &g_handle);
  if(ret != UPNP_E_SUCCESS) {
    printf("UpnpRegisterClient failed\n");
    return ret;
  }

  /*
   * Do some real work.
   */

  /* Unregister yourself with the library. */
  ret = UpnpUnRegisterClient(g_handle);
```

Figure 19.1 Control Point Application Code Listing *(Continues)*

```
  if(ret != UPNP_E_SUCCESS) {
    printf("UpnpUnRegisterClient failed\n");
  }

  /* Clean up the library. */
  UpnpFinish();

  return 0;
}
```

Figure 19.1 Control Point Application Code Listing

Now you can turn to the specific interfaces needed to discover, invoke, and subscribe.

Discovery

There are several different ways for a control point to discover a device. A search for all root devices causes all devices in range to return a response; a search for a specific service type returns responses from all devices that have the specified service; or a search for a specific device UDN generates a response from the single device you're looking for. Fortunately, the same control point interface supports all of these search methods:

```
int UpnpSearchAsync (IN UpnpClient_Handle Hnd,
                     IN int Mx,
                     IN const char *Target,
                     IN const void *Cookie);
```

`Hnd`—Handle to a registered UPnP client handle, generated from UpnpRegisterClient().

`Mx`—Maximum number of desired responses.

`Target`—Search string to look for. It may be a device UDN, service type, or device type.

`Cookie`—User-specified Cookie to be returned when the callback notify function is called with a search result.

Returns: UPNP_E_SUCCESS if successful, UPnP specification defined error code if not.

For the Super Toaster, since you know the UDN of the device you are developing, you search based on that value. Note that when using less restrictive search patterns, such as a service type, or for all root devices, the control point application must filter the search results for the specific device or service type desired.

With this interface, you can add discovery capability to your control point application by adding a callback function that looks at the event type, which can be any of the values listed in Table 19.1.

The code listing in Figure 19.2 shows the additions of these event types. When you find your Super Toaster device, you save information about the device for use when invoking actions later. Take special note of the different structures provided for each event type. For complete details on these structures, please refer to the `upnp.h` header file.

Table 19.1 descriptionType values

Type	Description
UPNP_DISCOVERY_SEARCH_RESULT	A search result was received from a UPnP device.
UPNP_DISCOVERY_ADVERTISEMENT_ALIVE	A device advertisement matching a previously specified search target was received.
UPNP_DISCOVERY_ADVERTISEMENT_BYEBYE	A bye-bye announcement from a device matching a previously specified search target was received.
UPNP_DISCOVERY_SEARCH_TIMEOUT	A recently initiated search timeout has expired.

```
/*
 * Function: upnp_callback
 *
 * Parameters: event type, pointer to the DOM event structure
 *             pointer to a user provided coookie
 *
 * Returns: UPNP_E_SUCCESS if everything worked
```

Figure 19.2 Control Point Application Device Discovery Callback *(Continues)*

```
 *
 * Description: This function will be called by the UPnP Library
 *              whenever it has information for you about search
 *              request, action invocations, or subscriptions.
 */
int upnp_callback(Upnp_EventType EventType, void *Event, void *Cookie)
{
  printf("upnp_callback: start\n");

  /* Switch on the event type. */
  switch(EventType) {
    case UPNP_DISCOVERY_ADVERTISEMENT_ALIVE:
    case UPNP_DISCOVERY_SEARCH_RESULT:
    {
      struct Upnp_Discovery *disc =
             (struct Upnp_Discovery *) Event;

      printf("Device found at location: %s\n", disc->Location);

      break;
    }

    case UPNP_DISCOVERY_SEARCH_TIMEOUT:
      printf("upnp_callback: search timeout\n");
      break;

    case UPNP_DISCOVERY_ADVERTISEMENT_BYEBYE:
    {
      struct Upnp_Discovery *disc =
             (struct Upnp_Discovery *) Event;

      printf("Device byebye at location: %s\n", disc->Location);

      break;
    }

    default:
      printf("upnp_callback: unhandled event type: %d\n",
            EventType);
      break;
  }

  printf("upnp_callback: end\n");

  return UPNP_E_SUCCESS;
}
```

Figure 19.2 Control Point Application Device Discovery Callback

With this capability you can now find your SuperToaster device! For your quick-and-dirty control point application, you'll just add this capability directly to the main function. If this were a real product quality-control point, you'd surely have a fancy user interface of some kind to support the interaction with the device. In fact, due to the user interaction of a control point application, they can often become larger and more complex than their device counterparts.

```
int main()
{
  int ret=0;
  int timeout=0;

  /* First initialize the UPnP Library. */
  ret = UpnpInit(NULL, 0);
  if(ret != UPNP_E_SUCCESS) {
    printf("UpnpInit failed\n");
    return ret;
  }

  /* Next, register yourself as a Client. */
  ret = UpnpRegisterClient(upnp_callback, &g_handle, &g_handle);
  if(ret != UPNP_E_SUCCESS) {
    printf("UpnpRegisterClient failed\n");
    return ret;
  }

  /* Send out a search request for your device. */
  ret = UpnpSearchAsync(g_handle, 5,
            "uuid:00A0C96EFAF4SuperToaster-1", NULL);
  if(ret != UPNP_E_SUCCESS) {
    printf("upnpSearchAsync returned ret: %d\n", ret);
    return ret;
  }

  /*
   * Do some other work.
   */

  /* Unregister yourself with the library. */
  ret = UpnpUnRegisterClient(g_handle);
```

Figure 19.3 Searching for Your Device *(Continues)*

```
  if(ret != UPNP_E_SUCCESS) {
    printf("UpnpUnRegisterClient failed\n");
  }

  /* Clean up the library. */
  UpnpFinish();

  return 0;
}
```

Figure 19.3 Searching for Your Device

Note that you use the specific UDN of your Super Toaster device, which is created from the MAC address of the machine on which the device is running. Obviously this code is not going to be portable to other environments, but unlike the other more generic search methods, you're guaranteed to find only one device.

When you run the control point application, you can see it discover your device:

```
upnp_callback: start
      Device found at location:
 http://192.168.0.1:1973/supertoaster.xml

upnp_callback: end
```

Next, you can turn your attention to invoking actions on the device.

Invoking Actions

Once discovered, the UPnP library provides the capability to invoke actions on a device. There are two methods for doing this: one invokes the action synchronously and the other invokes the action asynchronously, providing the return value (if and when complete) through your callback function. The following interfaces support the ability to invoke actions on a discovered device:

```
int UpnpSendAction (IN UpnpClient_Handle Hnd,
                    IN const char *ActionURL,
                    IN const char *ServiceType,
                    IN const char *DevUDN,
                    IN IXML_Document *Action,
                    OUT IXML_Document **RespNode);
```

Continues

`Hnd`—Handle to a registered UPnP client handle, generated from `UpnPRegisterClient()`.

`ActionURL`—Action URL of the device service.

`ServiceType`—Specified Service Type that contains the action being invoked.

`DevUDN`—This parameter is not used.

`Action`—This DOM document represents the SOAP action invocation.

`RespNode`—Pointer to a returned DOM document representing the SOAP action response.

Returns: UPNP_E_SUCCESS if successful, UPnP specification defined error code if not.

`UpnpSendAction()` is a synchronous call and returns only after an action response or after the UPnP Device Architecture-specified 30-second maximum response time has passed. `UpnpSendActionAsync()`, on the other hand, is an asynchronous call that returns immediately, with the action response being returned through the previously registered client callback function.

```
int UpnpSendActionAsync (IN UpnpClient_Handle Hnd,
                         IN const char *ActionURL,
                         IN const char *ServiceType,
                         IN const char *DevUDN,
                         IN IXML_Document *Action,
                         IN Upnp_FunPtr Fun,
                         IN const void *Cookie);
```

`Hnd`—Handle to a registered UPnP client handle, generated from `UpnpRegisterClient()`.

`ActionURL`—Action URL of the device service.

`ServiceType`—Specified Service Type that contains the action being invoked.

`DevUDN`—This parameter is not used.

`Action`—This DOM document represents the SOAP action invocation.

Continues

Fun—Function pointer to a callback that will receive the action response notification. *Cookie*—User-provided data that will be passed into the callback function.

Returns: UPNP_E_SUCCESS if successful, UPnP specification defined error code if not.

UpnpSendActionAsync() has the added ability to invoke an entire series of actions and then not have to wait for their response after calling each one, with the UPNP_CONTROL_ACTION_COMPLETE event type specified to the callback function. For your simple control point application, you'll use the synchronous UpnpSendAction() interface.

Before you can invoke the action, you need to create the SOAP packet requesting the invocation. This can be seen in the code below, but all SOAP request packets have the following body format:

```
<u:actionName xmlns:u=serviceType>
<paramname>paramvalue</paramname>
<paramname>paramvalue</paramname>
...
```

Figure 19.4 lists code to invoke the GetTotalSlices action.

Note that in the call to UpnpSendAction, you must provide the complete control URL for the device on which you're invoking the action. You have hard-coded this information here, but normally would retrieve the information from manually parsing the XML device description document for the device.

Invoking actions with parameters is only slightly more complicated, as you need to package the input parameters into the SOAP request packet. Figure 19.5 lists code to invoke the SetTotalSlices action, providing the input parameter specified by the user.

```
  /* Create your DOM document for the action. */
  strcpy(actionxml, "<u:getTotalSlices xmlns:u=\
"urn:schemas-intoast-com:service:lifetimestats:1\">");
  action = ixmlParseBuffer(actionxml);

  ret = UpnpSendActionAsync(g_handle,
http://192.168.0.1:1973/upnp/control/lifetimestats1,
            "urn:schemas-intoast-com:service:lifetimestats:1",
            NULL, action, upnp_callback, NULL);
```

Figure 19.4 GetTotalSlices Action Invocation

```
/* Create your DOM document for the action. */
strcpy(actionxml, "<u:setTotalSlices xmlns:U=\
      "urn:schemas-intoast-com:service:lifetimestats:1\">
<totalSlices>5</totalSlices>");
action = ixmlParseBuffer(actionxml);

ret = UpnpSendActionAsync(g_handle,
      "http://192.168.0.1:1973/upnp/control/lifetimestats1",
      "urn:schemas-intoast-com:service:lifetimestats:1",
      NULL, action, upnp_callback, NULL);
```

Figure 19.5 Invoking SetToasterTime

With the completion of these actions, you now have the capability to add action invocation support for all of the service actions for your Super Toaster. The remaining capabilities that you need to add to the control point application are subscriptions and eventing.

Subscriptions and Eventing

Like action invocation, the UPnP library supports both synchronous and asynchronous subscription interfaces. This is helpful when you'd like to automatically subscribe to all device services but aren't interested in waiting for the result of each subscription request.

There are two parts to managing subscriptions in a control point application. The first is making the first subscription request, the second is renewing the subscriptions when they expire. The latter part does require a fair amount of careful subscription management to make sure the subscriptions don't expire before being renewed.

The following interfaces support subscription in your control point application.

```
int UpnpSubscribe (IN UpnpClient_Handle Hnd,
                   IN const char *PublisherUrl,
                   IN OUT int TimeOut,
                   OUT Upnp_SID SubsId);
```

Hnd—Handle to a registered UPnP client handle, generated from `UpnpRegisterClient()`.

PublisherURL—The Subscription URL of the device service.

Continues

`TimeOut`—Specifies the requested subscription time. On return, this variable will contain the subscription time returned from the device.

`SubsId`—On return, this variable will receive the subscription ID.

Returns: UPNP_E_SUCCESS if successful, UPnP specification defined error code if not.

`UpnpSubscribe()` is a synchronous call that blocks until a subscription response is received from the device in question. Alternatively, the UPnP library supports an asynchronous subscription interface.

```
int UpnpSubscribeAsync (IN UpnpClient_Handle Hnd,
                        IN const char *PublisherUrl,
                        IN int TimeOut,
                        IN Upnp_FunPtr Fun,
                        IN const void *Cookie);
```

`Hnd`—Handle to a registered UPnP client handle, generated from `UpnpRegisterClient()`.

`PublisherURL`—Subscription URL of the device service.

`TimeOut`—Specifies the requested subscription time. On return, this variable will contain the subscription time returned from the device.

`Fun`—Pointer to a callback function that is notified of the result of the subscription request.

`Cookie`—User-provided data that is passed to the callback function when invoked.

Returns: UPNP_E_SUCCESS if successful, UPnP specification defined error code if not.

Based upon the value returned from the device for the subscription timeout, you'll need to renew the subscription before that time expires. A synchronous and asynchronous interface is provided for this purpose.

```
int UpnpRenewSubscription (IN UpnpClient_Handle Hnd,
                           IN OUT int *TimeOut,
                           IN Upnp_SID SubsID)
```

`Hnd`—Handle to a registered UPnP client handle, generated from `UpnpRegisterClient()`.

`TimeOut`—The Requested subscription time. On return, this variable will contain the subscription time returned from the device.

`SubsId`—The Subscription ID to renew.

Returns: UPNP_E_SUCCESS if successful, UPnP specification defined error code if not.

```
int UpnpRenewSubscription (IN UpnpClient_Handle Hnd,
                           IN int TimeOut,
                           IN Upnp_SID SubsId,
                           IN Upnp_FunPtr Fun,
                           IN const void *Cookie);
```

`Hnd`—Handle to a registered UPnP client handle, generated from `UpnpRegisterClient()`.

`TimeOut`—The Requested subscription time. On return, this variable will contain the subscription time returned from the device.

`SubsId`—The Subscription ID to renew.

`Fun`—Pointer to a callback function that is notified of the result of the subscription request.

`Cookie`—User-provided data that is passed to the callback function when invoked.

Returns: UPNP_E_SUCCESS if successful, UPnP specification defined error code if not.

Armed with these functions, you're ready to add subscription support to your device. When the asynchronous calls are complete, you'll receive a callback notification with one of the following responses:

- UPNP_EVENT_SUBSCRIBE_COMPLETE
- UPNP_EVENT_UNSUBSCRIBE_COMPLETE
- UPNP_EVENT_RENEWAL_COMPLETE

Additionally, when an event is received from the device, the registered callback function is be invoked with the UPNP_EVENT_RECEIVED event type specified.

Figure 19.6 lists the complete code to the very simple toaster control point with added support for subscription and eventing for your Super Toaster device.

```
/*
 * Filename: toastercp.c
 */
#include "toastercp.h"
#include "sample_util.h"

UpnpClient_Handle g_handle=-1;

/*
 * Function: upnp_callback
 *
 * Parameters: event type, pointer to the DOM event structure
 *             pointer to a user provided coookie
 *
 * Returns: UPNP_E_SUCCESS if everything worked
 *
 * Description: This function is called by the UPnP Library
 *              whenever it has information for you about search
 *              request, action invocations, or subscriptions.
 */
int upnp_callback(Upnp_EventType EventType, void *Event, void *Cookie)
{
  printf("upnp_callback: start\n");

  /* Switch on the event type. */
  switch(EventType) {
    case UPNP_DISCOVERY_ADVERTISEMENT_ALIVE:
    case UPNP_DISCOVERY_SEARCH_RESULT:
    {
      struct Upnp_Discovery *disc =
           (struct Upnp_Discovery *) Event;

      printf("Device found at location: %s\n", disc->Location);

      break;
    }
```

Figure 19.6 Complete Simple Control Point Code Listing *(Continues)*

```
case UPNP_DISCOVERY_SEARCH_TIMEOUT:
  printf("upnp_callback: search timeout\n");
  break;

case UPNP_DISCOVERY_ADVERTISEMENT_BYEBYE:
{
  struct Upnp_Discovery *disc =
       (struct Upnp_Discovery *) Event;

 printf("Device byebye at location: %s\n", disc->Location);

  break;
}

case UPNP_CONTROL_ACTION_COMPLETE:
{
  struct Upnp_Action_Complete *action =
       (struct Upnp_Action_Complete *) Event;
  char *tmp=NULL;

  printf("Action Complete with return code: %d\n",
        action->ErrCode);

  tmp = SampleUtil_GetFirstDocumentItem(
            action->ActionResult,
            "totalSlices");

  if(tmp != NULL) {
    printf("Total Slices: %s\n", tmp);
  }

  free(tmp);

  break;
}

case UPNP_EVENT_RECEIVED:
{
  struct Upnp_Event *event = (struct Upnp_Event *) Event;
  char *tmp=NULL;

  printf("Event Received!\n");
```

Figure 19.6 Complete Simple Control Point Code Listing *(Continues)*

```
      tmp = SampleUtil_GetFirstDocumentItem(
                event->ChangedVariables,
                "totalSlices");

      if(tmp != NULL) {
        printf("totalSlices changed to: %s\n", tmp);
      }

      break;
    }

    case UPNP_EVENT_SUBSCRIBE_COMPLETE:
    case UPNP_EVENT_UNSUBSCRIBE_COMPLETE:
    case UPNP_EVENT_RENEWAL_COMPLETE:
    {
      struct Upnp_Event_Subscribe *sub =
           (struct Upnp_Event_Subscribe *) Event;

      printf("Subscribe Response received with return code:
           %d\n", sub->ErrCode);

      break;
    }

    case UPNP_EVENT_SUBSCRIPTION_EXPIRED:
    {
      struct Upnp_Event_Subscribe *sub =
           (struct Upnp_Event_Subscribe *) Event;

      printf("Subscription expired\n");

      break;
    }

    default:
      printf("upnp_callback: unhandled event type: %d\n",
           EventType);
      break;
  }

  printf("upnp_callback: end\n");

  return UPNP_E_SUCCESS;
}
```

Figure 19.6 Complete Simple Control Point Code Listing *(Continues)*

```
int main()
{
  int ret=0;
  int timeout=0;
  Upnp_SID sid;
  IXML_Document action=NULL;
  char actionxml[250];

  /* First, initialize the UPnP Library. */
  ret = UpnpInit(NULL, 0);
  if(ret != UPNP_E_SUCCESS) {
    printf("UpnpInit failed\n");
    return ret;
  }

  /* Next, register yourself as a Client. */
  ret = UpnpRegisterClient(upnp_callback, &g_handle, &g_handle);
  if(ret != UPNP_E_SUCCESS) {
    printf("UpnpRegisterClient failed\n");
    return ret;
  }

  /* Send out a search request for your device. */
  ret = UpnpSearchAsync(g_handle, 5,
            "uuid:00A0C96EFAF4SuperToaster-1", NULL);
  if(ret != UPNP_E_SUCCESS) {
    printf("upnpSearchAsync returned ret: %d\n", ret);
    return ret;
  }

  /* Wait a bit. */
  sleep(5);

  /* Subscribe to a service. */
  ret = UpnpSubscribe(g_handle,
            "http://192.168.0.1:1973/upnp/event/lifetimestats1",
            &timeout, sid);
  if(ret != UPNP_E_SUCCESS) {
    printf("UpnpSubscribe failed with ret: %d\n", ret);
    return ret;
  } else {
    printf("UpnpSubscribe succeded with timeout: %d\n", timeout);
  }
```

Figure 19.6 Complete Simple Control Point Code Listing *(Continues)*

```
  /* Wait a bit. */
  sleep(5);

  /* Create your DOM document for the action. */
  strcpy(actionxml, "<u:getTotalSlices xmlns:U=\
        "urn:schemas-intoast-com:service:lifetimestats:1\">");
  action = ixmlParseBuffer(actionxml);

  ret = UpnpSendActionAsync(g_handle,
        "http://192.168.0.1:1973/upnp/control/lifetimestats1",
        "urn:schemas-intoast-com:service:lifetimestats:1",
         NULL, action, upnp_callback, NULL);

  /* Wait a bit. */
  sleep(5);

  /* Create your DOM document for the action. */
  strcpy(actionxml, "<u:setTotalSlices xmlns:U=\
        "urn:schemas-intoast-com:service:lifetimestats:1\">
        <totalSlices>5</totalSlices>");
  action = ixmlParseBuffer(actionxml);

  ret = UpnpSendActionAsync(g_handle,
        http://192.168.0.1:1973/upnp/control/lifetimestats1,
            "urn:schemas-intoast-com:service:lifetimestats:1",
            NULL, action, upnp_callback, NULL);

  /* Wait a bit. */
  sleep(5);


  /* Unregister yourself with the library. */
  ret = UpnpUnRegisterClient(g_handle);
  if(ret != UPNP_E_SUCCESS) {
    printf("UpnpUnRegisterClient failed\n");
  }

  /* Clean up the library. */
  ixmlDocument_free(action);
  UpnpFinish();

  return 0;
}
```

Figure 19.6 Complete Simple Control Point Code Listing

Finally, when exiting, it is appropriate to unsubscribe from all the device services to which the control point application is subscribed. This can be done through the following interface:

```
int UpnpUnSubscribe (IN UpnpClient_Handle Hnd,
                     IN Upnp_SID SubsId);
```

Hnd—Handle to a registered UPnP client handle, generated from `UpnpRegisterClient()`.

SubsId—Subscription ID to renew.

Returns: UPNP_E_SUCCESS if successful, UPnP specification defined error code if not.

Advanced Topics

In this brief introduction of building control point applications, a fair amount of detail and additional work was left out. Obviously, your control point application will work only for your Super Toaster device. Often, control point applications either need to support a broad set of devices or may need to manage a large set of similar devices, such as the home with multiple Super Toasters.

The Intel SDK also supports a wide variety of additional interfaces to set the maximum number of subscriptions, the maximum timeout value for an accepted subscription, and a series of utility APIs to allow the control point application to request and download specific files such as device and service description documents for parsing from a device. Often, it is not a good idea to assume that just because a specific service type is supported, then all actions and state variables in that service are similarly supported. This is actually fairly common for UPnP A/V devices, with their large set of optional actions and state variables.

For the control point application developer, it is highly recommended to take a closer examination of the sample TV control point application included in the Intel SDK. There you'll find examples of many of these advanced interfaces.

Summary

This chapter introduced you briefly to the necessary interfaces for development of a control point application. Discovery, Control, Subscription, and Eventing were all covered, providing the basis for development of advanced control point applications.

Part V

Future Topics

Chapter 20

Simple Control Protocol

This chapter begins its survey of technologies influenced by the UPnP architecture with an overview of Microsoft's Simple Control Protocol (SCP). SCP brings the UPnP device architecture to very small low-cost devices that wouldn't normally be able to afford a full UPnP stack. Devices such as light bulbs, lamps, and wall switches are prime examples of devices in this class. This chapter presents an overview of SCP, focusing on how it maps into the UPnP Device Architecture.

Why SCP?

Perhaps the most frequent device implementer criticism of the UPnP architecture is the cost involved in supporting the technology. The requirement that a device have a full-featured TCP/IP network stack and HTTP 1.0 compliant web server in particular can be cost prohibitive to many devices. Furthermore, not all devices may have access to a high-speed IP-based home network. Yet, you'd still like these devices to be able to communicate not only with each other, but also with existing UPnP nodes on the network. This is the role that SCP fills: It supports a lightweight implementation of UPnP technology style device protocols intentionally designed to run over low-bandwidth communication networks such as home power line networks. SCP also attempts to unify the home automation control network market, which is currently split between a set of proprietary protocols.

SCP Device Architecture

As illustrated in Figure 20.1, SCP devices consist of two major parts, the communication subsystem and the application subsystem. You will learn about each of these in succession.

Communication Subsystem

The SCP communication subsystem implements the core SCP protocol and physical interface. This subsystem consists of two subcomponents: the Communication Protocol Controller (CPC) and an EEPROM containing description and persistence data for the device.

The CPC implements support for communication on the network and interfaces directly with the PHY that supports the physical media to which the device is connected. Although initial implementations are targeted toward power line networks, there is no requirement in SCP that this always be the case. SCP requires only that the physical medium used supports a communication model where all devices can receive all transmissions.

Application Subsystem

The other major component in an SCP device, the application subsystem, implements the core user-level functionality for a device. For

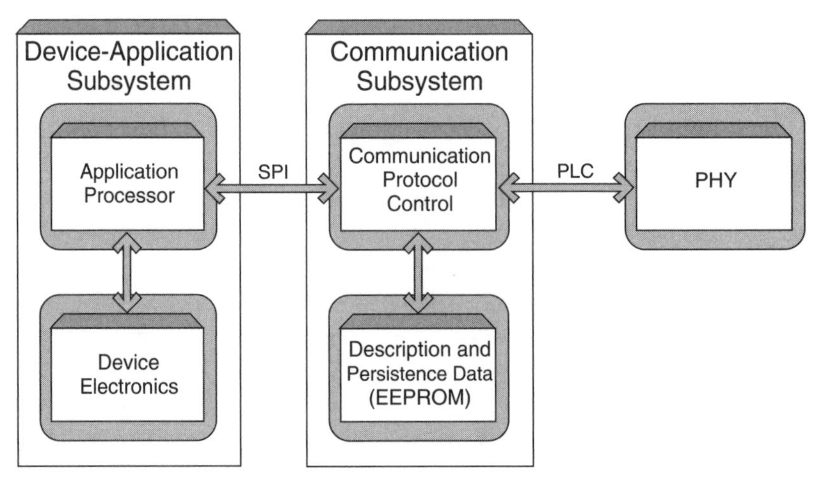

Figure 20.1 SCP Device Architecture

example, a thermostat control panel would have the control logic for handling user interaction in the Application Subsystem.

The application subsystem is typically implemented on a separate micro-controller and then interfaced with the communication subsystem via the Serial Peripheral Interface (SPI), on which the application subsystem is the master, performing initialization and communicating with the communication subsystem.

The specific protocol interface over the SPI is well defined, and Microsoft provides header files to which SCP device application developers can implement. Although there is no requirement that you use this same interface, it certainly can guarantee a wider choice of off-the-shelf communication subsystems for use in your SCP device.

SCP Discovery

Because SCP is not implemented on IP-based networks, the discovery mechanism is quite a bit different than UPnP device discovery. This section briefly covers details of the SCP discovery process and specific device characteristics needed to support this process.

Device Characteristics

Every SCP device contains a nodeID, a networkID, a Device Serial Number (DSN), and a Private Ownership Key (POK). The node ID is unique within a logical network of SCP devices, while the network ID is unique within a given physical network and denotes the specific logical network the device is on. The combination of the network ID and node ID provides a unique ID for the device across the entire physical network.

The 136-bit POK and 128-bit DSN are assigned when the device is manufactured. The DSN is similar to the UPnP UDN and is guaranteed unique for all SCP devices, while the POK is used for SCP security and can only be extracted from the device through a direct physical connection (that is, USB to a PC).

Physical and Logical Networks

SCP typically consists of one physical network (in the case of a power line network, the power lines in the home) and many logical networks. Logical networks are groupings of root devices within a localized area. For example, in an apartment complex building, one physical network exists for each building, with each apartment representing a unique logical network.

Logical network identifiers are not required to be unique beyond the physical network to which they apply. This means that bridging of physical networks is not supported. The number of logical networks supported on any given physical network is a function of the size of the network ID value used in the communication subsystem.

Microsoft's reference implementation for Power Line Communication supports up to 1022 logical networks (10 bits) and 2046 individual nodes (11 bits) on the logical network.

Address Space Arbiter

SCP device initialization relies on a special network node called the Address Space Arbiter (ASA). This node behaves in a similar fashion to a DHCP server on an IP-based network. It looks for SCP nodes on the network, and when it finds them assigns the network and node IDs for the device. The combination of the node ID and network ID make up the logical network unique device address.

In the case where no ASA is present, devices are allowed to set the network and node IDs manually, much like Auto-IP allows for the device to set its own IP address. In general, it is expected that most nodes will not have the intelligence to do so.

Node Presence

Unlike UPnP, SCP devices don't send out or receive device announcements when entering or leaving a logical network. To avoid sending messages to a device that may not exist on the network, SCP devices have the ability to detect the presence of another node on the network. The application processor often performs this task when setting up a subscription to ensure the device is on the network before sending out the subscription request.

SCP Logical Device Model

The SCP logical device model borrows heavily from UPnP technology. SCP root devices are allowed to have embedded sub-devices, with each device exposing a set of services with a series of actions and properties. SCP properties are the same as UPnP service state variables.

One of the primary differences between SCP and the UPnP architecture is that instead of having friendly alphanumeric names for services and actions, SCP devices carry a unique 16-bit integer identifier for each service and its associated actions and properties. This is a by-product of the extremely small amount of storage memory available in SCP devices.

Unlike UPnP devices, all SCP devices have a standard set of properties that must be implemented. These properties are never explicitly advertised in SCP service descriptions but are required to be supported on all SCP devices.

It is through these required properties that SCP supports discovery in a similar way to UPnP technology. SCP devices support properties to retrieve device and service descriptions, determine what actions are supported by the device, and even retrieve a presentation page for the device.

Table 20.1 gives some of these standard properties. It is clear that many of the required SCP properties map directly into the UPnP device model. Internally, this data is stored as tables in the device's EEPROM.

For table properties, the value of each property is merely the base index into an array of values that represent the actual data you're interested in. For example, the traditional XML UPnP device description document is stored as a series of entries in a table, one entry for each node value in the document. To access this data in your SCP device, you must first get the base index to the array of description data, and then iterate through the table to get the node values in the document.

Table 20.1 Required SCP Properties

Property Name	Description
DeviceSerialNumber	The manufacturer's assigned serial number for the device
PresentationData	The UPnP presentation page html in a byte array
DeviceDescription	UPnP Device Description table descriptor
ServiceDescription	The device's Service Description table descriptor
PropertyDescription	The device's Service Property (i.e., state variable) table descriptor
ActionDescription	The device service Action Description table
Routes	Routes table descriptor
Subscriptions	Subscriptions table descriptor
EventSource	Special edge-sensitive evented property that any node can set and any node can monitor

Eventing

Properties, just like UPnP state variables, can be evented. SCP supports two different models for property eventing: Level Sensitive and Edge Sensitive.

Level Sensitive eventing can specify an interval at which the value of a property is monitored for eventing. For example, if your SCP device has an analog dial, you may not want to event the property associated with that dial at every measurable change of the dial. Instead, you could support a Level Sensitive value of 10 that would event the property every 10th measurable change. This significantly reduces unnecessary network traffic and processing overhead for both the device sending the events and others receiving them.

Edge Sensitive events are evented at every measurable change of the property; this is the traditional UPnP model of eventing.

Outgoing Operations

To support the retrieval of property values such as the DeviceDescription, SCP defines a series of asynchronous device operations dubbed "outgoing operations" that one device performs on another device on the same logical network. Supported outgoing operations (from the perspective of your device to another) include:

- Action invocation on a remote device
- Device/service description requests
- Property value retrieval
- Subscription management

Your device uses these outgoing operations to communicate and discover other devices the same way that a UPnP control point would invoke actions, retrieve device and service description documents, and subscribe to property events.

Incoming Operations

At the other end of the pipe, so-called "incoming operations" are received by your device's communication protocol controller and queued for processing by the application subsystem. These requests are processed synchronously and support the following capabilities (viewed from your device's perspective):

- Signaled completion of some previously requested operation on a remote device

- The return of requested property data from another device
- Result of a remote action invocation
- Subscription verification

Through the combination of outgoing and incoming operations, your device can support the same set of operations that a more traditional UPnP device would; the primary difference is that these requests are not sent or received as XML SOAP packets, thus reducing the need for costly and complex parsing of XML packets on your SCP device.

To summarize the use of incoming and outgoing operations, here is an example of Device A retrieving the device description document from Device B:

1. Device A creates an outgoing operation to query the standard device property DeviceDescription, which has a predefined 16-bit integer identifier of 0xFFF7.
2. Device B receives an incoming operation from the CPC and sees that someone has requested the DeviceDescription property. Device B returns to Device A the value of the DeviceDescription property, a "baseID" that indicates the start the device description property data.
3. Device A creates another outgoing operation to query the value of the baseID.
4. Device B retrieves an incoming operation from the CPC and returns property values for the baseID, which includes an "itemCount" indicating the total number of entries in the DeviceDescription Property table.
5. Device A queries each baseID to baseID + itemCount -1 entries in the table to retrieve the device description(s).

At the end of this process, Device B has a complete device description representation of Device A, in the same way that UPnP devices do.

SCP and UPnP Differences

It should be clear now that SCP devices support the same device model as traditional UPnP devices. Yet aside from differences in implementation, there are some unique capabilities provided by SCP devices that are not available with UPnP devices.

Property Routes and Subscriptions

One of the shortcomings of UPnP devices is their inability to communicate directly to each other without having control point capability built into the device, an overhead not easily afforded by most embedded devices.

SCP solves this problem by creating the notion of a property route. Stated simply, a property route is a link between a property on one device and an action or property on another device.

For example, if you have an SCP-based light switch and light bulb, the light bulb would like to know when the state of the light switch has changed so that it can adjust its power state accordingly. A property route could be set up between the light switch state (off or on) and an action on the light bulb that sets the light bulb to the provided power state. When the user turned the light switch on, the power state action on the light bulb would be invoked with the state of the light switch passed as a parameter.

Property routes provide a unique and powerful capability to set up associations between disparate devices. For example, in the light bulb scenario, a single light switch can have defined property routes to every light bulb in a given room (or even the entire house). With one flick of the switch, all SCP light bulbs would receive the notification and turn on or off accordingly.

Property routes can also be thought of as one-way mapping between a subscribed property and its subscriber. Property routes can either be directed point-to-point or broadcast to multiple devices on the network. Information about what routes a device currently has set up is stored in its EEPROM. Due to limited storage space, most devices will have a limited number of routes they can support.

In fact, SCP property routes are nothing more than a special case UPnP service subscription that, unlike a normal UPnP subscription, allows the subscription of specific properties in a service. Property routes can be aggregated together to form traditional service-based UPnP subscriptions.

Route Creation

There are two ways to create property routes between devices. The first is through an intelligent control point style SCP node that has the ability to discover all devices on the network, allowing the user to create routes between logical devices found on the network. A tool to perform this task is included with the SCP SDK.

The other, more interesting way to create property routes is to do so at manufacture. Recall your light bulb and light switch example. If these two devices were manufactured and sold together, the light switch could come right of the box with the EEPROM preprogrammed to include a route to the included light bulb, ensuring that the two devices work together.

With home automation one of the most common uses for SCP devices, the latter scenario is actually very common, and it is certainly a scenario that traditional UPnP devices could not support.

Event Source Property

One of the most interesting differences between UPnP and SCP devices is the Event Source Property, a required SCP property, listed in Table 20.1. Simply put, the EventSource property is a many-to-many public property that any device can write to, and all other devices receive notification of its change.

Viewed from the perspective of UPnP technology, the EventSource property is like an automatically subscribed evented state variable that is open for all devices on the logical network to set via a standard and required exposed interface.

The power for such a property is almost infinite. Think of a home control center that would like to quickly and easily turn off all devices in the home. If the devices on the network were monitoring the EventSource property, by simply setting the state of the one EventSource property to off, every receiving device in the home would receive the event change notification and be turned off.

The SCP specification does not indicate any specific uses for the EventSource property, leaving it open and available for device implementers to use.

Security

Another differentiating feature of SCP that UPnP technology does not currently provide is security. SCP requires all transmissions to be encrypted when using a shared logical network key in open air, but relaxes the requirement in directed wired networks. The primary difference is how the logical network key is exchanged.

The three levels of security are:

- No security
- Low security
- High security

No security is the default setting for SCP, and no key exchange is performed. Low Security supports unsecured distribution of the logical network key, while High Security supports secured distribution of the logical network key using each device's POK.

All devices on the same logical network are required to operate using the same logical network key. For more information on details of the specific security algorithms used in SCP, refer to the SCP SDK.

SCP and UPnP Interoperability

Because SCP and the UPnP architecture share the same basic device model, it is easy to see that SCP and UPnP devices should be able to interoperate. The glue that binds the two networks together comes in the form of an SCP-to-UPnP bridge.

This application layer bridge simply discovers SCP devices on the SCP physical network, retrieves their device and service description information, and creates matching XML documents to advertise and proxy the SCP devices on the UPnP network. UPnP devices can then discover and communicate with SCP devices through this proxy.

The bridge is actually a special root node that exists on a logical SCP network that searches for and discovers all other root nodes on the same SCP network. This means that when SCP devices are bridged, it is done on a logical network basis only. To bridge all devices on the physical SCP network, a root bridge must exist on every SCP logical network.

SCP devices cannot discover, see, or communicate with UPnP devices; the bridging is unidirectional only.

Table 20.2 summarizes the mapping between SCP and UPnP devices using the familiar six phases of the UPnP Device Architecture.

Table 20.2 SCP to UPnP Device Mapping

Feature	Simple Control Protocol	UPnP
Addressing	Address Space Arbiter assigns device address and defines logical segments within a physical network.	DHCP or Auto-IP
Discovery	Search by specific device or look for all unassigned root devices.	Uses Simple Service Discovery Protocol (SSDP) to obtain the device description URL
Description	Root Device Description Property	XML Device Description
Control	Actions and Property Routes	Actions and state variable associations.
Events	Property subscriptions to track individual properties	Service-based subscriptions
Presentation	HTML Presentation Property	HTML presentation URL
Security	Three levels of logical network security	No security

SCP SDK

To support the development of SCP Devices, Microsoft has released an SCP SDK, complete with documentation, sample code, and a variety of tools and other utilities. Here you'll find a brief overview of the tools and capabilities provided by the SCP SDK.

Emulation Environment

One of the most useful tools provided with the SCP SDK is an emulation environment for which you can run your SCP devices on the PC. Included in the emulation environment is a fully emulated communications subsystem based on Microsoft's reference implementation CPC. All of your SCP device application code can be developed on the PC and then built to run in the emulation environment.

The emulation environment also includes a library linkable with user-level Windows (C++/C#) applications that allows you to create a user interface to your device, simulating user interactions with the physical hardware. This allows for quick and easy profiling of different user interfaces without requiring running hardware.

Sample Devices

The SCP SDK comes with two sample devices: an SCP light bulb and an SCP light controller (that is, a light switch). Both contain C code that would go on a real SCP application processor. The SDK also contains example user applications that use the aforementioned application library to interact with the sample devices.

Property Route Manager

Also shipping with the SCP SDK is a Property Route Manager that acts as a universal control point of sorts that discovers SCP devices and allows you to set up property routes between different SCP devices.

Using the Property Route Manager, you can set up a route between the light controller's On/Off property and the light bulb's Set Intensity action. Clicking on the light switch then causes the light bulb to turn off or on.

Tools

The SCP SDK also comes with quite a few useful tools and samples, some of which were described in the previous section. Recall that every SCP device needs to have an EEPROM binary image that stores the devices description document, its service descriptions, and reserved space for the devices properties and run-time code.

Remember also that SCP devices all have a required set of properties that must be present in every SCP device. When creating an SCP device description document in the traditional UPnP format, it is not necessary to include these required augmented properties, because a tool exists to do this instead.

The Upnp2SCP utility takes a given UPnP device or service description document, creates a modified version that includes the additional SCP augmented properties, and then creates a binary `.dat` file that is the binary representation (to be stored in EEPROM) of the device description document and its associated service descriptions.

Then, using the veeprom utility, you can create a virtual-EEPROM binary file that includes this information, as well as other configuration information you can specify in an `.ini` file (such as the length of time between advertisements, and so on).

The SDK also comes with a few Windows programs that are helpful for debugging. These include ScpMon to monitor SCP traffic over the SCP network, and CpCDebug, used to debug commands going to and from the communication subsystem and the device application. Also included is a utility to download flash images to the ITRAN IT800 PLC Transceiver (the default supported communication processor package), if your device happens to be based on that chip.

Summary

This chapter provided you with a high-level overview of the Simple Control Protocol, introducing its device model, describing how it maps to the UPnP architecture, and discussing additional unique features that SCP-specific devices support. Finally, you learned how SCP devices can be bridged to a UPnP technology-based network. Although not perfect for all devices, SCP certainly provides significant advantages to the very small, embedded device makers who would still like their devices to interoperate with the many UPnP devices already in the home. Finally, the chapter finished with a discussion of the SCP SDK, and the tools and capabilities included in it. For more information on SCP, the reader is encouraged to seek out the SCP SDK and look through the excellent documentation and examples contained within. For more information on SCP, please visit: `http://www.microsoft.com/windows/scp/`.

Part VI

The Appendixes

Appendix A

UPnP API Quick Reference

The following table summarizes the most used functions introduced in this book, including a short description of the function and the most commonly encountered error codes. This table is also included as a PDF file on the CD-ROM for easy printing for posting on the wall or other convenient location while you code.

Function	Description	Error Codes
Chapter 12: Adding Device Discovery		
int UpnpInit (IN const char *HostIP, IN unsigned short DestPort)	Initializes and binds the UPnP stack to the specified HostIP and Port. Must be called before any other functions.	UPNP_E_SUCCESS UPNP_E_INIT
int UpnpSetWebServerRootDir(IN const char *WebDir);	Initializes web server to serve files from the specified location	UPNP_E_SUCCESS UPNP_E_INVALID_ARGUMENT

Continues

Function	Description	Error Codes
int UpnpRegisterRootDevice(IN const char *DescUrl, IN Upnp_FunPtr Callback, IN const void *Cookie, OUT UpnpDevice_Handle *Hnd);	Given an XML device description document, a callback function pointer, and a user provided cookie, registers the specified root device with the UPnP stack, returning a device handle.	UPNP_E_SUCCESS UPNP_E_INVALID_DESC
int UpnpSendAdvertisement(IN UpnpDevice_Handle Hnd, IN int Exp);	Sends advertisements for the specified device, with a periodic interval of seconds specified by Exp.	UPNP_E_SUCCESS UPNP_E_INVALID_HANDLE
int UpnpUnRegisterRootDevice (IN UpnpDevice_Handle Hnd);	Unregisters and cleans up resources used by the specified device, sending bye-bye announcements for the device.	UPNP_E_SUCCESS UPNP_E_INVALID_HANDLE
int UpnpFinish( );	Performs the reverse of UpnpInit, and cleans up any library-allocated resources and shuts down the internal web server.	UPNP_E_SUCCESS UPNP_E_FINISH
int UpnpRegisterRootDevice2(IN Upnp_DescType descriptionType, IN const char *description, IN size_t bufferLen, IN int config_baseURL, IN Upnp_FunPtr Callback, IN const void *Cookie, OUT UpnpDevice_Handle *Hnd);	Alternate registration that, based upon descriptionType, supports specifying the device description document on disk, in memory, or via a URL. Meaning of description and bufferLen parameters depends on specified descriptionType. Given a function pointer callback and user provided cookie, returns a device handle.	UPNP_E_SUCCESS UPNP_E_INVALID_DESC UPNP_E_FILE_NOT_FOUND UPNP_E_EXT_NOT_XML

Continues

Function	Description	Error Codes
Chapter 13: Defining Device Services		
Upnp_Document UpnpParse_Buffer(IN const char *dom_str)	Given a character string, converts into a DOM document.	NULL
char * SampleUtil_GetFirst DocumentItem(IN Upnp_ Document ActionRequest, IN char *NodeName);	Utility function that, given a DOM document, returns the text value of the specified Node-Name.	NULL
Chapter 14: Subscriptions and Eventing		
int UpnpAddToPropertySet(IN OUT Upnp_Document *PropSet, IN char *ArgName, IN char *ArgVal);	Updates the provided PropSet with the specified argument name and value.	UPNP_E_SUCCESS NULL
int UpnpNotifyExt(IN Upnp DeviceHandle Hnd, IN const char *DevID, IN const char *ServID, IN Upnp_Document PropSet);	Sends out events containing the provided property set to all subscribed control points for this device.	UPNP_E_SUCCESS UPNP_E_ INVALID_SERVICE
int UpnpAcceptSubscriptionExt(IN UpnpDeviceHandle Hnd, IN const char *DevID, IN const char *ServID, IN Upnp_Document PropSet, IN Upnp_SID SubsId);	Accepts the subscription for the specified device and service handles; provides a property set of evented state variables for the service.	UPNP_E_SUCCESS UPNP_E_ INVALID_SERVICE
int UpnpAcceptSubscription(IN UpnpDeviceHandle Hnd, IN const char *DevID, IN const char *ServID, IN char **VarName, IN const char **NewVal, IN int cVariables, IN Upnp_SID SubsId)	Accepts the subscription for the specified device and service handles; provides pointers to matching size arrays of state variable names and values.	UPNP_E_SUCCESS UPNP_E_ INVALID_SERVICE

Continues

Function	Description	Error Codes
int UpnpNotify(IN UpnpDeviceHandle Hnd, IN const char *DevID, IN const char *ServID, IN char **VarName, IN const char **NewVal, IN int cVariables)	Sends out events for the specified device and service; provides pointers to matching size arrays of state variable names and values.	UPNP_E_SUCCESS UPNP_E_INVALID_SERVICE
Utility Functions		
Upnp_Document UpnpParseFileAndGetDocument (IN char *xmlFile);	Loads and converts the specified XML file into a DOM document.	NULL
Upnp_DOMString UpnpNewPrintDocument(IN Upnp_Node OperationNode);	Converts a provided DOM document back into a character string.	NULL
int Util_getAndSetNodeValue(IN OUT Upnp_Document *RootNode, IN const char *ParentName, IN const char *ElementName, IN const char *NewValue);	Provided a parent and child element name, updates the text node value with the provided character string, returning an updated DOM document.	UPNP_E_SUCCESS 1 in case of error
int Util_getMacAddress(IN char *InterfaceName, IN int len, OUT char *macAddress);	Gives the MAC address of the specified interface.	UPNP_E_SUCCESS
Chapter 19: Developing Control Point Applications		
int UpnpRegisterClient (IN Upnp_FunPtr Callback, IN const void *Cookie, OUT UpnpClient_Handle *Hnd);	Registers an application with the UPnP Library for client (control point) functionality, returning a handle that can be used in future client calls.	UPNP_E_SUCCESS UPNP_E_INVALID_PARAM
int UpnpUnRegisterClient (IN UpnpClient_Handle *Hnd);	Unregisters a previously registered client application, cleaning up associated resources.	UPNP_E_SUCCESS UPNP_E_INVALID_HANDLE

Continues

Function	Description	Error Codes
int UpnpSearchAsync (IN UpnpClient_Handle Hnd, IN int Mx, IN const char *Target, IN const void *Cookie);	Searches for the specified Target device, and calls registered callback handler when device responses are received.	UPNP_E_SUCCESS UPNP_E_INVALID_HANDLE
int UpnpSendAction (IN UpnpClient_Handle Hnd, IN const char *ActionURL, IN const char *ServiceType, IN const char *DevUDN, IN Upnp_Document Action, OUT Upnp_Document *RespNode);	Invokes the action specified by the DOM-formatted SOAP request packet on the specified device and service. Blocks until response received.	UPNP_E_SUCCESS UPNP_E_INVALID_URL UPNP_E_INVALID_ACTION UPNP_E_INVALID_PARAM
int UpnpSendActionAsync (IN UpnpClient_Handle Hnd, IN const char *ActionURL, IN const char *ServiceType, IN const char *DevUDN, IN Upnp_Document Action, IN Upnp_FunPtr Fun, In const void *Cookie);	Asynchronously invokes the DOM-formatted SOAP request packet on the specified device, calling the provided callback function upon completion.	UPNP_E_SUCCESS UPNP_E_INVALID_URL UPNP_E_INVALID_ACTION UPNP_E_INVALID_PARAM
int UpnpSubscribe (IN UpnpClient_Handle Hnd, IN const char *PublisherUrl, IN OUT int TimeOut, OUT Upnp_SID SubsId);	Sends a subscription request to the specified publisher URL and desired timeout value. Blocks until completion.	UPNP_E_SUCCESS UPNP_E_INVALID_URL UPNP_E_SUBSCRIBE_UNACCEPTED
int UpnpSubscribeAsync (IN UpnpClient_Handle Hnd, IN const char *PublisherUrl, IN int TimeOut, IN Upnp_FunPtr Fun, IN const void *Cookie);	Asynchronously makes a subscription request to the specified device with requested timeout length. The provided callback function is called when a response is received.	UPNP_E_SUCCESS UPNP_E_INVALID_URL UPNP_E_SUBSCRIBE_UNACCEPTED
int UpnpUnSubscribe (IN UpnpClient_Handle Hnd, IN Upnp_SID SubsId);	Cancels a previously accepted device subscription, freeing up resources.	UPNP_E_SUCCESS UPNP_E_INVALID_SID

Appendix B

References

This appendix includes the various resources we drew upon to write this book, such as the UPnP Device Architecture specification, various Internet RFCs and drafts, and published papers; pointers to web-based resources, such as the UPnP Forum web site and web sites for related standards; and a list of recommend books for learning more about the fundamental technologies upon which the UPnP architecture is built.

UPnP Device Architecture

Universal Plug and Play Device Architecture, Microsoft Corporation, 1999. http://www.upnp.org/download/UPnPDA10_20000613.htm.

IETF RFCs

RFC 1034, *Domain Names—Concepts and Facilities*. P. Mockapetris, 1987.

RFC 1035, *Domain Names—Implementation and Specification*. P. Mockapetris, 1987.

RFC 1123, *Requirements for Internet Hosts—Application and Support. (format for dates, such as the HTTP Date: header)*. Ed., R. Braden, 1989.

RFC 1766, *Tags for the Identification of Languages. (format for language tag, such as HTTP's Accept-Language header)*. H. Alvestrand, 1995.

RFC 1945, *Hypertext Transfer Protocol—1.0*. R. Fielding, H. Frystyk, and T. Berners-Lee, 1996.

RFC 2045, *Multipurpose Internet Mail Extensions (MIME) Part One: Format of Internet Message Bodies*. N. Freed, N. Borenstein, 1996.

RFC 2046, *Multipurpose Internet Mail Extensions (MIME) Part Two: Media Types*. N. Freed, N. Borenstein, 1996.

RFC 2047, *Multipurpose Internet Mail Extensions (MIME) Part Three: Message Header Extensions for Non-ASCII Text*. K. Moore, 1996.

RFC 2048, *Multipurpose Internet Mail Extensions (MIME) Part Four: Registration Procedures*. N. Freed, J. Klensin, J. Postel, 1996.

RFC 2049, *Multipurpose Internet Mail Extensions (MIME) Part Five: Conformance Criteria and Examples*. N. Freed, N. Borenstein, 1996.

RFC 2131, *Dynamic Host Configuration Protocol*. R. Droms, March 1997.

RFC 2136, *Dynamic Updates in the Domain Name System (DNSUPDATE)*. Ed., P. Vixie, S. Thomson, Y. Rekhter, and J. Bound, 1997.

RFC 2279, *UTF-8, a Transformation format of ISO 10646*. F. Yergeau, 1998.

RFC 2365, *Administratively Scoped IP Multicast*. D. Meyer, July 1998.

RFC 2387 *The MIME Multipart/Related Content-type* (format for representing content type, such as the MIMETYPE, e.g., mimetype element for an icon.). E. Levinson, 1998.

RFC 2396 *Uniform Resource Identifiers (URI): Generic Syntax*. T. Berners-Lee, R. Fielding, L. Masinter, August 1998.

RFC 2616, *Hypertext Transfer Protocol—1.1*. R. Fielding, J. Gettys, J. Mogul, H. Frystyk, L. Masinter, P. Leach, and T. Berners-Lee, 1999.

IETF Internet Drafts

Cheshire, S., "Dynamic Configuration of IPv4 link-local addresses." draft-ietf-zeroconf-ipv4-linklocal-01.txt, 10/2000.

Goland, Y. and J. Schlimmer, "Flexible XML Processing Profile (FXPP)." draft-goland-fxpp-01.txt, 6/2000.

Cohen, J., S. Aggarwal, and Y. Goland, "General Event Notification Architecture Base: Client to Arbiter." draft-cohen-gena-p-base-01.txt, 9/6/2000.

Stapp, M. and Y. Rekhter, "Interaction between DHCP and DNS." draft-ietf-dhc-dhcp-dns-12.txt, 3/10/2000.

Goland, Y. and J. Schlimmer, "Multicast and Unicast UDP HTTP Messages." draft-goland-http-udp-04.txt, 10/2000.

Goland, Y., T. Cai, P. Leach, Y. Gu, and S. Albright, "Simple Service Discovery Protocol/1.0, Operating without an Arbiter." draft-cai-ssdp-v1-03.txt. 10/28/1999.

Articles and Papers

Miller, B., T. Nixon, C. Tai, and M. Wood, "Home Networking with Universal Plug and Play." *IEEE Communications Magazine*, December 2001.

"Understanding Universal Plug and Play." Microsoft Windows ME white paper, 2000.

Waldo, J., A. Wollrath, G. Wyant, and S. Kendall, "Events in an RPC-Based Distributed System." *Sun Microsystems Lab Technical Report*, November 1995.

Shrader, B., "A proposed definition of 'Ad hoc network'." Royal Institute of Technology (KTH), Stockholm Sweden, May 8, 2002.

Bettstettter, C. and C. Rennder, "A Comparison of Service Discovery Protocols and Implementation of the Service Location Protocol." Institute of Communication Networks, D-80290 Munich, Germany, September 2000.

Web Sites

Site	URL
Document Object Model (DOM)	http://www.w3c.org/DOM/
Open Sound System (OSS) for Linux	http://www.opensound.com/linux.html
Extensible Markup Language (XML)	http://www.w3c.org/XML/

Continues

Site	URL
Hypertext Markup Language (HTML)	http://www.w3c.org/Markup/
Hypertext Transport Protocol (HTTP)	http://www.w3c.org/Protocols/
Intel's UPnP Site	http://www.intel.com/labs/connectivity/upnp/index.htm
Internet Engineering Task Force	http://www.ietf.org/
Linux SDK for UPnP Devices	http://upnp.sourceforge.net/
Microsoft's UPnP Site	http://www.microsoft.com/hwdev/tech/nonpc/UPnP/default.asp
SOAP/XML Protocol	http://www.w3c.org/2000/xp/Group/

Other Online Documents and Standards

Title	Description	URL
Address Resolution Protocol	Overview of ARP	http://whatis.techtarget.com/definition/0,,sid9_gci213780,00.html
HTTP Made Really Easy	A nice tutorial on HTTP that explains the basics of HTTP communication and teaches the practical details of writing HTTP clients and servers	http://www.jmarshall.com/easy/http/
ISO 8601	Specifies numeric representations of date and time, 12/21/2000	http://www.iso.ch/iso/en/CatalogueDetailPage.CatalogueDetail?CSNUMBER=26780
UPC	Uniform Product Code—a 12-digit, all-numeric code that identifies the consumer package	http://www.uc-council.org/main/ID_Numbers_and_Bar_Codes.html
Understanding DHCP	Cisco's DHCP tutorial	http://www.cisco.com/warp/public/779/smbiz/service/knowledge/tcpip/dhcp.htm

Continues

Title	Description	URL
Web Services/SOAP and CORBA	A comparison of SOAP and CORBA	http://www.xs4all.nl/~irmen/comp/CORBA%20vs%20SOAP.html
XML Tutorial	A tutorial on the basics of XML	http://www.xml.com/pub/a/98/10/guide4.html

Recommended Books

Comer, Douglas, *Internetworking With TCP/IP Volume 1: Principles Protocols, and Architecture*, Fourth edition, Upper Saddle River, NJ: Prentice Hall, 2000.

Comer, Douglas (with D. Stevens), *Internetworking With TCP/IP Volume II: Design, Implementation, and Internals*, Third edition, Upper Saddle River, NJ: Prentice Hall, 1999.

Comer, Douglas (with D. Stevens), *Internetworking With TCP/IP Volume III: Client-Server Programming and Applications, BSD Socket Version, Second edition*, Upper Saddle River, NJ: Prentice Hall, 1996.

Holzner, Steven, *Inside XML*, Indianapolis: New Riders Publishing, 2001.

Kosiur, Dave, *IP Multicasting*, New York: John Wiley & Sons, Inc., 1998.

Pressman, Roger S., *Software Engineering: A Practitioner's Approach*, New York: McGraw-Hill, 2001.

Stevens, Richard W., *TCP/IP Illustrated, Volume 1: The Protocols*, Reading, MA: Addison-Wesley, 1994.

Stevens, Richard W., Gary R. Wright, *TCP/IP Illustrated, Volume 2: The Implementation*, Reading, MA: Addison-Wesley, 1995.

Glossary

Action A command presented by a service that can be invoked by control points. A service typically has many actions. Each action has a set of optional input and output parameters and an optional return value.

Ad-Hoc Network A network where there are no preexisting infrastructure devices and services (such as a DHCP server) and the network nodes themselves make up the network. Devices use other means, such as Auto-IP, to acquire IP addresses, and are then able to communicate.

Address Resolution Protocol (ARP) A network protocol that maps a network level address, such as an IP address, to its corresponding data link address, such as an Ethernet addresses. UPnP devices use ARP to find out whether an address selected with Auto-IP is currently used by any other devices.

Addressing The process by which a UPnP device acquires and releases its address. Addressing is the first step in UPnP networking—a device must acquire an address before it can advertise itself.

Administrative Scope A way to limit the reach of multicast data. A special range of IP multicast addresses, 239.0.0.0 to 239.255.255.255, is called the administratively scoped IPv4 multicast address space.

Within this range, addresses are partitioned to have predefined semantics about how broadly the data will propagate. Administrative scoping provides a simple way to contain IP multicast communication within the administrative boundaries of an organization.

Advertisement A message from a device to control points announcing that the device is now available.

All Hosts Group A particular multicast IP address, 224.0.0.1, used to address all of the multicast hosts that are directly connected to the same network as the sender.

Argument A parameter for an action exposed by a service. Each argument may be an input argument or an output argument, but not both. One of the output arguments may be designated as the action's return value.

Auto-IP A method by which an endpoint on an IP network automatically chooses an IP address and subnet mask in the absence of a central service, such as a DHCP, to manage addresses. This method is described in the Internet Draft, the "Dynamic Configuration of IPv4 Link-Local Addresses."

Chunked (Transfer) Encoding A method used by HTTP servers that breaks the response into smaller chunks and sends them in a series. Such responses are identified by including the `Transfer-Encoding` header with the value set to `chunked`.

Control The method invocation process where control points invoke methods provided by a device's services. The control protocol used between UPnP control points and devices is the Simple Object Access Protocol (SOAP).

ControlURL Each service listed in a device description document has an element, the `<controlURL>`, that provides the URL where all control messages for that service are to be sent.

Control Point An entity on the network that invokes the functionality provided by a UPnP device. The control point may discover devices, retrieve device and service descriptions, invoke actions on services, query for state variables, and receive events from services.

Cookie User-specific information stored on a client computer by a web site so that the information can be passed to the server on future requests. Cookies are often used by stateless protocols, such as HTTP, to maintain state on the client to pass to the server with each request.

Decentralized Discovery An approach to service discovery whereby there is no central store to maintain information about resources, their location, and their availability. Instead, each client directly queries the network and each resource responds directly to these requests.

Description A phase of UPnP device operation that allows devices to present information about themselves and the services that they provide, in the form of XML-based device and service description documents, to control points on the network.

Device A logical container for services. A device can acquire an address, can be discovered, can provide information about itself in the form of a device description document, and can provide a presentation page. Control actions and eventing work directly with services, however. A device may contain other embedded devices.

Device Control Protocol (DCP) *See* device description document.

Device Description (Document) A document, expressed in the XML-based UPnP Template Language, provided by UPnP devices that contains information about the device (such as manufacturer name, model name, serial number, and so on), a list of services provided by the device, and a list of any embedded devices. Control points retrieve the device description document to learn about the device and its services. UPnP device vendors fill in placeholders in a device template standardized by one of the working committees.

Device Type A formal definition of a logical device, as expressed in a device description document. Standard device types are defined by working committees of the UPnP Forum.

Discovery A phase of UPnP device operation that allows control points to search for devices and services on the network and find ones that meet its search criteria.

Document Object Model (DOM) An API for HTML and XML documents that defines the object model for these documents. The W3C has specified the DOM API in a language-independent way and has been implemented in many different programming languages. With the DOM programmers can access, change, delete, or add just about anything found in HTML or XML documents.

Dynamic Host Configuration Protocol (DHCP) A client/server protocol that provides a framework for passing configuration information to hosts on a TCP/IP network, including the host's IP address, subnet mask, default gateway, and domain name server.

Embedded Device A device logically contained within another device. Any embedded devices are listed in a device's description document.

Event A notification message sent by a service to control points that indicates a change in one or more of the service's state variables.

Event Key A value maintained by the publisher of event messages for each subscriber as an error detection mechanism to ensure that subscribers have received all event messages sent.

EventSubURL Each service listed in a device's description document has an element, the `<eventSubURL>`, that provides the URL where control points can register to receive events from the service. The GENA protocol is used to manage subscriptions and send event messages.

Evented State Variable A service will send event notifications to control points when this state variable changes. State variables are marked as evented or not in the service's description document.

Eventing The phase of UPnP device operation where services send notifications of changes to state variables to control points.

General Event Notification Architecture (GENA) A protocol that implements a publisher/subscriber system whereby a subscriber may request, renew, or cancel a subscription. Event notification messages are sent from the publisher to subscribers.

Host Group A group of endpoints on an IP network that receive multicast data from a sender. Each host in the logical group shares a common multicast address and receives any data sent to the multicast address. The membership in this logical group can change over time.

HTTPMU HTTP over multicast UDP. HTTPMU allows sending HTTP messages to many recipients simultaneously. HTTPMU enables a group communication model using HTTP-style request/response messages.

HTTPU HTTP over unicast UDP. With HTTPU, a host can send an HTTP-formatted message to another host without the expense of setting up a TCP connection.

HTTP Resource A network-based service that is accessed via the HTTP protocol. The SSDP protocol is used to discover HTTP resources.

Initial Event Message A special event message sent when a control point first subscribes to receive events from a service. This special first message includes the names and values for all evented variables provided by the service and allows the subscriber to initialize its model of the state of the service.

Initial Request Line The first line of an HTTP request that includes the HTTP method, the path of the requested resource, and the version of HTTP being used.

Infrastructure Network *See* Managed Network.

Internet Gateway Device (IGD) The first device standard produced by one of the UPnP Forum working committees. The IGD supports sharing of Internet connections, advanced connection-management features, management of host-configuration services, and support for transparent Internet access.

Lease (of an IP address) An agreement, between a server managing IP addresses and a client acquiring an IP address, that the client may use the IP address for a limited period of time. The server assigns the address to the client. Once the lease expires, the server may assign the address to another client.

Managed Network A network supported by devices and services, such as a DHCP server, dedicated to the operation of the network (as opposed to an ad-hoc network that has no such supporting devices or services).

Marketing Committee A committee of the UPnP Forum that undertakes joint member promotion of UPnP, including representing the UPnP Forum at industry trade shows.

Moderation of Events An extension to the UPnP Template Language that specifies a limit for the rate at which events are sent from a publisher to subscribers. It is used for state variables that would otherwise change too rapidly for eventing to be useful.

Notification *See* Event.

Phases of UPnP The sequence of operation of UPnP devices consisting of addressing, description, discovery, control, eventing, and presentation.

Presence Announcement In SSDP, resources announce their presence on the network, letting potential clients know of their availability.

Presentation A phase of UPnP device operation that allows devices to provide a Web page for manual control and administration.

Presentation Page UPnP Devices can use their embedded web servers to provide a web interface for manual management and control of the device. An administrator using a web browser can load the device's Presentation URL and view information about the device and control it.

Publisher In a Publisher/Subscriber system, the publisher is a source of event messages delivered to subscribers, who register to receive them. For UPnP devices, the services can publish state change events to control points.

Publisher/Subscriber Model A software design pattern used to implement event notification. In this model, the publisher is the source of events and grants a client a subscription when it registers interest in receiving events provided by the publisher. Upon the occurrence of an event, the publisher delivers an event notification to the subscriber.

QueryStateVariable A predefined action implemented by every service to provide access to its state variables.

Related State Variable Every input argument to an action is associated with one of the service's state variables—its related state variable.

Return Value The output argument to an action that has been designated as returning the result of the action. Only one of an action's arguments may be its return value.

Root Device A logical device that is not embedded in any other logical device.

SCPD *See* UPnP Service Template.

SCPDURL The URL for a service's description document. Each service listed in a device description document has an SCPDURL pointing to the service's description document.

Service The basic unit of functionality provided by UPnP devices. A service provides actions that can be invoked by control points and state variables that can be used to model the state of an underlying physical device.

Service Description Document An XML document expressed in the UPnP Template language that provides the formal definition of a logical service. Standard service description templates are defined by the working committees of the UPnP Forum and are filled in by device vendors.

ServiceId A sub-element of a service element in a device description document, the `<serviceId>` uniquely identifies a service. For standard services defined by a UPnP Forum working committee, the serviceId begins with `urn:upnp-org:serviceId:` followed by a service ID suffix.

Service Type A service type is a URI that identifies the type, or function, of a particular resource. SSDP provides the mechanisms for discovering resources by service type. Service types for UPnP devices and services are defined by UPnP working committees for each standard device type. Standard service types are denoted by `urn:schemas-upnp-org:service:` followed by a unique name assigned by the working committee, a colon, and an integer version number.

Simple Object Access Protocol(SOAP) A protocol that brings together XML and HTTP to provide a Web-based messaging and remote procedure call mechanism. XML is used to express the contents of the messages, while HTTP is used to send the messages to their destination.

Simple Service Discovery Protocol (SSDP) A protocol for discovery of HTTP-based resources on the local area network that doesn't require any configuration, management, or administration.

ssdp:alive A message from a UPnP device joining the network that advertises the availability of one of its devices or services. When joining the network, the device advertises all of the devices and services it is providing. The `ssdp:alive` message is sent using a GENA `NOTIFY` method over the SSDP multicast channel.

ssdp:bye-bye A message sent by a device being removed from the network that notifies control points that the device or one of its services are no longer available. One `ssdp:bye-bye` message is sent for each `ssdp:alive` advertisement previously sent out by the device.

State Change (Event) A notification, sent from a service to a control point, that one or more of its evented state variables has changed.

State Table A service's state variables.

State Variable A variable, maintained by a service, that has a name, type, optional default value, optional constraint values, and which may trigger events when its value changes. State variables may be used to model the state of a physical device.

Steering Committee The high-level directing body of the UPnP Forum. The Steering Committee provides business leadership and makes decisions for the UPnP Forum. As the organization's management team, the Steering Committee oversees the working committees for defining device descriptions.

Subscriber In a publisher/subscriber software design pattern, the subscriber is the recipient of event messages sent by the publisher. In UPnP, control points can subscribe to state change events from services.

Subscriber List A list of registered subscribers in a system that implements a publisher/subscriber software design pattern.

Subscription An agreement between a publisher and a subscriber in a publisher/subscriber design that the subscriber will receive requested events from the publisher.

Subscription ID An identifier, generated by the publisher, that the subscriber presents when referencing a subscription. For example, the subscriber might present the subscription id when renewing or canceling a its subscription.

Subscription Cancellation A message, sent by a subscriber, such as a UPnP control point, to a publisher, such as a UPnP service, to discontinue its subscription for events.

Subscription Expiration The end of a time-based agreement between a publisher and a subscriber. When a subscription expires, the subscriber is removed from the subscription list and the publisher stops sending events to the subscriber.

Subscription Renewal A message, sent by a subscriber to the publisher, to keep a current subscription active, perhaps by extending the time of subscription expiration.

Technical Committee A group in the UPnP Forum that consists of technical representatives from various companies. The technical committee handles technical issues from working committees. They are responsible for the technical "big picture."

Time to Live (TTL) Field A field of the IPv4 header that controls the number of times, or "hops," that an IP datagram is allowed to traverse a router. Changing the TTL value at the source of communication will extend or contract the reach of the IP datagram.

Uniform Resource Identifier (URI) An identifier that provides a conceptual mapping from an identifier to a particular resource on the Web. For example, a particular URI might reference the home page for a particular organization whose contents changes over time, while the URI for the page remains the same. URIs are further classified as Uniform Resource Locators and Uniform Resource Names.

Uniform Resource Locator (URL) A URI that identifies a resource by specifying its location rather than identifying the resource by name or other attribute. Many URL schemes are named after protocols, such as http, ftp, and gopher.

Uniform Resource Name (URN) A label for a resource that is required to remain globally unique and persistent even when the resource ceases to exist or becomes unavailable.

Unique Service Name (USN) An SSDP header and associated value provided in SSDP messages that uniquely identifies an SSDP service.

UPnP Device Architecture A document that defines the protocols and conventions for communication between UPnP control points and devices.

UPnP Device Template An XML document derived from the UPnP Template Language that lists what a particular device type must include in its device description document, including device type, required embedded devices (if any), and required services. Standard UPnP device templates are defined by UPnP Forum working committees.The device template is completed by a device vendor.

UPnP Forum A cross-industry group created to guide the creation of the UPnP standards. The UPnP Forum consists of more than 550 companies, including industry leaders in consumer electronics, computing, home automation, home security, appliances, printing, photography, computer networking, and mobile products.

UPnP Implementer's Corporation (UIC). An independent company created by the UPnP Steering Committee, the UIC manages the conformance testing of devices to UPnP standards, administers the UPnP certification process, licenses tests to UIC members, reviews the manages the test results, and issues certificates of conformity to devices that pass the tests.

UPnP Service Template An XML document derived from the UPnP Template Language that lists what a particular service type must include in its service description document, including actions, parameters, and state variables. Standard UPnP service templates are defined by UPnP Forum working committees. The service template is completed by a device vendor.

UPnP Stack The set of protocols used by UPnP devices.

UPnP Template Language An XML schema that defines the elements and attributes used in UPnP Device and Service Templates. The UPnP Template Language is defined by the UPnP Device Architecture.

Working Committee An organizational elements of the UPnP Forum, formed as needed by participants to define standard device types.

XML A meta-language with which to develop markup languages that specify the structure of data and how various elements of the data relate. XML is becoming the de facto Internet standard for the representation of information.

Zero Configuration Network A network where the user is not required to configure devices before they are used on the network.

Index

100 Continue response, 47

A

A/V
  architecture, 360
  control point, 381
  media renderer, 375
  media server, 363
  playback, 375
  streaming content, 361
  support, adding, 385
action, 18, 463
  request and response, 122
actionList, 104
ActionName, 247
ActionRequest, 246
address
  conflicts, resolving, 70
  multicast, 37
  multi-homed, 45
  selection, auto-IP, 69
Address Resolution Protocol, *See* ARP
addressing, 21, 23, 463
  and UPnP devices, 65
  protocols, 32
ad-hoc network, 463
  auto-IP, 70
administration
  web-based, 169
administrative scope, 463
advertisement, 87, 464
  interval, 348
AL (alternate location) header, 51
all hosts group, 38, 464
Allegro Software
  SDK vendor, 174
allowedValueList, 107
announcements
  duplicate, 348
API, 297
  alternative, 311
  quick reference, 451
application subsystem
  SCP, 436
application-based control, 169
  example, 198
architecture, 17, 25
  A/V, 360
  and security, 13
  SCP, 436
  standards-based, 6
argument, 464
ARP, 463
Atinav Incorporated
  SDK vendor, 174
audio playback
  example, 382
audio/video, *See* A/V
auto-IP, 32, 66, 69, 464
  limitations of, 71
  retry limit, 73
AV Wizard
  development tool, 411
AVTransport service, 374

B

binding,SOAP, 114
bye-bye, 188, 209

C

Cache-Control header, 91
caching
  HTTP support for, 48
callback
  GENA, 132
Callback function, 206
cancellation, 288
certification
  of devices, 9
character encoding
  client/server agreement, 157
chunked encoding, 45, 464
class diagram
  service, actions, and state variables, 28
  UPnP device, 26
client authentication, 112
communication
  decentralized, 79
  multicast, 32
  point-to-point, 32
  property route, 442
  subsystem, SCP, 436
  transport, GENA, 131
config_baseURL, 213
ConnectionManager Service, 368
connections, persistent, 47
connectivity
  device, 5
ContentDirectory service, 364
control, 22, 24, 464
  application-based, 169
control point, 18, 464
  A/V, 381
control point application
  developing, 413
control point development
  advanced topics, 431
control service, example, 199
controlURL, 27, 121, 464
conventions
  for device implementation, 188
cookie, 207, 465

D

daemon service
  UPnP is not, 203
data types, UPnP, 231
datagram
  limited propagation of, 38
DCP, 465
de-allocating resources, 209
debugging, 205
decentralized discovery, 465
denial-of-service
  vulnerability, 15
description, 21, 23, 465
  device development step, 343
description document
  overview, 93
  rules, 96
description phase, 94
descriptionURL, 27
development tool
  AV Wizard, 411
  Device Sniffer, 217
  Device Spy, 356
  Device Validator, 355
device, 25, 465
  address, obtaining, 71
  addressing, 65
  certification, 9
  control, 6
  embedded, 103, 346
  embedded and root, 20
  localization, 155
  service list, 101
  standardization process, 11
  SW requirements spec, 165
device architecture
  error codes, 250
device control protocol, 25, 465
device description
  example, 188
  in device description document, 193
device description document, 465
  complete example, 199
  dynamically generated, 217
  structure, 97
  template, 190
  updating, 351
device design
  advanced topics, 346
device discovery
  problem description, 187
device mapping
  SCP-to-UPnP, 445
device registration, 201
device service description
  overview, 227
Device Sniffer
  development tool, 217
Device Spy
  development tool, 274, 356

device state
  inconsistent, 212
device type, 465
device UDN, 350
Device Validator
  development tool, 355
DHCP, 32, 66, 167, 466
DHCP lease, 67
digital signature, 112
discovery, 22, 23, 465
  in control point development, 416
  overview, 76
discovery mechanism
  SCP, 437
discovery response, SSDP, 84
document
  retrieving, 108
Document Object Model, *See* DOM
DOM, 58, 465
  creating on-the-fly, 298
  node, 60
  overview, 256
DOM document
  converting string to, 251
duration
  subscription, 289
Dynamic Host Configuration Protocol, 466

E

ease-of-use
  vs security, 13
embedded device, 20, 346, 466
embedded platform, 175
emulation environment
  in SCP SDK, 445
encoding rules, SOAP, 114
encryption, 112
envelope, SOAP, 114
error
  action response, 126
  codes, 250
  in SOAP request, 120
  notification not sent, 38
event, 28, 466
  in a distributed system, 129
event information
  run-time, 169
event key, 133, 466
event message
  overview, 145
  XML-based, 133
event moderation, 136
event notification, 148
  requirement, 169
evented state variable, 133, 466
evented variable, 27
eventing, 22, 24, 466
  device development step, 345
  in control point development, 423
  SCP, 440
  UPnP template language, 135
eventSubURL, 27, 285, 466
exception
  SOAP, 120
expiration information, 91

F

flash memory, 347
friendlyName, 194

G

GENA, 89, 466
  overview, 131
  using with UPnP, 132
General Event Notification Architecture, *See* GENA

H

handler
  action request, 248
hardware interface library, 167
hnd
  handle parameter, 207
home maintenance
  user scenario, 7
host group, 37, 466
HostIP, 205
HTTP, 5, 31, 40
  request in SOAP, 117
  status codes, 42
  transaction structure, 40
HTTP 404 not found, 222
HTTP methods
  GENA, 132
HTTP resource, 467
HTTPMU, 32, 467
HTTPMU discovery request, 81
HTTPU, 467

I

IGD, 467
imagining the future, xv
implementation example, 163
implementer
  responsibilities, 188
independence, 6
infrastructure network, 467
initial event message, 29, 133, 467

initial request line, 467
Intel
  SDK vendor, 176
Intel SDK
  installation, 177
  using in applications, 182
Intel Tools for UPnP Technologies, 217
interface
  administrative, 6
  wired/wireless, 347
Internet Gateway
  certified device type, 12
Internet Gateway Device, *See* IGD
interoperability
  UPnP and SCP, 444
interval
  advertisement, 289
invoking actions
  control point development, 420
IP address
  dynamically assigned, 212
IP multicast, 37
IP network address support, 167
IPv4, 37
IRL, 41

J

Java
  supported versions, 174

K

key
  event, 137

L

language tag, 156
Lantronix
  SDK vendor, 175
LastChange
  state variable, 362
lease
  DHCP, 67
lease (of an IP address), 467
library
  HW interface, 167
  initialization, 203
lifetime statistics, 306
  example, 196
  module, example, 268
  service document, 233
  trackability required, 168
linkable library, 445
Linux SDK, 173
localization, 155
  support, 321
logical device model
  SCP, 438
logo certification, 173

M

main(), 201
managed network, 467
mapping
  device, SCP-to-UPnP, 445
mapping requirements
  to device description doc, 189
Marketing Committee, 467
media server, 363
media, *See* A/V
memory consumption, 347
message envelope
  SOAP, 115
message-based protocol
  SOAP, 112
Metro Link
  SDK vendor, 175
Microsoft
  SDK vendor, 175
moderation of events, 136, 468
movie watching
  user scenario, 7
M-SEARCH, 81
multicast
  address, 37
  communication, 32
multi-homed address, 45
multiple root device
  pros and cons, 191
MX request header, 50

N

namespace requirement, 189
namespace, SOAP, 114
network
  ad hoc, 6, 70
  zero-configuration, 6
network event notification
  example, 197
network support
  for multicast, 38
networked lifestyle, xv
non-evented state variable, 30
notification
  event, 148
NOTIFY, 87
notify
  GENA, 132

nt and nts
GENA, 132

O

object model, 24
output parameters
multiple, 259

P

packet
return, structure, 259
parameters
output, multiple, 259
persistent connections, 47
phases of operation
of UpnP devices, 21
phases of UPnP, 468
platform
embedded, 174, 175
platform independence, 6
Platform-Independent Data Representation
SOAP, 112
point-to-point communication, 32
presence announcement, 87, 468
presentation, 22, 24, 468
device development step, 346
presentation page
advanced topics, 340
creating, example, 322
dynamic creation, 324
getting for a device, 152
hidden, 349
implementing control from, 155
overview, 319
UPnP, 151
presentation page UPnP, 468
presentationURL, 199
property route, 442
protection
device re-entry, 349
protocol
addressing, 32
common device control, xvi
leveraged in UPnP, xvi
protocol stack, 32
GENA, 131
publisher, 468
publisher/subscriber model, 468
overview, 130

Q

QueryStateVariable, 468
quick reference
UPnP API, 451

R

range
limiting in multicast, 38
related state variable, 27, 468
remote procedure call, *See* RPC
RenderingControl service
actions, 378
state variable, 376
renewal, 287
request headers, 82
request structure
check validity of, 251
request/rResponse mModel, 40
requirements
client/server, 49
response header
SSDP, 84
USN, 85
response time
search, 83
retrieving documents, 108
return SOAP packet
structure, 259
return value, 27, 239, 469
root device, 20, 469
RPC implementation, 112
RPC representation, SOAP, 114
rules
description document, 96
discovery response, 86
SOAP encoding, 114
run-time event information, 169
run-time loadable shared object, 203

S

S (sequence) header, 51
SCP architecture, 436
SCPD, 469
example, 197
scpd, 103
SCPDURL, 469
SDK, 173
SCP, 445
search response time, 83
search types, 83
security
provided in SCP, 443
SOAP, 112
solution, 14
vs ease-of-use, 13
security vulnerability
SSDP service bug, 14
segmentation fault, 229
semantics
subscription, 286

service, 18, 469
  device development step, 344
  UPnP, 25
service action
  forms of, 229
service action handlers
  complete example, 261
service description
  template, 284
service description document, 103, 469
service list
  device, 101
service subscription
  overview, 284
service type, 469
serviceID, 197, 248, 469
services defined
  in device description document, 195
serviceStateTable, 105, 236
serviceType, 196
sid
  GENA, 132
Siemens
  SDK vendor, 176
signed message, 112
Simple Object Access Protocol, *See* SOAP
Simple Service Discovery Protocol, *See* SSDP
SOAP, 469
  HTTP conventions, 117
  overview, 113
SOAP request
  posting, 197
specVersion, 104
SSDP, 15, 78, 470
SSDP request header
  SSDP, 82
ssdp:alive, 89, 470
ssdp:bye-bye, 91, 470
standardization process
  for devices, 11
standards
  technical and legal, 9
state change (event), 470
state table, 20, 470
state variable, 20, 236, 470
  AVTransport service, 371
  ConnectionManager service, 368
  evented, 133
  LastChange, 362
  non-evented, 30
  RenderingControl service, 376
state variables
  adding ranges to, 241
statistics
  lifetime, 196
steering committee, 470
streaming content, 361
String variable, 107
subscribe
  GENA, 132
subscriber, 470
subscription, 28, 470
  cancellation, 143
  device development step, 345
  example, 137
  in control point development, 423
  process, 137
  renewal, 141
  URL, 285

T

tag
  language, 156
TCP, 31
TCP/IP, 5, 31
  foundation of UPnP devices, 65
Technical Committee, 471
technology
  underlying, 35
template
  device description document, 190
terminology, 17
thread manager, 347
Time to Live (TTL) Field, 471
tool
  AV Wizard, 411
  Device Sniffer, 217
  Device Spy, 356
  Device Validator, 355
Tools for UPnP Technologies
  development tools, 184
transport service, A/V, 370
TTL field, 38

U

UDN, 194, 350
UDP, 31
UIC, 472
Uniform Resource Identifier, *See* URI
Uniform Resource Locator, *See* URL
Uniform Resource Name, *See* URN
Unique Service Name, *See* USN
unsubscribe
  GENA, 132
UPnP
  analogy to Microsoft COM, 18

architecture and security, 13
data types, 231
device localization, 155
presentation page, 151
stack, 472
UPnP device
implementation example, 163
UPnP Device Architecture, 472
UPnP Device Template, 472
UPnP Forum, 8, 472
committees, 10
launched, xv
UPnP Implementer's Corporation, 15, 472
UPnP Service Template, 472
UPnP Standard
foundation for home networking, 4
What is it?, 5
Why?, 4
UPnP Template Language, 472
upnp.h
error codes defined in, 250
Upnp_Action_Request, 246
Upnp_Subscription_Request, 295
UpnpFinish(), 210
UpnpSendAdvertisement(), 207
UpnpUnRegisterRootDevice(), 209
URI, 36, 471
URL, 36, 471
absolute, 45
presentation, 320
URLBase
device description document, 193
URN, 36, 471
user scenarios, 6
USN, 78, 472

V

validity
duration of, 110
value
return, 239
variable
evented, 27
related state, 27
state, 236
video, *See* A/V

W

web server
built-in, 31
web-based administration, 169
example, 199
working committee, 472

X

XML, 5, 52, 473
attributes, 57
CDATA sections, 57
document prolog, 53
elements, 56

Z

Zero Configuration Network, 473

"Why does Intel Press exist? As the pace and depth of Intel's new technology introduction increases, the brains that are closest to the technologies—often its creators—must fulfill their responsibility of disseminating the information to the developer community. This is critical to Intel's success. We are 'building block' suppliers and our success depends on the industry's informed and effective use our of our building block technologies."

Patrick Gelsinger
Senior Vice President and Chief Technology Officer
Intel Corporation

Real-World Advice on USB Design

USB Design by Example

A Practical Guide to Designing I/O Devices

By John Hyde

ISBN 0-9702846-5-9

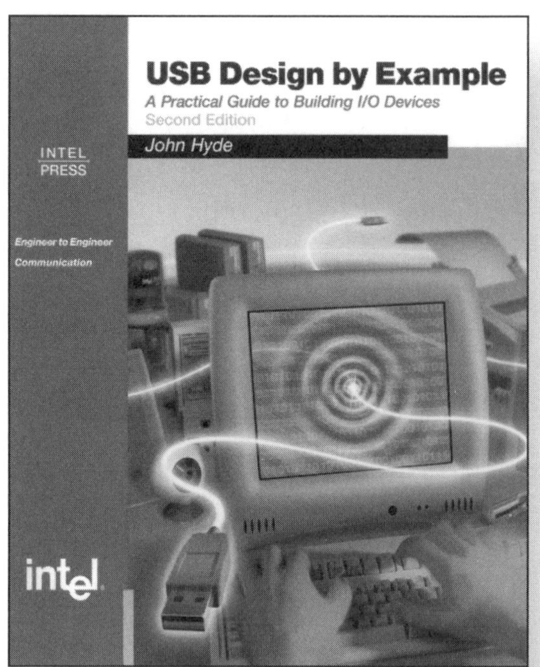

USB Design by Example
A Practical Guide to Building I/O Devices
Second Edition
John Hyde
INTEL PRESS
Engineer to Engineer Communication
intel

John Hyde, a twenty-three year veteran of Intel Corporation and recognized industry expert, goes well beyond all the Universal Serial Bus specification overviews in this unique book, offering the reader the golden opportunity to build unparalleled expertise, knowledge, and skills to design and implement USB I/O Devices quickly and reliably. Through a series of fully documented, real-world examples, the author uses his practical customer training experience to take you step by step through the process of creating specific devices. As a complete reference to USB, this book contains design examples to cover most USB classes—HID, communications, audio, mass-storage, and hub—and provides insights into high-speed USB 2.0 devices, including a device driver for a vendor class called blockio.

> *"We could implement a USB design with this book alone."*
>
> *Chris Gadke,*
> *Design Engineer, Tektronix, Inc.*

Serial ATA Storage Architecture and Applications

Designing High-Performance, Low-Cost I/O Solutions

By Knut Grimsrud and Hubbert Smith

ISBN 0-9717861-8-6

Serial ATA, a new hard disk interconnect standard for PCs, laptops, and more is fast becoming a serious contender to Parallel ATA and SCSI. Computer engineers and architects worldwide must answer important questions for their companies: "Why make the change to Serial ATA? What problems does Serial ATA solve for me? How do I transition from parallel ATA to Serial ATA and from SCSI to Serial ATA?" The authors of this essential book, both Intel Serial ATA specialists, have the combined expertise to help you answer these questions. Systems engineers, product architects, and product line managers who want to affect the right decisions for their products undoubtedly will benefit from the straight talk offered by these authors. The book delivers reliable information with sufficient technical depth on issues such as Phy signaling and interface states, protocol encoding, programming model, flow control, performance, compatibility with legacy systems, enclosure management, signal routing, hot-plug, presence detection, activity indication, power management, and cable/connector standards.

"This book provides explanations and insights into the underlying technology to help ease design and implementation."

Rhonda Gass, Vice President, Storage Systems Development
Dell Computer Corporation

Introduction to PCI Express†

A Hardware and Software Developer's Guide

By Adam Wilen, Justin Schade, and Ron Thornburg

ISBN 0-9702846-9-1

Written by key Intel insiders who have worked to implement Intel's first generation of PCI Express chipsets and who work directly with customers who want to take advantage of PCI Express, this introduction to the new I/O technology explains how PCI Express is designed to increase computer system performance. The book explains in technical detail how designers can use PCI Express technology to overcome the practical performance limits of existing multi-drop, parallel bus technology. The authors draw from years of leading-edge experience to explain how to apply these new capabilities to a broad range of computing and communications platforms.

"This book helps software and hardware developers get a jumpstart on their development cycle that can decrease their time to market."

Ajay Kwatra, Engineer Strategist, Dell Computer Corporation

Building the Power-Efficient PC

A Developer's Guide to ACPI Power Management

By Jerzy Kolinski, Ram Chary, Andrew Henroid, and Barry Press

ISBN 0-9702846-8-3

An expert author team shows developers and integrators how to address the increasing demand for energy conservation by building power-managed PCs. Learn from key engineers responsible for the development of ACPI Power Management the practical knowledge and design techniques needed to implement this critical technology. The companion CD includes sample code, complete power management documentation, Intel® power management tools, and links to references.

Learn how to build power-efficient PCs from the experts

IXP1200 Programming

The Microengine Coding Guide for the Intel® IXP1200 Network Processor Family

By Erik J. Johnson and Aaron Kunze

ISBN 0-9712887-8-X

As very deep submicron ASIC design gets both more costly and time-consuming, the communications industry seeks alternatives providing rich services with higher capability. The key to increased flexibility and performance is the innovation incorporated in the IXP1200 family of network processors. From engineers who were there at the beginning, you can learn how to program the microengines of Intel's IXP12xx network processors through a series of expanding examples, covering such key topics as receiving, processing, and transmitting packets; synchronizing between hardware threads; debugging; optimizing; and tuning your program for the highest performance.

Increase your performance with this hands-on coding guide

The Virtual Interface Architecture

A Guide to Designing Applications for Systems Using VI Architecture

By Don Cameron and Greg Regnier

ISBN 0-9712887-0-4

The VI architecture addresses the long-standing problem for systems that need an efficient interface between general-purpose computers and high-speed switched networks. In this book, Intel architects outline the motivation, benefits, and history of the Virtual Interface Architecture. Code examples guide you through the syntax and semantics of the VI Provider Library API. With this reference, hardware and software engineers can apply the VI Architecture to development of scalable, high-performance, and fault-tolerant systems.

Design scalable, high-performance, fault-tolerant systems

About Intel Press

Intel Press is the authoritative source of timely, highly relevant, and innovative books to help software and hardware developers speed up their development process. We collaborate only with leading industry experts to deliver reliable, first-to-market information about the latest technologies, processes and strategies.

Our products are planned with the help of many people in the developer community and we encourage you to consider becoming a customer advisor. If you would like to help us and gain additional advance insight to the latest technologies, we encourage you to consider the Intel Press Customer Advisor Program. You can **register** here:

www.intel.com/intelpress/register.htm

For information about bulk orders or corporate sales, please send email to **bulkbooksales@intel.com**.

Other Developer Resources from Intel

At these Web sites you can also find valuable technical information and resources for developers:

developer.intel.com	general information for developers
www.intel.com/IDS	content, tools, training, and the Early Access Program for software developers
www.intel.com/software/products	programming tools to help you develop high-performance applications
www.intel.com/idf	world-wide technical conference, the Intel Developer Forum